Teaneck

THE DEMETRIUS LEGEND
AND ITS LITERARY TREATMENT
IN THE AGE OF THE BAROQUE

Ervin C. Brody

Rutherford • *Madison* •

THE DEMETRIUS LEGEND
AND
ITS LITERARY TREATMENT
IN THE
AGE OF THE BAROQUE

Fairleigh Dickinson University Press

Quotations from *A History of Russia* by V. O. Kluchevsky, published by
E. P. Dutton & Co., Inc., are reprinted with permission.

To the memory of my father and mother

Contents

Preface

In coining the phrase *Weltliteratur,* Goethe had in mind a national theme which, like Faust, by its universality has become the literary property of all nations. The great German poet visualized a huge tree, rooted in the earth of one nation, whose branches spread far and wide, fructifying the soil of other nations.

Such a universal theme is the Demetrius legend, which grew out of the turbulent events known in Russian historiography as the Time of Troubles (1598-1613). Demetrius, third son of Ivan the Terrible, Tsar of Russia, is generally assumed to have been killed or to have accidentally stabbed himself to death in an epileptic fit in 1591 at the age of nine. Yet twelve years later, in 1603, a young man appeared in Poland who asserted that he was Demetrius, Ivan's son, and that he had miraculously escaped the murderers sent by Boris Godunov, now Tsar Boris, to kill him. Helped by the Poles, two Popes, the Jesuits and some disgruntled Russians, Demetrius won the Muscovite throne by conquest in 1605. However, a brief eleven months later he was killed in an uprising led by the principal boyars of Russia. This was a period of national tragedy, as one civil war followed another with the appearance of new pretenders to claim the throne now occupied by the self-proclaimed Tsar Vasilij Šujskij, and with the intervention of foreign powers.

These chaotic events were watched with great attention in the various countries of Western Europe. Some of these countries understood the difficult situation of the Muscovite State and attempted to take advantage of her internal weakness. Yet these events were not only of historical importance, of interest for politicians, and a matter of diplomatic play for foreign governments. The intrigue, the secretly woven plots of contending political parties, the extinction of a famous dynasty which had ruled Russia over seven hundred years, the struggle for succession, the thunder of battles between Russians, Poles, Cossacks, Swedes, Germans, Hungarians, and even French and Englishmen, and the magic name of Demetrius, which gradually became a symbol of rebellion, had an unusual fascination for the people of the age. Here was an adventure story taken from real life, more interesting than fiction since it was true and, because of the exotic quality which remote Russia still retained for most foreigners, doubly attractive for the contemporary reader. This was still the age when tales of the extrordinary and adventurous were the favorite literary fare, and even if Cervantes wrote the first part of *Don Quixote* (1605) to poke fun at their exaggerations, the average reader still felt that he had merely added one more, indeed the most successful, to the growing number of these unusual tales. This was the age of Shakespeare's historical dramas, full of intrigues, pretenders, and usurpers, and *Hamlet,* the most famous of the Elizabethan revenge tragedies, was staged in London in 1603, the same year that Demetrius first appeared in Poland to launch his "campaign of revenge" against Boris Godunov, Tsar of Russia. Thus, it is understandable that the legend woven around the mysterious figure of Demetrius at once became popular, and so attractive that over a hundred tragedies, melodramas, and harlequinades have been written on the subject, not counting the great numbers of novels, poems, and operas. The unsolved riddle of this unusual personality has constantly attracted historians too, and, as a recent study by Yale historian George Vernadsky[1] shows, they have continued to return to this subject.

This book attempts to study the Demetrius legend in history as well as in some selected dramatic works of world and Russian literature. Central to the legend and to much of the literary interest in it are the origin, personality, and motivation of Demetrius himself, and his figure as it is treated in historiography and in dramatic literature is the focal point of the present study.

Answers to the following questions will be sought: What part did contemporary events of the country in which a writer adopted the Demetrius legend play in his artistic efforts? Did the ideology of his age suggest to the playwright solutions for the treatment and organization of historical material which so

---

1. George Vernadsky, "The Death of the Tsarevich Dimitry; a Reconsideration of the Case," *Oxford Slavonic Review* 5, (1954): 1–19.

often seemed contradictory? How did his aesthetic sensibility overcome the rigid limits of facts and events which historians of the time extracted from the past? Did he exercise selection from the various possibilities and *dramatis personae* which the events offered on the basis of certain peculiarities of his period or on the basis of his dramatic needs? How much did the psychology with which he illuminated Demetrius's mask, his behavior, his relationship to Marina Mniszek, his clash with Godunov and Šujskij owe to the *Weltanschauung* of his particular country and age? Finally, how was the writer's specific choice influenced by the work of his predecessors and what were the links between them? A cause and effect relationship between the evolution of the literary portrait of Demetrius and its historicity, between psychology and tradition, between aesthetic license and actual events, underlies the investigation, which explores the artist's subjective interpretation of these particular events of the Time of Troubles.

The first chapter gives a historical review of the period from the writings of prominent Russian and foreign scholars and from the reports of contemporaries. This is not an attempt to write a full record of the age or to furnish a key to its complex nature, which has defied generations of scholars, but rather to provide the reader with the essential facts, as well as their basic interpretation by contemporary witnesses and historians, which in turn served the dramatists as a historical basis for their literary endeavors. Once this has been done, the Zeitgeist of the century recalled, and the background evoked, the stage will be properly set for a discussion of the Demetrius dramas. We will then see the essential and protean Demetrius in history and literature, both individual and universal, true and false, hero and villain, rebel and tyrant, saint and sinner, humanist and soldier, royalist and republican, Russian and Westerner, Orthodox, Catholic, and Protestant—a unique blend of historical facts, popular legends, and literary imagination.

The second and third chapters concentrate on the dramatic reflection of the Demetrius legend in the age of the baroque. While a great deal of scholarly literature already exists on the artistic use of the subject by later dramatists—especially German and Russian,[2] the first two important dramas treating the his-

---

2. Emanuel Salgaller, *The Demetrius-Godunof Theme in the German and Russian Dramas of the Twentieth Century* (Ph.D. dissertation, New York University, 1956).

torical Demetrius, composed in the beginning of the seventeenth
century in Spain and England, have never been analyzed historically. Although highly successful in its time, Lope de Vega's
El Gran Duque de Moscovia y emperador perseguido has remained virtually unnoticed in the last three hundred years. This
play is important for the students of both Russian and Spanish
literature since it represents the first attempt in Western European drama to treat a theme from Russian history, a country
which until the fifteenth century had been considered the home
of the legendary Scythians and Sarmatians. And in John
Fletcher's *The Loyal Subject,* the reflections of the stormy reign
of Ivan the Terrible and the hidden Demetrius motif have been
completely overlooked by literary critics and historians, both
Russians and Westerners.

Lope uses the Demetrius legend as his central theme, follows
the trend of historical events, and his main protagonists are well-
defined, although occasionally idealized and highly distorted,
historical figures of the period. Fletcher's treatment is entirely
unorthodox; the theme touches, mixes, synthesizes, and even
confuses historical personalities and events. Therefore, while
in Lope's play we follow the actions closely, treat the plot in
detail, analyze the dramatist's craft in his artistic efforts to
superimpose a Spanish world on the historical Russian-Polish
material throughout the entire *comedia,* our main interest centers on the identification of the curiously camouflaged historical
personalities, certain events of the Russian Time of Troubles,
and the discovery of the hidden Demetrius motif in Fletcher's
drama. A number of scenes connected with the moralizing of
Archas, the main hero of the drama, the spectacular variations
on the theme of honor, the militant behavior of Archas's virtuous daughters, the duke's attempts to seduce the girls, all this
is of little interest to us, since these are stock situations and
characters usually present in Fletcher's creative workshop.
While we are enchanted by what Lope tells us of his Spanish-
Slavic heroes and their fairy-tale adventures in a world of
baroque make-believe, we are, in turn, fascinated in trying to
remove the veil with which Fletcher hides his protagonists and
their exploits and to discover the authentic contemporary Russian historical material in his play.

In the fourth chapter the further development of the Demetrius legend in the German and Russian dramas of the modern

age will be briefly reviewed.[3] In addition to the individual merits of the plays, the relation of the German and Russian dramas to one another and to their respective sources will also be considered. It will be seen that Schiller, the most characteristic representative of the *Sturm und Drang* period, and Hebbel in the nineteenth century continue the baroque tradition of the Demetrius legend, and even some of the Russian dramas reflect to a greater or lesser degree the baroque sensibility.

The conclusion will investigate the suitability of the theme for treatment as a tragedy and point out the baroque characteristics of the corpus of the Demetrius dramas. Attention will be given to the extent to which each age and country in which the Demetrius legend has been treated, has reinterpreted it in terms of its own ideological attitudes and artistic preferences. Finally, the relationship between historical source and artistic product will be shown. It will be seen that, taken together, the Demetrius dramas of the corpus provide an intellectual and spiritual biography of the Russian Time of Troubles and illustrate the argument that the basic life of a period is best understood through its literature.

In regard to orthography, I retain the spelling of contemporary sources where it does not disturb an intelligent reading of the text, since it transmits both the spirit and color of the age. The names of the protagonists are spelled according to the use of the historian or dramatist whose work is being discussed or quoted. While I refer to our hero as Demetrius, Lope calls him Demetrio, Paul Ernst, the German dramatist, Demetrios, and the Russian playwrights, Dimitrij.

Except for such common nouns as Tsar, Tsarevich, and the like, accepted forms in the English language, the rules of transliteration of the Slavic Department of Columbia University have been consistently followed. Thus, the reader will find the names "Tolstoj," "Puškin," "Xomjakov," "Ključevskij," and so on in this study, even if variants of these names are used in other works with greater frequency.

---

3. Some of the more recent German Demetrius dramas remained in manuscript and still some others were presumably destroyed or lost during the Second World War.

Acknowledgments

This book was based on a doctoral dissertation under the title *Events of the Russian Time of Troubles in Two Baroque Dramas: Lope de Vega's El Gran Duque de Moscovia and John Fletcher's The Loyal Subject* at Columbia University. I would like to express my sincere gratitude to Professor William E. Harkins and Professor Harold B. Segel for their kind help during the preparation of the dissertation. I am especially indebted to Professor Emilio González-Lopez for his constant encouragement and interest in my work.

I also wish to thank the following publishers for having given me permission to quote from published works:

Las Americas Publishing Company, for permission to quote from Emilio González-Lopez, *Historia de la Literatura Española, Edad Media y Siglo de Oro*, 1962.

Ediciones Atlas, Madrid, for permission to quote from Lope de Vega, *El Gran Duque de Moscovia y Emperador perseguido*, 1952.

C. H. Beck'sche Verlagsbuchhandlung (Oscar Beck), Muenchen, for permission to quote from Karl Vossler, *Lope de Vega und sein Zeitalter*, 1932.

B. Behr's Verlag GmbH, Hamburg, for permission to quote from Friedrich Hebbel, *Demetrius*, 1904.

G. Bell and Sons Ltd., London, for permission to quote from John Fletcher, *The Loyal Subject*, 1908.

J. M. Dent & Sons, Ltd., for permission (world rights) to quote from V. O. Kluchevsky, *A History of Russia*, trans. C. J. Hogarth (New York: Russel and Russel, 1960). Originally published in the U.S. by E. P. Dutton & Co., Inc.

Librairie Arthème Fayard, Paris, for permission to quote from Constantin de Grunwald, *La vrai histoire de Boris Godunov*, 1961.

The Polish Review, for permission to quote from Ervin C. Brody, The Demetrius Episode in a Drama of Lope de

Vega," Winter, 1968, and "Schiller's Vision of the Slavic World in his Demetrius Fragment," Winter 1969.

Routledge & Kegan Paul Ltd., London, for permission to quote from Alexander S. Pushkin, *Boris Godunov,* trans. Alfred Hayes, 1918.

Tulane Drama Review, for permission to quote from A. A. Parker, "The Approach to the Spanish Drama of the Golden Age," September 1959.

Universitaet Zuerich, for permission to quote from Adele Ott, *Die italienische Novelle im englischen Drama,* 1904.

The University of Pennsylvania Press, for permission to quote the *Hispanic Review,* J. H. Arsona, "La introducción del gracioso en el teatro de Lope de Vega," January 1939.

The University of Wisconsin Press, for permission to quote from *The English Works of Giles Fletcher, the Elder,* edited by Lloyd E. Berry (Madison: The University of Wisconsin Press; © 1964 by the Regents of the University of Wisconsin).

World Publishing Times Mirror, for permission to quote from Gerald Brenan, *Literature of the Spanish People from Roman Times to the Present Day,* Meridian Books, 1957.

THE DEMETRIUS LEGEND
AND ITS LITERARY TREATMENT
IN THE AGE OF THE BAROQUE

1

The Demetrius Legend in History

Introduction

"The history of a nation belongs to the poet,"[1] wrote Puškin shortly before beginning his work on *Boris Godunov,* obviously suggesting that only the sensitive artist can truly feel, understand, and recreate the authentic pulse-beat of a historical period. Yet Puškin must also have felt, as his own example shows, that without thorough historical research the poet cannot "revive the past century in all its truth."[2] Thus, it is only by respecting historical truth and "by asking questions of the past"[3] on the one hand, and by approaching this historical material with his subjective intuition and emotion on the other that the poet can hope, in Puškin's interpretation, to avoid presenting a dry, uninspired, and monotonous narrative, and create, instead, a living historical drama.

An acquaintance with the facts, events, and circumstances of the puzzling period known as The Time of Troubles in Russian history is a *sine qua non* for a detailed discussion of the Demetrius dramas. While the Rankean ideal of absolute objectivity is impossible since the selectivity and arrangement of evidence, and occasional comment are clearly subjective, it is still worth while attempting to accommodate various opinions, to cover pitfalls with planks of relative objectivity in order not to permit one viewpoint to dominate the others.[4] Thus, the possibility of seeing the age in retrospect will be explored by quoting authoritative opinions, and tracing the evolution of certain trends regarding the interpretation of the Time of Troubles in historiography.

General Characteristics of the Age

There were several characteristic elements in the political and social structure of the European states of the sixteenth and early seventeenth century which were generally identical, such as the struggle between kings and great nobles for power, uncertainties about succession to the throne, and especially religious conflicts. In general the age was characterized by a growing sense of anxiety and insecurity. There was a shift of power from one class to another. Unemployment rose and, as a result, social unrest was noticeable.

One important characteristic of the sixteenth century derives from the fact that it was an era when most of the nations of modern Europe assumed the form in which we find them today. In the continuous struggle between the king on the one side, and feudal nobility and Church on the other, we can observe a contrasting development throughout the century. In most of the major Western nations and in Muscovy, royal power had greatly increased and, in alliance with the minor nobility and middle classes, it effectively destroyed the moderating influence of the great nobles and reduced them to reluctant supporters of its policy or forced them into complete isolation. This created a perfect political climate for the growth of absolute monarchy illustrated not only in the case of the Muscovite state but also in Tudor England and Valois France. Yet in other countries, especially those in the Carpathian and Baltic regions, we notice another example, in which all levels of nobility united to preserve their privileges and to secure effective limitations of the royal powers. In those countries the sixteenth century was the golden age of the nobility with its credo of liberalism and the republican autonomy.

Succession to the throne created problems in many countries. Since a sustained consideration of this question is outside the scope of this study, I merely point to the pattern of dynastic succession in England, France, and the Muscovite State of this time.

The most important characteristic of the century was its religious struggle. As a result of the Reformation and Counter-Reformation, Christian Europe became divided into a Protestant North and a Catholic South. Absolutist kings of the North welcomed the Reformation as an end to the interference of the

Church in state matters and created national churches; merchants found the air of individual freedom exhilarating, and peasants hoped that the new dispensation would liberate them from the yoke of feudalism.

While the Muscovite State did not benefit from the great cultural currents of European Renaissance and the refreshing spiritual innovations of the Reformation, and had to wait another century to become part of the European community, it is appropriate to review briefly the intellectual and religious turmoil in Poland, Russia's immediate neighbor to the west, since that country played a significant part in the events of the Time of Troubles. The Reformation nearly conquered the country: the upper classes became Protestant, the Parliament (Sejm) almost attained a Protestant majority, and the royal court itself was a center of unorthodox tendencies. At this time Protestantism denoted progress, intellectual and social superiority, while Catholicism came to be identified with the lower classes and the less educated, backward elements. However, this situation suddenly changed because of the efforts of fervent and able men, and Catholicism, passing from retreat to offense, attained an intellectually more advanced and morally more attractive state. The Jesuits, who came to Poland about 1564, became a powerful national force, influential in politics, distinguished in social activities, and predominant in education.

In his recent book *La vraie histoire de Boris Godunov,* French historian Constantin de Grunwald sums up the religious situation in Europe at the time of the death of Ivan the Terrible:

Au moment où disparaissait Ivan le Terrible, l'Europe entière était engagée dans la guerre de religion. En France, la lignée des Valois s'étaignit dans une ambiance de luttes sanglantes: l'heure d'Henri IV, le grand pacificateur n'était pas encore venue. En Angleterre, la reine Elisabeth préparait l'exécution de sa rivale Marie Stuart, espoir des catholiques; en Autriche la Contre-Reforme prenait son premier élan. Plus à l'est en Pologne . . . le catholicisme avait déjà assuré son triomphe.[5]

Ivan the Terrible

Many of the Demetrius dramas are seen as a clash between Boris, the usurper, and Demetrius, the real or alleged heir. Yet both Boris's rule and the appearance of the alleged Demetrius are only the last two links in the chain of events which began when Ivan IV killed Tsarevich Ivan, his eldest son, who was re-

garded as the unquestionable successor to the throne. This senseless murder, done in a moment of uncontrollable rage, created
a power vacuum and pushed—following the brief tenure of the
weak and unwilling Feodor, Ivan IV's younger son—the dominating figure of Boris Godunov on to the throne. Thus, consideration of Ivan IV's complex figure may be regarded as a
Vorgeschichte, a kind of overture, to the Demetrius dramas, and
some historical dramatists, such as Lope de Vega and Aleksej
K. Tolstoj, also begin the story there.

Ivan's awesome figure has inspired a host of legends. The
most difficult problem is the historical assessment of his controversial character. The historians differ radically on his evaluation, yet their interpretations are based not so much on contradictory evidence; they rather differ because of their conflicting
moral and ethical viewpoints.

There are three schools of opinion about Ivan IV's reign.
The traditional view, based mainly on moral absolutism, initi-
ated by native chroniclers and foreign contemporaries and continued by modern scholars, depicts him in negative terms.[6] For
this school, Ivan has become the incarnation of all that is evil
in man, a modern Nero in a Muscovite caftan.

Another viewpoint is that of panegyric by Soviet biographers,
who not only defend Ivan from his accusers, seen as traitors
(Kurbskij), adventurers (Taube and Krause, Ivan's *guards* of
German origin), and bourgeois historians (Karamzin), but
praise him as a heroic builder of centralized Russia, a great
administrator, and a talented diplomat.[7]

Standing somewhere between these two extremes are those
who seek neither to vindicate nor to condemn Ivan, but to understand and to explain his actions within the temper of his time,
stressing the political issues of his struggle with the great boyars,
and calling him the first Tsar who recognized the full significance
of his authority. This opinion is more balanced, since it is based
on a scientific approach and attempts to give equal attention to
Ivan's positive and negative qualities.[8]

If two foreign opinions—one by Sonia E. Howe, an English
scholar who collected the reports of contemporary English
visitors to Russia, and a more recent one by Grunwald—are
juxtaposed, it will be noticed that the earlier tendency to see
everything Russian in dark colors, and, conversely, to praise the
West indiscriminately by comparison, gradually turns into a more
objective view which reflects the viewpoint of the third school.

Thus Howe sums up contemporary English opinions of six-teenth-century Russia in the following strong indictment:

During Ivan's reign Muscovy had become a byword for oppression and corruption among the foreigners . . . and the numerous records of that period . . . relate the terrible state of unhappy Russia. Many of these writers do not fail to express their gratitude for the blessings enjoyed by their own country, and profound pity for the Russians . . . they strongly condemn the immorality and callous brutality rampant.[9]

Grunwald, on the other hand, tries to find the clue to Ivan's reign in the spirit of the age:

Ce serait une grosse erreur de considérer Ivan . . . comme un phénomène unique en son genre, comme un réprésentant typique d'une nation russe portée . . . à la violence et à la cruauté. Pour éviter des interprétations aussi arbitraires, nous devons situer ce souverain dans son époque: celle de la Renaissance. . . . Avec un léger décalage chronologique, le Tsar Ivan apparaît alors comme un équivalent russe de Louis XI, d'Henry d'Angleterre, d'Isabelle d'Aragon ou de César Borgia. Il y avait en lui, comme en ces personages, un élément pathologique qui finit par dégénerer en cruauté. Mais il était, lui aussi, un des hommes les plus instruits de son temps, un artiste. . . . S'il y a quelque chose de spécifiquement russe en lui, c'est peut-être la démesure de ses passions.[10]

A list of those specific events in Ivan's reign which created the instability of its social fabric and precipitated the chaos of the Time of Troubles can be drawn up as follows:

1. His persecution of the great boyars, among them many able statesmen and military figures, which created a tremendous gap in the ranks of the higher nobility. The latter deserted Russia in great numbers to enter the service of Poland or fled elsewhere.

2. This persecution of the boyars not only weakened the state but almost desolated the central provinces and Ivan found it impossible to raise enough soldiers for his wars.

3. The process of political transformation created social and economic changes which, in turn, produced acute discontent, especially among the ousted elements, who sought to regain their former positions. As long as the central authority remained strong, this discontent was kept in control, but a governmental crisis was likely to set in motion a political and social upheaval.

4. Finally, Ivan's frequent debauchery and savage temper gave rise to a lowering of morals among the great boyars in his Court.

Although his evaluation is negative, I conclude with a summary of Ivan's reign by Klučevskij, the well-known Russian historian:

[Ivan] was a thinker rather than a doer. . . . Even without him the life of the Muscovite Empire would have developed precisely as it had done before his day . . . without him Russian development would have escaped many of the shocks. . . . The chief point to notice, therefore, is his *negative* importance. . . . The one-sided, self-seeking, opinionated bent of his political ideas combined with his nervous irritability to deprive himself of all practical tact, political perspective, and grasp of realities, with the result that, though he made a successful beginning of the work of completing the structure of the State . . . he insensibly ended by shaking that structure to its foundation. . . . In short, the Tsar sacrificed both himself, his dynasty and the welfare of his realm to his ferocity and self-will.[11]

Boris Godunov

Boris Godunov is one of the two main protagonists of the Demetrius dramas. There is a cause and effect relationship between the two main heroes. On the one hand, Boris could not have become the Tsar of Russia without the death of Tsarevich Demetrius and, on the other hand, the alleged Demetrius could not have conquered the throne of Moscow without the downfall of the House of Godunov.

Boris's controversial character has defied an objective approach so far. He was either looked at through the eyes of that famous trinity: Karamzin, the official historian of the early nineteenth century, Puškin, the most celebrated poet of the period, and Musorgskij, the composer of the Russian nationalist school, as an introspective guilt-ridden monarch who, having "attained the highest power" finds the "crown of Monomax"[12] too heavy, because the price he had paid to become the Tsar was a monstrous crime; or he was regarded, especially in the interpretations of Pogodin and Platonov, Russian historians of the nineteenth and twentieth centuries, not as the villain and intriguer of the history books and dramas, but rather as a brilliant statesman, deeply interested in European culture, who died, not because of any pangs of conscience, but simply because the political, social, and administrative tasks of the period proved overwhelming for him.[13]

When Ivan IV died in 1584, Boris was 33 years old. He was the most enduring favorite of the terrible Tsar and had survived fifteen years of close, although at times uneasy, relationship with him. It is characteristic that Boris first found favor in the eyes of Ivan IV about the time when the *opričnina*[14] began to disintegrate and it is possible that the abolition of this sinister state security organ was originally his idea.[15]

Boris was completely devoted to Ivan IV[16] and thus succeeded in maintaining the latter's confidence. He pushed his way further by marrying the daughter of the notorious Maljuta Skuratov, one of Ivan's favorites in the *opričnina,* in 1570. Ten years later Ivan's younger son Feodor married Boris's sister, Irene, and the Tsar made Boris a prince. About this time a friendship developed between Boris and Tsarevich Ivan, the presumptive heir to Ivan IV's throne, and when the Tsar killed his eldest son in 1581, Boris tried, though in vain, to shield the unfortunate Tsarevich from his father's blows. The repentant Tsar later remembered Boris's intervention with gratitude and, before his death, appointed him as one of the five members of the Council of State to advise in matters of government Tsarevich Feodor, whom he deemed unfit to govern alone.

After the death of Tsar Ivan IV and in the early stages of Tsar Feodor's reign, a growing rivalry developed among the historical pentarchy of this Council, of which Boris, due to his consummate diplomatic talent, ultimately emerged victorious. As the remaining sole adviser of Feodor, Boris reached the summit of his influence and represented the real power in the State, since the weak Feodor would do nothing without his advice. He held his own court within the Kremlin with the same brilliance as the Tsar, and his wisdom, skill, and ability were stressed by contemporaries and modern historians alike. It seemed that, after the stormy reign of Ivan the Terrible, Muscovy would return to normalcy under Boris's guidance.

Feodor's peaceful reign was interrupted by the catastrophe at Uglič in 1591, in which Tsarevich Demetrius, Feodor's younger brother, presumably lost his life. Since this event is of crucial importance for the understanding of the Demetrius dramas, we will consider it in some detail with special emphasis on Boris's role in this affair.

Ivan the Terrible married Maria Nagoj as his seventh wife in September, 1580, and she bore the monarch a son, named Demetrius, on October 19, 1583. Thus, when Ivan IV died on March 17, 1584, Demetrius, his youngest son, was just a few months old. On the very night of Ivan's death the uncertainty of succession already involved the partisans of the young Demetrius in a bloody fratricidal clash with the adherents of Feodor, his older brother. The question of who should inherit the throne arose from the fact that Feodor was physically and mentally unable to govern, while Demetrius was a mere babe. Thus, it was evident that whoever of these two ascended the throne would not be able to rule by himself and his powerful protectors would have to govern for him.[17] Bogdan Belskij, appointed by Ivan as Demetrius's guardian, made an initial effort to put the infant Demetrius on the throne, but his attempt was thwarted and the other boyars who remained faithful to Tsar Feodor decided to send Demetrius, his mother, and the Nagojs, his relatives, to Uglič, a little town, about a hundred miles north of Moscow on the Volga, in order to prevent a recurrence of such disturbance.

In Uglič the Nagojs lived in honorable exile, separated from the splendor of the capital, having lost, at least for some time to come, their chance to share in the reign of the country. Maria, Demetrius's mother, seemed to have accepted the change in her fortune without complaint, but her strong-willed brothers, rich boyars only yesterday and now reduced to the existence of captives in a provincial town, represented a potential danger for Feodor and Boris. They could not forget that they were guarding the future Tsar and it seemed to them that, were it not for Boris, the evil spirit of the feeble Feodor, they could return to their former distinguished position in Moscow. Thus, presumably the Nagoj brothers did their best to instill hatred in Demetrius for Boris and it was probably not difficult to preach hatred to a child who, according to contemporary accounts, soon developed certain traits characteristic of his father's cruel nature.

We must assume that his agents kept Boris informed of what was happening in Uglič, since he had sent his confidant Mixail Bitjagovskij to that city as a treasurer and comptroller to oversee the activities of the Nagojs. Bitjagovskij was obviously regarded as hostile by the Nagojs and quarrels over financial matters must often have occurred between them.

It was in the tense atmosphere of this city that, at noon on May 15, 1591, Demetrius's mother heard a cry in the courtyard, and when she rushed out, she found her son with a mortal wound in his throat. In her frenzy she accused Bitjagovskij of murdering the young Tsarevich and this so excited the local crowd that they killed Bitjagovskij, his son, and about ten others who were suspected of participation in Demetrius's murder. For her conduct she was later forced to take the veil as nun Marfa, and it is under this name that we meet her in most of the Demetrius dramas of world literature.

Boris's complicity or innocence in the death of Tsarevich Demetrius has not been satisfactorily solved up to this very day, and the controversy concerning his role began almost immediately after the bloody affair in Uglič.

A few days after Demetrius's death a commission consisting of Vasilij Šujskij, Andrej Klešnin, Elizar Vylušgin and the Metropolitan Gelasi was sent by Tsar Feodor and Boris to Uglič to conduct an investigation concerning the cause of the catastrophe and the subsequent riot. Later an official document (*sledstvennoe delo*) was issued,[18] which contains a record of the interrogation of witnesses at Uglič, of various petitions submitted to the Commission, and the final decision by the Moscow authorities. With the exception of Mixail Nagoj, the Tsarina's brother, who steadfastly maintained that Demetrius had been murdered by Osip Voloxov, Nikita Kačalov, and Daniel Bitjagovskij (Mixail's son) on Boris's order, all the other witnesses asserted that the Tsarevich stabbed himself to death in an epileptic fit, and this involuntary suicide has become the official version of the catastrophe at Uglič.[19]

Contemporary literature, however, had an entirely different view of this event. The old Russian annalists sharply contradicted the official inquiry, found Boris guilty, and their opinion was that the disorder which later swept over the Russian land was God's punishment for Boris's crimes.[20] Yet modern historians find the chroniclers' view emotionally unstable, politically biased, and completely untrustworthy.[21]

If we now turn to a review of the most important accounts of foreign contemporaries such as Giles Fletcher, Queen Elizabeth's ambassador to Tsar Feodor; Jerome Horsey, another English diplomat and traveler; Martin Baer, a German Lutheran pastor; George Peyerle, an Augsburg merchant; Jacques Margeret, a French mercenary, who first fought in Boris's army and later became the bodyguard of the alleged Demetrius; Marina Mniszek, the wife of the alleged Demetrius; Samuel Maszkiewicz, a Lithuanian nobleman in the Polish army; Isaac Massa, a Dutch geographer; Hetman Stanislas Żółkiewski, Marshal of the Polish army; and Barezzo Barezzi, a Jesuit father, we find that they contain a unanimous condemnation of Boris.[22] However, in his lucid review "The Death of the Tsarevich Dimitry; a Recon-

sideration of the Case," the historian Vernadsky discounts the
reliability of these accounts since none of these foreigners, except
Horsey, was present in Russia at the time of Demetrius's death
and therefore they could only record what they had heard from
others.[23]

In modern historiography, especially in the eighteenth century,
the belief in Boris's guilt continues for a long time, and historians
base their consideration on the information conveyed by the
Russian chronicles and foreign contemporaries.[24]

In the nineteenth century, however, Russian historical thought
undergoes an important evolution regarding Boris's role in the
drama of Uglič. Due to a gradual awakening of national consciousness after the Napoleonic wars and a remarkable flowering
of Russian historiography in the second half of the century, there
is a growing preoccupation with the past and an attempt to rein-
vestigate critical periods in the nation's history. It is no longer
the exclusive domain of those scholars who, relying on the disputed evidence of partisan chroniclers, unquestioningly proclaim
Boris's guilt. The portrait of a sinful Boris is still painted with
the traditional brush, continues to haunt the authorized version,
and still represents the favorite literary approach. Yet, first tim-
idly, then gradually and increasingly, dissenting and protesting
notes jar this unanimity, and, even if they fail to shatter completely the hard-core opinion, they still emerge as a fresh and
powerful trend in historiography, showing the necessity for a
new and objective reappraisal of Boris's role on the basis of
documentary proof (the official inquiry was first published, as
the reader will recall, in 1819) and not on mere rumor. Thus the
century closes in a growing tension between these two anti-
thetical views.[25]

In the present century the trend toward Boris's moral rehabilitation continues with renewed vigor. Scholars begin to pay more
attention to a judicious reinterpretation of the official inquiry,
and, after the Second World War, the predominant view is either
doubt of Boris's guilt or outright rejection of the accusation
against him. An unquestioning acceptance of Boris's guilt is
hardly ever encountered in the historiography of the postwar
decades.[26]

Returning to our historical narrative we find that, in spite of
the excitement generated by the catastrophe in Uglič, the murder
of Tsarevich Demetrius was, after a while, apparently forgotten.
Therefore, when Tsar Feodor died in 1598, the most logical

contender to the throne was still Boris, despite the fact that he was not one of the old nobility and the great boyars of the period feared and hated him. Yet, when he was offered the crown, according to some historians he refused with mock humility and pretended to forsake the sinful world to find solace and seclusion among the austere walls of a monastery. However, after a mass demonstration in his favor, Boris relented and accepted the crown. Although Boris's election was a legitimate act by the National Assembly (*Zemskij Sobor*), his enemies still whispered that he had secretly resorted to bribery and threats to secure the throne and that the demonstration had been planned by his political lieutenants.

Boris began his reign with apparent popular approval and continued the wise and firm rule which he had shown during Feodor's nominal authority. He avoided foreign conflicts, worked hard to build up the country peacefully, and looked after the welfare of the people. Yet it seemed that fate was against him, since none of his constructive plans succeeded. Even in his family life he experienced tragedy when the young Danish prince, his daughter's bridegroom, fell ill and died. Finally a national disaster occurred when the whole land was struck by a severe famine in the years 1601-1603. Although Boris did his best to alleviate the famine by distributing grain to the hungry and giving employment to the needy, he did not have sufficient resources to feed all, nor enough public works to support the great number of jobless, and the situation gradually assumed the proportion of a real catastrophe. As the Russian historian Platonov points out:

... hordes of famine-stricken people as well as bandits wandered all over the country, plundering, burning, and killing. Famine and highway robbery, were "the beginning of the calamity" for Russia.[27]

Against this background of confusion and discontent, the most prominent boyars, Boris's great enemies, who unsuccessfully had tried to force the Tsar to grant them greater rights and to accept a certain limitation of his own power, decided to stir up the nation by spreading the news that the report concerning the circumstances of Tsarevich Demetrius's death had been false; that Boris's agents had been ordered to kill Demetrius, but confused and nervous, they had killed a wrong boy instead, and that the real Demetrius escaped and was now about to reappear to conquer the throne which, by right of birth, belonged to him. To this

whispering propaganda Boris's answer was the arrest of the
leading boyars on charges of conspiracy and treason. Under
these conditions, in 1604, news reached Moscow that a man who
claimed to be Tsarevich Demetrius had appeared in Poland,
organized an army with Polish support, and was now marching
against Boris, the usurper of the Muscovite throne.

In the final phase of Boris's life one setback followed another. His diplomatic moves to Poland to stop the Pretender
failed and his huge army, aside from some meaningless victories,
could not decisively defeat the little band of emigré Russians,
Polish adventurers, and disgruntled Cossacks which formed the
troops of the alleged Demetrius. When, on April 13, 1605,
Boris suddenly died, he carried his dream of establishing a
House of Godunov with him into the grave, since Feodor, his
son, who succeeded him, could not halt the final disintegration
of his crumbling Empire. After Basmanov, the commander of
the Russian army, decided to forsake his oath to Boris and to
swear allegiance to the Pretender on May 7, 1605, even before
his coronation the alleged Demetrius became virtually the Tsar
of Russia.

The Emergence of the Alleged Demetrius

In the gallery of historical figures of the Time of Troubles,
the last portrait is that of the alleged Demetrius, the main hero
of the dramas to be discussed in this study, whose personality
has been one of the greatest enigmas of Russian history. The real
origin and true identity of this person has never been, and may
perhaps never be, satisfactorily explained, yet it has continued
to puzzle historians, to fascinate playwrights and novelists, and,
in the last three-and-a-half centuries, to excite the imagination of
people attracted by mystery and unusual adventure.

The exact details between the presumed escape of the alleged
Demetrius in 1591 and his phoenix-like reappearance in Poland
are not known. He probably explained them several times, but
no written record was left.

The definite date when Demetrius appeared in Poland is not
known either. The earliest date—1600—is indicated by Margeret, while Boris learned of his existence only in 1604.[28]

Demetrius must have come to Adam Wiśniowiecki, the Polish
magnate in Brahin, at the latest in the early autumn of 1603,
because we find the first mention of his name in a letter dated

November 1, 1603, by Rangoni, the Papal Legate in Poland, to Pope Clement VIII.[29] According to most contemporaries, Demetrius at first worked as a page, servant, and cook until he revealed himself to be Ivan IV's son who had escaped from Boris's assassins.

There are two versions of this revelation. In Marina Mniszek's diary it is recorded that the alleged Demetrius, feeling himself to be dying, sent for a priest, and after confession, told the priest that he was not the person the people at Wiśniowiecki's estate thought he was, and a document hidden in his bed, which the priest was to read only after he died, contained the explanation of his origin. Yet the priest felt it was his duty to inform Adam Wiśniowiecki of this strange event and the latter forced the alleged Demetrius to reveal his "true" identity.[30]

The other version, transmitted by Baer, reflects the color of a popular tradition. One day when Prince Wiśniowiecki took a bath, his young valet forgot to bring him something, and Wiśniowiecki, annoyed, slapped him on the face. The young valet began to weep and said: "Prince Adam, if you only knew who I am, you would treat me differently." When the amazed Wiśniowiecki asked him to identify himself, the valet answered that he was Tsarevich Demetrius, Ivan IV's son. Then he related the story of his miraculous escape and showed a gold cross, adorned with diamonds, which he had received at his baptism.[31]

Wiśniowiecki believed the alleged Demetrius's story, took him to his brother Constantin, who, in turn, introduced him to George Mniszek, his father-in-law, the powerful Palatine of Sandomierz. When Mniszek heard that the alleged Demetrius was Ivan IV's son who sought to conquer the Muscovite throne usurped by Boris, and saw how Demetrius was attracted to Marina, his daughter, he decided to support his claim, hoping to be richly repaid by Demetrius after the latter has regained his empire. He knew well Sigismund III, king of Poland, and after informing the king of Demetrius's presence in Poland asked for his help, which would involve the recognition of the alleged Demetrius as well as assistance for the latter's campaign against Boris.

The alleged Demetrius met the King of Poland on March 15, 1604, and asked the latter's support for the recovery of his empire. He promised his true gratitude to the Polish King and nation if Sigismund would aid him.[32] Sigismund's attitude in the Demetrius affair is not clear to historians. According to some scholars, he recognized Demetrius and promised his help,[33] while according to others he decided to remain neutral but permitted his nobles to act in Demetrius's favor if they so wished.[34] Although most of the Polish nobles showed skepticism and even hostility to Demetrius's claim,[35] some were not unhappy at the opportunity of seeing the proud Boris humiliated, and others were attracted by the possibility of free plunder in rich Moscow.

In the view of the majority of historians, it is clear that, except for the Mniszek's clique, Poland was not originally responsible for the conspiracy to put the Pretender on the Russian throne.

Whether the original idea of using the alleged Demetrius against Boris for their ulterior motive came from the Jesuits, or whether the Pretender played a comedy with them and even with the Popes for achieving his aim is again one of the controversial questions of Russian historiography.

Several contemporaries, Protestants for the most part, and most of the Russian historians, suspect a Jesuit plot, and, although they add that in this diplomatic game of chess the alleged Demetrius proved smarter than the Jesuits, they still feel that it was the century-old policy of the Papal Court to eradicate the schism in Russia which used the Pretender for its purpose.[36] On the other hand Pierling, the Jesuit father, a specialist of the Russian Time of Troubles, tries to prove that the Jesuits did not initiate any plot against Moscow. He indicates the unfavorable reaction of Clement VIII to the emergence of the alleged Demetrius, and stresses the fact that the Jesuits visited the Pretender only after Sigismund had already given his unofficial blessing to the claimant of the Muscovite throne.[37]

Yet Pierling did not succeed in whitewashing his Order. In his popular history *Boris Godunov,* Stephen Graham accuses the Jesuits of duplicity:

It did not seem to them beyond the power of faith . . . to bring Russia into the true fold. In their reasoning the most striking point of departure was that in Russia all depended on the will of . . . the tsar. . . . Since Possevino's [the Pope's emissary to Ivan the Terrible] mission, the hope of converting Russia has been kept alive. . . . With the rise of Dimitry, the faith seemed justified. To some pious Catholics it must have seemed that God had saved Dimitry from the dead in order that Russia might be saved . . . by the mechanism of their conscience they were predisposed toward the Pretender. 'The cause of Christ always justifies the means.' It did not so much matter if Dimitry was an impostor. . . . What mattered was that he would bring Russia into the Catholic communion.[38]

On March 19, 1604, the alleged Demetrius met Rangoni, the Papal Legate in Poland, for the first time, asked his recommendation to the Pope, and promised to make a common crusade against the Turks.[39] In his efforts to win the support of the Jesuits, the clever Pretender did not overlook the fact that a ready promise to abjure Orthodoxy in favor of Catholicism might seem suspicious and he deemed it preferable to undergo a gradual conversion only after a studied inner struggle. The two Polish Jesuits who introduced Demetrius into Catholicism were Sawicki and Grodzicki, and, according to Pierling, the Pretender was converted on April 17, 1604.[40]

However, several of Demetrius's later acts, such as asking the Jesuits' permission to accept the blessing from the hand of an Orthodox priest at his coronation, marrying Marina according to the Greek rite, and choosing Protestants as his immediate collaborators, question the sincerity of his conversion. Kostomarov, the Russian historian, goes even so far as to doubt the fact of the Pretender's conversion.[41]

The alleged Demetrius wrote his famous letter to Clement VIII on April 24, 1604, informing him of his escape from the most cruel tyrant through the special providence of God, of his decision to join the Catholic Church, and asking the Pope's blessing, expressing his hope that perhaps God would use him to propagate His divine glory.[42] Yet, in spite of this letter, the alleged Demetrius still continued to profess openly only the Orthodox faith, and, except for vague promises, he did nothing to encourage the high hopes of the Jesuits, who followed him to the Russian capital, for the restoration of the Catholic religion in his country.

As a conclusion to this incident of the alleged Demetrius's flirtation with Catholicism, I quote Pierling, who sees the following three stages in the Pretender's religious attitude:

1. A Cracovie, il a tout le zèle d'un néophyte et sa piété est exemplaire; 2. pendant la campagne, c'est la raison d'État qui prédomine et l'amour de la religion lui est subordonné; 3. parvenu au trône et mal entouré, il s'adonne à l'impiété et au désordre.[43]

The Pretender's relationship with Marina Mniszek can be summarized in a few words. In most accounts the alleged Demetrius is said to have fallen in love with Marina, while her feelings toward the Pretender were motivated more by ambition and vanity than by true love. Walter Flex, the German literary critic, calls her a "cold egoist" and, in Pierling's view, she showed "more calculation than passion."[44] Enraptured by the idea of becoming a queen, her true complexion was clearly revealed after the alleged Demetrius's death, when she tricked Tsar Vasilij and made her way to the camp of the second Pretender in order to pursue her claim to the Russian throne.

Was the Pretender's success due to the military help received from the Poles or to the moral support of Rome and the Jesuits? The answer is that the success of the alleged Demetrius was due to neither of these factors and must be sought elsewhere.

We have seen that the Pretender received no real aid from King Sigismund and the only help he obtained was from Mniszek and his clique, who interpreted Sigismund's neutral attitude as a carte blanche to go ahead on their own and who organized a small band of adventurers, of whom a considerable number later returned to Poland. The rest, never numerous enough to win an important battle, gave only halfhearted support to the Pretender, being more interested in looting the Russian countryside.

As for the Pope, the alleged Demetrius had hoped to obtain from him, as a result of his "conversion" and vague promises, some material support, similar to that given previously by Rome to Stephen Bathory, king of Poland, for his campaign against Ivan IV, or at least some strong moral support. Yet despite the zeal of the Jesuits, Clement VIII remained aloof, and, apart from pious rejoicing and giving thanks to God for His divine intervention in favor of the Catholic faith, he did not provide any actual assistance for the Pretender.

The success of the alleged Demetrius was due to a coincidence of two factors. One was the emotional climate of the country, expressed in the discontent of the Russians—mostly those of the southern frontiers, remote garrisons as well as the banished nobles from the central provinces, and escaped serfs—with Boris's government. These discontented Russians could only welcome the Pretender, from whom they all expected an improvement in their situation.

The other factor lay in the concept of the Russian people concerning the divine nature of the tsar and in their strong attachment to their seven-hundred-year-old dynasty. Thus, as Ključevskij explains, the Russians could never really accept the election of Boris, since the image of an elected Tsar seemed to them not a result of political necessity, but an infringement of the elementary laws of nature "as grave an irregularity as an elected father . . . or mother," and they could only regard such a tsar, no matter how well he governed, as a usurper, "while even a single sign of a 'born tsar' in the person of a newcomer, however unknown his origin, was sufficient . . . to inspire them with respect."[45]

In addition, the mysterious death of Demetrius created conflicting rumors, "of which the popular imagination selected the most congenial," since what the people really desired was "that the Tsarevich should . . . reappear . . . and dissipate the gloomy uncertainty"[46] in which they have lived ever since Tsar Feodor's rule came to an end. In Ključevskij's summary:

As always in such cases, men were disposed to believe that villainy had failed, and . . . Providence had acted as the guardian. . . . In the eyes of the harassed nation the terrible fate of Boris . . . and his family was a striking manifestation of the eternal justice of God, and helped, more than anything else, to bring about the success of the pretenders.[47]

Having seen the cause of the alleged Demetrius's success, let us now consider his downfall. Why was it that the people were so easily influenced to turn and to rend the Sovereign whom they had so enthusiastically welcomed only eleven months previously?

The bloody events of May 17, 1606, are regarded by some sources as the result of a spontaneous uprising created by general dissatisfaction, yet there was a conspiracy behind the scenes prepared for a long time.

Platonov feels that the alleged Demetrius must have shocked the conservative elements, the boyars, and the well-to-do in Moscow with his plebeian ways and lack of dignity, breach of tradition, neglect of religious rites, his habitual rides to the church on horseback, and concludes:

. . . but the climax came at the time of his marriage. A great number of Poles had come to Moscow . . . to attend the wedding and . . . they were lodged in private houses. The guests assumed an air of superiority and . . . hurt the feelings of their hosts. . . . On the day of the wedding the Poles were invited to the Palace, and they [the Russians] were not even admitted to the Kremlin. . . . In addition . . . the populace was aroused . . . that the new Tsaritsa had not become Orthodox, and that the wedding . . . had taken place . . . in defiance of custom, on the eve of a holiday.[48]

In addition, the Polish guests brought so many mercenaries

with them that rumors of an impending Polish military occupation of the Muscovite capital were spread among the people.

Yet the popularity of the alleged Demetrius with the masses
was still so strong that the conspirators did not dare to move the
townsmen openly against the Kremlin but pretended to lead
them against the Poles under the excuse that the armed Poles
were murdering the innocent Russians. In view of the arrogant
conduct of the Polish soldiers, it was easily believed by the
majority of the population. For the immediate purpose of killing the alleged Demetrius, according to Soviet historian Pokrovskij, they despatched a specially selected small detachment
"which was readily admitted to the very sleeping quarters of the
tsar because it was headed by the foremost boyars of Moscow."[49]

That the chief cause of the alleged Demetrius's downfall cannot be attributed to a spontaneous uprising is borne out by his
continued popularity and by the willingness of the Russian people,
especially of those outside of Moscow, to support the second
Pretender, whom they identified with the first Demetrius. The
plot to kill Tsar Demetrius was hatched by the great boyars,
who had never intended to let him actually rule Russia unless he
agreed to be their tool, since, as Pokrovskij explains, the original
rebellion of the nobles was not launched in favor of the alleged
Demetrius, but against the usurper Boris. Since Demetrius refused to listen to them, retained his independence, took his high
office seriously, and governed intelligently, the boyars decided,
almost from the very first days of his accession, to overthrow
him. In Ključevskij's words we must listen to a testimony by
Vasilij Šujskij, the mainspring of the boyar revolt, who, at a
meeting of his fellow conspirators, said that he had known all
the time that the alleged Demetrius was not Ivan IV's son:

The "great" boyars were forced to create a pretender for the purpose of
dislodging Boris, and thereafter to dislodge the pretender for clearing
the road to the throne for a member of their own circle.[50]

Who Was the Alleged Demetrius?

In our attempt to establish the identity of the alleged Demetrius on the basis of historical sources, the first problem we face
is whether Tsarevich Demetrius died or escaped in Uglič on
May 15, 1591. For, if Ivan IV's son died in Uglič, the Tsar

crowned in Moscow on July 31, 1605, was obviously an impostor, whereas if Tsarevich Demetrius escaped, he could have become the legitimate Tsar of Moscow in 1065.

According to the official report Tsarevich Demetrius died in an epileptic fit. Yet Šujskij, the head of the commission which investigated the circumstances of the affair in Uglič, made three contradictory statements concerning the Tsarevich's death. These statements were obviously motivated by Šujskij's changing political fortune and they cannot be regarded trustworthy.

Yet in Boris's letter to Sigismund, in which the former attempts to identify the alleged Demetrius as a certain Gregory Otrep'ev, a runaway monk and evildoer, we find curious references to Ivan's "seventh, and therefore not legal wife," and to the alleged Demetrius, that "even if that criminal were really Prince Dmitri . . . risen from the dead, being the son of the . . . illegal wife, what could he do in our Kingdom"[51] Thus, Boris is clearly not sure whether the alleged Demetrius is or is not Ivan IV's son, for why would he speak of the legality of the true Demetrius's claim if he were convinced that the alleged Demetrius is not Ivan's son?

While the statements of Boris and Šujskij are interesting as historical documents of the time, their obvious bias discounts their validity, and they do not advance our investigation concerning the death or escape of Tsarevich Demetrius. Much more important could be the testimony emanating from, and centering around, the nun Marfa, Demetrius's mother. Marfa's testimony can be divided into two distinct groups: the first, made at the emergence of the alleged Demetrius, and the second made at his death.

According to some historians, when Boris, informed about the appearance of the alleged Demetrius in Poland, asked Marfa whether she could tell him anything about her son's death in Uglič, she answered that she did not know whether Demetrius was alive or not. According to others, Marfa replied that her son had been spirited away out of Russia, and she believed him to be still alive.[52]

Did Marfa recognize and accept the Pretender as her son? The meeting with Marfa must have been the most crucial moment for Demetrius. He was already recognized by Ignatius, the new Patriarch, but this was hardly enough, for Ignatius was only recently promoted by the Pretender himself to replace Jov,

the old Patriarch, who was Boris's protégé. In the eyes of the
tradition-bound Russian masses the most convincing proof of his
claims lay in "his mother's" recognition.

In the opinion of most contemporaries, Marfa recognized
the Pretender as her son, while modern historians are divided
on the genuineness of her sentiments.[53]

The last time Marfa was mentioned in connection with the
alleged Demetrius occurred shortly before or after the latter
was killed by the conspirators. Asked by Šujskij's clique whether
the Pretender was her son, she answered, according to some,
that her son had died in Uglič and she accepted the alleged
Demetrius only because everyone seemed to like him, while, according to others, her reply was: "You should have asked me
when he was still alive; now, obviously, he is no longer mine."[54]

Summarizing Marfa's testimony we can see that it was rather
confused. This must have been due to her emotional state, long
confinement in a convent, and obvious hatred of Boris. In his
popular history *Der falsche Demetrius,* Pantenius aptly mentions:

Man kann . . . aus der Tatsache, dass sie Demetrius anfangs als ihren
Sohn anerkannte ebensowenig schliessen, dass sie ihn fuer ihr Kind hielt,
wie der Umstand, dass sie ihn spaeter verleugnete, zu dem Schluss
berechtigt, sie habe ihn von vornherein als Betrueger erkannt.[55]

The contemporary Russian chronicles unanimously report that
Tsarevich Demetrius had been killed in Uglič and the alleged
Demetrius was an impostor.[56]

The original source of Tsarevich Demetrius's escape from the
assassins in Uglič is Adam Wiśniowiecki's report to King Sigismund, which Rangoni, in a Latin translation, forwarded to
Clement VIII on November 8, 1603. The most important part
of the report concerns the resourcefulness of Demetrius's devoted tutor, who, having discovered the plan to murder the
young prince, thwarted Boris's assassins by substituting another
child for Demetrius.[57]

Of the great number of contemporaries believing the alleged
Demetrius to be Ivan's son, the most important testimony comes
from Jacques Margeret, who knew the Tsarevich well: "Je con-
clus qu'il estoit le vray Demetrius Ionnes, fils de l'empereur
Ionnes Basilides, surnommé le Tyran."[58] The impressive roster
of authoritative contemporaries causes Pierling to exclaim:

Est-il donc tout à fait impossible que Démétrius ait été le vrai fils de
Jean IV, sauvé à Ouglitch? . . . Le roi de Pologne . . . se prononce
en sa faveur. . . . Les pontifes romaines Clement VIII et Paul V . . .
entrent dans la même voie. . . . Henri IV, roi de France, fait écrire à
Margeret . . . l'histoire du souverain. . . . L'extrême facilité avec la-
quelle cet accord universel dissipe les rumeurs, contraires à Démétrius, ne
donnerait-elle pas le droit de poser ce dilemme: ou l'Europe entière s'est
trompée, ou Démétrius était le vrai fils de Jean IV?[59]

Yet in all fairness it must be pointed out that it was not the
whole Europe which was deceived, nor could the opposite view
be described as mere rumors, because there were many who did
not believe in the story of the alleged Demetrius. There are contemporary Dutch, English, and German sources which regard
the Pretender as false although they usually present both the
positive and negative sides of Demetrius. As indicated before,
there was also a strong body of opposition among the Polish
nobles.[60]

It is appropriate at this point to draw an interim balance concerning the earliest opinions about the validity of Demetrius's
claim. Disregarding politically motivated and contradictory opinions, we can state that: (1) The majority of the Russians
accepted him; (2) The Russian chroniclers condemned him;
(3) The Jesuits, two Popes, and the Polish clergy regarded him
as authentic; (4) The Polish nobles, with the exception of the
Mniszek group, were against him; (5) King Sigismund was
generally in favor of him; and (6) With few exceptions the
Protestants were against him.

Thus, it can be seen that the judgment of Demetrius's claims
was colored by religious, dynastic, social, and nationalistic considerations and, in some cases, by purely egoistic motives. The
enthusiasm of the Russian people for Demetrius, in whom they
saw the legitimate heir to the throne and from whom they expected an improvement in their wretched social condition may be
contrasted to the attitude of the Russian chroniclers who, partly
out of ignorance, political partisanship, fierce patriotism and its
consequent xenophobia, and religious conservatism, regarded the
Pretender as Satan's vessel. With the exceptions mentioned
above, the Catholic contemporaries favored him for his promise
of bringing the true faith to Russia, while the Protestant writers
of the period judged him rather on the basis of "factual" information about his alleged escape from Boris's henchmen in Uglič.

In the eighteenth century the main lines of the interim balance still hold. The Catholic countries continue to regard the alleged Demetrius as Ivan's son while in Russia the official version identifying him with Otrep'ev dominates. Yet as the example of Gerhard F. Mueller, the German scholar who taught at St. Petersburg, shows, in this great process of world history ideological lines are crossed and previous opinions repudiated.[61]

In contrast to the scarcity of historical works devoted to the problem of the alleged Demetrius in the eighteenth century, in the nineteenth century an increasing number of articles, historical studies, monographs, and even many-volumed histories were published on this subject. In addition to the two-hundred-year-old official version, other opinions are also voiced, and the protean character of Demetrius gradually unfolds itself in a fascinating display of recurrent historical reinterpretation. Toward the end of the century some iconoclastic voices even dare to proclaim such an unprecedented opinion as that the Pretender might after all have been the legitimate son of Ivan the Terrible.

While Karamzin faithfully follows the chronicles and gives us nothing new about Demetrius, in his *Cerkovnaja istorija* (*History of the Church*, 1823), Metropolitan Platon was the first to express the view that it was not Otrep'ev's idea to become a Pretender, and it is possible that the Pretender was not Otrep'ev but someone else, put up by a clever intriguer operating behind the scenes. According to Platon, the Poles masterminded the idea of creating a Pretender for the purpose of gaining political influence in Russia. Pogodin identifies the Pretender as Otrep'ev and believes that the Jesuits engineered the plot.[62]

The investigation of Solov'ev, a Russian historian of the nineteenth century (1857), is important because it forms a bridge between the works of previous scholars and those of the future generation. While Solov'ev believes that the Pretender was Otrep'ev, he was the first who paid attention to the character and psychology of the alleged Demetrius. The firm behavior of the Pretender, his sincere belief in his rights, and his last fervent appeal to the conspirators to take him to the people to review his case dispassionately, convinced Solov'ev that this claimant was not a conscious impostor. If he was a cheater, this historian states, he, in turn, was so cleverly cheated by some skilled intriguer that he came to believe fully in his royal origin.[63]

The most significant work of the century on the Demetrius

riddle is Kostomarov's exposé *Kto byl pervyj Lžedimitrij?* (Who Was the First False Demetrius?), written in 1864, in which the author attempted to prove that the Pretender was not and could not have been Otrep'ev. The main argument of this treatise is that obviously it was easier for Boris's government to discredit a well-identified criminal and defrocked monk than a nameless pretender whom the people could, because of the mystery which anonimity creates, identify with Tsarevich Demetrius. Thus, Boris's government put the label of Otrep'ev on the alleged Demetrius to prevent the possibility of such an identification.

Kostomarov states that the Pretender was completely convinced of his royal origin. When Šujskij spread the news that the Pretender was not Ivan's son, the alleged Demetrius was not afraid to summon an assembly of the whole nation to examine the charges against himself. Had there been any proof that Demetrius was Otrep'ev, he could have been easily dethroned on this occasion. Even more important was the fact that, after the assembly unanimously sentenced Šujskij to death, the alleged Demetrius generously pardoned him. The Pretender must have been aware of the fact that Šujskij knew more about the Uglič affair than anyone else and that Šujskij was the next in line to the throne in case he (the alleged Demetrius) were dethroned. Thus, Kostomarov asks, if Demetrius had not been absolutely convinced of his right, would he have spared the life of such a dangerous foe? Another important step, adds Kostomarov, was his despatching Mikhail Skopin-Šujskij as his deputy to invite Marfa to meet him in Moscow. Would an impostor dare to send a blood relative of Vasili Šujskij, who recently denounced him as a defrocked monk, as his confidant for such an important mission? Even at the time of the *coup d'état,* the conspirators still did not know who the alleged Demetrius was, otherwise why would they have asked him: "Who are you? Who is your father?" Before killing him, the conspirators could have taken him, as he himself had asked, in front of the assembly of the people to let him prove his origin. Why did the Šujskij clique, not call Otrep'ev's mother, brother, uncle, and all those who knew him to testify against the claim of the alleged Demetrius?

Having proved that the alleged Demetrius was not Otrep'ev, Kostomarov attempts to answer the question of who he might have been. He could not have been educated by the Jesuits because he did not know Latin well enough, nor did he show the zeal for Catholicism which a disciple of Jesuits would presumably have displayed. He could not have been Polish either, because he spoke Russian as a born Great Russian. Could he have been the son of Ivan the Terrible? It is not absolutely impossible, answers Kostomarov, admitting that it would have been easier to save Tsarevich Demetrius than to fabricate him anew. Yet the author cannot accept this hypothesis either, for in that case the real Demetrius would have rewarded, during his reign, all those who had helped him to escape, and, while he was in Poland, would have been able to provide more substantial proof of his origin than he actually did. Finally, Kostomarov comes to the conclusion that the alleged Demetrius was created by the boyars' party, enemies of Boris.[64]

How deep is the mystery which surrounds the origin of the Pretender and how difficult is it for a conscientious scholar, even in possession of certain documentary proofs, to take a positive stand without having second thoughts is shown by Pierling's example. The author of *Rome et Démétrius* (1878) does not come to a definite conclusion regarding the identity of the alleged Demetrius, but the selectivity of his sources and the mechanism of his belief incline him to regard the Pretender as Ivan's son. Yet after additional investigation of the subject twenty-three years later in his new book *La Russie et le Saint-Siège* (1901), Pierling abandons his previous belief and feels that the alleged Demetrius was not Ivan's son. However, even on this occasion he is not fully convinced that this is the ultimate truth and cautiously qualifies his statement.[65]

Although earlier we had to discount Pierling's claim that at the beginning of the seventeenth century the whole of Europe believed in the miraculous escape of Tsarevich Demetrius, we must still admit that by far the greater number of foreign contemporaries, probably due to the zeal of the Jesuits in this period of victorious Counter-Reformation, came to accept the fabulous story of this Russian phoenix. This was, as we have seen, in sharp contrast to Russian historiography, which for two centuries and a half unquestioningly accepted the traditional view about the identity of the alleged Demetrius with the impostor Otrep'ev.

Yet, as Aleksej S. Suvorin, editor of the *Novoe Vremja* (New Times) and publisher of Chekhov's short stories points out, in private conversations among Russian historians and scholars, and even among people interested in the manifold, and often contradictory, texture of their past history, the possibility that the true Tsarevich had ascended the throne in 1605 and that Šujskij and his cohorts had killed the last offspring of the House of Rjurik was often discussed. This view could not be advanced openly because of the prevailing censorship in the press and the traditionally hostile attitude of the Church and government to the alleged Demetrius. However, despite this official ban, some intrepid researchers cautiously proceeded to remove the time-honored veil from this secret, and the cloud which oppressed objective historical investigation for three centuries slowly began to lift.

Suvorin's article (1894)[66] is distinguished by a new approach to the riddle of the elusive Demetrius, a journalistic urge of sensationalism, and a fantastic plot to justify his speculation, and, at the same time, strange as it may seem, by a partial return to Karamzinian tradition.

Comparing the Pretender to Xlestakov, the hero of Gogol's famous comedy *The Inspector General*,[67] Suvorin posits that the Pretender appeared not because he was useful to the Poles, Jesuits, or boyars, but because the temper of the time conjured him. Suvorin defends Karamzin's view that the alleged Demetrius was identical with Otrep'ev, who is the key figure in this legend, and crops up in every historical account.

Epilepsy plays an essential part in Suvorin's portrait of the Pretender. Since Tsarevich Demetrius was epileptic, it is important to note, the author adds, that the alleged Demetrius had all the traits of an epileptic too, as reflected in his sudden change from generosity to savagery, his grandiose dreams, and in his excessive sensuality.

Why did the boyars choose Otrep'ev, Suvorin asks. Not because of similar age or appearance, but because of their identical way of life. Since Otrep'ev was convinced that he was the rightful monarch, no preparation was needed to put him on the throne.

In Suvorin's hypothesis Tsarevich Demetrius had an epileptic fit in Uglič on May 15, 1591. He cut himself with the knife he was playing with, he was lying motionless, and appeared to be dead, but he was not really dead. His mother cried, his uncles used the occasion to settle accounts with the Bitjagovskij clique, the agents of Boris Godunov in Uglič, and the enraged population killed the enemies of their beloved Tsarevich. Yet Demetrius regained consciousness, and the Nagojs, the uncles and protectors of Demetrius, were faced with their harsh responsibility of having incited a massacre. They could not admit that Tsarevich Demetrius did not die and therefore decided to spirit him away lest he be seen by the population. Afanasij Nagoj took Demetrius to Yaroslavl in a boat on the Volga and hid him somewhere. Later he went to Jerome Horsey, the English traveler-merchant-diplomat in Russia asking him for some medicine for the Tsarevich who still might have needed it. Back in Uglič the Nagojs found a boy who had recently died and was similar in age to Demetrius and whom they displayed for the Šujskij commission which came from Moscow to investigate this case. In the meantime the real Demetrius grew up in various monasteries and took the name of Otrep'ev. The great boyars knew of him, but only when Boris became a tyrant did they begin to tell Demetrius of his past and to prepare his comeback to the throne. As if in a dream Demetrius recalled his almost forgotten life in Uglič. The boyars preached to him hatred of Boris, but the intelligent boy soon realized that they only wanted to use him for their own selfish purpose. Later he went to Poland and the rest of his story is known. To the obvious question of historians why Demetrius did not give details about his past, Suvorin replies that Demetrius hated both his wanderings in the monasteries, and the mask behind which he had to hide. Perhaps, muses Suvorin, Demetrius wanted to reveal all this to the people before the conspirators killed him, and this may explain his persistently repeated request to be taken to the people.[68]

Although Suvorin's plot is fantastic, it is not without logic. Suvorin refers to the article of Evgenij Ščepkin, a Russian historian, "Wer war Pseudodemetrius I?," in which two Otrep'ev families are described, and comes to the conclusion that if we can regard the Pretender as an adopted child of one of the Otrep'ev families, the Demetrius riddle may be considered as solved.[69]

Suvorin's view concerning the possibility of the identity of Demetrius of Uglič with the Demetrius of Sandomierz was shared by Kazimierz Waliszewski, a Polish-French historian, and D. S. Šeremetev, a Russian historian, with different motivations.[70]

Thus, the present century begins with an opposition of two cautiously formulated views, one affirming, the other denying the hero's identity with Tsarevich Demetrius. In order to bring this historical investigation up to date a few additional works must be mentioned, although they have no direct relevance to the Russian Demetrius dramas, the last of which appeared at the beginning of this century.

Having studied the official report (*sledstvennoe delo*), I. S. Beljaev, a Russian historian, states (1907) that not the real Demetrius, but another boy was killed in Uglič, and therefore the Pretender could have been Ivan IV's son.[71]

The most scientific, detailed, and lucid analysis of the official report was made by Vladimir Klejn (1913), a specialist of the affair in Uglič, who restored this much-maligned state paper to its full historical trustworthiness. It is difficult to disagree with the admirable logic which informs every page of this historical document. He holds that Demetrius killed himself in an epileptic fit, and comes to the conclusion that unless new contemporary accounts of unquestionable validity showing the contrary are discovered, the findings of this report cannot be disregarded.[72]

A brief essay by E. V. Tatiščev, Platonov's student, "K voprosu o smerti Tsarevicha Dimitrija" (On the Question of Tsarevich Demetrius's Death) (1922), mentions two important facts. First, the author found records in the Kirill Belozerskoj Monastery, according to which on May 15, 1592, i.e., on the first anniversary of the Uglič affair, the nun Marfa, Demetrius's mother, made a donation to the memory of her dead son. In Tatiščev's view this document would prove without any doubt that Demetrius died, and the Pretender was an impostor. Second, he quotes from a statement by Andrej Nagoj, dated November 19, 1617, in which the latter speaks about a horse which he took from his younger brother Mixail at the time "when Tsarevich Demetrius was killed." To evaluate this statement according to its trustworthiness, continues the author, we must recall the circumstances under which it was written. This was Andrej Nagoj's last will before his death, in which he used Demetrius's murder as a casual point of time reference. In the opinion of the Russian historian it is impossible to believe that, in his last solemn hours, the dying Nagoj had any reason to distort the truth of events which had occurred some twenty-eight years earlier.[73]

Vernadsky's article, mentioned before, is the last important historical contribution to the Demetrius legend. Although the author does not speculate on the identity of the alleged Demetrius, his warm endorsement of Klejn's analysis clearly reveals his conviction that Tsarevich Demetrius died in Uglič and therefore Demetrius of Sandomierz could not be Demetrius of Uglič.

Thus, the historical contradictions continue and the present stand of scholarship admits three interpretations:

1. The romantic school (Suvorin, Waliszewski, Šeremetev, Beljaev) believes that the alleged Demetrius could have been Ivan IV's son.

2. The scientific school (Platonov, Tatiščev, Klejn, Vernadsky) holds that Tsarevich Demetrius died and therefore the Pretender was not identical with Ivan's son.

3. The Soviet school affirms that Tsarevich Demetrius died and the alleged Demetrius was a political adventurer, agent of the Poles and the Vatican.

"Every historical work reflects a certain philosophy of life and a certain period of time," said Pokrovskij[74] and, as an illustration of this thesis one can see how, from the various historical portraits of the alleged Demetrius, the political, social, and religious aims of the government, under whose aegis it was produced, can be deduced.

It is impossible not to understand why Boris's government called the Pretender a criminal and why, for Šujskij's annalist, he was Satan's vessel. To the historian of the eighteenth century, who himself had to skate on the thin ice of political uncertainty because of the chaotic succession created by recurring palace revolutions, the alleged Demetrius could not expect a fair trial either. Ščerbatov, an eighteenth century Russian historian who disagreed with many of Peter I's progressive reforms, could not but see in the alleged Demetrius an avowed partisan of Western culture and a forerunner of the corruption of traditional Russian morality. The fear of Jacobinism in the wake of the French revolution, the official acceptance of the Pretender's bust carved by Karamzin, the court historian, and later the reactionary conservatism of Nicholas I continued to prevent an objective appraisal of the problem. It was only during the relatively liberal government of Aleksandr II that Kostomarov dared to submit his iconoclastic theory. The sympathy with which the reactionary Suvorin regarded the alleged Demetrius might come as a psychological shock to students of history. But his Karamzinian hate of Boris Godunov, usurper of the throne, and his desire to maintain the legitimacy of succession might explain his stand.

In the Soviet era the changing colors of the portrait of the

alleged Demetrius may be linked to the oscillation of governmental policy. The Pokrovskian "rebellion of the nobles" which
spearheaded the uprising against Boris is now replaced by the
rebellion of the masses to become the dominant trait of the Time
of Troubles with strong xenophobian overtones. And, it is not
without interest to note, as seen from the Soviet stage, the various interpretations of the alleged Demetrius have completed
a full circle, and, after his three-hundred-and-fifty years of wandering in Russian historiography, the hero of the legend returned to his point of departure and once again donned his
original mask. There is hardly any difference between the version
of contemporary Russian annalists seeing him as Satan's vessel,
opening the door for a foreign invasion of the Muscovite State,
and that of *Outline of History of the USSR* regarding him as
a tool of the Polish-Lithuanian magnates and of the Vatican
preparing a disguised military intervention in Russia.[75] Without
its religious implication, the Soviet still sees the alleged Demetrius in this mystery story with his cloak stitched in Rome, and
his dagger tempered in Cracow. It is possible that the encomium
of Soviet historians, to whitewash Ivan IV and to present him as
a wise leader of Russian expansionism, could not have permitted
an objective judgment of the man who promised to give Russian land away to the very nation which blocked Muscovite expansion to the West in the sixteenth and seventeenth centuries.

Whether or not the alleged Demetrius was the real Tsarevich, he was definitely a man of the Renaissance and of the
Reformation. He had many visible specks on his moral armor,
such as his vanity for high titles, his sensuousness, his intrigue
with the Poles and Jesuits, and his extravagant gifts for his
favorites. Yet Solov'ev speaks of his "brilliant talent," of his
skill in statescraft, of his plans to send the boyars abroad to
learn the ways of the West, and sees in him a forerunner of
Peter's progressive reforms.[76] Pierling stresses his interest in humanism and culture, his fascination for rhetoric, languages, and
literature, mentions his civilizing and scientific projects, his plans
to bring foreign engineers and craftsmen into Russia, and points
out his educational zeal in building schools and colleges.[77]

This explains why, in some of the Demetrius dramas, he is
regarded as a kind of Russian Prometheus who stole the light of
civilization from the West to illuminate the dark and vast Russian
plains. Unfortunately this light was brutally extinguished by the
jealousy, superstition, and backwardness of the boyars of the pe-

riod, and Russia had to wait another century until Peter the Great finally succeeded in building a lasting cultural bridge to the West.

NOTES

1. D. D. Blagoj, *Tvorčeskij put' Puškina* (Moscow-Leningrad: Akademii Nauk SSSR, 1950), p. 416.

2. *Ibid.*

3. A phrase of Vissarion Belinskij (1811–1848), a leading Russian literary critic and political thinker. *Ibid.*, p. 46.

4. Pavel O. Pierling, *Rome et Démétrius* (Paris: E. Leroux, 1878), p. xii.

5. Constantin de Grunwald, *La vraie histoire de Boris Godunov* (Paris: A. Fayard, 1961), p. 55.

6. S. F. Platonov, *Drevnerusskija skazanija i povesti o smutnom vremeni XVII veka*, 2d ed. (St. Petersburg: Tip. M. A. Aleksandrova, 1913), p. 172; George Peyerle, "Beschreibung der Moscowitterischen Rayse," trans. Nikolaj Ustrjalov, *Skazanija sovremennikov o Dimitrij Samozvance* 5 vols.; (St. Petersburg: 1834–1837). 2:1–2; N. M. Karamzin, *Istorija Gosudarstva Rossijskago*, 11 vols., 5th ed. (St. Petersburg, 1845), 9:259.

7. R. Wipper, *Ivan Grozny*, trans. J. Fineberg (Moscow: Foreign Languages Publishing House, 1947), p. 13; C. Baxrušin, *Ivan Groznij* (Moscow: Gosizdat, 1945), pp. 3, 5, 65.

8. S. M. Solov'ev, *Istorija Rossii s drevnejšix vremen*, 11 books (Moscow: Izd. social 'no-ekonom. lit., 1960), 4:7; S. F. Platonov, *Ivan Groznij* (St. Petersburg, 1923), pp. 12–14; Charles Ziegler, *Ivan IV dit le Terrible* (Paris: Science Historique, 1957), p. 2; H. Vallotton, *Ivan le Terrible* (Paris: A. Fayard, 1959), pp. 8, 294, 305.

9. Sonia E. Howe, *Some Russian Heroes, Saints and Sinners* (London: Williams and Norgate, 1913), p. 229.

10. Grunwald, p. 23.

11. V. O. Ključevskij, *A History of Russia*, trans. C. J. Hogarth, 5 vols. (New York: Russel and Russel, 1960), 2:103.

12. A. S. Puškin, *Boris Godunov*, a drama in verse. Rendered into English verse by Alfred Hayes (London: K. Paul, Trench, Trubner & Co., Ltd., 1918), pp. 28, 55. The crown of Monomax is the famous gift of the Byzantine Emperor Constantine IX to Vladimir Monomax, Grand Prince of Kiev (1113–1125), as emblem of Russian sovereignty.

13. M. Pogodin, "Ob učastii Godunova v ubienii Tsarevicha Dimitrija," *Istoriko-kritičeskije otryvki* (Moscow, 1846); S. P. Platonov, *Boris Godunov* (Prague, 1924).

14. The institution of the select men of Ivan IV; a kind of state security organ and private army.

15. Stephen Graham, *Ivan the Terrible* (New Haven: Yale University Press, 1933), p. 255.

16. Platonov, *Drevnerusskija*, p. 304.

17. Solov'ev, 4:192–94.

18. The official report (sledstvennoe delo) was first published in *Sobranija gos. gram. i dogovorov* (1819), vol. 2; later Suvorin published it in his book *O Dimitrii Samozvance* (St. Petersburg: 1906), pp. 181–221; the third edition was prepared by Vladimir Klejn in 1913. See n. 72.

19. Šujskij changed this version several times. His final statement, issued after his coronation in 1606, was that Demetrius had been murdered by Boris's agents in 1591.

20. Platonov, *Drevnerusskija,* pp. 23, 177, 180, and 275.

21. *Ibid.,* p. xvi; Vernadsky, p. 6.

22. Giles Fletcher, "Of the Russe Commonwealth," *The English Works of Giles Fletcher, the Elder,* ed. Lloyd E. Berry (Madison: The University of Wisconsin Press, 1964), p. 205. The original edition was published in 1591; Jerome Horsey, "A Relacion of Memoriall Abstracted of Sir Jerome Horsey, His Travels," *Russia at the Close of the Sixteenth Century,* ed. Edward A. Bond (London: Hakluyt Society, 1857), p. 257; Martin Baer, "Chronicon Muscovitum continens res a morte Joannis Basilidis Tyranni" trans. Ustrjalov, 1:4; George Peyerle, Ustrjalov, 2:2; Jacques Margaret, *Estat de l'Empire de Russie et Grande Duche de Moscovie* (Paris, 1606), p. 18; Marina Mniszek, "Dnevnik Maryiny Mniševka," trans. Ustrjalov, 4:2; Samuel Maszkiewicz, "Dnevnik Samuila Maskevica," trans. Ustrjalov, 5:3; Isaac Massa, *Histoire des Guerres de la Moscovie (1601–1610),* 2 vols. (Brussels, 1866), 1:46; Hetman Stanislas Żółkiewski *Expedition to Moscow, a Memoir,* trans. M. W. Stephen (London: Polonia Publications, 1959); Barrezo Barezzi, *Relazione della segnalata e come miracolosa conquista del paterno Imperio conseguita dal serenissimo giovine Demetrio Gran Duca di Moscovia: L'anno 1605* (Venice, 1605).

23. Vernadsky, p. 8.

24. De la Rochelle, *Le Czar Demetrius, Histoire Moscovite* (Paris: 1716), pp. 6–8; Gerhard F. Mueller, *Sammlung Russischer Geschichte,* 9 vols. (St. Petersburg: 1732–1764), 5:52; P. Ch. Levesque, *Histoire de Russie* (Paris, 1782), p. 220; Le Clerc, *Histoire de la Russie ancienne,* 2 vols. (Paris, 1783), 2:381; M. M. Scerbatov, *Istorija Rossijskaja ot drevnejšix vremen,* 7 vols. (St. Petersburg: 1770–1791), 6:2.

25. Karamzin, 10:75; Solov'ev, 4:317–42 and Kostomarov, *Sobranie sočinenija,* 21 vols., (St. Petersburg; Izd. Lit. Fonda, 1903), 4:16. The first dissenting voice came from Mixail Pogodin, who felt that Demetrius's death was not necessary for Boris. (Pogodin, p. 278.) He was supported by N. S. Arcybašev, "O končine Careviča Dimitrija," *Vestnik Evropy,* Nos. 9–12 (1830), pp. 241–66; by N. Ustrjalov, i:vii; and by E. A. Belov, "O smerti Careviča Dimitrija," *Žurn. Min. Narod. Prosv,* 168 (1873): 1–44, and 279–320.

26. Platonov, *Boris,* pp. 7, 8, 169, 174, 182; M. N. Pokrovskij, *History of Russia,* trans. and ed., J. D. Clarkson and M. R. M. Griffiths (New York: International Publishers, 1931), p. 169; Karl Staehlin, *Geschichte Russlands,* 2 vols. (Berlin: 1923), 1:315.

27. Platonov, *History of Russia,* trans. E. Aronsberg (New York: The Macmillan Co., 1925), p. 146.

28. Margeret, trans., *Ustrjalov,* 3:77; Herman Skribanowitz, *Pseudo-Demetrius I* (Berlin: 1913), p. 9.

29. Pierling, *Rome,* p. 175.

30. Marina Mniszek, *Ustrjalov,* 4:4.

31. Baer, Ustrjalov, 1:33.

32. Pierling, *Rome,* p. 180.

33. Alessandro Cilli, *Historia di Moscovia* (Pistoia: 1627), p. 12; *Tragoedia Muscovitica, sive de vita et morte Demetrii,* apud Grevenbruch (Coeln: 1608), p. 64.

34. Pierling, *Rome,* p. 39.

35. *Russkaja Istoričeskaja Biblioteka,* izd. Arxeografičeskoj kommissii, vol. I; (St. Petersburg: 1872), pp. 1, 5, 10, 16, 38.

36. De Thou, "Historiarium sui temporis," trans. Ustrjalov, 3:131; Massa, p. 26; Karamzin, 10:77; Solov'ev, 4:404; Kostomarov, 4:61–65.

37. Clement VIII wrote on the margin of Rangoni's report "Sarà un alto re di Portugallo risuscitato." Pierling, *Rome,* p. 9.

38. Stephen Graham, *Boris Godunov* (London: Ernest Benn, 1933), p. 180.

39. Pierling, *Rome,* p. 182.

40. *Ibid.,* pp. 20–37.

41. Kostomarov, *Kto byl pervij Lžedimitrij?* (St. Petersburg, 1864), p. 34.

42. Pierling, *Rome,* pp. 157–58.

43. Ibid., p. 150. Giertych points out that Demetrius was gathering troops under the pretext of war against Turkey, but actually he was supporting an anti-royalist rebellion in Poland. Introduction to Żółkiewski, p. 26.

44. Walter Flex, *Die Entwicklung des tragischen Problems in den deutschen Demetriusdramen von Schiller bis auf die Gegenwart* (Dissertation, Friedrich Alexander Universität, Erlangen, Hofbuchdruckerei, Eisenach H. Kahle, 1912), p. 38.

45. Ključevskij, 3:51.

46. *Ibid.,* p. 56.

47. *Ibid.*

48. Platonov, *History,* p. 151.

49. M. N. Pokrovskij, p. 192.

50. Klijučevskij, 3:31.

51. Sonia E. Howe, *The False Dmitri* (London: Williams and Norgate, 1916), pp. 11–13.

52. Massa, p. 115; Karamzin, 9:83–84; Solov'ev, 4:411; Kostomarov, *Sobranie,* p. 101.

53. Baer, in Ustrjalov, 1:48–49; Peyerle, in Ustrjalov, 3:146; Karamzin, 11:127–128; Solov'ev, 4:429; Kostomarov, *Sobranie,* 4:143.

54. De Thou, in Ustrjalov, 3:158; Karamzin, 9:169; Kostomarov, 4:223.

55. Theodor H. Pantenius, *Der falsche Demetrius* (Bielefeld-Leipzig: 1904), p. 88.

56. Platonov, *Drevnerusskija,* pp. 46, 58, 195, 229.

57. S. J. Pierling, *La Russie et le Saint-Siège* 3 vols. (Paris; Plon-Nourrit et Cie, 1896–1901), 3:431–44.

58. Margeret, *Estat,* p. 175; Peyerle, Ustrjalov, 2:2; Marina Mniszek, Us-strjalov, 4:2.

59. Pierling, *Rome,* p. xx.

60. Baer gave a list of people who denied Demetrius's claim. Ustrjalov, 1:102–3; Horsey, p. 261; Żółkiewski, p. 34. In a letter to King Sigismund, the Polish Chancellor Jan Zamojski wrote that Demetrius's story sounds like a comedy by

Plautus or Terence. Quoted by Skribanowitz, p. 82. There were a few voices who maintained that it was impossible to decide whether or not Demetrius was true. De Thou, Ustrjalov, III, 3:168; Grevenbruch, *Tragoedia,* p. 114.

61. Rochelle, p. 3; Mueller's testimony is contradictory. First he stated that the alleged Demetrius was Otrep'ev (5:200–8), then he declared that Demetrius was Ivan's son. (Quoted by Pierling, *Rome,* p. xxii.)

62. Platon, *Cerkovnaja istorija* (Moscow: 1823), pp. 167–79; Pogodin, p. 309.

63. Solov'ev, 4:403.

64. Kostomarov, *Kto byl,* pp. 11, 13, 17, 18–19, 50–63.

65. Pierling, *La Russie,* p. 399.

66. Suvorin, *O Dimitrii Samozvance* (On the False Demetrius) (St. Petersburg, 1905), pp. 1–114.

67. Suvorin follows Kostomarov's *Kto byl,* p. 49.

68. After reading Suvorin's hypothesis, the historian Bestužev-Rjumin wrote to D. S. Šeremetev, who was also trying to solve the Demetrius puzzle: "For you the important thing is that it was the real Tsar Demetrius and that this problem can now be discussed openly." (Suvorin, p. iv.)

69. Evgenij Ščepkin, "Wer war Pseudodemetrius I?" *Archiv der Slavischen Philologie* 20 (1898): 224–325; 21 (1899): 99–169 and 558–606; and 22 (1900): 321–432. This is the most comprehensive survey of the literature concerning the identity of the Pretender.

70. K. Waliszewski, *La crise revolutionnaire,* 2d ed. (Paris: Plon-Nourrit et Cie, 1906), pp. 53–54. Šeremetev believed that it was the last Rjurik who came to his tragic end when Šujskij and his followers stormed the Kremlin on May 17, 1606, and the conspirators knew well that they killed the son of Ivan the Terrible, their rightful Tsar, and not the runaway monk of the Čudov monastery. See Suvorin, pp. iv–v.

71. I. S. Beljaev, quoted by Vernadsky, p. 14.

72. Vladimir Klejn, "Ugličskoe sledstvennoe delo," *Zapiski imp. Moskovs. Arxeologičeskago Instituta* 25 (1913).

73. E. V. Tatiščev, "K voprosu o smerti Careviča Dimitrija," *Sbornik statej po russkoj istorii posjaščennix S. F. Platonovu* (St. Petersburg: 1922), pp. 219–26.

74. Pokrovskij, p. ix.

75. *Outline History of the USSR* (Moscow: Foreign Languages Publishing House, 1960), p. 72.

76. Solov'ev, 4:403; V. S. Ikonnikov, *Neskol'ko zametok po voprosam smutnago vremeni* (Kiev: Tip. Imperatorskago Universiteta, 1916), pp. 60–61.

77. Pierling, *Rome,* p. 77. After finishing this manuscript I read Philip L. Barbour's *Dimitry, Called the Pretender.* The author feels that "unprejudiced and careful investigation of available sources leads not only to the inescapable conclusion that Dimitry himself was convinced that he was genuine, but also to the presumptive truth that in some way he really was." (Boston: Houghton Mifflin Co., 1966), p. 327.

2

Lope de Vega's *El Gran Duque de Moscovia y Emperador Perseguido*

Introduction

The earliest literary adaptation of the Demetrius legend, *El Gran Duque de Moscovia y emperador perseguido,* a drama in three acts, was written by Lope de Vega, founder of the Spanish national theater.[1]

A brief outline of the plot is as follows: In an outburst of anger Basilio, Great Prince of Muscovy, kills his son Juan and he himself dies the same day. Since Teodoro, Basilio's other son, is unfit to rule, Cristina, Teodoro's wife, appoints Boris, her brother, to govern until Demetrio, son of Teodoro and Cristina, grows up. Boris, the new governor, usurps the power and decides to kill Demetrio. However, Lamberto, Demetrio's tutor, and Rufino, Lamberto's servant, thwart the attempt and Demetrio escapes. Later Demetrio and Rufino enter a monastery, but flee when Boris discovers Demetrio's presence there. Later Demetrio and Rufino work as peasants in Livonia and become servants for the Count-Palatine, to whom Demetrio reveals his identity. With the help of Sigismundo, the king of Poland, Demetrio reconquers his empire and marries the Count-Palatine's daughter.

The attraction which Lope felt for the Demetrius saga was not only its historical actuality, its contemporary reality, but also its dramatic character,[2] which appealed to his imagination and artistic instinct. The feudal lord who becomes a tyrant is a favorite theme of Lope (*Fuenteovejuna, Peribañez*), and he devoted several *comedias* to the wise and just king who severely condemned wanton and immoral noblemen (*Los novios de Hornachuelos, El mejor alcalde, el rey*). In his Demetrius drama the tyrant-nobleman goes even further and attempts to murder the legitimate heir to the throne to become the monarch. This is a theme which rarely appears in Lope's theater since treachery against the king could hardly be accommodated with Lope's exalted ideas about royal majesty. Yet the richness of dramatic events which characterizes the miraculous escape of the Russian Tsarevich and his subsequent extraordinary adventures must have been too great a temptation for the Spanish playwright and led to his decision to put them on the stage. Thus, history served merely as a frame into which Lope cast his quickly moving romantic extravaganza and baroque chiaroscuro.

If the tyrant was one of Lope's favorite themes, so also was the innocent and persecuted hero. "In einer stattlichen Gruppe Lopescher Dramen," writes the German literary critic Karl Vossler in *Lope de Vega und sein Zeitalter,* "steht der . . . unterdrueckte . . . Mensch im Vordergrund . . . Unglueck und Leid besonders wenn sie einen Schuldlosen treffen sind . . . ein dankbarer Gegenstand."[3]

Another reason for dramatizing Demetrius's adventures must have been Lope's keen sense for the stage. "Lope . . . hatte eben mit einem Publikum zu tun," wrote Grillparzer, the famous Austrian playwright, a great admirer of Lope, "dass durch seine Romanzen und Ritterromane . . . an das Bizarre . . . ja Wunderliche gewoehnt war und es von dem Dichter forderte."[4] Thus, the spectacle of a tyrant persecuting an innocent hero who is the legitimate heir and later the king of the country must have touched the audience and moved it to compassion. We can illustrate this melodramatic situation with a scene from the play when Lope's Demetrio, wrapped in rags, is introduced by the Count-Palatine to King Sigismundo of Poland to ask the latter's support for his campaign to reconquer his throne:

> Rey: ¿Quiere verme roto?
> Conde: Quiere
>   Que cuanto más te moviere
>   A compasión, más lo estima.[5]

In addition to the combination of tyranny and innocence, Lope's dramatic convention demanded that the hero should not accept the injustice, but fight back bravely regardless of the odds against him. In Vossler's words:

Dem Jammer und Unrecht sich nicht zu beugen . . . sondern tapfer dagegen zu reagieren, das ist in Lope's Sinn die . . . buehnengemaesse Haltung. Nirgends sind seine Spiele frischer als dort wo er die Abwehr eines Unrechts . . . zu zeigen hat. Der Gegenschlag . . . ist nicht nur in der grossen Geschichte seines Volkes, sondern auch im taeglichen Leben der fruchtbare . . . dramatische Moment.[6]

Thus, the basic theme of the *comedia* is usurpation of power, persecution of the innocent prince, and punishment of the tyrant by the legitimate emperor, who at the end of the play regains his crown.

Problems of Dating, Sources, and Scholarship

As it was the case with many of his other plays, Lope probably wrote *El Gran Duque* directly for performance on the stage,[7] and it was first published only several years later in the *Séptima parte de las Comedias de Lope de Vega* in 1617. Américo Castro, a Spanish literary historian, indicates that there was another copy of this *comedia* dated 1613 and entitled *Los nuevos sucesos del Gran Duque de Moscovia*.[8] However, the exact date of the composition of the play is not known, nor can it be definitely established when it was performed for the first time.

WESTERN-EUROPEAN CONTRIBUTION

The first tentative dating of Lope de Vega's Demetrius *comedia* can be found in the preface which Moritz Rapp, a German *hispanista* of the last century, wrote to his translation of this drama in 1868. Rapp believed that the Spanish dramatist created *El Gran Duque* at a time when the alleged Demetrius was still alive, which would make the terminus *ad quem* not later than mid-1606. The German translator also noted the discrepancy between the ending of the drama and the historical events in Moscow:

Sehr merkwuerdig ist aber, dass das Stueck in Moskau ganz anders zu Ende lief als es in Madrid auf der Buehne agiert wurde. Der Moench Otrepief trat seinen Kamp gegen Zar Boris 1604 an und bald darauf muss das Stueck geschrieben . . . worden sein, denn schon 1605 wurde der falsche Demetrius ermordet und die Kunde davon konnte noch nicht in Spanien sein als der Dichter . . . [sein Drama] schrieb. Sonst haette er sein Stueck nicht zur Verherrlichung der Legitimitaet . . . aufgefuehrt.[9]

In his *Observaciones Preliminares* to the seventh volume of Lope's works (1896), the distinguished Spanish literary historian Menéndez y Pelayo disagrees with Rapp's speculation about the date of the composition and argues that Lope could not have written his *comedia* during the life of his hero, whose reign was so brief. He correctly states the year of Demetrius's death as 1606 and adds that ten years later Lope's *comedia* was already published. Regarding the date of the staging, the Spanish literary critic asserts that

we cannot establish when the *comedia* was played for the first time, but it should have taken place considerably earlier, since in the play the false Demetrius (whom Lope shows as authentic) remains alive in peaceful possession of his empire. Thus, the news of his death did not reach Spain at once.[10]

A study of the sources for Lope's *comedia* will help us to come closer to the date of the composition. While Rapp refers to some specific details of the play which Lope must have obtained from Russia without naming definite sources, Menéndez y Pelayo is more precise:

Which of the many reports circulating throughout Europe about this extraordinary event did Lope read? Most probably he read the pamphlet of the Italian Barezzo Barezzi (1606) and perhaps some Spanish reports based on Barezzi's account.[11]

The title of Barezzi's brochure is *Relazione della segnalata e come miracolosa conquista del paterno imperio, conseguita dal serenissimo giovine Demetrio, Gran Duca di Moscovia. L'anno 1605.* S. Ciampi, the Italian literary historian, thinks that Barezzi is a pseudonym and attributes this pamphlet to Antonio Possevino, the Jesuit father who visited Russia as the Pope's envoy to mediate peace between Ivan the Terrible and Stephen Bathory, King of Poland, in 1581,[12] and wrote *La Moscovia,* an account of his visit.[13]

Father Possevino was in touch with the Jesuits in Poland as well as with Czyrzowski and Lawicki, the two Polish Jesuits who accompanied Demetrius in his campaign in Russia against Boris Godunov, and he received information about events which occurred in Russia of the time.[14]

Menéndez y Pelayo does not think that Lope used *Tragoedia Moscovitica, sive de vita et morte Demetrii,* a contemporary anonymous account of Demetrius's adventures, written in 1608, because this pamphlet already mentioned Demetrius's death. The Spanish scholar points out that another hypothesis is possible—and the historical errors in the drama seem to reinforce it—that Lope did not use a printed record, but oral information from some Polish or Spanish Jesuits living in a Polish college, the only likely channel through which, at that time, news could have come from such a remote country to Spain.

In spite of the disagreement of this Spanish scholar I feel that Lope might have read *Tragoedia* and used it for the description of the court, character, and death of Basilio (the historical Ivan IV), the accidental murder of Tsarevich Juan (the historical Tsarevich Ivan), and Boris's participation in the assassination of Demetrio's double. However, some episodes of *Tragoedia,* such as Boris's active role in the murder, the replacement of Demetrio with another boy and not with the tutor's own son, and the tutor's doubt about the alleged Demetrio's origin, are at variance with the drama and therefore this brochure can be regarded only as a possible supplementary source.

While Menéndez y Pelayo correctly guessed Barezzi's work, either in the Italian original, or in a possible Spanish version as Lope's source, Emile Gigas, a Danish scholar who treated this problem in his "Etudes sur quelques *comedias* de Lope de Vega" (1933) did not seem to know anything of Barezzi's work as a source for Lope's drama, and merely suspected some kind of information from a Jesuit source.[15]

In agreement with Rapp, Gigas also felt that Lope had certain specific knowledge of the Slavic world and enumerated a few instances of Russian *couleur locale* in the play, such as the mention of Tsar Basilio's iron stick, the sign of his authority, the royal titles of Boris, and references to sable martens.

Gigas died at the time when his article was published and he could not know that, in another article written almost at the same time as his, "La fuente de El Gran Duque," the German *hispanista* Gertrud von Poehl believed that she had found the Spanish source for the Demetrius drama.[16] On the basis of abundant historical details in Lope's play, Poehl came to the conclusion that the Spanish playwright must have used a written account. However, his treatment of the alleged Demetrius as an authentic prince contradicts Russian tradition and shows indirectly that his information must have come from a country where the Pretender's royal birth was recognized. Such a country, Poehl continues, was Poland, and therefore Lope's direct source was either a Latin, Italian, or Spanish account, languages which Lope understood, presumably drawn from the original Polish report.

Poehl later examined the Spanish translation of Barezzi's work, done by Juan Mosquera, a Spanish Jesuit, in 1606, entitled *Relacion de la Señalada y como milagrosa conquista del paterno imperio*[17] and published her findings in another article, "Quellenkundliches zur Geschichte des Ersten Falschen Demetrius."[18] In her view, "Mosquera hat *nicht genau* uebersetzt," but rendered an "Ueberarbeitung" and created a "literarisch frisiertes Werkchen." Since all the changes that Mosquera made can be found in Lope's play, Poehl is convinced that Lope's direct source was not Barezzi, but Mosquera. It is important to point out the most active change in Mosquera's recasting, which concerns the saving of Tsarevich Demetrius from Boris's assassins. Thus, if we juxtapose Barezzi's Italian original:

Mise dunque il Gouernatore a dormire in un medisimo letto con Demetrio, un figliuole dell'istessa eta, et fatezza, senza dire ad alcuno cosa veruna; et come fu addormentato, fece portare Demetrio secretamente fuori del letto. Venuto il tempo determinato di ammazzare Demetrio i sudetti mandati da Boris, pensando coprire il misfatto coll'oscurita della notte, andarono al letto di Demetrio e strangolarono quell' altro figliulo, credendo che fosse Demetrio.[19]

with Mosquera's Spanish version:

. . . el Gouernador y ayo de Demetrio determinó con vn notable engaño salvar la vida a este Principe de cuya fidelidad se le auia cõfiado y pospuló la de vn solo hijo que tenia, de la mesma edad, talle y faciones de Demetrio; hecho digno por cierto de eterna memoria. Tomó pues a su propio hijo y acostoló en la mesma cama de Demetrio y estando los dos muchachos ya dormidos, sacó a Demetrio de la cama y dexó a su hijo en su lugar durmiendo en ella. . . .[20]

we notice that, while in Barezzi's original the tutor replaced Demetrius with a "boy of the same age and similar appearance," Mosquera lent epic proportion to the tutor by having him replace the young prince with his own son, who was subsequently strangled. This change is retained in Lope's play, who gave the name Lamberto to the anonymous tutor of Mosquera's pamphlet.

We also find an important change between Mosquera's account and Lope's *comedia* as far as religious ideology is con-

cerned. Lope's drama is completely silent about the introduction
of the Catholic faith in Russia, an idea which plays such an
important part in Mosquera's account. Poehl feels that Lope's
main aim was to entertain his audience and that therefore the
historical background did not deserve the attention of the playwright, who might have felt that the inclusion of this idea would
have burdened the exposition of the *comedia*. Lope takes for
granted, Poehl adds, that the action occurs in a Catholic country. Boris, for example, in his letter to the Pope declares that
he is a good Catholic, and Rodulfo, Boris's confidant, tells
Sigismundo in his ambassadorial message that the Conclave will
excommunicate the impostor who tries to pass for Demetrius.

Poehl indicates Possevino's *Moscovia* as a definite source for
Mosquera's brochure but she leaves unexplored the possibility
of a direct influence of Possevino's work on Lope. The Spanish
playwright may have obtained from *Moscovia* valuable information concerning the atmosphere of Basilio's court, the character of this Tsar, the details of Tsarevich Ivan's accidental
murder, and the facts of Basilio's death. Boris is referred to
only by his rank and Demetrio is not mentioned at all. However,
this book could not have been Lope's main source, since it was
written before Tsarevich Demetrio's death or escape and can
be regarded, like *Tragoedia,* only as a possible complementary
source.

Poehl feels that the date of Lope's drama must be 1606, the
year when Mosquera completed his recasting of Barezzi's
pamphlet. The German scholar now attempts to narrow down
even further the date of the composition and indicates that the
license for printing Mosquera's work was issued on May 20,
1606, and that in chapter 13 of this account, which is an entirely independent addition by Mosquera, it is mentioned that
the two sons of George Mniszek, the Palatine of Sandomierz, participated in the procession of Corpus Christi in Valladolid, Spain, on May 25, 1606. Thus, Poehl argues that Mosquera's account could not have appeared before that date, that
is, before the Pretender's death. In Poehl's interpretation, both
Rapp and Menéndez y Pelayo were mistaken in thinking that
Lope wrote his play while Demetrius was still alive. The Spanish
public acclaimed in the theater the triumphant Demetrius at a
time, Poehl concludes, when he had already been murdered in
Moscow.

As Poehl has proved, then, Lope used not Barezzi's Italian

account, but its Spanish recasting by Mosquera, and therefore
Barezzi as Lope's main source can be omitted. It is not even
sure whether Lope knew Barezzi's brochure at all.

Mosquera's pamphlet was unquestionably one of Lope's main
sources. The poisoning of Teodoro, Basilio's older son, the way
in which Demetrio is saved, the close relationship between Demetrio's tutor Lamberto, and Demetrio, Demetrio's reception
by Sigismundo and Rodulfo's change of heart—all these important details convincingly prove it. Yet Poehl is not right when
she asserts that all Lope had to do was to follow Mosquera,
since the latter gave the Spanish playwright all the raw material
he needed, and the rest was due to Lope's invention. Even if we
did not know of any other possible source and accepted Poehl's
assurance that Lope invented all that which he did not find in
Mosquera, there would still remain some historical details whose
origin remains a matter for conjecture.

In a further discussion concerning Lope's sources, the Dutch
scholar J. A. Van Praag polemicizes with Poehl in his article
of 1937, "Más noticias sobre la fuente de 'El Gran Duque',"[21]
and attempts to show that Mosquera's *Relacion* was not the only
source for Lope. He believes that the play could also have been
based on the fourth part of *Histórica pontifical y católica* by Luis
de Bavía, first published in Madrid in 1613.[22] In chapter 86 of
the fourth part of this work Demetrius's peregrination is re-
counted, while a later chapter treats Demetrius's triumph and
death.

Bavía knew Barezzi's account of Demetrius, but it seems to
Praag that the Spanish historian also consulted other sources
for the compilation of his work. As we have already seen in
both Mosquera's account and Lope's play the German knight
sacrifices his own son to save Demetrio's life, while Barezzi
mentions only that a boy of similar appearance was sacrificed.
In Bavía's work, however, Praag finds both statements juxtaposed:

Some people say that the tutor replaced Demetrio with his own son and
saved the prince's life with his son's death. Others say that it was not his
son but a boy of similar appearance who was brought there to deceive
the murderers.[23]

Lope, like Mosquera, presents Demetrio not as son, but as
grandson of Basilio. Bavía fell into the same error, the Dutch
scholar tells us, but in chapter 92 he corrects himself: "Basilio

left two sons, Teodoro and another small boy, and he entrusted the latter to Bielsio, a chief baron."[24]

Praag also cites other details from Bavía's work which are mentioned by both Mosquera and Lope, but not by Barezzi, such as the recognition of Demetrius by Boris in the monastery and several minor ones.

According to Praag, Bavía used not only written sources, among them perhaps the *Tragoedia,* but also knew personally some eyewitnesses of the tragic events in Moscow, and his report is of special interest because Boris is shown objectively.

Praag affirms that Lope knew Bavía's work and consulted it while writing his own play. As a proof he cites such episodes as the cause of Teodoro's madness and especially the intrigue of Isabela, the wife of Juan, Basilio's son, episodes which are similar in Lope's play and in Bavía's account.

Thus, Praag concludes, Lope's play could not be dated before 1613, the year in which the fourth part of Bavía's work was published, and the Dutch scholar implies that Lope wrote his play knowing that Demetrio was dead.

In a summary of the research done so far on this drama, made by American scholars of Spanish literature Morley and Bruerton in *The Chronology of Lope de Vega's Comedias* (compiled in 1940), we find that Praag's view is "a doubtful hypothesis at best when we consider that the story closes with the impostor alive and triumphant." They cautiously date the play as 1606 with a question mark and believe that "Lope could have derived everything but the astrologer's episode from Mosquera or from part III of Bavía's *Histórica Pontifical* (1608) with the possibility that it circulated in MS earlier."[25]

I disagree with Morley and Bruerton and find Praag's conclusion convincing, although his argument is not completely scholarly either, in that he wrote his article without consulting Mosquera's brochure and judged the latter merely on the basis of Poehl's information. Furthermore, he did not give a full analysis of Bavía's report, did not go far enough in comparing the atmosphere and the character description and, especially, did not point out the textual similarities between the source and the *comedia* in detail. However, his championing of Bavía's book as one of Lope's main sources is fully justified, and I believe that, in addition to, and perhaps even more than Mosquera, *Histórica Pontifical* is to be regarded as the main source of *El Gran Duque.*

To reinforce my opinion I point out the following similarities between Bavía's book and Lope's Demetrius drama:

The movement of Lope's plot follows closely Bavía's report, especially in the description of the atmosphere of the Court, the accidental murder of Tsarevich Juan, Basilio's death, Godunov's character, the tutor's role in saving and guarding Demetrio, the latter's life in the Palatine's kitchen, the audience with the king, and the military campaign.

The general historical background which Bavía depicts is far superior to the somewhat parochial and limited horizon of Mosquera's brochure. This is especially true of the twilight period of interregnum after Basilio's death, of Boris's clever maneuvering behind the scenes of the power struggle, and of the chaotic conditions which threaten to erupt in a civil war, of Boris's election as tsar, and of his fear of losing power. Thus, some of the historical phenomena in Lope's play which would remain unexplained if we accepted Poehl's hypothesis uncritically, find a satisfactory solution in Bavía's account. Even such a casual detail as the one we find hidden among the many cogent arguments in Rodulfo's ambassadorial message to Sigismundo about the father of the alleged Demetrio, a monk who is still alive, is reflected in Bavía's account.

Insofar as textual borrowings are concerned, the following juxtapositions reveal that Lope relied somewhat more heavily on Bavía than on Mosquera:

A. Motifs which occur in both Mosquera and Bavía and can be found in Lope's drama:

1. In both sources the tutor admonishes Demetrio to maintain his reserve ("recato") in the world, while in Lope's play we hear Boris ask the monk Demetrio, who obviously remembers his tutor's advice, to drop his reserve ("deja el recato.")[26]

2. The tutor also urges Demetrio to regain his father's empire ("el paterno imperio," "estado imperio," "imperio paterno") and Lope uses the phrase "paterno imperio" in the farewell advice of Lamberto to the Prince.[27]

3. At the time of Boris's visit to the monastery, Demetrio finds himself in danger ("peligro") and, in the monastery scene of the play, Rufino mentions that Demetrio was in great "peligro" and the latter replies that he is still in "peligro."[28]

4. The Lithuanian sponsor of Demetrio's claims to the throne asks permission ("licencia") of King Sigismundo for

Demetrio's visit and, in the play, the Palatine calls in Demetrio and Rufino who have been waiting outside the King's chamber: "Ya espera / El Rey y licencia os da."[29]

5. The reports mention that Demetrio stirred the pity ("movio a *lástima*") of the king and the others at the Court. Lope retained the verb, while the noun suggested a homophonic substitution to him in the scene when the Palatine tells the king that Demetrio, dressed in rags, wants to see him: "Que cuanto más te moviere / A compasión más lo *estima*." (italics supplied)[30]

B. Some motifs occurring only in Mosquera which we find in Lope:

1. The Jesuit father mentions that the tutor has taught and instructed ("enseñado y maestrado") Demetrio with such care as corresponded to a prince ("convenia a tal Principe"). In the play Cristina, Demetrio's mother, tells him that she has invited Lamberto so that the latter "te enseñe / Actos de principe."[31]

2. The tutor sees that Demetrio has already grown up ("ya de buena edad") and urges him to recover ("recobrar") his empire. In the play Lamberto tells Demetrio "Ya es tiempo . . . cobrando el paterno imperio."[32]

3. The tutor loves Demetrio as his son ("como a hijo") and brings him up with more care than a father ("más que padre"). In the play Lamberto addresses Demetrio "hijo" and, after Lamberto's death, we hear Demetrio lament him: "¿Espira mi padre?"[33]

4. After Lamberto's death, Demetrio feels himself abandoned and in great danger ("Q corria su vida si se descubria quien era"). In the play he exclaims: "¿Que puedo hacer / Para asegurar mi vida . . .?" and "Si digo que soy rey, cierta es mi muerte . . ."[34]

5. After Boris's visit to the monastery, Demetrio decides to move to another place because of fear ("de . . . miedo"). In the play Rufino, Demetrio's companion, tells the Prince that Boris's appearance in the monastery created "justo miedo."[35]

6. The Palatine advises Demetrio to cross the Boristhenes (the Dneper) with caution ("vigilancia") and, having passed it, according to Mosquera's account, Demetrio's army goes through a great forest ("selva"). In the play, we hear the Palatine warn Demetrio to cross the river with "cuidado y vigilancia" and the latter replies that he is even more preoccupied with the "oscuras selvas" which await him on the other side.[36]

C. Some motifs occurring only in Bavía's account which we find in Lope.

1. *Histórica Pontifical* mentions an English savant who has spoken to Boris about Tacitus. In the play we hear Boris refer to Tacitus in his conversation with the astrologer.[37]

2. Bavía indicates that Demetrio is now sixteen years old, and, in the play, Boris mentions that he has been ruling for sixteen years. This is not a real proof, but a numerical coincidence, since Boris was not crowned the year Demetrius was born.[38]

3. The tutor tells Demetrio that he was a child ("niño") when he was saved. Lope describes Demetrio as "niño" in the first act.[39]

4. The tutor mentions that Boris has tyrannized his states ("tiranizado sus estados"). In the play Rufino reports to Lamberto that Boris "tiranizo los estados."[40]

5. After the tutor's death, Bavía narrates, the prince was left without a guide and a pilot, with whom he had hoped to reach a safe port ("sin la guia, y principal piloto con quien avia cobrado esperanza de tomar buen puerto . . .") In the play Demetrio laments Lamberto's death: "En él murio mi esperanza / Padre, amparo, confianza / Luz, maestro, norte, puerto."[41]

6. In connection with Demetrio's wanderings Bavía speaks about the conversation of *pícaros* concerning various aspects of life. This passage might have suggested to Lope the picaresque elements in Demetrio's adventures.[42]

7. Out of Bavía's description concerning Demetrio's audience with Sigismundo, in which the Polish King heard his plea with such sympathy ("No fué mal oido Demetrio aunque la grandeza del caso hazia dudar"), Lope might have constructed a witty question based on the relationship of the two verbs "oir" (to hear) and "ver" (to see) : "¿Qué hará el oir / Señor, si te mueve el ver?"[43]

8. Bavía attributes to an unequal number ("desigual numero") of soldiers the outcome ("sucesso") of the first phase of Demetrio's decisive battle. In the play Rufino explains to the desperate Demetrio that ". . . el exceso / Nos puso en tan mal suceso . . . porque son cien mil / Y acá veinte mil no son."[44]

9. Bavía states that Demetrio thought highly of the Cossacks ("en que ponia la mayor confianza de la vitoria") and, in reference to these soldiers, Lope twice stressed their good fighting

qualities ("gente diestra"). Yet as Bavía implies, the rich Boris might have bribed them ("les pagaron o compraron"), and in the play Margarita, the Palatine's daughter, tells Sigismundo that the Cossacks are leaving Demetrio because Boris is bribing them with money "con el dinero en la mano / A todos llamando está / Los cosacos . . . le [Demetrio] han dejado." At times even the smallest nuances of Bavía's indications are reflected in Lope's drama. Bavía is not sure whether Boris really did buy the Cossacks ("no digo que aora") and the sensitive Lope finds it important to follow Bavía in this minute detail as Margarita says "Oigo decir que . . ."[45]

10. The shameful flight of the Cossacks from the battlefield is described by Bavía as "They turned their backs shamefully to the enemy" ("bolvian vegonçosamente las espaldas"), and, in the play, Demetrio shouts to his fleeing men: "¿Adónde, soldados, vais / Vuelta la espalda al traidor . . .?"[46]

11. In Boris's characterization Bavía uses the noun "industria" (cleverness, ingenuity). In the play Boris mentions that he is in his high office because of his cleverness "por industria" and later Orofrisa, Boris's wife, urges him to take steps against Demetrio by using his cleverness: "¿Para que es la industria . . . ?"[47]

12. Bavía indicates that, after Teodoro's death, Boris shrewdly pretended that he did not want the crown and let the other claimants destroy one another with mutual recriminations. The people became excited ("alborotado") seeing the dissension among the pretenders and were afraid of the possibility of a civil war. Lope uses the word "alborotar" four times in connection with the discontent of the Russians over Boris's tyranny.[48]

Scholars have continued their speculation concerning the dating of the play and in a recent research, "Las fuentes de El Gran Duque," J. Vernet, a Spanish researcher, states that

If only this Demetrius, who was murdered on May 17, 1608, existed, the dating could be determined on the supposition that Lope wrote his *comedia* before learning of Demetrio's death. Yet the problem is complicated by the emergence of another Pretender after the assassination of the first Demetrius. Certain political parties in Russia wanted to identify this new Pretender with the first Demetrius.[49]

It is Vernet's view that, due to the contradictory reports coming from Russia, usually through Polish channels, about the fate of Demetrius after Šujskij's *coup d'état* and the emergence of

the second Demetrius, Lope might not have known which version
to believe. Thus, the puzzling offer of the triumphant Demetrio
to give military aid to King Sigismundo against Charles of
Sweden at the end of the play, which Vernet feels is at variance
with history, might conceivably be a reflection of events connected with the second Demetrius. For Lope and many of his
West-European contemporaries, Vernet adds, the first and second
Demetrius might have seemed the same person.

I am not sure whether Vernet read carefully enough Lope's
sources—Barezzi, Mosquera, and Bavía—in which such an alliance (Russia and Poland) is emphasized. Yet Vernet's speculation on linking the events connected with the first and second
Pretender is still possible and contemporary historical sources
reinforce it. Margeret, Demetrius's French bodyguard, reported
that there were "rumors that Demetrius was not killed . . . but
someone else was in his place," and, in her collection of contemporary British and Dutch accounts, Howe states that many
believed in the second miraculous escape of the Pretender.[50]

The emotional climate of the country where the alleged Demetrius was received with so much enthusiasm a short while before
might have proved contagious. In the overheated atmosphere of
the Counter-Reformation it could not have seemed strange at all
to a Jesuit of Mosquera's blind faith and unquestioning religious
philosophy that divinity intervened again to save the just from
the wicked. At the end of 1606 the Roman Curia continued to
choose the kind of news concerning the confused situation in
Muscovy which pleased it best, clinging to the hope that Demetrius was still alive. E. Šmurlo, a specialist in the relations between the Holy See and the Slavic world, informs us that: "Pope
Paul V . . . refusa longtemps de croire au fait accompli. . . . Ce
n'est qu'à fin de 1608 qu'ils se convanquirent définitivement . . .
qu'il fallait renoncer à jamais au rêve si longtemps caressé de
voir de nouveau le tsar Démétrius au pouvoir."[51]

Vernet seems to have overlooked a reference in the play which
may perhaps be linked with the appearance of the second and
even a third Pretender. In his address to Sigismundo, Rodulfo,
Boris's ambassador, reproaches him with the fact that, because
of the support the Polish king gave to Demetrio, there are
already a thousand Demetriuses waiting for their chance. ("A su
ejemplo también otros aspiran / Y hay mil Demetrios ya.")[52]

In the final part of his article Vernet suggests that Lope might
have modified the tradition of the printed sources and might

also have used oral reports from members of the Spanish embassy returning from Persia, who in 1608 spoke to the second Demetrius, obviously believing him to be the first Pretender.

Can we establish the date when the news of the death of Demetrius reached Spain? We know that the earliest account of his death was published in Amsterdam, entitled *Légende de la vie et de la mort de Démétrius* (1606), which, under the title *The Reporte of a Bloudie and Terrible Massacre in the Citty of Mosco,* was republished in London in 1607.[53] Yet the first printed report of his death was published in Spain only in the fourth part of Bavía's *Histórica Pontifical* in 1613. Thus, there is a gap of seven years and Praag is probably correct when he finds it incredible that it would have taken so long for the news to reach Spain. The Spanish Jesuits must have known of Demetrius's death earlier since, as Poehl indicates, the annals of the Jesuits contained this news from 1606 on. Still it is quite likely that they were in no hurry to spread this information, so unfavorable for their purpose, in Spain. Hence, we cannot tell exactly when the Spaniards learned about this news. As far as Lope is concerned, Poehl feels that he found out about this event only many years later, and perhaps this explains why, in 1617, his Demetrius drama was published without any alteration. To the obvious question why Lope did not change his play at the publication of the *Séptima parte de las Comedias de Lope de Vega* in 1617, which included the Demetrius play, when he already knew about Demetrius's fate, Praag answers that, even if Lope had wanted to change the ending, which he, as a good playwright, would never have done lest the play lose all its dramatic force, he could not have done it for the simple reason that he had no part in the publication of the *Séptima parte* of his *comedias*.

In addition to the sources we can also apply internal evidence to establish the date of the drama.

In his article "Alusiones a Micaela Lujan," Américo Castro refers to the second "great moments of passion" in Lope's life, Micaela Lujan, the Camila-Lucinda of his sonnets, and connects it with the efforts of scholars to fix the date of the Demetrius drama. After analyzing eighteen of Lope's plays, in which he found Lucinda as one of the protagonists, the latest of which was *La batalla del honor,* dated 1608, Castro feels that Lope's Demetrius drama must have been written about this time.[54]

While Castro applied the right analytical tools, he still did not go deep enough and apparently mistook Margarita, the

Count-Palatine's beautiful daughter, for Lucinda, the peasant girl, in the play. The Spanish scholar quotes from the second act of the play when Demetrio exclaims:

¡Qué bellíssima mujer / A cuánto mira sujeta!
Dichoso el que amaneciere / Con tan lindo sol al lado,

and presents these lines as if they were addressed to Lucinda, but actually they are spoken to Margarita, whom Demetrio later marries.

In his chronology of Lope's plays Buchanan, a literary researcher (1922), places the date of the Demetrius drama between 1603 and 1613. However, reviewing Buchanan's work, Montesinos, another Spanish scholar, disagrees with these dates and suggests 1603-1606. Fichter, a literary historian (1924) feels that the date should be between 1603-1606, for "Lope would hardly have written of Lucinda after 1608 ¡Qué bellíssima . . .!" Fichter fell into the same trap, as Américo Castro did before him, because these words, as pointed out above, are not directed to Lucinda.[55]

While the terminal dates, 1606, 1608, and 1613, which these three scholars indicate may be correct, the initial year—1603— cannot be justified. Lope could not have written his drama earlier than May-June, 1605, *i.e.,* before the date when Basmanov, the commander of the Russian army, went over to Demetrius's side; this occurred on May 7, 1605.

In his article on Lope's "Belardo-Lucinda plays" (1937) Bruerton mentions Castro's "Alusiones" and states that "we cannot . . . take 1608" as the last date of plays which contain references to Lucinda, pointing out that there are at least four cases of Lope's use of such references after 1608.[56]

Finally, Morley and Bruerton in *The Chronology* have examined *El Gran Duque* from the point of view of its versification and believe that the composition of the Demetrius drama would be an "anomaly after 1613."[57]

Most of the researchers linked their opinion with the date of the death of the alleged Demetrius, under the impression that Lope could not have written the Demetrius drama if he had known about the death of the young prince, otherwise the Spanish playwright would not have glorified the Russian prince as a legitimate emperor. I feel that this view proceeds from a mistaken notion, since I am convinced that the problem is not the date of the death of the alleged Demetrius, or whether Lope knew or did not know about it, but rather Lope's belief in Demetrio's authenticity, and his dramatic sense that this Russian prince, alive or dead, was worthy of being represented on the Spanish stage of the early seventeenth century.

I suggest that Lope believed in his unusual hero and that Demetrius's death did not change his belief, and I am also convinced, in spite of the opinion of most researchers to the contrary, that Lope knew of the pretender's death. Among Lope's possible sources I mentioned the *Tragoedia* published in 1608, in which the anonymous writer describes Demetrius's death. Lope may or may not have read this account, but without any doubt Lope did read the fourth part of Bavía's *Histórica*, the first edition of which was published in 1613, and, by that time, *i.e.,* seven years after the death of the alleged Demetrius, Lope must have been informed of the events of this Slavic Saint Bartholomew's night, May 27, 1606, in Moscow. But, even if we suppose that Lope still did not know of Demetrius's death until 1613, which is quite difficult to believe, after reading the fourth part of Bavía's history there could not be the slightest doubt that Lope learned of the catastrophe. Immediately following the description of Demetrio's military campaign, which was one of Lope's main sources of information, Bavía also depicts Demetrio's coronation, the gradual discontent of Moscovites over Demetrio's preference for foreigners, and finally the uprising against him, and his murder. It is unthinkable that Lope could have ignored this important information. Therefore, it is impossible to accept Poehl's view that Lope learned about Demetrio's death only many years after the event and that, as late as 1617, he published his drama without any change because he still remained in the dark about the fate of his hero.

In reporting Demetrio's murder Bavía added

But the Muscovites' hate of Demetrius continued. They published a catalogue of his crimes . . . without mentioning the evidence with which Demetrius had proved his authentic birth, evidence which they had accepted, the Muscovites now called him an impostor and not the true Demetrius. They even attempted to prove their charges and found alleged parents and brothers of Demetrius who asserted that his name was Gregorio Estrepio. . . . Yet who can assure us of the trustworthiness of these statements?[58]

The above passage is, in my opinion, decisive for the proper understanding of Lope's concept of Demetrio. The Spanish dramatist read both Mosquera (who did not show the tragic end of Demetrio) and Bavía (who did), but as we can see from the above quotation Bavía blamed the unenlightened Muscovite mob for this deed.

Convinced of the young Pretender's royal origin and moved by his undeserved tragic end, Lope decided to bring to the stage the miraculous adventures and famous deeds of this Russian prince. He ended the play at the apogee of Demetrio's career after his victory on the battlefield not because he did not know the subsequent fall of his hero, but in spite of it. His evident affection for Demetrio played a more important part in the concept of the drama than approximation to, or *mimesis* of, historical truth.

In addition Lope's dramatic concept required the fulfillment of poetic justice. One of the keys to the interpretation of the Spanish drama of the period can be found in the frustration the villain experiences in the execution of his evil attempts and in the triumph of the carrier of a just cause. Thus, the guilty Boris should suffer, but the innocent Demetrio should not. As A. A. Parker points out in his article, "The Approach to the Spanish Drama of the Golden Age," it is a principle of literature and not a fact of experience that

[the] plot is constructed on the principle of poetic justice. . . . In real life evil men may prosper and virtuous men may suffer. But in literature it was, in seventeenth-century Spain, considered fitting that wrongdoing should not go unpunished and virtue unrewarded. . . . Nobody should be punished without deserving it.[59]

Thus, aside from his evident attachment to his unusual hero, Lope's fine dramatic sense did not permit him to portray a virtuous hero suffering an undeserved death on the stage. His Spanish audience of the early seventeenth century would not have liked or understood such an ending.

Moreover, Lope's theater was optimistic, and a tragic end, a negative portrait in somber colors rarely occupied his artistic brush. Essentially Lope had an untragic view of life. According to Vossler:

Das etwa der Abstieg oder seelische Untergang eines Menschen . . . zum Hauptgegenstand . . . einer Buehnenwerk gemacht werden koennte, kam ihm nicht in den Sinn. Wieweit er von negativ getoenten Lebensbildern entfernt ist, ersieht man vielleicht am besten daraus, dass er sogar den tragischen Mythen des Altertums eine Wendung ins Heitere zu geben pflegte.[60]

That belief in Demetrio continued unshaken in spite of his personal tragedy and was not limited to Lope's drama in Spain is proven by *El principe perseguido Infeliz Juan Basilio,* a play by Belmonte, Moreto, and Martines, based on *El Gran Duque,* staged in 1651, *i.e.,* almost half a century after Demetrius's death, in which this Russian prince is still shown to be the legitimate successor to the throne.

Thus, my conclusion is that Lope wrote the Demetrius drama in 1613, after having read the fourth part of Bavía's *Histórica Pontifical;* it is of course also possible that this part was earlier available in manuscript, and in this case the date of the play's composition may be earlier.

RUSSIAN CONTRIBUTIONS

Because of the use of a Russian theme in the play, it is appropriate to review Russian scholarship on Lope's Demetrius drama.

Lope is mentioned in Russia as early as 1735 in a poem by Tredjakovskij.[61] Subsequently several of his plays were translated in the nineteenth and twentieth centuries, but there is no full translation of his Demetrius drama up to this day. P. O. Morozov translated into prose the first act of this play under the title *Velikij gercog Moskovskij i gonimyj imperator* in 1912, but even this translation has remained in manuscript.[62]

There is an interesting study by M. P. Alekseev, an important Soviet scholar, well known for his essays on world- and Spanish literature, entitled "Boris Godunov i Dimitrij Samozvanec v zapadnoevropejskoj drame" (Boris Godunov and the False Demetrius in West-European Drama), dated 1936.[63] The Soviet reviewer gives us much useful information about previous Russian scholarship on this drama, and his characterization of Lope's Demetrio is especially successful. He is surprised to find Lope generally so familiar with Russian life in the Time of Troubles and, in his opinion, Lope has created a well-written and interesting work.

Alekseev thinks that idealization of the character of Demetrio is the result of Lope's sources, and that the Spanish dramatist looked at Demetrio through the eyes of the Jesuits. We have no proof, states the Soviet critic, that Lope knew the fate of his hero in history, although it hardly seems possible that news of Demetrius's murder had not reached Spain by the time Lope wrote his *comedia*. Yet even if Lope had known the true fate of his hero, Alekseev asserts, he still would not have changed the end, since to do so would have robbed the drama of its ideological content.

Unfortunately Alekseev's analysis is rather superficial on the whole and the Soviet scholar relies too much on what other critics have said; he repeats their mistakes and seems to have read Lope's drama quite casually.

Alekseev thinks that Lope did not have sufficient information concerning certain details, and to this circumstance the Soviet critic attributes some of Lope's historical errors, such as the presence of a German knight and a Spanish servant at the Muscovite Court. However, Lope shows both Lamberto, the German knight, and Rufino, the Spanish servant, living not at the Muscovite Court but in the country, and he uses this fact to imply a difference between the moral atmosphere of the wicked Court and the innocent country. Second, both Barezzi and Mosquera, as well as many other contemporary sources which differ among themselves only in details, indicate a German knight (or doctor or tutor) as Demetrius's savior. Third, the introduction of Rufino is a typical example of how Lope wove a Spanish element into a drama set in a foreign country.

Alekseev refers to both Barezzi's original and Mosquera's version, indicating that Lope followed them faithfully. However, unlike Poehl, he does not point out the vital difference between the original and the translation, and treats them as if they were of exactly the same tenor. Thus, the Soviet scholar maintains that in both Barezzi's *Relazione* and Mosquera's *Relacion* as well as in Lope's drama we have an identical description of the murder plot against Demetrio who is saved by his tutor, the latter replacing the Prince with a boy of similar appearance. However, this version appears only in Barezzi's brochure, while Mosquera and Lope, as indicated before, treat the saving of Demetrio differently.

Alekseev further mentions that Demetrio, on his tutor's advice, enters a monastery. Yet in the play, Lamberto does not give Demetrio any such advice, but, on the contrary, urges him to reconquer his empire. According to Alekseev, in both the

sources and the drama, Demetrio reveals himself to Wiśniowiecki, who, in turn, introduces Demetrio to the Palatine of Sandomierz. This is true only of the sources; in the drama Demetrio
reveals himself directly to the Palatine and Wiśniowiecki is never
mentioned.

After Alekseev, the most important Soviet scholar on Lope's
Demetrius drama in N. I. Balašov, who has devoted two studies
to this problem. One is "Lope de Vega i problematika ispanskoj
dramy XVII. veka na vostočnoslavjanskie temy" (Lope de
Vega and the Problems of Seventeenth-Century Spanish Drama
on Eastern Slavic Themes), and the other, "Renessansnaja
problematika ispanskoj dramy XVII veka na vostočnoslavjanskie
temy" (Renaissance Problems of Seventeenth-Century Spanish
Drama on Eastern Slavic Themes), both written in 1963. The
second study complements the first.[64]

The Soviet author feels that, in addition to the reports of
Barezzi, Mosquera, and Possevino, Lope may also have heard
verbal accounts from some Poles, Russians, and even Ukrainians
who lived in Poland and Russia at the time of the Demetrius
affair.[65]

In a fascinating analysis Balašov departs radically from the
opinions of all previous scholars, and raises important questions
concerning Lope's doubts as to the authenticity of Demetrio, as
well as concerning the title and ideological content of the drama.
He first tentatively places the date of the drama between 1606
and 1613 and then fixes it in the summer of 1606. Following
Menéndez y Pelayo's hypothesis Balašov argues that Lope wrote
the drama before news of Demetrio's death reached Spain.

In the opinion of the Soviet scholar Lope does not portray
Demetrio as an ideal hero, but appends attributes of hopelessness
and adventurism to his behavior, and even goes so far as to have
Boris expose and accuse Demetrio through Rodulfo's clever
embassy to Sigismundo. However, Balašov does not mention the
fact that throughout the drama Boris and Rodulfo are regarded
as untrustworthy and that Rodulfo's exposé not only did not
change Sigismundo's friendly attitude to Demetrio, but even
strengthened the attachment of the Polish king to the Pretender's
cause. In a letter to the Count Palatine, Sigismundo described
Rodulfo's report as a "thousand lies" and ordered that Boris's
ambassador be severely punished.[66]

Since Balašov presents his facts in such a way as to imply
some vague doubt on Lope's belief in Demetrio's authenticity,

we are left somewhat confused as to whether, in his final interpretation, Lope did or did not believe in Demetrio.

The Soviet scholar indicates that Lope's drama was first entitled *Los nuevos sucesos del Gran Duque de Moscovia* since the
manuscript of 1613 bears that title, and feels that Lope changed
it after he had learned of Demetrio's death to its present title
as a reflection of his reaction to this news.

Unfortunately Balašov's suggestion raises more questions than
it hopes to settle. He fails to support his hypotheses by any facts
or additional arguments, nor does he attempt to comment on
whether Lope made, at the time when he changed the title, any
alterations in the original text. The Soviet scholar may have
overlooked the fact that Lope had nothing to do with the publication or the title-changing of his *comedias* in 1617. His plays
were published, as Hugo A. Rennert, a Lopean specialist, mentions in his *Life of Lope de Vega,* by the bookseller Miguel de
Siles in Madrid without Lope's participation.[67]

However, if this case represented an exception and Lope did
give some instructions that the title be changed to its present
one, would he not also have wanted to use the opportunity to rewrite some part of the play? While Balašov's argument is basically correct that the title *Los nuevos sucesos* does not make
sense, after the massacre of May 27, 1606, became known, I
feel that it was not Lope but his bookseller who, using simple
common sense, altered the title to bring it somewhat closer to
reality.

Balašov argues that the original title of the *comedia* was
Los nuevos sucesos, yet the word "nuevos" (new, recent) seems
to imply that it was not the original title and might have been
preceded by an earlier version which was simply entitled "los
sucesos" (the adventures) of the Great Duke of Muscovy, to
which the 1613 version, *Los nuevos sucesos,* might have been
either a sequel, or a recasting of the first version. Although we
do not know of such a play, a great number of Lope's *comedias*
were lost and such an earlier version might have been among the
lost plays.

In a number of Lope's plays the title is repeated at the end of
the last act. Thus, if the original title was *Los nuevos sucesos,* we
should expect to find it in the text. Yet, we find only that, at the
end of the *comedia,* Sigismundo proclaims "Dando fin a los
sucesos / Del Gran Duque de Moscovia," which may reinforce
my argument. Of course, the counter-argument may be raised

that the text came down to us in a corrupted version and there are some passages in the play which may justify this supposition and therefore its authenticity cannot be proved.

Analyzing Lope's *comedia* further, Balašov contradicts all previous opinions that Lope saw Demetrio through the eyes of the Jesuits. He mentions that Mosquera was a calumniator of Russia, yet argues that Lope consciously "distilled his muddy sources," discarded the calumny and showed himself diametrically opposed to Mosquera in the most essential part of the drama. Balašov claims that the *raison d'être* of Lope's drama was a direct rebuttal of the Catholic point of view contained in the writings of Possevino and Mosquera. The Spanish playwright completely eliminated the references to the main idea of the Jesuits, continues the Soviet critic, and we find not one word in the Demetrius drama regarding the conversion of Orthodox Russia and Demetrio's secret adherence to Catholicism. According to Balašov, Lope regarded the attempt to introduce Catholicism by force in Russia as reactionary and consequently repudiated it. Although Lope, Balašov adds, did not reject the principles of faith directly and was reserved in expressing his disrespect to the Church, the Demetrius drama seems to demonstrate that Lope was basically indifferent and at times even hostile to Catholic policy. The Soviet reviewer builds up an image of Lope, man of the Renaissance, who was interested in strengthening national and state unity and wished Russia to become such a progressive state as has never existed in Spain. In his attempt to solve the puzzling appointment of Rufino as Prince of Cracovia, an appointment which Demetrio, the new ruler of Muscovy, could not have made since Cracow was the capital of the powerful Polish state, the Soviet literary critic maintains that, since an anti-Polish tendency of the drama was unconceivable, Lope, the Spanish humanist, was ridiculing the Jesuits with this strange appointment.

While the broader issue of the Catholic tone of the Demetrius play will be discussed in the subchapter "The Spanish World in Lope's Demetrius *Comedia*," I will consider some of Balašov's statements at this point. The Soviet critic tries to separate Lope, who represents for him the humanistic Zeitgeist of the century, from Possevino and Mosquera, who hide behind narrow religious values. While Lope did considerably change his sources, I am convinced that he still continued to represent both the humanistic aspects of the Renaissance and the religous and national ideals of his country. Lope's humanism is one which is impregnated by a special Spanish genius, an important part of which is a synthesis of medieval and pagan elements.

To deny Lope's Catholicism and to claim that he was hostile to the Church is unthinkable, for he was one of the staunchest supporters of the Catholic church of his time. The great number of religious plays, dramas of lives and saints, and *autos sacramentales* which Lope, who in 1614 was ordained a priest and was received into the Congregation of Saint Peter in 1625, wrote completely disprove Balašov's thesis and show that Lope was in sympathy with the religious spirit of his age and country.

Balašov is correct in his assertion that it is surprising to find that Lope maintained silence about the introduction of the Catholic faith in Russia. We may agree or disagree with Poehl, who felt that Lope was simply not interested enough in the historical background, and that the omission of all the religious references was due to his stage sense of not retarding the development of his fast-moving drama. However, we may find a better answer if we consider the problem not only from the viewpoint of Lope the playwright, but also from the personal experiences and beliefs of Lope the man. For Lope, the man and soldier who participated in the disastrous naval battle of the Spanish Armada in the English channel in 1588, the real danger to Spain came from expanding Protestantism and the Turkish incursions. Lope the playwright wrote about the struggle against Protestantism in several of his works (*Los españoles en Flandes, Don Juan de Austria en Flandes,* etc.), in some of which the theme even degenerated into personal invective against certain important Protestant personalities (*Corona trágica* against Queen Elizabeth, *Dragontea* against Sir Francis Drake, etc.). The same national and religious fervor informs his plays written against the powerful Turks who had recently invaded Hungary and threatened to engulf the whole Catholic world (*El cerco de Viena por Carlos V*).

On the other hand, Lope did not regard Russian Orthodoxy as a danger, because, in contrast to the Protestant and Moslem search for more *Lebensraum,* Russia did not attempt to export her spiritual merchandise to the West and was content to preserve the purity of her Orthodox faith within her national boundaries. In addition, the curious Lope must have known enough of Russian history to recall such outstanding events as Russia's subjugation by, and ultimate victory over, the Tartars and her willingness to join a crusade against the Turks, and this awareness might have caused him to regard Russia as a potential ally of Catholicism in its struggle against the Crescent Moon. This may explain why, in the drama, Lope chose to regard Russia as a Catholic country and made Boris refer to himself as "principe . . . católico." Another reason may have been Lope's creative principle of looking at people and countries not as they really were but through the pure tint of his poetic illusion and thus transforming them in harmony with his view of the world. If, as Balašov maintains, Lope had been religiously indifferent, he would have maintained the same detachment toward the Protestant and Mohammedan world as well, and would not have written such strong denunciations of these religions.

The Soviet critic is again right in his statement that Lope should have known that Cracow was the capital of the powerful Polish state, and not part of Russia, but he is certainly wrong in his interpretation of this lapse. Every scholar of Lope agrees that he was careless in his geography and often committed elementary errors. He believed that Cathay was near the River Ganges (*Angélica en el Catay*), he once called the Don an African river, and even made Sultan Suliman ruler of the New World (*El cerco de Viena por Carlos V*). Vossler mentions that Lope's naïveté went so far that "he made Mohammedans speak as if they were Spanish Catholics".[68] Rapp feels that Lope probably wrote this drama in a single day, as was often his custom, and, at the end of the play, he must have felt a physical and intellectual exhaustion which might also explain this amusing mistake.

Balašov implies that Lope was a political revolutionary against the authority of the King and the Church, and he was often persecuted by the Inquisition. Since Lope did not dare to defy Philip II openly, Balašov maintains, he had to hide behind Aesopian language in portraying the powerful Spanish king in the mask of Basilio, the tyrant of Russia. As far as the Inquisition was concerned, which distrusted the nonconformist Lope, he pacified it, according to Balašov, by including one reference to the Pope in the drama.

It is obvious that in Lope's tremendous artistic forest not all the trees are of the same size and therefore it is not difficult by a subjectively limited approach to select a few dramas and to quote some examples which would seem to prove Balašov's thesis concerning Lope's alienation from the policy of the Catholic church and his defiance of the Spanish monarchy. However, when Lope's entire creative production is considered in an objective scholarly analysis, Balašov's interesting modern approach must be disregarded, for the Spanish playwright will stand before us not as a revolutionary, or as a reactionary, but as a man of his age, spirit, and conventions. Lope often professed democratic sentiments, yet these were not politically but morally and metaphysically motivated. He, like many others of his age, had occasional clashes with the Inquisition, but certainly was not persecuted by it constantly.[69]

Obviously influenced by Soviet historical interpretation, which regards the alleged Demetrius as an international adventurer in the pay of his interventionist Polish masters, Balašov attempts to force Lope's Demetrio into an ideological straitjacket, an interpretation which is alien to the purity of the Spanish playwright's artistic conception. Thus, in Balašov's analysis, Lope's innocent and naïve prince appears as an anti-hero of a modern adventure drama involved in a hopeless and unpopular campaign. To fit his thesis Balašov wishes to transform Sigismundo, a highly idealized, majestic, and generous king in Lope's *comedia,* into a treacherous monarch. Also Lope's Margarita, who courageously follows Demetrio to the battlefield, is unconvincingly metamorphosed by Balašov into a cold, heartless egoist similar to Puškin's Marina Mniszek in *Boris Godunov.*

Balašov justifiably reproaches the trio of Barezzi-Mosquera-Bavía for their religious fanaticism and distorted viewpoints, but his own literary essays occasionally also lack scholarly detachment and factual objectivity.

In his most recent study, *Očerki istorii ispano-russkix literaturnyx otnošenij XVI-XIX vv.* (Outline of History of Spanish-Russian Literary Relations in the Sixteenth and Seventeenth Centuries) (1964),[70] Alekseev repeats the same views which he expressed twenty years earlier concerning *El Gran Duque.* Demetrio is still the ideal hero, the viewpoint is Jesuitic, and the tutor continues to replace Demetrio with another boy. The only rectification in his recent book is that Alekseev no longer juxtaposes Barezzi-Mosquera as Lope's sources of equal value, but asserts that Lope followed Mosquera. Yet, if this is true how can Alekseev still maintain Barezzi's view about Demetrio's double?

It is interesting that Alekseev, although now familiar with Balašov's views, since he mentions them, does not review them critically. From the fact that he himself does not offer anything new, or alter Balašov's opinion, it must be assumed that the present stand of Soviet scholarship on Lope's Demetrius drama, and by extension on Spanish literature of the Golden Age, is divided between the opinions of these two scholars, although the fact that Balašov was invited to read his iconoclastic view at the Congress of Slavists in Sofia (1963) appears to tip the balance in his favor as the current Soviet literary spokesman on this subject.

Dramatis Personae

GENERAL OBSERVATIONS

> It was typical of the popular nature of his genius that he showed little interest in moral qualities that differentiate people: his characters are built on the way of life or profession. That is to say he does not give us misers, hypocrites . . . but peasants, soldiers, nobles, mayors, kings, who, according to the role cast for them, are either good or bad.
>
> Brenan, *Literature of the Spanish People.*[71]

In his historical dramas Lope apparently is seeking to understand a whole epoch from the actions of certain protagonists. As Vossler points out: "Im Grunde bedeutete fuer Lope die Exemplare der Menschheit mehr als die Exemplare der Moral, der Politik und Weltgeschichte."[72]

In this drama we can observe the protagonists acting out the role which is characteristic of their social status, sex, rank, and profession. On leaving the Court in Lamberto's custody, Demetrio promises his mother that he will not forget the fact of being her son ("ser hijo vuestro"); replying to Basilio's reproach Isabela says that she is what she is ("soy quien soy"), implying that she is behaving like a woman; and, urging Demetrio to regain his throne, Lamberto tells him "become what you are" ("a quien eres, correspondas.")[73]

It is interesting to notice that when the protagonists are about to do something extraordinary, they assure themselves that they are merely continuing a traditional custom of their particular sex or social class. Thus, when the childless Isabela decides to begin her intrigue with Rodulfo, her excuse is that she will not be the first to give an alien child to her husband and, after he decided to kill Demetrio, Boris mentions the fact that many great monarchies came into being as a result of political murder.[74]

In general there is hardly any character description or psychological motivation in Lope's play. Little light is thrown on the intimacy of personality in his individual conscience and not much is said about the essence of human nature. This superficiality of characterization is due to Lope's understanding of the nature of the Spanish stage of his time when a fast-moving extraordinary plot was the most important dramatic element.

Although Lope's Demetrius drama is essentially one of action and not of character, we find many important deviations from this general rule. The characters are not of one piece. Some are complex, changing and developing, while others retain their basic traits with little alteration, and still others remain, from the time they first appear on the stage, practically unchanged.

We also find certain revelations of human nature in Teodoro's philosophy, the Count-Palatine's contemplation, Boris's apologia, and Demetrio's occasional meditation. While action is still the predominant element of the play, and dialogue is often used merely to accompany action, we frequently surprise our heroes in their reflective attitudes.

It is important to note the different motifs for the action of the protagonists. Lope's positive figures function as the upholders of social order and are possessed by a desire to restore justice in a fragmented world. They act out the roles assigned to them by their community. This is especially well illustrated in the hierarchical structure of the pyramid-like Polish society. Belardo, the simple Polish Lithuanian peasant, is just as dignified and humble to his feudal lord, the Palatine, as the latter is to King Sigismundo, while the Palatine is just as cordial and respectful to Belardo as the Polish king is to him. The positive characters are often idealized, historically distorted, and therefore less concincing.

The negative characters, however, are motivated by individual passions and weaknesses. Boris's lust for power forces him to commit a logical crime, and the mad passion of Rodulfo for Isabela makes him Boris's accomplice, since the latter promises Isabela's hand for Rodulfo's services. The negative characters are described more realistically, are closer to history, and are more believable.

The foregoing exposition explains Lope's dramatic practice of creating character pairs, *i.e.,* certain similarities among some of the positive and some of the negative protagonists who appear in parallel situations and repeat one another's thoughts and deeds. This is especially true of Teodoro, who sets the moral tone of the play and some of whose ideas are repeated by Lamberto, Demetrio, and even Belardo.

A consideration of the characters of *El Gran Duque* promises us a key with which to open a little the door of Lope's artistic laboratory. Since he based his drama on the historical data furnished by his sources, the first group of names in his list belong to historical protagonists. Then he invented personages whose existence might have been justified by the actions and events of the drama. Finally, Lope completed the roster with figures who really have nothing to do with the historical occurrences of the time, but whom he found useful because of his artistic conventions, dramatic requirements, secondary plots, and stage effects.

BASILIO (IVAN THE TERRIBLE)

Among the historically recognizable protagonists we find Basilio, who corresponds to Ivan IV. Basilio sets the tone of the whole drama and the consequences of this tragic action lead to the destruction of the more than seven-hundred-year-old House of Rjurik and the introduction of Boris's tyranny.

Vossler mentions that ". . . der Typus Nero von jeher die Phantasie des Volkes angeregt hat und ein dankbarer Buehnenkoloss war."[75] In a great many plays, Lope used tyrants because they represented the spirit of an age which saw so many of them, but at the same time they also served as theatrical conventions, since they created confusion and chaos by their capricious deeds.

Most likely Lope used Possevino's *Moscovia* or Bavía's *Histórica* as his source. Possevino mentions Ivan's impetuous character and describes his arbitrary action with the first two wives of Tsarevich Ivan, whom he forced to take the veil.[76]

In a fairly accurate historical description Lope shows Basilio at the end of his life as an impatient, violent, gloomy and sullen tyrant. There is an exaggeration in his actions and speech, and even a suggestion of buffoonery.

Everybody trembles at his court because no one knows whom his iron stick will strike next. His stick is not only a material object in the play, but also his symbol. It is like a personified Fate, menacing the life of the whole court, and Lope subtly utilizes its effect by gradually intensifying its threat.

Yet, if Basilio is portrayed as a villain in the first scene, Lope shows him with sympathy in a scene of jealousy with Isabela. Although it may be due to Basilio's suspicious nature that he goes around the palace eavesdropping, he now acts as the upholder of the family's honor and a wise old man of the world. However, this sensible behavior soon leaves him, and he again becomes the impatient tyrant. Since his words do not persuade, his rage of self-assertion explodes in a brutal physical act.

In the final flash of lucidity of one about to die, Basilio understands that with his death the whole Court will be paralyzed. The dramatic repetition of the word "nadie" (nobody) in his farewell to the world in general suggests that he deems no one worthy of continuing his reign and he foresees the doom of the Muscovite state.

BORIS GODUNOV

Of all of the characters in the drama Lope best understood Boris, whom he described as a highly dynamic character in all his historical complexity. In the first act he appears just as much frightened as all the others in the hallucinating atmosphere of the terrible Tsar's palace. After the death of Juan and Basilio, Boris senses a windfall in his fortune, and becomes a wily courtier. And, when he has been appointed to govern, he usurps the power and acts as a tyrant.

Thus, the first impression of Boris is favorable. When Cristina informs him of Juan's murder, Boris sympathizes with her ("¡Qué hazaña tan vil y fea!") and echoes her fears. He even shows himself anxious for Teodoro's safety and finds God's punishment as the reason for Basilio's accidental killing of Juan. ("Esta es permision de Dios / Porque el reino te quitaba / Tu padre y á Juan le daba.")[77] Yet in retrospect, it becomes clear that in these comments Lope is ironical, since later Boris, although with different motivation, commits the very acts of which he earlier accused Basilio.

In the play, Boris seeks historical justification, based on reasons of state, for his seizure of power. This Russian Machiavelli feels that, after Basilio's death, chaos may threaten the land in the competition for the throne of other claimants, perhaps from those who have been appointed to co-govern with him, all of whom are unworthy of such high position. Thus, for the welfare of the nation, he decides to eliminate all other potential claimants to the throne; as he sees it, Russia will benefit from his enlightened and progressive rule.

Unlike the Demetrius dramas of Puškin, Aleksej K. Tolstoj and Henry von Heiseler, Lope did not create a *Seelendrama* about Boris. The Spanish playwright is interested in following Boris's rise to power, his desire to establish a ruling House of Godunov, his tenacious defense and ultimate loss of the throne. Lope convincingly depicts Boris's positive and negative qualities and this realism is shattered only when the last melodramatic scene ends in his suicide. Lope's realistic portrayal of Boris stems from his familiarity with the temper of the time. In sharp contrast to Russian tradition, we find hardly any accusation against Boris because of his political crime. Even when Demetrio calls him the greatest tyrant, it does not change Boris's portrait because this statement is owing partly to Lope's occasional baroque exaggeration and partly to dramatic effects, since the greater the villain, the more impressive must be the hero's performance in conquering him. Lope lived in an age of political Machiavellism, in which reasons of state permitted, invited, and justified political murder. In Boris's portrait Lope synthesized the general political phenomena of the epoch: the power struggle, the social transformation of the land, and the individual traits of this monarch—his ambition, lust for power, administrative skill, and love of family.

It is not the discovery of his crime that brings about Boris's loss of power, but the fact that Demetrio is still alive. No matter how well Boris has governed, or how much happiness he has brought to the people, once the legitimate successor of royal origin appears on the scene, according to the code of the society of the early seventeenth century, Boris must be regarded as a usurper. Thus, in Boris's downfall and Demetrio's success, Lope reveals the habitual reflex of a people conditioned to rise for legitimate succession in preference even to their individual welfare.

DEMETRIO (TSAREVICH DEMETRIUS)

The most important historical distortion in Lope's drama is in the origin of Demetrio, who is shown as Tsarevich Teodoro's son and Ivan IV's grandson. In this case it was not Lope who altered history but his sources—Barezzi and Mosquera—whom he followed. It is difficult to find a satisfactory explanation for this curious mistake. In a letter of July 10, 1605, written in Latin by Possevino to Demetrius, the word *father* in reference to Ivan the Terrible is several times changed to *grandfather* (avus). This reference might have confused Lope's sources. There was also some rumor that Tsar Feodor (the Teodoro of the play) had a son, whom at birth Boris Godunov replaced with a girl in order that he (Boris) could succeed Feodor. During the reign of Demetrius, a certain Ilja Korovin, a Cossack, appeared, and pretending to be Feodor's son, claimed the throne. It is not impossible that Possevino-Barezzi might have heard of this story. According to Praag, Lope knew of the error, but preferred to perpetuate it for its greater dramatic force, because Demetrio, Teodoro's son, had the moral obligation of avenging his father as a matter of honor.

In the accounts of Possevino, Barezzi, Mosquera and Bavía, it is God who plans, thinks, acts, fights, and wins, and Demetrius is merely His instrument who serves to carry out His instructions on earth. If at times Demetrius appears to be a superman, it is because he is God's chosen envoy; if he seems immortal, it is because he is equipped with God's special passport; and if he finally emerges invincible, it is because he is protected by the shield of divinity.

Lope retained the general sense of this Catholic *Leitmotif* and the intervention of providence in Demetrio's fate. In his drama the future Tsar speaks of God with great devotion, believes in the importance of serving Him, and implores divine help before meeting Boris's army.

Yet simultaneously Lope also modified the preponderant religious viewpoint by softening the severity, relaxing the asceticism, and humanizing the saintliness of the figure. Thus, if Lope still wrote a *Vita,* he shifted the emphasis from the almost holy portrait of this Prince to a heroic and popular ruler of Russia. In his portrait we see more of the earthy garment of a man than the purple robe of a saint. If the spirit of Demetrio occasionally soars skyward, his feet remain solidly on earth. He is no Count Orgaz who represses the call of his senses in order to reach heaven, but rather a cosmopolitan and heroic Velasquezian Ambrosio Spinola who wants to find pleasures in this world too. Thus, Demetrio now appears as an amalgam of religious and worldly elements. The cassock of the monk becomes too tight for this Tsarevich because Lope has enriched him with pagan and sensuous traits. The mixture and interrelationship of these two distinct spheres—the mystique of the Catholic church and the joyous wonders of the Renaissance—cast Demetrio in a unique baroque mold.

It is interesting to observe Lope's art in gradually effecting Demetrio's transformation from a poor monk of a wretched monastery to a man of the world. Demetrio leaves the bare walls of his spiritual abode, doffs his cowl and black cape, hangs them on a tree, departs through an orchard, and crosses the mountain to a new world. A guard remarks that Demetrio left his monk's garment as a snake leaves its skin, implying that the Russian Prince has already outgrown the monastery. The orchard, symbol of the joyous and earthly spirit of the Renaissance, is the key to this scene.

Demetrio's few faults do not blur his total portrait as a brave, majestic, wise, and chivalrous figure. Lope's genius is reflected in bringing Demetrio down to earth while still retaining his ideal qualities. He is made of the same cloth as all the other men in his camp and the difference is merely of degree, not of kind.

TEODORO (TSAREVICH FEODOR)

In the play Teodoro (the historical Tsarevich Feodor) appears as Ivan IV's older son and Juan (the historical Tsarevich Ivan) as his younger son, while in history the opposite is true. In this respect Lope consciously distorted reality, for his sources clearly indicate that Juan was the older son. He introduced this change to heighten dramatic tension in connection with the problem of succession.

Teodoro is Lope's most unusual character in the drama. He sees the obvious truth and expresses it with disconcerting simplicity, and thus he becomes, willy-nilly, the champion of freedom of expression at a Court which has long since lost this habit.

Although his thinking is impregnated with Catholic faith, he is not a religious mystic because the issues he defends are social and moral. By holding up a Stendhalian undistorted mirror, he tears off the mask of hypocrisy from the others at the Court. Yet Teodoro does all this with such youthful innocence that, at times, we wonder whether he is not a predecessor of the little boy in Hans Christian Anderson's *The Emperor's New Clothes.*

From Cristina's discourse with Demetrio we learn that much benefit to the state was expected from Teodoro's cleverness and that he early showed signs of virtue, justice, and good government. Yet partisans of Juan, his younger brother, poisoned him so that he should not succeed. This is by far the strongest indictment of the Muscovite Court, because the heir to the crown is eliminated for the very reason that would most eminently qualify him for this high position.

It is one of the ironies which Lope unfolds with such skill that Cristina, who often speaks of Teodoro tenderly, accuses him of lack of wisdom ("le falta el entendimiento"),[78] while it is really Cristina who shows little prudence in her hasty move to name Boris governor. Indeed, we find that *entendimiento*—which is best rendered here *philosophical wisdom*—is Teodoro's most outstanding characteristic.

The play opens with a duel of wits between father and son, in the course of which Basilio hurls at Teodoro a torrent of insulting epithets. Again we are aware of Lope's irony, for many of these epithets are more applicable to Basilio than to Teodoro, and if there is a moral judgment involved in this scene, it is Basilio who stands convicted.

A typical display of Teodoro's ideas is seen in his conversation with a tailor. Teodoro asks the tailor to sit down, and when the tailor is afraid to do so in the presence of royalty, he denounces the hypocrisy of the world which, scornful of man's spiritual equality, makes a difference between man and man. The Russian prince wants to break down the artificial barriers created by class and rank and seeks to reestablish man's dignity according to his usefulness. He praises the tailor's skill and calls him a friend. The social and democratic tone is unmistakable in this episode.

Thus, we are not surprised that, far from seeking the throne for himself, he regards it as an imposition and dismisses it as a bad joke.

The episode with the dogs—which bark at those who feed them—may be seen as another excuse to express a philosophical insight. Teodoro sees in them the flattering courtiers who eat at the table of the prince yet constantly clamor for more rewards. The wider implication of this episode in the fundamental meaning of the play is reflected in the attitude of Boris, who flatters Cristina in order to obtain a high position—that of the *de facto* ruler in Muscovy—but once having attained it, he aims at becoming, and indeed becomes, the *de jure* emperor.

Does Teodoro only pretend to be an idiot as an escape mechanism from the realities of life around him? Vossler believes that Lope comes close to the borderline between tragic madness and higher sensibility, but does not cross it. Teodoro is really a court jester in a royal robe, but he is also a sensitive poet who derives pleasure out of sounds, forms, and colors.

Teodoro's quest for the understanding of the universe, his existential anxiety, his longing for the Horatian *beatus ille que* way of life, and his prophetic insight make him a morally attractive figure, the like of whom would be difficult to find anywhere else in the enormous artistic production of Lope.

However, knowing Lope's recurrent irony in this drama, it is interesting to speculate on the possibility whether or not he used the poisoning of Teodoro on purpose to express his belief that, in order to be able to formulate such abundance of ethical ideas in a corrupt world, one must be half mad. It is important to point out that Teodoro's prototype, the historical Russian Tsar Feodor, was a kind of saintly fool. If we accept Lope's conscious irony in creating this remarkable figure, for which his sources contributed almost nothing, Teodoro cannot be regarded as Lope's spokesman for formulating a definite ethical belief. Most students of Lope would assure us that the Spanish playwright never had such a purpose. Yet Lope might have used Teodoro in the same way as Cervantes used the half-baked hero of *El Licenciado Vidriero* for making a few comments on certain aspects of human life which he himself would have wanted to make.

There are strong similarities between Lope's Teodoro and Aleksej K. Tolstoj's delicate, saintly, and truthful Tsar Feodor in the second part of Tolstoj's dramatic trilogy. Distinct similarities may also be discovered between Lope's hero and Sigismundo, the Polish prince, in Calderón's *La Vida es Sueño* and it is quite possible that the other great playwright of the Spanish Golden Age used certain traits of Teodoro for the creation of his own protagonist.

KING SIGISMUNDO OF POLAND

The most important Polish historical figure, King Sigismund III, is a completely idealized and historically distorted figure. All of Lope's sources praised highly this Catholic King and Lope faithfully followed them. Sigismundo's principal role is to introduce a fresh moral climate after the suffocating atmosphere at the Court of the two tyrannical Emperors of Muscovy. The friendly, respectful, and lyrical tone which characterizes the spiritual climate of Sigismundo's palace reflects both the aesthetic and moral superiority of the Polish Court over that of Ivan the Terrible and Boris Godunov. Sigismundo stands for generosity, justice, and majesty. He is the symbol of a noble king offering his personal help to an innocent and unjustly persecuted emperor. It is his high mission to be the father of his nation and, indeed, he regards Demetrio as his son, and when the Palatine joins Demetrio's army, leaving his daughter Margarita behind, Sigismundo naturally takes over the role of her father as well.

Sigismundo is a wise and experienced statesman who does not judge rashly the authenticity of Demetrio's claims on mere rumors and warns the Palatine that the story of Demetrio's miraculous escape may not be true. However, when the Palatine convinces him that Demetrio is the legitimate heir to the crown of Muscovy, Sigismundo receives him with tenderness. As a sensitive monarch—who himself was born in prison and thus can sympathize with the unfortunate situation of the Russian Prince —he asks the Palatine whether it would not be a good idea to dress the Russian Tsarevich in a princely garment in the forthcoming audience with him, in order to raise his morale.

Lope also shows him in the role of a military leader who knows how to assess the value of an army. His personal courage is reflected by his decision to aid Demetrio with his presence on the battlefield.

THE COUNT-PALATINE (GEORGE MNISZEK OF SANDOMIERZ)

Another idealized and historically distorted figure is the Count Palatine. His noble conduct, poetic sentiments, baroque view of life, and deep Catholic faith make him a distinguished knight of the age.

In Demetrio's campaign the Palatine functions as his aide-de-camp, planning his strategy and mapping his military moves. He cautions Demetrio to cross carefully the treacherous Dnieper. When the enemy is in sight, he urges Demetrio to retain the initiative by attacking first. Finally, as befits Demetrio's closest collaborator, he crowns the Tsarevich with a laurel of green leaves as the Great Duke of Muscovy after the victory.

It is the Palatine who reflects the peculiar mixture of earthly Renaissance elements and the baroque sentiment of the fugitive-ness of existence. In a scene of deep symbolical significance the Palatine appears against the background of a late summer land-scape hunting deer with javeline. This exciting game—a favorite pastime of both Spaniards and Poles—among forest and rivers fills him with pleasure as he follows the tracks and sound of the animal. Yet the fast deer eludes him and runs toward the river and disappears behind the dense thicket. The flight of this proud and graceful, yet highly vulnerable animal—the king of the forest—seems to symbolize for the Palatine both the dignity and the ephemeral nature of existence, both the beauty and rich-ness of life and the inevitable fact of death. As the deer is seek-ing safety from the hunter's darts, among all the joys and pomp of this exuberant nature, the Palatine soberly reflects on the Carthusian *momento mori.*

OTHERS

Among other historical figures of the first group is Cristina, Teodoro's wife and Demetrio's mother in the play. In history she corresponds to both Maria Nagoj, Demetrio's mother, and Irina Godunova, Tsar Feodor's wife. Margarita is the historical Marina Mniszek, wife of the alleged Demetrius, still another idealized and distorted figure. Isabela is Juan's wife, while in history she is Elena Šeremetova, Tsarevich Ivan's third wife. Orofrisa, Boris's wife, is historically Maria Grigorevna, daugh-ter of Maljuta Skuratov, the infamous *opričnik* of Ivan the Terrible. We find no explanation for this fantastic name and, according to *Los nombres en las comedias de Lope de Vega* by Morley and Tyler, this is the only instance when Lope used it.[79] Juan and Isabela, Boris's children, correspond to the historical Feodor and Ksenija.

In the second group we find Rodulfo, Lope's invention, one of the assassins unnamed in the sources whom Boris sent to

Uglič. Lope went beyond the conventional cloak-and-dagger episode, clothed Rodulfo in a Spanish costume, and used him in connection with Isabela's intrigue and in some events of Boris's rule. He is a strange and complex person because of the great number of roles that Lope assigned to him. Vernet identifies him as the historical Vasilij Šujskij, while Balašov sees in him Basmanov, Demetrius's bodyguard. Both interpretations are only partly correct, since they do not account for all phases of Rodulfo's activities. He also functions as Semon Godunov, Boris's police chief, and the ambassador of Boris to Sigismundo.

The source for Lamberto is the unnamed tutor in the account of Barezzi-Mosquera. His German nationality was indicated in Lope's sources, but Lope generally uses Germans in his plays as symbols of loyalty and perseverance. The Spanish dramatist was also a great admirer of Charles V, the famous Catholic king of the House of Habsburg. It is possible to assign to Lamberto a historical role as the protector of the child Demetrius, in which case he may be identified with Bogdan Belskij, a great favorite of Ivan the Terrible. Another historical possibility is to see him as Afanasij Nagoj, who, according to some speculation, saved the child in Uglič. If we regard Lamberto as one of the Nagojs, his wife Tibalda and his son César can be explained historically as part of the historical Nagoj family who took care of the upbringing and the education of the child Demetrius in Uglič, to which city he was honorably exiled after the death of Ivan the Terrible.

Vossler describes him as a somber figure, a person of a different world. His unbelievably inhuman act of sacrificing his own child to gain eternal fame revolts the sensibility of a twentieth-century man, but Lope's drama must be judged according to the conventions of the Spanish stage of the early seventeenth century. Henry Richard Lord Holland, an English Lopean scholar of the early nineteenth century, points out in his book *Some Accounts of the Lives and Writings of Lope Felix de Vega Carpio and Guillen de Castro,* that such an "extraordinary and embarassing situation [is] produced not for the purpose of exhibiting the peculiarities of character . . . but with a view of astonishing the audience with a strange, unexpected, unnatural conduct."

Lamberto compares his sacrifice to that of the biblical Abraham and it is true that a certain saintliness characterizes him. Lope may have found some indication of the religious traits of

Lamberto in his sources. Bavía describes the unnamed German tutor of Demetrio as follows: "Quien dize que era ayo de Demetrio, vn cauallero Aleman; esto es lo más cierto, y quien que vn Sacerdote Moscouita." It is not impossible that Lope fused the features of the German knight—in the play we see him approve of Demetrio's fencing practice with César—and the Moscovite priest to create Lamberto's composite figure.[80]

Rufino, the Spanish servant, is Lope's invention and serves to render the play more Spanish by the introduction of a *gracioso,* one of Lope's most conventional figures. On the basis of Mosquera's account, Poehl calls Rufino a synthesis of two persons: the knight who carried Demetrio to a safe place after the assassination attempt and the monk who accompanied him to Livonia. Lope glorifies Spain by showing Rufino's loyalty, courage, and wisdom, and by stressing his active participation in the *reconquista* of Russia.

The Duke of Arnies is also Lope's invention, but he may have been conjured up out of Mosquera's account. The great number of knights at the Muscovite court may be seen at Lope's attempt to create a Spanish milieu, but even more interesting is to see them as members of the historical pentarchy who governed in Feodor's name after Ivan IV died. Two of them, Conrado and Augusto, accompany Teodoro, report, talk, and listen to him. Perhaps they were assigned to protect Teodoro after he had lost his sanity. In the play Cristina appoints certain unnamed persons to be co-regents with Boris for Teodoro. Two other knights —Tiano and Severio—make their appearance in Poland and it may be assumed that they have fled from Boris's tyranny to that country. Historically it is well attested that many Russian noblemen fled to Poland during Boris's rule. Eliano and Finea, Boris's agents to murder Demetrio during the latter's military campaign, also have distinct historical prototypes.

The last group includes those persons for whom we find no historical parallel. These are Lisena, Margarita's companion, and a group of peasants, Belardo, Febo, and Lucinda. In their *Los Nombres en las Comedia de Lope de Vega* Morley and Tyler show Lisena as German although she is Polish-Lithuanian. These authors made another mistake in calling the group of peasants Russians while they are also Polish-Lithuanians.[81] Other figures of this group are harvesters, a tailor, an astrologer, and servants. Lisena merely functions as a reward for Rufino, as Grillparzer, in his essay on Lope, wittily remarked: "Am

Schlusse des Stueckes bekommt jeder der Maenner ein Weib, es mag hergenommen werden woher es wolle."[82]

Finally, there is a reference in the play to "Estefano," whom Morley and Tyler identify as Russian, though he is, in history, Stephen Bathory, the Polish king of Transylvanian-Hungarian origin.

The *Comedia*

Lope "never intended that his *comedias* should be printed and coldly analyzed in the scholar's study," Rennert mentions in his *Life of Lope de Vega,* ". . . his plays were destined to be represented on the stage." He divided the Demetrius drama into three acts without any further division into scenes. In an attempt to cut a path among "the wild flowers of his garden"[83] Rapp in his translation and Hartzenbusch in his edition of Lope's dramas divided the acts into scenes.

In the Demetrius drama, as in his other *comedias,* Lope disregarded the classical unities of time, place, and action, and let tragic and comic elements freely mingle.

El Gran Duque describes the events beginning on November 19, 1581, the day Ivan IV killed his son Ivan, and ending sometime in May, 1605, after Basmanov's change of heart in favor of the alleged Demetrius (May 7, 1605). Thus, Lope's *comedia* deals with twenty-four years of Russian history.

Chronology is often disregarded and events are telescoped. In the play Ivan IV dies on the same day as his son Ivan, while in history he died on March 18, 1584. Contrary to history, Teodoro (Feodor) never appears as a Tsar in the drama, because immediately after Ivan IV's death Cristina appoints Boris to govern the country.

Demetrio, whom Lope calls "niño" (child) without indicating how old he is, already participates in the events of the first scene of the first act. Yet in reality, Demetrius was not born until October 19, 1583, and could not have played a part in this scene, which occurs on November 19, 1581.

The question of chronology cannot be solved satisfactorily and it would be naïve to insist on an exact rendition of historical truth. Apart from the fact that Lope's sources were imperfect and biased, in view of the great number of plays which he produced we cannot expect from the Spanish playwright the careful and minute historical preparation which characterizes, for example, Friedrich Hebbel's dramatic fragment or Aleksandr N. Ostrovskij's Demetrius tragedy. In addition, as Rapp suggested, Lope may have written this play, as he did so many others, in one day. Lope did not polish his Demetrius *comedia*, but improvised it. Each playwright of historical drama distorts historical truth to a certain extent and reinterprets the events according to his ideological bias and artistic convention. This is what Lope did; he retained, and only slightly modified, historical events, except when they clashed with his dramatic needs.

The Plot of the Play and Lope's Dramatic Art

First Act. *Cristina tells Demetrio that Juan's followers poisoned Teodoro so that Juan could succeed Basilio. The poison did not kill Teodoro, but made him unfit for governing. Cristina is afraid that an attempt may be made on Demetrio's life to prevent him from succession since Juan has no children to succeed him. She entrusts Demetrio to Lamberto to bring him up in secrecy. Basilio surprises Isabela and Rodulfo as they embrace and slaps her for her infidelity. Juan reproaches his father and the latter, in anger, strikes him dead. Basilio himself dies from grief the same day. Cristina appoints Boris to govern, but the latter usurps the power and sends Rodulfo to murder Demetrio. Warned by Rufino, Lamberto replaces Demetrio with César, his son, and the assassins kill César, mistaking him for Demetrio. In the meantime Demetrio, Lamberto, and Rufino escape.*

From a historical viewpoint this is the most important act, showing the chain of events at the Muscovite Court which precipitated the Time of Troubles. Lope acquaints us with the fearful atmosphere of Ivan IV's reign, the character of which is well summarized by Cristina's hysterical cry: "¿Quién ne tiembla?" Violence, intrigue, and jealousy reflect the fight for power. The attempt to kill Teodoro may be linked with the brutality of the *opričnina*, since Teodoro is punished for his noble qualities and presumably he was in the way of the *opričniki*, who favor Tsarevich Juan to succeed Ivan the Terrible because of his savage nature. Isabela's intrigue leads to the accidental murder of Juan and one fateful event follows another in rapid succession. There is a moral degeneracy gnawing away the strength of the Court and this implies that fresh forces outside the Court are needed to revitalize it. Thus, Cristina invites Lamberto, the German knight who lives in the country, to take care of the education of Demetrio. The introduction of the Spaniard Rufino at this point may be seen as Lope's attempt to give Spain an important role in the future regeneration of Muscovy.

The tense atmosphere of the Court, where murder and death are rampant, is contrasted to the peaceful climate of Lamberto's home, where friendliness reigns. An especially warm scene of youthful exuberance between the two friends, Demetrio and César, precedes the catastrophe and lends great poignance to the senseless murder of the latter. This is the only Demetrius play in world literature in which the attempt to murder Demetrius is acted out on the stage.

Although Boris emerges at the end of the first act as the uncontested ruler of Russia, the future is not completely bleak, for Demetrio has escaped from the assassins, and Rufino, in the role of a Greek chorus, predicts that God will return his kingdom to Demetrio.

On the subject of Teodoro's poisoning, Mosquera mentions, enigmatically and unhistorically, that this younger son was poisoned for reasons of succession, so that he should not compete with his older brother. However, this statement, as Mosquera himself admits, must be attributed to rumors ("se dixo"),[84] for, at the time of Possevino's visit to Russia, Ivan, the older son, was in good health and regarded as the unquestioned heir to Ivan IV. Why should the younger son, not in the immediate line of succession, be poisoned? How could Teodoro have competed with his older brother for the throne? Although there was no firm law of succession in Russia at the time, and the tsar regarded the whole country as his personal property and considered himself entitled to name a successor of his own choice, the custom had been for the eldest son to succeed. It is obvious that Barezzi's information, on which Mosquera based his version, was incorrect because, in another passage, Barezzi indicates that Juan was inclined to goodness and clemency, while, in reality, Juan followed his father's footsteps in cruelty and debauchery.

Lope must have changed Mosquera's version concerning the age of Teodoro and Juan because it did not make sense to him. Accepting the story of poisoning, he sacrificed historical truth for a good dramatic situation, since in his *comedia,* in which Teodoro appears as the older son, the partisans of the younger brother poison Teodoro to obtain the crown for their candidate, who otherwise could not have become the tsar. Lope's solution is more logical and must have been more convincing for his Spanish audience, who knew next to nothing of life and conditions at the distant Russian Court.

The most tragic event of the first act is the accidental murder of Juan, historically attested by all of Lope's possible sources. In Barezzi's version the argument between father and son arose because of the latter's wife, although she was not guilty of any dishonesty. By omitting the qualifying clause Mosquera gave an entirely different implication to Barezzi's report: "The father, quarrelling one day with Juan, his older son, because of the latter's wife, wounded him gravely." In Poehl's opinion, Lope the dramatic poet, not, perhaps, Lope the man, could not interpret these laconic words of Mosquera otherwise than to suppose a scene of infidelity and jealousy. Praag denies that this situation was Lope's invention and believes that Lope followed Bavía's account, which the latter had borrowed from Possevino's *Moscovia*. According to Possevino, one day Ivan IV came into the room of his son's wife, who, being pregnant, was dressed only lightly, and in his anger over this indecency, he slapped her. As a result of this incident she had a miscarriage. The Tsarevich reproached his father for his violent behavior and Ivan IV, stung by his son's accusation, struck him fatally.[85]

It seems to us that, beyond the interpretations of Poehl and Praag, Lope has introduced a typical Spanish motif of honor and jealousy in the material supplied by his sources. Leaving the problem of honor aside for the moment, we can see how Lope built the greater part of the first act with remarkable theatrical efficiency into the orbit of a characteristic Spanish drama. He invented Isabela's barrenness, filled her with envy for her more fortunate rival (Cristina) and motivated her attempt of infidelity, which triggered all the historical consequences. Thus, instead of the historical theme dominating the action, it is rather the other way around and "theme is largely a pretext for the action," as Pring-Mill points out in his introduction to *Lope de Vega 5 Plays* "something whose implications in the given situation are being exploited chiefly for their dramatic possibilities."[86]

Second Act. *After years of wandering Lamberto dies. Demetrio and Rufino become monks. News reaches Boris that Demetrio is alive and he decides to investigate the report. Boris arrives at the monastery in which Demetrio lives, and orders Rodulfo to kill him. Demetrio and Rufino manage to escape, work with Lithuanian harvesters, and become kitchen help for the Count Palatine. When they hear that a revolution has begun against Boris in Russia, Demetrio reveals his identity to the Palatine and asks for his support.*

The second act lacks the sweep of the momentous historical events of the first and there is a considerable slackening of pace which permits the protagonists to formulate their thoughts and to reflect upon their problems. Thus, theme is no longer subordinated to action, but gains equality as a principle of dramatic construction. When Lamberto sounds the call for the *reconquista,*

> Ya es tiempo, Principe ilustre / Que volviendo por
> tu honra
> Por tu vida, por tu fama / A quien eres correspondas
> Cobrando el paterno imperio.[87]

Lope is as much attracted by the ethical values at issue as by the theatrical tools with which the final result is achieved.

If in the second act Lope separates himself from his sources, and becomes relatively free of the straitjacket of history, he gains in spontaneity, and we see him at his best as a truly creative artist. He is no longer limited to the ready-made material Mosquera and Bavía gave him and shows much greater individuality in devising and creating the plot.

Since Lope is not so much concerned with the destiny of Russia in this act, the story becomes simpler and the majority of the protagonists are no longer members of a knightly court, but the modest men and women of a rural community. Lope seems to feel more at ease now that he can create new complications, introduce a romantic motif, and mix tragic and comic elements.

Although this act contains the most dramatic confrontation of the play, that between Boris and Demetrio, it is handled with much greater lightness and grace than the other two. It is due to the fairy tale quality of the plot in this act, almost entirely Lope's invention, with which he carries his audience into an idealized world, and prepares for a sudden turn in the fortune of his hero.

The accidental appearance of the Palatine and his pretty daughter is the key to the transformation of an almost lethargic

Demetrio into an active hero. This casual meeting suggests to him the idea of recruiting a powerful ally for his campaign, and his plans already include matrimony with Margarita.

Lope focuses attention on the development of the two protagonists, puts them in various new situations in order to see their character reflected in the opinion and attitude of others, gradually intensifies their struggle, and paves the way for the final duel. Suspense created by a chain of unusual situations is maintained: it is characteristic that, at the end of this act, we are not permitted to know the outcome of the important discussion between Demetrio and the Palatine. Through providential intervention the solution of the conflict is hinted at, but Lope still retains enough roadblocks (Boris's large army is intact), provides possible further complications (the love of the Duke of Arnies for Margarita), and unforeseeable events (will the Polish king support Demetrio?) to hold our interest and to prevent a facile untimely conclusion that virtue will ultimately be rewarded and vice punished no matter what.

The classical opposition between the evil court and the innocent country continues, becomes heightened, and is radically altered. While out of the twenty-seven scenes of the first act twenty occur in the aristocratic court, only three of the twenty-five scenes of the second act take place in the Kremlin, and all the others are set in the country. With this fudamental shift, both the atmosphere and the tone of the *comedia* change. A certain democratization may be seen in the scenes which show Demetrio among the simple monks of the monastery, the peasants and harvesters of the Lithuanian countryside, and the servants of the Palatine, sharing their life, participating in their work, and enjoying their natural gaiety.

Structurally it is in the mid-point of the *comedia* that Lope introduces, before Demetrio's meeting with the Palatine, an enchanting rural scene filled with joy and gaiety. It is at this stage that the play shakes off both the heaviness of the atmosphere of the Court and the rarefied air of the monastery, and earthly pleasures of song, dance, and hunting against a broad and sunny landscape dotted with rivers and forest become dominant.

In harmony with the changed atmosphere, the tone becomes more lyric, suave, and jesting. The cheerful and mellow tunes of the folksong break the severity and monotony of the *Te Deums* of the monastery, and the comic gestures of Rufino and the racy jests of Febo are carried out with such exuberant zest as to suggest by their inherent optimism that the attainment of world harmony cannot be far away. It is only appropriate that, at the end of this Brueghelian scene, the optimistic Rufino points to a happy ending of Demetrio's adventure.

> Señor, camina
> Que si un alma es advina / Tu serás emperador . . .[88]

Balašov finds that this act is decisive for the understanding of Lope's relation to Russia and to the problem of the king's power in Spain and Muscovy. He characterizes the tone as Falstaffian and having the same function it has in Shakespeare's *Henry IV;* he stresses the importance of familiarity with the life of the people and folk environment as positive factors in the character formation of the future king. Balašov is especially fascinated with the scene in which the future Russian emperor cleans and sweeps in the monastery.

The most interesting part of the second act is the confrontation between Boris and Demetrio. In Mosquera's account Lope read that Boris, at the time of his visit to a monastery, noticed a monk who looked like Demetrio and the playwright transformed this passage into a vivid and highly dramatic scene with typical baroque elements.

Demetrio overhears a conversation mentioning that the Great Duke is coming to visit the monastery. He hardly has time to express to Rufino his anxiety concerning this visit when Boris, Orofrisa, and Rodulfo arrive. Among the monks Boris immediately notices Demetrio, comments on his noble qualities ("De hombre noble muestra indicio"), and asks him whether he is of noble birth ("¿Eres hombre de valor?")[89]

This scene gives Lope an opportunity to display most efficiently his baroque thesis of deceiving with the truth ("engañar con la verdad.") Although in his reply Demetrio truthfully informs Boris of his origin, his words are so cleverly constructed that Boris is unable to plumb the *double entendre.* "I was the son of someone who was not without any use and value . . . because he was a slave and a noble."

> Hijo fui de quien no fué / Sin servicio y sin valor
> Porque fué . . . esclavo y señor.[90]

The description fits Teodoro perfectly in his dual role: a man of royal blood who, at the same time, is also a slave of others because of his inability to govern; others, therefore, rule for him, and ultimately rule him.

Demetrio also describes his mother in the same simple, yet enigmatic way: "My mother was not a prophet, and I do not think that she was even prudent, because, being trustful, she gave away her fortune, and left me poor."

> Mi madre no era profeta / Ni aún pienso que fué discreta,
> Porque fué muy confiada / Dió su hacienda, y me dejó / Pobre . . .[91]

Again, it is a remarkable portrait of Cristina, who did not foresee the dangers which her hasty move of giving Boris the reins of the empire entailed and thus ruined herself and her son.

It is now Boris's turn to attempt to outwit Demetrio by asking the latter to pray for him, while, at the same time, his thoughts are already turned toward eliminating this mysterious person. Yet Demetrio is not deceived, as his answer indicates: ". . . no pasa día ninguno que no me acuerdo de vos," which means that he knows well from which direction he may expect danger, while, on the surface, he is simply complying with Boris's request to pray to God for him ("Con mil ruegos le importuno . . .").[92] Boris remains in doubt concerning the true identity of this monk and expresses his uncertainty in the following words:

> Parece un santo . . . y parece / A Demetrio.[93]

In addition to this verbal duel between the two antagonists, this episode is important because it reflects the attitude of the simple monks and the guards concerning Boris and Demetrio, the present and the future ruler of Russia.

At the beginning of the scene Boris, the Great Duke of Muscovy, is received in all reverence. The Master of Novices praises his zeal and comments on his royal character. The Abbot humbly expresses his gratitude to Boris for the high honor of his visit. Yet everything is changed when Boris tries to bribe the Abbot to kill the monk Demetrio. Not only does the Abbot indignantly refuse to do so, and calls Boris's rule unjust, but his sympathy is evoked for the monk Demetrio, whose life he would like to save. Boris's guards also feel the injustice when they are ordered to kill an innocent man, and they cannot hide their satisfaction when they discover that the monk Demetrio has escaped.

Thus, the noble image of Boris begins to sink and, as more and more people learn of his unjust acts, he comes to be hated by all. In the meantime Demetrio, by his simple nobility and modesty, wins the sympathy of the people with whom he comes into contact.

The end of the second act is a pearl of the baroque theater. Demetrio seeks entrance to the Palatine to reveal his origin, but is surprised by Margarita, who asks this "kitchen help" who he is. Demetrio decides to play the clown and tells Margarita that he is the crown prince of Muscovy and that he wants to marry her. Again, Demetrio deceives with the truth, but this time Margarita, with her feminine intuition, senses that this unusual story, although presented as a joke, may still be true, and permits him to see her father.

Third Act. *The Palatine introduces Demetrio to King Sigismundo, who offers Demetrio military support. Boris sends Rodulfo to Sigismundo to denounce Demetrio and also sends Eliano and Finea, his agents, to kill him. Yet his plans fail and, defeated by Demetrio in a battle, he commits suicide. All hail Demetrio, the new Great Duke of Muscovy.*

In its wealth of historical detail this act is similar to the first, but artistically it is the weakest of the three. Some structural imperfections and occasional unpoetic language point to the possibility of a corrupted version.

Lope skillfully manages to maintain suspense until the end of the *comedia*. The optimism generated for Demetrio's cause in the second act is not permitted to grow unchecked. Boris is shown, for obvious dramatic reasons, as a powerful adversary, and the final outcome remains in doubt until his suicide. Thrusts and counter-thrusts follow one another in breathless succession as the two protagonists battle each other in various situations until the climactic confrontation.

Lope uses the love scenes, which in so many of his dramas drown history, as secondary, and makes Margarita's tender words contrast with the prevailing martial mood. To create a logical solution, to tie up all the loose strands, and to bring together the destinies of Demetrio and Margarita, Lope has the latter participate, in some way, in the dangers of war.

A major deviation from his sources is Lope's description of Boris's death. Lope reached maximum intensity of tragic effect by placing Boris in a quasi-individual combat against Demetrio on the battlefield and making him die in front of the latter. In this way Lope achieved a dramatic confrontation and illustrated in personal and concrete terms the victory of justice over wickedness. Another deviation from his sources is the description of the death of Orofrisa and of Boris's children on the battlefield.

The little insight we gain into the characters of the protagonists comes once more through the mirror of their actions, and Lope seems, in this final act, to be seeking a meaning in their deeds in order to establish an equilibrium between theme and action as dramatic principles.

The Spanish World in Lope's Demetrius *Comedia*

GENERAL OBSERVATIONS

In Vossler's opinion, what he calls "der nationale Grundzug" is one of the most important traits of Lope's *comedias*. The German critic feels that

Nur stofflich, nicht formal, d.h. nicht geistig greift Lope ueber das spanische Denken, Glauben und Trachten hinaus. Eine ausserspanische, ausserkirchliche Welt hat er niemals anerkannt. Er kehrt ihr den Ruecken, als waere sie nicht.[94]

Lope wrote *El Gran Duque,* like so many of his other historical plays, against the background of a Spain elevated to her greatest might by the imperial policy of Charles V and Philip II and their attempt to impose a Spanish way of life on Europe. This imperial idea informs Lope's dramatic art and the term *hispanizar* (to turn into Spanish) in this sense may be applied to most of his historical dramas whose action occurs in a foreign land. Thus, in his *Arte nuevo de hacer comedias* (A new method for writing *comedias*), when Lope posits his first and second rules as "to imitate the actions of men" and "to paint their customs," he means Spanish men and Spanish customs.

In his *Lope de Vega,* Marcel Carayon, another Lopean scholar, states:

Niemand war soweit wie Lope von einer dokumentarischen Auffassung der Kunst entfernt. Selbst in den ausserhalb Spaniens spielenden Komoedien ist sein Menschenschlag ausgesprochen spanisch: soviel vermoechte ueber ihn die Umgebung, in der er lebte.[95]

Lope identified himself with the ideals of his country, with the total life of the Spanish people, and this identification forms the basis of his dramatic concept. González-Lopez, a Spanish literary historian, points out that Lope even transformed into Spanish material themes taken from foreign literature and history.[96] Thus, although in his Demetrius *comedia* Lope treats a theme from Russian history with Russian and Polish historical figures against a Russian and Livonian landscape, he sees the theme, the figures and the landscape through a Spanish mirror.

It is the national character of the Spanish society of kings and peasants, soldiers and artisans, but especially of knights, with their almost incredible loyalty to the monarch and unconditional belief in divine providence, which we see reflected on Lope's stage. In the words of Vossler:

Er laesst die Menschen der fernsten . . . Laender fuehlen, denken, reden, und handeln als waeren es Spanier des Barock, herrschaftliche, ehrbeflissene Menschen, voll persoenlichen und nationalen Geltungsdrang.[97]

Lope was able to create this sentiment only because he, more than any other poet of his time, became the living symbol of the aspiration and historical justification of Spain. Lope's glorification of Spain is best reflected by the imperial idea inherent in *El Gran Duque*. Spain is represented by one of his heroic men—Rufino—in the glorious deed of reconquering a country which Lope insists on regarding as Catholic.

Yet it is not only in the theme itself, the legitimate right of Prince Demetrio to reconquer his throne, in which the Spanish world is revealed, but also in the ideas and precepts of which the protagonists are the standard-bearers and which Boris and his clique violate. This shifts the intellectual, spiritual, and social focus even farther from the lands in which the action occurs, Poland and Russia, and brings it closer to Spain.

Thus, the protagonists of the drama are not only the Russian Ivan the Terrible, Boris Godunov, Demetrius, and the Polish Sigismund, the Palatine, and Margarita, but also their Spanish counterparts in the historical and poetic world of Lope. However, in spite of their complex nature, these protagonists are not abstract persons of any time and place, but men and women with concrete qualities incarnating the national sentiments of Spain, rooted in a soil and age with traditional Spanish concepts in the conditions and beliefs of the Iberian peninsula superimposed on the Slavic personalities of the Russian Time of Troubles. Thus, when Lope makes various characters of the *comedia* praise the unjustly persecuted Demetrio, it is the panegyric of a Spanish hero in a Russian costume; when he stresses King Sigismundo's generosity, he has the noble qualities of a Spanish king before his eyes; and when he speaks of the Boristenes (Dnieper), he visualizes the Guadalquivir or another Spanish river transplanted into the Slavic world. The Demetrius drama of Lope is a vast eulogy of Spain and the Spanish way of life, and its protagonists are not only the Russian-Polish but also the Spanish people.

What are those ideas and precepts of the Spanish world that we find in Lope's Demetrius drama? They can be summarized as a spiritual unity of three immutable sentiments: honor, Catholic faith, and monarchy.

HONOR

Honor in Spanish drama can be defined as the dignity, reputation, and equality of all men. Its conventional code is so strict that, as Butler Clark states in *Spanish Literature,* "it replaces the abstract 'Necessity' of allegorical drama."[98] It almost ceases to be a manifestation of an individual sense of dignity to become an opinion, since it expresses the relation of the individual to society: What do others think of us?

We have already seen how Lope transformed his sources and created a typical Spanish motif from Isabela's intrigue in the first act, and we will now consider it within the honor code of the Spanish drama.

There are three persons involved in this situation: Isabela, whose behavior arouses Basilio's suspicion; Basilio, whose motive, in the light of Isabela's accusation, appears suspect; and Juan, who is deceived by Isabela and therefore distrusts Basilio. It is interesting to note that Lope assigns almost no role to Rodulfo, the corespondent of Isabela's indecent conduct, obviously stressing indirectly that he is merely a pawn in Isabela's design.

First, it is Basilio who, seeing the intimacy between Isabela and Rodulfo, feels that his own honor is hurt through the damage that the honor of his son has suffered:

Parece que la abrazó / Mancha en mi honor sufro yo,[99]

and who, in reproaching her, poses as the defender of his son's reputation:

Causa he tenido;
Que sospecho que el honor / De mi hijo tratas mal.[100]

However, the shrewd Isabela attempts to wriggle out of this situation by accusing her father-in-law of, in turn, jealousy and dishonorable conduct toward herself:

. . . Esos celos han nacido / Quizá de que me pretendes.[101]

Her dishonest conduct, and perhaps even more, her bold reference to his tyranny and to his debauchery provoke Basilio to slap her for "el santo honor."[102] It is important to note the use of the adjective, with which Lope intensifies the significance of the noun.

Basilio feels that with this physical chastisement of Isabela the honor of his family is avenged. However, the episode is far from finished because Isabela's painful cries bring Juan and others into the room. After listening to her complaint, it is now Juan's turn to assert that, as a result of his father's action, his own honor has been soiled:

Tu, que me has de dar honor / Me le vienes a quitar.[103]

Juan feels that dishonor to him is reflected, as in a mirror, in the way his wife has been treated:

Sabes que el espejo ha sido / En que se mira mi honor.[104]

The situation is further complicated in this case by the fact that Juan is faced with Basilio in the dual quality of the latter: both as his father and as his king. Juan must obey Basilio both as his son and as his vassal. In general Lope exalted the extraordinary quality of the king who can do no wrong and pointed out, as in *Los Vargas de Castillo,* that the subject must accept the damage done to his honor. Yet there are also exceptions to this rule in Lope's theater. At times he must have felt so strongly about the sanctity of honor, as in *Los novios de Hornachuelos,* that even the absolute monarch is not permitted to overstep this limit. In *El Gran Duque* we also find an exception to this rule, although Lope in this episode stresses more Basilio's role as Juan's father than as king.

There follows a battle of wits between Isabela and Basilio concerning the interpretation of the word *celoso,* with its various meanings of jealousy, longing, and envy. Isabela accuses Basilio that he "anda celoso de mi" in the sense that he covets her, while Basilio replies to Juan that he (Basilio) is "celos de tu honra" in the sense that he, the father, is jealously guarding his son's honor. When Juan, not knowing whom to believe, asks Isabela's explanation of this strange occurrence, she shrewdly misleads him by giving a different twist to Basilio's words: "Si, / Pues te la quiere quitar," implying that Basilio is eager to rob Juan of his honor by seducing his wife. This equivocal way of speaking, lending itself to various interpretations, is a typical trait of Lope's baroque art and continually recurs in this drama.[105]

Isabela outwits Basilio, and it is in vain that the latter, defeated in this skirmish of sophistry, tries to withdraw behind the unassailable Castillian curtain of paternal authority:

No hay que dar / Satisfaciones de mi / Yo soy tu padre.[106]

Juan is not content with this explanation and regards it as an indirect admission of his father's guilt, since he is well aware of Basilio's previous record of voluptuousness. Thus, in demanding satisfaction Juan further stresses his father's guilt in this affair.

This act of demanding satisfaction is reminiscent of a ritual of purification in the sense of washing off the stain cast on someone's honor. However, Juan feels powerless against his father, but warns him that if he were not his father, he (Juan) would strike him for his dishonorable conduct.

Juan must be satisfied that with a verbal chastisement, *faute de mieux,* he regains his honor in the opinion of the others. But now the pendulum of the strict Spanish honor code swings once

again in the other direction. Basilio's paternal dignity has been
shattered and, in order to regain it, he must punish his son. In
addition, Basilio also feels that his authority as an absolute
monarch has been brought into question by the disobedience of
his son and vassal. Thus, both as his father and his king, he
must now chastise Juan:

> Si a elle dile el bofeton / Por lasciva e insolente,
> A ti por inobediente . . .[107]

Balašov, the Soviet literary critic, feels that the situation
between Lope's Basilio and his two sons Juan and Teodoro was
suggested to the playwright by a similar situation which had
existed between Philip II of Spain and Don Carlos, his son.
Naming Helena, the historical third wife of Tsarevich Ivan,
as Isabela, Balašov thinks that Lope associated this episode in
the play with the legend of the rivalry between Philip II and
Don Carlos for Queen Isabela, the second wife of Philip II.[108]
  This interesting speculation was originally made by Rapp in
1868; adding a footnote to the pertinent passage of his translation of the drama, Rapp asked: "Sollte der Dichter nicht
beilaeufig an Don Carlos gedacht haben?" As his authority
Balašov refers to Altamira y Crevea's *Historia de España,* but
in that book the Spanish historian rather denies the rumors of
Carlos's illicit love with his stepmother. Much more obvious is
the supposition that the Soviet reviewer was thinking of Schiller's
powerful *Don Carlos,* in which the German playwright, influenced by Protestant sources, brilliantly dramatized the complex
relationship between the erstwhile bridegroom and later stepson
and passionate admirer of Philip II's wife.
  I think, however, that Balašov's theory of an identification
of Basilio with Philip II in Lope's mind is untenable in view
of the great esteem in which Lope held this Spanish king. In his
Arte nuevo Lope refers to Philip II as the prudent king, and
in his play *Pobreza no es vileza* he makes a simple Spanish
soldier assert that Philip is the guardian of his honor. Could
this Spanish king have served as a prototype for Basilio, whom,
as Balašov himself admits, Lope treats without sympathy? If
Lope was thinking of an Iberian prototype, it is likely that
Pedro el Cruel, king of Portugal (1357-67), a cruel and sensuous emperor, was his choice.[109]

CATHOLIC FAITH

In Lope's architectural plan of the cosmos, God and the Catholic idea precede everything else. Kings, governors, judges, and other dignitaries can only follow Him at a respectful distance. This Catholic idea constitutes the second element of the spiritual unity of the Spanish man of Lope's era.

The entire world depends on God's will, and nature, in a harmonious order, reflects God's will and becomes its instrument. Human society follows this natural order, and in Lope's *Weltanschauung* there is a strong similarity between the structure of society and nature. In Lope's eyes Spaniards were the chosen people of God, invested with the mission of propagating the Evangelium and of imposing the Catholic faith all over the world.

The Catholic idea can be seen in *El Gran Duque* in its three aspects: 1. the religious tone which informs the entire *comedia,* 2. the providential intervention which accompanies Demetrio throughout his life, and 3. the concept of repentance, according to which even the greatest sinner will be pardoned if he sincerely repents. The Catholic idea, expressed with a human accent, thus becomes the moral dimension which gives profundity to the dilemmas of the individuals, and it also represents the spiritual scenery against which the play develops.

The religious tone pervades the drama so strongly that it can be noticed even in the habitual conversation of almost everyone in the *comedia*. Yet there is an important difference between the manner in which the positive and negative characters use the name of God. The latter—Basilio, Isabela, Rudolfo, and Boris—mention divinity casually and mechanically, as phrases of convention only, uttered at random, without any depth of religious and moral implication, and go even so far as to invoke God's help in the execution of their nefarious plans.

The positive characters—Teodoro, Cristina, Lamberto, Rufino, César, and Demetrio—never use God's name for a trifling reason. In their speech the invocation of God is always a fervent appeal, profoundly felt and mysteriously experienced, and carries with it moral and social implication. Since the two Russian kings—Basilio and Boris—are shown as tyrants, we often hear the positive characters seek God to ask His justice and protection against the wickedness of these kings. Lope's thesis that God is the king of kings is well illustrated in this drama, in which we see a continuous frustration of the tyrants by God.

Like his Jesuit sources, which stressed the miraculous elements in Demetrio's life (Barezzi: *miracolosa,* Mosquera: *milagrosa* in the titles of their brochures) and attributed his successful campaign to divine intervention, Lope retained this sense of providence in history, and by emphasizing in his comedy that God guided Demetrio through all the dangers, he offered to his spectators a long chain of providential events.

Vossler calls the concept of repentance Lope's "religioese Zuversicht" and adds that:

Die starre Entfremdung oder Feindseligkeit zwischen Gesellschaft und Einzelwesen, wie wir sie heute kennen, ist in einer Zeit, in der die christliche Kirche faehig war, auch den abseitigsten Verbrecher zu retten, erspart geblieben. . . . Dem Verbrecher . . . steht die Krone des Maertyrers und Heiligen jedeszeit zur Verfuegung, sofern er die Glaubensstaerke besitzt.[110]

This third aspect of the Catholic idea, although indicated partly in his sources, becomes greatly intensified in that Lope strongly emphasizes Demetrio's magnanimity in pardoning repenting sinners. Yet he also employs it as a means of heightening stage effects, because he makes Demetrio first pardon the smaller sinner, Eliano, followed by the greater sinner, Rudulfo, the murderer of César; and, as we learn from Demetrio, he even intends to pardon Boris.

Conversely, we see as the drama develops how one by one the partisans of Boris repent their misdeeds, and even Boris himself professes repentance in his final gesture, although this is obviously not a full repentance in a religious sense or he would not kill himself.

MONARCHY

The final element of the spiritual unity of the Spanish world is the idea of an absolute monarchy, which, in Lope's dramas, dominated the pattern of society.

Lope regarded the Spanish monarchy as a kind of universal empire and Emperor Charles V as a spiritual head of a chosen state. The king represented and imitated God, and God helped the king in fulfilling his duties. One may speak of a commonwealth of divinity and monarchy, a union from which comes the suggestion for the moral conduct of the monarch. Thus, in most of Lope's dramas the king appears as the incarnation of justice, guarantee of social balance, and source of honor. It is his high mission to be the father of his nation. His person is connected with the idea of divine origin of authority, which is the basis of absolute monarchy. Yet Lope also indicated that an unjust king can be deposed—as in his play *La Reina Juana de Nápoles*—and he also limits his sovereignty by an essential objective: the welfare of the nation expressed in national unity— as in another drama, *El hijo por engaño*.

In Lope's Demetrius drama we meet three Russian monarchs —Basilio, Boris, and Demetrio—and one Polish king, Sigismundo. While Lope uses Demetrio and Sigismundo to illustrate his ideal of the good king, he also employs the negative traits of Boris and especially of Basilio, in the very contrast these two tyrants represent, to reinforce his argument.

When Basilio threatens Teodoro with his stick in the first act, the original edition of the *comedia* (1617) has the following note: "Este baston traen los Duques de Moscovia por cetro."[111] While this is historically incorrect, since, as nearly as we can ascertain, such an iron staff is mentioned only in connection with Ivan IV, and the identification of the sceptre with the staff does not appear anywhere else in Russian history, it is with this sceptre-stick that, in Lope's drama, Basilio kills Juan. Lope cleverly paints the psychology of Basilio in this episode. Basilio is a tyrant who does good and evil without discrimination, and, because of this ingrained habit, he can no longer distinguish one from the other. Thus, these diametrically opposite qualities fuse and become one in his mind, and it is shown that he does not know with which of the two, the royal sceptre or the tyrant's stick, he will punish Juan:

A ti por inobediente / Por este cetro o baston.[112]

In Lope's view the highest symbol of justice can degenerate into a murderous tool when wielded by a tyrant.

The final statement of this powerful scene is expressed by Teodoro, the jester and moral chronicler of the Court, who indicates that as a rule, at a coronation ceremony in Moscow, a staff is given instead of a sceptre to the new monarch, and, in a play of words—in which *dejar* means to let, to permit, but also to abandon and, by extension, to kill—he says that with his staff Basilio has just "crowned" the heir to his empire in death:

En Moscovia es el baston / Cetro y insignia real
Y éste le dan por señal / En nuestra coronacion:
Y ansi el Duque lo ha mostrado / Pues con el baston le dió
En señal que le dejó, / Heredero de su estado.[113]

In addition to the spiritual unity of the Spanish world so prominently displayed in *El Gran Duque,* Lope included in this drama such typical elements of his Spanish theater as an astrologer, a *gracioso,* and peasants, and also created a picaresque theme.

THE ASTROLOGER

We cannot tell whether the astrologer episode was entirely Lope's invention or, as Praag suggests, Lope just happened to read about it in Bavía's history while working on this *comedia,* or, as Morley and Bruerton assert, it was more like a commonplace of folklore than a conscious borrowing.

The Catholic church had bitterly fought the astrologers in the religious Middle Ages, indicates Frank G. Halstead, an American *Lopista,* in his article *The Attitude of Lope de Vega toward Astrology,*[114] and finally, as a compromise, decreed that, while the stars could incline the will, they could not force it.

In the opinion of such literary critics as Luis Astrano Marin in *La vida azarosa de Lope de Vega* and Rennert and Castro in *La vida de Lope de Vega,*[115] the Spanish playwright was exceptionally interested in astrology and his attitude in such plays as *Roma abrasada* and *La mayor corono* was that of a credulous and superstitious man. However, when all of Lope's artistic output is considered, Halstead explains, the preponderant evidence is that the Spanish playwright was neither credulous nor superstitious.

These clashing attitudes of Lope on the subject of astral influence are artistically, although somewhat ambiguously, spelled out in the Demetrius drama. The positive viewpoint— that is, the triumph of the stars—is depicted in a scene between Boris and the astrologer. The news that Demetrio, the legitimate ruler of the land, is alive and coming against Boris has already spread far and wide in Russia and, under strict orders of Boris, the police are alerted to arrest everybody who dares to speak about Demetrio's military campaign. An astrologer who publicly proclaimed that Demetrio was alive is arrested and brought to Boris for interrogation. After an animated debate, in which Boris and the astrologer each refers to the teaching of such authorities as Tacitus, Seneca, and Erasmus to prove his subjective point of view and to disprove that of his adversary on the reliability or untrustworthiness of the prophecy of the stars, Boris orders that the astrologer be hanged. Thus, at this point it would seem that belief in the stars is not justified, since the man who professed positive views is to be hanged. But in the final analysis the stars do triumph, because Demetrio is alive and conquers his throne, and to the unlucky astrologer may be accounted postmortem the dubious moral satisfaction of having guessed right.

We may perhaps see, as Richard H. Lawson does in his article "El Gran Duque . . . A Likely Source for Lessing,"[116] a human agent of fate in the astrologer who, by proclaiming that Demetrio was alive, predicted Boris's downfall. The author quotes from Rudolf Schewill's *The Dramatic Art of Lope de Vega* as follows: "It is also of interest that Lope . . . suggests lines along which the subsequent drama of fate, which the Germans call *Schicksalsdrama,* was conceived."[117]

I am inclined to believe that, in this particular case, Lope extolled astrology merely in order to intensify dramatic effects. The Spanish dramatist used this scene for a double purpose: he wanted, on the one hand, to illustrate by a concrete example the widespread belief of the Russian people in the miraculous escape of Demetrio which was mentioned in the preceding scene by Rodulfo, and, on the other hand, to show the definite change in Boris's character, who, after sixteen years of just and peaceful rule, becomes a tyrant, and hangs an innocent man for proclaiming the truth. It is interesting to note that the historical Boris Godunov was a very superstitious man, attributing great importance to the prediction of the stars, and, at the time of Demetrius's appearance, he thought that sorcery had been used to raise Demetrius from the dead.

In general, the attitude of Lope's Boris to signs around himself is equivocal. He eagerly accepts those auguries which are favorable to him, and refuses to believe those which run counter to his wishes. When, for example, Rufino, who happens to overhear Boris's secret conversation with Rodulfo about the plot to murder Demetrio, is seized, and when, upon his interrogation, Boris becomes convinced that he is "mute" and cannot reveal the plot, the Russian ruler assigns this incident to his lucky star and regards it as a heavenly approval of his just claims to the throne. (". . . ¡ Cuánto debo al cielo soberano! / Con justa causa la corona emprendo / Pues quiere que secretos que la intenten / Los hallen mudos porque no lo cuenten.")[118]

The negative point—that is, the denial of astrological science —can be culled from various statements in the play connected with the ebbing and rising of Demetrio's fortune. When Lamberto dies, the unhappy Demetrio, feeling the severity of the tragic loss, exclaims that he was born under a cruel star. ("En dura estrella nací.")[119] On another occasion, at the time of Boris's surprise visit to the monastery, when Demetrio's life is in danger, Rufino laments the severity of the stars. ("Tu estrella me maravilla / Toda sujeta a traidores.")[120]

These statements reflecting the low points in Demetrio's adventures are, however, offset by the eulogy with which the Palatine hails him after the turn of the tide in the decisive battle against Boris. (". . . Con tal valor ha vuelto a la batalla / Que la gente que ya vencida huia / Le van siguiendo, y á su ejemplo hacen / Hazañas inauditas.")[121] This, I believe, is the authentic voice of Lope, in which he expresses his own opinion that, by a courageous application of free will, man can control his destiny. In the words of Halstead: "Lope was a reasonable man, with knowledge of astrological science. In the last analysis he believes 'Dichoso aquél que con prudencia sabe / Vencer su condición y ser bienquista / Que es la voluntad la mejor llave.' "[122]

The importance which Lope attributed to celestial signs in this play is another bridge linking *El Gran Duque* to Calderón's *La vida es sueño,* which is literally permeated with references to astrology.

PEASANTS

Lope especially distinguished himself in plays which deal with the simple life of the peasants in the country, as, for example, in *Fuenteovejuna* and *Peribañez.* In Brenan's phrase ". . . they have a matt, earthy tone like peasant pottery . . . [they] show remarkable power . . . conveying the corporate life of a whole community."[123]

The Polish-Livonian peasant scene has an irresistible charm, freshness, and humor. It is a little world by itself, entirely Lope's creation, and has nothing to do with his sources or history. The community is represented by its traditional, yet individualized types—Belardo, the man of common sense and simple taste; Lucinda, his good-hearted daughter, who looks at the wonders of the world with big, naïve eyes; and Febo, the country simpleton. The scene is not Spanish *costumbrismo,* but rather a decoration and embellishment of the *comedia.*

The esteem with which Lope regarded the existence of this simple folk of the earth on a remote hillside is perhaps best documented by the fact that, while the persecuted prince finds no safe refuge in the various monasteries, among the Polish-Livonian peasants he is in full safety. Vossler correctly explains the origin of these episodes with peasants in Lope's art:

Dass Lope . . . seine unschuldig Verfolgten so gerne bei Bauern einkehren und sich dort verbergen laesst, bei welcher Gelegenheit er die laendlichen Verhaeltnisse dieser Letzteren mit so viele Vorliebe ausmalt, ruehrt wohl von dem noch nicht ganz erloeschenen Geschmacke seines Publikums fuer die frueher so beliebte Schaeferpoesie her.[124]

The lyric atmosphere, lightness, and even carelessness that envelops this scene may at first appear to weaken the dramatic conflict, yet the inclusion of a bucolic intermezzo amid the breathless welter of violence, murder, and persecution does not seem artificial at all and represents a welcome change. Structurally it serves as a transition between the severity of life in the monastery and the worldly urbanity of the Count-Palatine's lordly mansion. The significance of this episode—which occurs almost exactly in the middle of the *comedia*—may be seen in the fact that it forms a bridge between the passive and persecuted, and active and happy Demetrio. It represents the turning point of his Odyssey, for it is at this stage that he decides to begin his *reconquista* through the active help of the Palatine.

Belardo is the head of the peasant community and his status is immediately recognized by the discerning Demetrio. He is willing to give food and shelter to the strangers provided that they want to work. Yet he is no dictator of his small world and, in a democratic fashion, asks his daughter's opinion before making a decision. He shares with Teodoro the habit of plain speech without hidden thoughts and ulterior motives. He has his own dignity and social rank and refuses to adorn his hat with false plumes, yet, as a good and wise father, he also understands the longing of his daughter for a pretty dress. Without knowing who they are, he invites the Palatine's party to share their simple meal, and, when he finds out that the newcomer is his feudal lord, he displays the typical Spanish traits of dignified vassal humility and asks them to honor his house with their presence.

In contrast to the rapidly changing values of the Muscovite Court, where there are no good or bad people since everything depends on blind chance and the dividing line between vice and virtue becomes increasingly fuzzy, Lope created in Belardo, frequently the spokesman of the Spanish dramatist in several of his *comedias,* the standard-bearer of constant and positive values, linked him as the *genius loci* to the earth of the Livonian countryside where he was born, and made him a symbol of his surrounding and origin. Lope stressed in him, in Vossler's phrase, "die Verwachsenheit des Einzelnen mit seiner Umgebung."[125]

Such is Lope's love for the simple life of the peasants that, in the analysis of Ricardo del Arco, a Spanish *Lopista,* even the language changes when he treats a rural scene: "Cuando en sus comedias surge el tema rústico, cambia el ritmo poético; se nota que el estro opera más fácil, espontáneo ye suelto."[126]

Mention must be made of the remarkable similarity in the tone and the atmosphere between the song of the Polish-Livonian harvesters in this *comedia* and the charming simplicity and fresh humor of the *Pieśni* (Songs) of Jan Kochanowski (1530-1584), the greatest Polish poet until Mickiewicz, and the *Sielanki* (Eclogues) of Szymon Szymonowicz (1558-1629), the Polish contemporary of Lope.[127]

EL GRACIOSO

One of the most important figures of the Spanish theater of the *Siglo de Oro* is the *gracioso,* an invention of Lope de Vega for the Spanish stage, although his predecessors may be seen in the *miles gloriosus* and other comic types of the Roman theater of Plautus and Terence. He is created in order to check and to break occasionally the dramatic tension by supplying comic elements on the stage. He also serves as a foil to the hero by putting in sharper relief the deeds and the attributes of the latter. He is characterized by popular wisdom, broad humor, and practical resourcefulness.

In the opinion of J. H. Arsona, a Spanish literary scholar, in *La Introducción del gracioso en el teatro de Lope de Vega,* Lope devoted much of his talent in developing and refining this type:

> trabajó en él más que en ningun otro personaje de toda su obra . . . empleó en su elaboración todo el talento de que le había dotado la naturaleza y virtió en el los rasgos más sinceros de su carácter.[128]

In Lope's Demetrius drama there are two types of *gracioso*: Rufino, the servant-companion-friend type, and Febo, the comical peasant.

Rufino, the Spanish guardian, servant, and friend of Demetrio, is an excellent example of the many-sided figure of the *gracioso* whom Lope succeeded in adapting to the constantly changing contours of the play. His resourcefulness is reflected in the spontaneous reaction to his interrogation by Boris, who has him arrested after discovering that Rufino had overheard his conversation with Rodulfo planning Demetrio's murder. There is a distinct echo of Sancho Panza's shrewdness in his playing the deaf and mute to Boris and Rodulfo. His frequent baroque exaggeration, a recurrent theme in the play, can be seen, for example, in his report to Lamberto concerning Boris's plot: "Sin aliento y aun sin vida / pues muertó un caballo dejo / Vengo a avisarte," alerting the German knight to the immediate danger to Demetrio's life, adding that "Que me venian siguiendo / De suerte que mis espaldas / Iban sintiendo sus pechos."[129]

His constant and insatiable hunger is his status symbol and he appreciates good food above everything else. He is literally dying from hunger at the poor monastery and cannot think of anything but food (". . . ¿cómo estamos Señor? / Muerto de hambre más que vivos")[130] and when they come to the Livonian peasants, instead of greeting them, his first question is whether there is anything to eat (¿Hay de comer?").[131] Even at the time of the idyllic song of the harvesters he cannot enjoy the gay scene because his one-track mind is set exclusively on food. His preoccupation with food reaches Gargantuan proportions when he is working as a kitchen-help in the Palatine's estate. The spectator hopes that, in the kitchen of the rich Palatine, Rufino will find an earthly paradise in the choice of food, but this is not the case: "Triste vida es cocinero / Pues cómo lo que no quiero / Y lo que quiero no cómo."[132]

A comic effect is attained by his exaggeration, especially when it is coupled with a Freudian slip of the tongue concerning his never-ending hunger. To Belardo's question whether he can cut the wheat well ("¿Segáis bien?"), Rufino assures him that he is able, with a single blow, to cut down . . . a six-pound bread ("De un golpe derribo . . . / Un pan de seis libros").[133]

The comic seriousness with which he answers the chamberlain's questions about the color of a dress, love, and jealousy serves as a foil to stress the romantic quality of Demetrio's affection for the Palatine's daughter.

Rufino's earthy realism and common sense often contrast with Demetrio's idealism. He always remains on solid earth, and, as J. K. Klein, a German literary historian pointed out, "el coloquio entre amo y criado . . . presente el carácter de un monólogo dialogado . . . al criado corresponde la acción, al galán la expresión poética."[134] This limited vision of the world and directness of approach gives Rufino a definite superiority over Demetrio in certain moments when the necessities of life are concerned. It is obvious that Lope wanted to illustrate the harmony with which the *gracioso*'s practical sense complements the hero's idealism and spirituality.

We find Rufino often criticize living and working conditions in the monastery and the kitchen almost in the sense of a contemporary labor union organizer. As a true Spaniard, Rufino, in the words of German *hispanista* Ludwig Pfandl in *Geschichte der spanischen Nationalliteratur,* "schafft der Auffassung des niederen Volkes Gewicht und Geltung . . . verkoerpert . . . in vielen Dingen den einfachen, gesunden Menschenvestand."[135] Thus, when Demetrio, hungry and in rags, sweeps the floor of the monastery, Rufino utters his social protest: "Pues barre un rey que atropellas / Tiempo en un pobre español,"[136] and in the kitchen where they have to clean and to scrape, his comment is equally critical: "Mire, a que oficio tan vilo / Le ha traido su destino."[137] As Dr. Maria Heseler, another German-speaking Spanish scholar, mentions in *Studien zur Figur des gracioso bei Lope de Vega und Vorgaengern* "der *gracioso* ist ueberhaupt gern ein wenig Philosoph, allerdings ein praktischer, der vorwiegend an Strasse und Leben geschult ist."[138] We hear Rufino philosophize about the unjust laws of the universe which oppress even kings, and also about honor and vanity.

Schewill calls the *gracioso* "a miracle of invention" and adds that "Lope has managed to put into the servant the unbounded resources of his wit and made him one of his chief claims to rank among the world's great comic playwrights."[139] We first admired his wit as he outplayed Boris and Rodulfo in the Kremlin, smiled at his comic farewell to the symbols of monastery life ("Adios, capilla / Adios, santo escapulario,"[140]) enjoyed his jokes among the Livonian laborers and in the Palatine's kitchen, and, finally, laughed at his puns at the cost of the chamberlain in the palace of King Sigismundo.

Heseler believes that Lope, himself, often hides behind the witticisms of the *gracioso* and uses him as his spokesman: ". . . der Autor den *gracioso* mehr als irgend eine andere Figur seiner *comedias* als Vermittler seiner Ideen, seines Witzes und Scharfsinnes gebraucht hat."[141]

It is important to note that Rufino is not only a *gracioso* of the conventional type, but also a true friend and a loyal subject of Demetrio. In the decisive battle Rufino fights bravely at Demetrio's side, guards and encourages him, and shares with him the fruit of victory.

The other *gracioso* in the play is Febo, a member of the Livonian peasant community. He is a peasant buffoon, a man of his place and social conditions. While Rufino is more cosmopolitan and can easily move from one social circle to another and blend with it, Febo is firmly planted on his native hill among his goats, and his philosophy of life centers around his immediate surroundings. He is jealous of newcomers, disrespectful of women, and a zealous guardian of his own small place in the world. His gross and racy humor is connected with the earth, hill, and domestic animals of his limited horizon. The high point of humor in the drama is reached when Febo and Rufino meet and match their wits.

A PICARESQUE THEME

The adventures, wanderings, and struggle for survival of Demetrio and Rufino may be considered as a picaresque theme. Yet it is only picaresque in form and not in the overall theme of the dream. If Demetrio is regarded as Teodoro's son, as he is in Lope's *comedia,* he cannot play the role of the *pícaro.* The *pícaro* is a rogue who has no social pedigree, no background, stands alone in the world, and, although he is not persecuted by anyone, he still has to grow up and shift in an indifferent, and often hostile world. Demetrio, however, is of royal origin, and his motive in wandering and hiding is not merely self-preservation, but the first positive step toward the recovery of his throne.

Nevertheless, because the adventures in Demetrio's life offer themselves ideally to a picaresque treatment, and because Lope, no doubt, must have been aware of the great success of the first two picaresque novels—*Lazarillo de Tormes* and *Guzmán de Alfarache*—a number of picaresque elements can be found in this drama. If we consider Demetrio as a child who grows up under difficult social conditions and makes his way by his wit through an unfriendly and dangerous world, trying to hide and outwit Boris and his henchmen, we then have the structure of a picaresque play.

Demetrio and Rufino enter several monasteries under various pseudonyms (Frayle Bernardino and Gil) to protect their identity and to find security. Their next adventures carry them to Livonian harvesters where they work under the fictitious names of Marzal and Bruto. Finally we find them in the kitchen of the Palatine in the role of *pícaros de cocina* (kitchen-helps), named Maese Andrés and Maese Pasquin. This last episode consists of genuine picaresque elements, in which wandering, hunger, food, eating, and the idea of working in a kitchen play a prominent part. Immediately preceding the revelation of his identity to the Palatine, Demetrio plays the clown with Margarita and this is still part of the picaresque theme.

Although Demetrio and Rufino are always together and work as a team, there is a great difference in their attitude and outlook on their social environment. Demetrio's dignity, symbol of his royal origin, is maintained even under the most trying circumstances. In the monastery he does his work silently; he does not participate in the crude jokes of Rufino and Febo among the peasants, and in the Palatine's kitchen he cleans the dishes just as calmly, although the other servants call him a *pícaro*. But in the concept of Lope, Demetrio's noble status remains unaffected in spite of his temporary humble position.

On the other hand Rufino acts out his picaresque role with great zest. I have already discussed him as a *gracioso* and there is a definite bridge between the functions of the two. As Montesinos points out: "Tiene [*el gracioso*] el buen humor del

pícaro, su alegría de la vida aunque está animado . . . de mejores
propósitos morales."[142] His constant hunger and sharp wit,
pointed out previously in the role of a *gracioso,* are typical picaresque elements. If only he would get the kind of food he likes,
and if only he would not have to scrape the dishes, the kitchen
would become his kingdom. As González-Lopez points out:
". . . la comida tiene el lugar que ocupaba el amor y el honor en
las de ficciones. La cocina llega a tener un lugar destacado."[143]

Unfortunately poor Rufino never really has a chance to satisfy his hunger. The monastery is poor, among the harvesters
Febo watches him with eagle eyes, and in the kitchen of the
Palatine he gets the wrong kind of food. In addition to this
misery, Rufino's free spirit suffers from claustrophobia because,
with the exception of the peasant episode, he is always closed
in among forbidding walls which bar his free movement. For
Rufino the life of a *pícaro* is the gayest, most amusing, and sweet-
est way of existence on earth. This is how Lope characterized
the picaresque life, and according to the article of Miguel Herrero, another Spanish scholar, *Nueva interpretación de la novela
picaresca,* Lope himself was eminently familiar with the picaresque literature of the time and, in some ways, he also was a
pícaro.[144] Thus presumably it is Lope himself who speaks through
Rufino and sings a veritable paean to the pleasures of the life of
the *pícaro,* who is as free as a sparrow to roam the countryside
at will, who can eat without any ceremony, never has a worry,
and would not change with a king:

> ¡Ay, dichoso picardia! / Comer provechoso en pié!
> ¿Cuándo un pícaro se ve / Que muera de perplejia?
> Ah dormir gustoso y llano / Sin cuidado y sin gobierno . . .
> Vida de rey fuera risa / Con esta vida ligera.[145]

Historical Reality or Poetic Illusion?

In the preceding chapter we saw that Lope has the spiritual
and social concept of Spain before his eyes when he speaks of
the Slavic world in the Demetrius drama.

Let me now ask the question: What Spain is it that Lope
sees? Is it the Spain of his own century? Does he depict a contemporary reality of his time? Do the Spanish elements of his
Demetrius drama superimposed on the Slavic world of the orig-

inal plot approximate life, customs, and mores of the Iberian peninsula of the late sixteenth and early seventeenth century?

To answer these questions the following points must first be raised: Did such a generous and noble king as Sigismundo exist in Lope's age? Could the prototype of Lamberto's sacrificing his own son for the higher idea of monarchy and glorifying himself in this unbelievable act live in the last decade of the sixteenth century? Can we visualize a Spanish prince of the period who just won an epic battle for an empire rushing to risk his life again and offering military assistance against a powerful foe out of sheer gratitude?

A careful consideration of these points would furnish the information that the Spanish prototypes of Sigismundo, Lamberto, or Demetrio did not exist in Lope's time, but belonged to a bygone period, one which Lope attempted to evoke. The extravagant sentiments of the heroes of Lope's Demetrius drama were not suggested by the age of the Spanish dramatist, but rather by an artificially recreated state of society and by certain ideas recalled from an earlier, more chivalrous and almost legendary time. As Vossler indicates:

Sollte man doch Komoedien, auch wenn Koenige und beruehmte Persoenlichkeiten darin vorkommen im allgemeinen nicht mit historischer Strenge auf ihre objektive Wahrheit pruefen, sondern nur etwa so wie unsere alten kastilischen Erzaehlungen hinnehmen, die anheben: Es war einmal ein Koenig und eine Koenigin.[146]

Thus, for Lope the Demetrius legend did not represent historical reality of the time of King Philip III of Spain, but rather a poetic transfiguration of life and ideas. In González-Lopez's analysis:

Toda su obra dramática está vestida con un bello ropaje poético; con una nota lírica de gran belleza, con un aliente poético que le da fuerza y grandeza y con un ambiente poético que se respira en toda su obra.[147]

Whence comes this "beautiful poetical garment" with which Lope's heroes are adorned? According to Fitzmaurice Kelly in *Lope de Vega and the Spanish Drama,* it comes from an epoch and community of the past:

He will see pass before him the entrancing pageant of a vanished age, a society vivid, picturesque, noble, blazoning its belief in God, the King, the Point of Honor, as empirious realities governing the conduct of an entire nation.[148]

To be more precise, it comes from the time and vigor of the Spanish Middle Age whose brilliance, grace, and charm continue to live in the literary recasting of the life and adventures of this Russian phoenix. It is essentially the reflection of the romantic spirit and the ideological current of the age of knights, the base and root of medieval society.

Lope created a synthesis of elements from the tradition of Spanish life of the Middle Age, and his most notable production is inspired by feudal Spain of the fourteenth and fifteenth centuries. The heroes of his Demetrius drama are presented to us as the incarnation of the chivalric spirit of this age and they stand before us as true contemporaries of the heroes of the Spanish legends of the period. Thus, Lope embellished the historical details of his sources with the flight of his fancy in the rich garden of the Spanish past, saw the events and the protagonists of the Russian Time of Troubles through the poetic mist of his fantasy, in which he recalled the spirit of the *romancero* and the heroic legends of the *El Cid* type. According to Vossler, in the dramas of Lope

die altspanische Heldenzeit mit besonderer Waerme und Farbenpracht zur Darstellung kommt. Mit der innigen Sehnsucht, die einen entschwundenen Zustand vergoldet, blickt Lope auf die Tage des Cid oder der *Reyes católicos* zurueck und lebt und webt in den Sagen, Legenden, Chroniken und Romancen seiner Vaeter. Er freut sich daran etwa so . . . als wie man nach Natur und Urspruenglichkeit, nach . . . arkadischen und paradiesischen Zeitalter sich sehnt.[149]

Lope goes even beyond the chronicles and *romanceros;* his poetical power invents incidents which these might not have contained, and thus he becomes an epic-popular poet of times gone by. Lope the dramatist proves himself to be a poet rather than a historian, and for him the essence of the Demetrius drama does not lie in the information conveyed by his sources, or in the contemporary reality of Spanish life, but rather in the gossamer web of his fertile poetic illusion. As A. A. Parker indicates, "an historical theme [for Lope] was . . . not [for] painting a historical picture . . . the fact that [the drama] portrays manners and customs of seventeenth-century Spain is . . . irrelevant to the theme."[150]

Lope and the Russian Time of Troubles

The title of the 1613 manuscript of Lope's Demetrius drama, *Los nuevos sucesos del Gran Duque de Moscovia,* implies that it was not his intention to write a historically accurate play, but rather to dramatize Demetrio's extraordinary adventures. The key to the manner in which Lope used the source material was invariably his artistic sense and the question he always asked himself was how to attain maximum dramatic intensity on the stage for the delight of the spectators. Therefore he omitted such descriptive and reflective passages of his sources as plans for the introduction of Catholicism in Russia—indeed, he treated Russia as if she were a Catholic country—and educational projects, as well as references to religious ceremonies and Demetrio's letter to Pope Clement VIII, all of which would unduly have burdened and retarded the fast development of the drama. Although he was not especially interested in the historical background of the period, he still retained his source material unless history clashed with his artistic preferences and conventions, in which case the source material had to yield. Considering the religious fanaticism with which his Jesuit informants conveyed the Demetrius legend and Lope's own geographical remoteness from the location of the actual events, the amount of authentic historical information contained in his drama is remarkable. Except for the idealized portrait of his Polish protagonists, his historical figures are shown with a measure of objectivity. It is interesting to note that it is exactly at the point when Lope injects a highly stylized internal Spanish motif of honor in the drama—the accidental murder of Tsarevich Juan—that historical truth attains its peak, and this fascinating scene, in the opinion of Fedorov, a Russian critic of Lope's Demetrius *comedia,* is "able to revive for the spectators the image of the historical Ivan the Terrible."[151]

REFLECTION OF THE HISTORICAL COMPLEXITY OF THE PERIOD

One of the most remarkable features of the drama is its constantly recurring uncertainty concerning some of the important historical events and a certain—perhaps even deliberate—vagueness in some of the statements made by the protagonists. It is possible that Lope wanted to alert the spectators by the deliberate use of an enigmatic manner of speech which was popular with the gallery of the Spanish stage of the period since it challenged the theatergoers to pit their cleverness against the hidden meaning of the play. It is also possible to believe, as Pring-Mill does, that the individual drama is linked outward to the structure of natural order "by subtle use of interlocking images which bring out analogical correspondences [between society and nature . . . individual human organism and body politic] . . . and constant use of generalized statements" and that these statements "should not be dismissed as platitudinous, but used as a key to the relationship between the general and the particular—between the abstract universal principle and the particular concrete situation facing the characters in the play."[152] Armed with this key the sensitive spectator would presumably seek the true meaning of the play in the universality of the theme illustrated by the action and its practical consequences rather than in the statements themselves.

The Time of Troubles is one of the most complex eras in Russian history and poses a great number of unsolved mysteries of identity and of riddles of psychology. One of such episodes concerns the actual or presumed death of Tsarevich Demetrius. The historical controversy regarding the mystery of the Uglič affair and its consequences find a fascinating reflection in the Demetrius *comedia* by a sense of constant vacillation and hesitation with which it is treated.

The spectator or reader of Lope's drama cannot tell who killed Demetrio's double, for the actions and statements of Rodulfo, whom Boris bribed to kill Demetrio, are contradictory. This murder and its sequences are dramatized in the following way:

1. Rodulfo orders the guards to kill the presumed Demetrio and one of the guards strangles him.[153]

2. In reply to Boris's question, Rodulfo later reports that he killed Demetrio by his own hands.[154]

3. In the monastery Rodulfo does not recognize Demetrio— at least it is not indicated in the scene that he does.[155]

4. Rodulfo falsely reports to Boris that the monk-Demetrio was killed. This event is not acted out in the scene, but logically follows from the plot.[156]

5. Rodulfo recognizes Demetrio in the camp of the latter. Amazed, he asks himself how it is possible that Demetrio is alive when he had killed him.[157]

This hesitation and uncertainty is very similar to the attitude of the historical Vasilij Šujskij, one of the prototypes of Rodulfo, who, on three different occasions, gave three different and contradictory versions of Demetrius's murder.

The greatest puzzle of the Time of Troubles—whether the man who appeared in Poland claiming to be the rightful heir to the throne of Muscovy was the real Tsarevich Demetrius, son of Ivan the Terrible—is reflected through the uncertainty and vagueness pervading the entire drama concerning the identity of the Pretender. The following episodes are worthy of mention:

1. On receiving the first news Boris refuses to believe that Demetrius is alive and assures Orofrisa, his wife, that Demetrio is dead.[158]

2. Doubts overcome Boris. He asks Rodulfo for assurance whether Demetrio is really dead. Although Rodulfo tries to reassure him, Boris is not convinced and decides to travel through Russia to investigate.[159]

3. In the monastery Boris is not sure whether the man who stands before him is a monk or Demetrio. But as his action indicates, he is inclined to believe that the man is Demetrio and orders Rodulfo to kill him.[160]

4. Boris now seems relieved and, in a conversation with Rodulfo, brands as false the news that Demetrio is alive.[161]

5. However, on receipt of a letter, Boris again changes his mind and now believes that Demetrio is alive. At this time, however, Rodulfo objects by saying that Demetrio may be an impostor, while Orofrisa cannot tell whether the man is Demetrio or not.[162]

6. Now Boris again shifts his position and calls Demetrio an impostor.[163]

7. Despite definite fresh news of Demetrio's military campaign against Boris, Orofrisa still insists that it is only a plot of the boyars, implying that Demetrio is an impostor.[164]

8. Rodulfo, Boris's ambassador to King Sigismundo, denounces Demetrio as an impostor.[165]

9. However, in the very next scene, Rodulfo is not so sure any longer and, in a conversation with the Duke of Arnies, an admirer of Marina, calls Demetrio "false or true."[166]

The historical vacillation should not create the impression that Lope was not firmly convinced of the authenticity of Demetrio's claim, for his overall sympathetic treatment of this Russian prince is an eloquent proof of his belief. It is rather due to the vagueness of his sources, to the influence of Demetrio's death as described and interpreted by Bavía, to his own objectivity, and mainly to his infallible dramatic sense in building up high tension and suspense by the introduction of the possibility of doubt. Thereby a certain element of mystery surrounds the hero, as Menéndez y Pelayo remarked: "El protagonista habla muchas veces como conviene a su misterioso carácter."[167]

The historical uncertainty continues with the events concerning the fate of Teodoro. We do not know exactly who poisoned him. According to Barezzi: "á cui da fanoiulla . . . fu fatto dare una beuenda . . ," to Mosquera: "al qual . . . le dierõ cierta comida," and to Bavía: "el padre le dio bebida . . . ," and Lope's drama reflects this imprecision when Cristina informs Demetrio that the poison was given to Teodoro by partisans of Juan. But in his talk with Sigismundo, Demetrio does not mention Juan's participation in connection with the plot and merely indicates that "envious knights" were the perpetrators of the crime.[168]

We do not know either whether the object of the poisoning was to kill Teodoro or to make him insane, since the information given by Cristina and Demetrio is contradictory. This may be due again to the vagueness with which the sources cautiously qualify their report ("segun se dixo," "como dizen.") It may also be the result of some subsequent rumor. Margeret, Demetrius's French bodyguard, mentions in his account that Tsar Feodor was killed by Boris.[169] The lack of precision concerning the poisoning is even reflected in the choice of the indefinite personal pronouns with which Lope describes the event. Cristina cryptically tells Demetrio "Que quite al hijo la vida / Quien quita al padre el imperio,"[170] in which statement the vague "quien" (who), together with the conditional-subjunctive clause beginning with "que", shows the ambiguity.

This hesitation over Teodoro's fate in the play is again quite similar to rumors circulating at the time according to historical literature. Boris refers to these rumors in Puškin's drama, *Boris Godunov.*

There is also contradictory information about the cause of the death of Juan, the historical Tsarevich Ivan. In a scene of the first act Lope indicates that the accidental murder of Juan was due to his disobedience, yet in the third act Demetrio reports to Sigismundo that the catastrophe was caused by the rivalry of father and son for the same woman.

LOPE'S POETIC INTUITION

The remarkable adherence to actual history which Lope shows in his drama denies the validity of Poehl's claim that all Lope had to do was to dramatize the material given to him by Barezzi and Mosquera, also the assertion of Morley and Bruerton that Lope could have derived everything but the astrologer episode from Mosquera or Bavía. These scholars obviously were not familiar with all the intricate details of this highly complex period of Russian history, otherwise they would not have made such sweeping generalizations.

Lope saw the events connected with the adventures of Demetrio at a triple remove. First it was Barezzi-Possevino who collected the material, partly from his own experience and partly from his correspondence with his Jesuit friends in Poland and Russia. Then came Mosquera and Bavía, who dressed up the information conveyed by Barezzi-Possevino with their typical Spanish pomp and baroque exaggeration. Finally Lope artistically recast and reinterpreted the information of his sources. It is worthy of note that there are a number of episodes and even historical facts in the play which may be attributed to Lope's highly developed poetic insight and almost uncanny sense of the *Zeitgeist* in approximation of contemporary reality, with little support from, and at times even in spite of, his sources. Some of these episodes are as follows:

1. Orofrisa refers to some boyar ("algun vassalo") who has nursed an impostor claiming to be Demetrio in order to dethrone Boris. This reference coincides with Boris's historical statements that setting up an alleged Demetrius was the job of the boyars.[171]

2. Basilio's description of Teodoro as half a woman ("medio mujer") reminds us of the almost feminine sensitivity of the historical counterpart of this Russian prince. Teodoro's desire to retire to a monastery agrees with Karamzin's evaluation of the historical Tsar Feodor whose rightful place was a cell or catacomb rather than a palace.[172]

3. In the monastery episode Mosquera and Bavía showed the abbot as a passive participant who meekly answers Boris's questions. However, in the play Lope changed him completely. The abbot not only refuses to kill the monk-Demetrio, but also utters such seditious sentiments as that Boris's law is unjust and wants to warn the monk-Demetrio of the danger. Solov'ev, the Russian

historian, mentions that when Boris ordered Smirno-Vasilev, a government official, to escort under strong guard Grigorij Otrep'ev, the alleged Demetrius, to the Kirill monastery for punishment, "powerful friends" alerted Otrep'ev and the latter managed to escape.[173]

4. In spite of his sources, which state that a Lithuanian nobleman dressed Demetrio according to his status, Lope makes him visit Sigismundo in rags. Historically, while Demetrius was in Poland, he participated in a Catholic religious ritual of collecting alms in rags.[174]

5. An interesting case of how a sensitive poet can discover historical truth in spite of his sources occurs in connection with Demetrio's lament over his lack of money and dwindling army when he is faced with the superior force and wealth of Boris in the play. ("Yo pobre, sin tesoro y sin ejercito / Pues que me falta gente cada dia.")[175] Since his sources thought very highly of the Polish king who supported Demetrio's campaign, an anti-Polish statement would have been inconceivable on their part, and therefore they carefully hid the fact that Demetrio's campaign was poorly organized and often he had no money to pay his soldiers. Yet the sources had to admit the well-known fact that many of Demetrio's Polish soldiers went home and, from this statement, Lope, the man of his time, perfectly understood the reason and indicated it in the play.

AN UNDISCOVERED SOURCE?

We also find a few historical references in Lope's drama for which there is no support from his known main sources and we simply cannot tell whether to credit his poetic insight or to search for another undiscovered source.

1. Rufino's constant hunger, as has been pointed out before, is a typical picaresque element. If this episode is entirely Lope's invention, it obviously needs no support from a source. Yet curious as it may seem, this hunger motif coincides with the great wave of hunger which swept over Russia in 1601-1603 just before the appearance of the historical alleged Demetrius in Poland. Could Lope have known about it or is it merely a coincidence?

2. In scene five of act three Boris is reading a letter about Demetrio's presence in Poland. It is historically attested that,

before beginning his campaign in Russia, Demetrius wrote to Boris offering him pardon if he repented and yielded the throne.[176] Another famous Demetrius play, by Friedrich Hebbel, opens with a scene in which Boris shows his friends a letter which he has just received from Demetrius.

We may presume that, in Lope's play, Boris is reading Demetrio's letter. Knowing human nature as well as Lope did, it is not unreasonable to assume that he thought that Demetrio, before entering on a risky military campaign, would write to his opponent in the same tenor as did his historical prototype.

3. In scene nineteen of act three a soldier reports to Demetrio that Orofrisa poisoned her two children, Juan and Isabela, "the beautiful."[177]

Isabela of Lope's play corresponds to the historical Ksenija Godunov who was famous for her beauty. Historical literature, *bylinys* (Russian historical songs), and even the Demetrius dramas of Aleksandr N. Ostrovskij, Aleksej K. Tolstoj, and Aleksej Suvorin mention this fact. How did this intimate detail reach Lope?

4. Isabela, Juan's wife, is shown by Lope as an ambitious and intriguing person. This characterization fits exactly Elena Šeremetova, her historical prototype who was one of the most notorious intriguers at the court of Ivan the Terrible.

STRUCTURAL PROBLEMS AND PUZZLING DETAILS

In addition to the above examples some structural oddities and a few puzzling details in the play should be pointed out:

1. In scene ten of act three Rodulfo assures the Duke of Arnies that Boris is marching with his army to the Boristhenes, the historical name of the river Dneper. How did Rodulfo know about this detail? Boris made this decision *after* he had sent Rodulfo away on his ambassadorial mission to Sigismundo. Perhaps something has been left out of the original manuscript of the *comedia,* or, what is more likely, Lope simply forgot about this confusing detail in the heat of bringing the play to an end.

2. In scene eighteen of act three we see Boris die in Demetrio's presence and, without any transition, in act nineteen a soldier appears reporting to Demetrio news of what has happened *after* Boris's death. Hartzenbusch, the Spanish editor of

this drama, remarked in a footnote: "Demasiado pronto lo ha sabido. Harto será que no falta algo en la escena anterior."[178] I agree with Hartzenbusch that something may have been left out in the preceding scene to create this structural ambiguity.

3. In the last scene of the third act Demetrio asks Rufino to marry Lisena, Margarita's confidante. Yet there is no previous indication that Lisena was on the battlefield. How did she manage to get there in time for the grand finale of the *comedia?* Lope does not give us any information about this detail and it is obviously a *deus ex machina* solution to reward the faithful Rufino. It is interesting to note that in his translation Rapp logically "improved" on Lope and, in this scene, replaced Lisena, who suddenly and miraculously materialized from thin air, by Finea, who has been with Demetrio's army for some time.

4. When Demetrio appears to be losing the battle against Boris, he exhorts his own men by saying "Demetrio soy, caballeros; / Que no soy encantador. . . ."[179] Since his army consisted mostly of Poles and Cossacks, his warmest supporters, fully convinced of his rightful claim to the Muscovite throne, it is difficult to understand why Demetrio had to tell them that he was not an impostor. Perhaps after reading the charges of the Muscovite mob against Demetrio in Bavía's account, Lope introduced the phrase "I am not an impostor" as a kind of preliminary defense of Demetrio's good name.

5. In scene seventeen of the third act we hear the Palatine praise the heroism of Demetrio who, by his courageous conduct, caused his fleeing army to return to battle and victory. But in the last scene of this act Rufino mentions that it was Rodulfo who, by his timely intervention, made Demetrio's soldiers return. Thereby we are left wondering whether it was Demetrio or Rodulfo who changed the tide of the battle.

Even more important is the question: What was Lope's reason for changing an important part of Mosquera's information which runs:

. . . vn valiente Moscouia llamado Basmanov . . . fué el primero q se le rindió. El qual con algunos militares de sus soldados se puso en medio de todo de exercito de Boris y a altas bozes dixo: Que el Principe Demetrio era su legitimo señor y heredero de Moscovia y . . . se puso en las manos de gēte de Demetrio.[180]

In accordance with history Mosquera clearly indicates that Basmanov brought Boris's army over to Demetrio's side, and yet

Lope, contradicting history, Mosquera, and even himself, makes Rodulfo-Basmanov bring back Demetrio's *own* army.

We cannot find a satisfactory explanation for this contradiction and must add it to the catalogue of several other puzzling structural problems, corruption of the original text, and even spelling errors.

6. In his ambassadorial message Rodulfo tells Sigismundo that his [Sigismundo's] support of Demetrio has caused worldwide indignation and even the Pope knows about this affair. ("Ya el Papa deste vil noticia tiene: / Descomulgarte en cónclave se trata.")[181] But who is to be excommunicated? King Sigismundo? The correct reading of the verb "descomulgar" together with the postpositive indirect personal pronoun of the second person singular *te* would indeed point to the Polish king. However, it is quite unconceivable that the Pope would have wished to excommunicate this pious and respected Polish king for his support of Demetrio. We must regard the indirect personal pronoun *te* as an error and replace it with *le* of the third person singular in order to change its meaning to read "to excommunicate the impostor." Although historically it still is not true, since the Pope had no intention of excommunicating the alleged Demetrius, who has just converted to Catholicism and from whom the Pope expected the extraordinary task of bringing the Orthodox Russians back to the Catholic faith, it sounded more logical for Rodulfo to imply that even the Pope did not believe in the claim of the alleged Demetrius and wanted to excommunicate him. By invoking the Pope's authority Rodulfo might have hoped to cause Sigismundo to abandon the alleged Demetrius.

There is no direct source material to support this curious quotation even in its corrected form, for the obvious reason that Mosquera and Bavía knew very well that Russia was an Orthodox country and therefore Boris could not have applied to the Pope to impose religious sanction against another person of the same Orthodox faith.

The origin of this puzzling statement may be found in chapter ninety-three of the fourth volume of Bavía's account, in which the Spanish historian reports the efforts of the Russian Patriarch (Job) who anathematized the alleged Demetrius and all those who supported him. Obviously Bavía had some difficulty to understand and translate into Spanish the essence of the Patriarch's message because his pertinent text runs as follows:

". . . descomulgar (digamoslo ansi) a todos los que no obedecen a Boris."[182]

Since Lope treated Russia as a Catholic country, he could not include in the play this reference to the Greek Orthodox rite because his religious Spanish audience would not have understood it, and therefore he simply changed it to conform to the spirit of the *comedia* and, instead of having the Orthodox Patriarch threaten to anathematize Demetrio and his supporters, he showed the Pope excommunicating the impostor for his evil deeds.

Some of these structural inconsistencies and puzzling details may perhaps be attributed to Lope's desire to rearrange the last act to accommodate the conflicting news he may have heard about the final events in Demetrio's adventures or even to a rearrangement already but not quite successfully accomplished. Rapp feels that these structural infelicities in the third act may be due to the physical exhaustion of the playwright:

Man glaubt ueber den unausgesetzten Arbeit des Meisters die physische Muedigkeit mit anzuschauen, die ihn gradweise unter dem fortschreitenden Werke mehr ergreift und das ist zuverlaessig eine dem Drama schaedliche Qualitaet.[183]

The True Demetrius and the False Sebastian

Lope wrote his Demetrius *comedia* for a Spanish audience which still remembered the events connected with the many pretenders to the crown of King Sebastian of Portugal (1557-1578), who presumably died in Africa while fighting a religious war against the Moors although his body has never been recovered. The circumstances of the death of this king were so mysterious that many patriotic Portuguese believed that Sebastian had escaped and, in a messianic fervor, they expected the return of their king. In the chaotic conditions created by the alleged death of Sebastian and the appearance of many pretenders, Philip II of Spain, nephew of John III, King of Portugal, made good his claim to the Portuguese crown by force of arms and punished the pretenders. The failure of these claimants to conquer the vacant Portuguese throne was regarded by the religious Spanish people as a divine judgment on their unjustified aspirations and in Spanish history they became known as the false kings.

Lope also considered these pretenders false, although in his play *La tragedia del Rey Don Sebastian y bautismo del principe de Marruecos* (written between 1593 and 1603) he did not actually treat the question of the false kings in much detail. However, it is interesting to note that in his Demetrius *comedia* there are various references to these pretenders. In addition to such general observations in the play that there have always been pretenders in the world, when the first news about Demetrio arrives, Boris compares him to the Portuguese pretenders who were punished by Philip. Later Rodulfo, Boris's ambassador, tells Sigismundo that because of his help to Demetrio, many new pretenders have already appeared. Lope might have had some information about other pretenders to the Russian throne and linked the events of the Russian Time of Troubles to the political confusion which reigned in Portugal after Sebastian's death and by this familiar reference he skillfully managed to bring this period of Muscovite history closer to his audience.

We should note that for Lope, the patriotic Spaniard, the reigning king of Spain, Philip II, became the legitimate ruler of Portugal after Sebastian's death. The various pretenders were impostors. In his Demetrius *comedia,* on the other hand, the reigning king, Boris, is false, and Demetrius is the authentic emperor of Muscovy. In this respect Lope's *comedia* is in complete contrast to the contemporary Russian chronicles and to the several Russian Demetrius dramas in which Demetrius is regarded as the false king.

In Lope's *comedia* Demetrius's royal origin is fully certified by Rufino, his private notary public, who has been his loyal companion and guardian ever since Cristina entrusted Demetrio to Lamberto's care. Rufino's statement is accepted unquestioningly not only because he is a heroic and faithful figure, but mainly because he is a Spaniard.

The Success and Influence of *El Gran Duque*

Lope's drama must have been popular. An indirect evidence of its success may be seen in another Demetrius play, *El principe perseguido. Infeliz Juan Basilio,* written by Luis de Belmonte, Augustin Moreto, and Antonio Martines in 1650.[184] Menéndez y Pelayo thinks that this play is a mere recasting of Lope's Demetrius drama and Ruth L. Kennedy, an American scholar, in *The Dramatic Art of Moreto,* mentions that *El principe per-*

seguido. Infeliz Juan Basilio is indebted to Lope for the plot, some of the characters, and a few fragments of dialogue.[185] I am in agreement with these scholars that this play is completely Lopean in spirit, although greatly inferior to *El Gran Duque.*

There was also a third Spanish play, *Hados y Lados hacen dichosos y desdichosos, Parecido de Rusia,* published anonymously in the seventeenth century, which may have been devoted to the Demetrius theme.[186] It is unavailable for comment, and therefore I do not know whether it was another reworking of Lope's play, perhaps drawing as well on *El principe perseguido. Infeliz Juan Basilio* by the above-named three authors, or an original *comedia* dealing perhaps with another aspect of Russian history.

A further evidence of the success of Lope's Demetrius drama is revealed by its adaptation for the Dutch stage. One adaptation, *Den groten gerthoge van Moskovien oft gheweldighe heerschaappije,* was made by Cornelis de Bie and performed in Lierre in 1672, while another, by Antonio Francisco Wouthers, was published in Bruxelles without date.[187]

I feel that the device for saving the boy Demetrio in Lope's drama is reflected in Rochelle's popular historical novel *Le Czar Demetrius* (1716). Richard H. Lawson argues that Gotthold E. Lessing's drama fragment *Das Horoskop* (1758) is indebted to Lope's play. Franz Grillparzer's drama *Ein treuer Diener seines Herrn* (1826) was also influenced by Lope's Demetrius *comedia.* Certain elements of this Spanish drama can also be observed in Aleksej S. Suvorin's *Tsar Dmitry the Impostor and Princess Ksenija* (1905). It is very likely that Calderón de la Barca used several motifs of Lope's drama in his famous baroque play *La vida es sueño.* I am also convinced that, in his *The Loyal Subject,* John Fletcher, the Jacobean playwright, utilized a great number of dramatic elements from Lope's Demetrius play.

NOTES

1. The edition used for this study is "El Gran Duque de Moscovia y emperador perseguido," Tomo Cuarto de las Comedias Escogidas de Frey Lope Felix de Vega Carpio, *Biblioteca de Autores Españoles,* 52 (Madrid, Edición Atlas 1952). It will be referred to as *El Gran Duque.*

2. Moritz Rapp, "Einleitung zu Lope de Vega," *Spanisches Theater,* 4 vols. (Leipzig, 1868), 3:10.

3. Karl Vossler, *Lope de Vega und sein Zeitalter* (Muenchen: Beck Verlag, 1932), p. 285.

4. Franz Grillparzer, "Studien zum Spanischen Theater," *Saemtliche Werke,* 20 vols. (Stuttgart: Cotta, 1893), 16:339.

5. Lope, III. 1.

6. Vossler, p. 287.

7. Hugo A. Rennert, *The Life of Lope de Vega* (New York: G. E. Stechart & Co., 1937), p. 428.

8. Américo Castro, "Aluciones a Micaela Lucan. . ." *Revista de Filológia Española,* 5 (1918): 278.

9. Rapp, p. 303. The year 1605 is incorrect.

10. Menéndez y Pelayo, "Observaciones Preliminares," *Obras de Lope de Vega,* 7 vols. (Madrid, 1896), 7:133.

11. *Ibid.,* p. 134.

12. S. Ciampi, *Esame critico con documenti inediti della storia di Demetrio di Iwan Wassiliewitsch* (Florence, 1827), pp. 4–5.

13. Antonio Possevino, *La Moscovia* (Ferrarra, 1592).

14. Mentioned by K. M. Obolenskij, Preface to the translation of Barezzi's "Relazione," *Čtenija v imper. obščestve istorii i drevnostej* 5 (Moscow, 1845): iv.

15. Emile Gigas, "Etudes sur quelques comédias de Lope . . ." *Revue Hispanique* 81 (1933): 177–89.

16. Gertrude von Poehl, "La fuente de El Gran Duque . . ." *Revista de Filología Española* 19 (1932): 47–63.

17. *Relacion de la señalada y como milagrosa conquista del paterno imperio consequida del serenissimo principe Ivan Demetrio, Gran Duque de Moscovia, en el año de 1605. Juntamente con su coronacion, y con lo que a hecho despues que fué coronado, desde el ultimo del Mes de Julio, hasta agora, recogido todo de varios y verdaderos avisos, venidos de aquellas partes en diversas vezes:* traducido de lengua italiana en nuestro vulgar Castellano. Por Juan Mosquera, religioso de la compañia de Jesus. En Valladolid en casa de Andres de Merchan, año de 1606.

18. Gertrude von Poehl, "Quellenkundliches zur Geschichte des Ersten Falschen Demetrius, Mosquera-Barezzo Barezzi," *Zeitschrift fuer Osteuropaeische Geschichte* 7 (1933): 73–85.

19. Barezzo Barezzi, *Relazione della segnalata e come miracolosa conquista del paterno-Imperio, consequita dal serenissimo giovine Demetrio, Gran Duca di Muscovia, L'anno 1605* (Venice, 1605), chap. 3, pp. 4–5.

20. Mosquera, chap. 3, folio (henceforth referred to as "f") 5a.

21. J. A. van Praag, "Más noticias sobre la fuente de El Gran Duque . . ." *Bulletine Hispanique* 39 (1937): 356–66.

22. *Histórica Pontifical y Católica,* compuesta y ordenada por el doctor Luis de Bavía. Capellan del Rey, nuestro Señor, en su Real Capilla de Granada. I have used the edition of 1652 (Madrid).

23. *Ibid.,* Pt. 4, p. 318.

24. *Ibid.,* p. 378.

25. S. Griswold Morley and Courtney Bruerton, *The Chronology of Lope de Vega's Comedias* (New York: The Modern Language Association of America, 1940), p. 39. The reference to part third is an obvious error, since it does not contain anything about Demetrius's escape and subsequent adventure.

26. Mosquera, chap. 3, f 6a; Bavía, Pt. 4, chap. 86, p. 319; Lope, II.

27. *Ibid.*, Lope, II.

28. *Ibid.*, f 6b; p. 320; Lope, II. 9.

29. *Ibid.*, f 7a; p. 321; Lope, III. 1.

30. *Ibid.*, f 7b; p. 321; Lope, III. 1.

31. Mosquera, chap. 3, f 6a; Lope, I. 6.

32. *Ibid.*, Lope, II. 6.

33. *Ibid.*

34. *Ibid.*, Lope, II. 3, II. 2.

35. *Ibid.*, f 7a; Lope, II. 9.

36. *Ibid.*, chap. 6, f 9a; Lope, III. 11.

37. Bavía, Pt. 4, chap. 86, p. 317; Lope, II. 19.

38. *Ibid.*, p. 319; Lope, II. 18.

39. *Ibid.*, Lope, I. 1.

40. *Ibid.*, Lope, I. 23.

41. *Ibid.*, p. 320; Lope, II. 3.

42. *Ibid.*, Lope, II. 20.

43. *Ibid.*, p. 321; Lope, III. 2.

44. *Ibid.*, p. 322; Lope, III. 16.

45. *Ibid.*, Lope, III. 15.

46. *Ibid.*, Lope, III. 16.

47. *Ibid.*, Pt. 4, chap. 86, p. 318; Lope, II. 4, III. 5.

48. *Ibid.*, Lope, II. 18, 19.

49. J. Vernet, "Las fuentes de El Gran Duque," *Cuadernos de Literatura* 5–6 (1949): p. 17–36. The date is a mistake, since Demetrius was killed on May 17, 1606.

50. Quoted by Nikolai Ustrjalov, *Skazanija sovremennikov o Dimitrii Samo- svance,* 5 vols. (St. Petersburg, 1834–1837), 3:97–98; Sonia E. Howe, *The False Dmitri* (London: Williams and Norgate, 1916), p. 63.

51. The correspondence between Cardinal Borghese in Rome and Paul Rangoni, the Papal Legate as well as Mgr. Simonetta in Poland, reflects the hopes and frustrations of the Catholic Church concerning Demetrius's fate. It is of special interest to note the dates of the official dispatches, since they refer to the second Demetrius as if he were the first.
From Cardinal Borghese to Rangoni:
Rome, September 30, 1606: ". . . V.S. apporta gran congettura della vita di Demetrio, ma pare poco verisimile ch'essendo egli fuggito da suoi stati."
October 7, 1606: ". . . abbiamo molti contrasegni della vita di Demetrio."
October 21, 1606 ". . . . se vive Demetrio, dovra conoscere il beneficio singolare assolutamente dalla mano di Dio."
December 9, 1606: ". . cominciamo a credere che Demetrio viva . . . porche vien scritto affermativamente da piu bande."
From Cardinal Borghese to Mgr. Simonetta:
December 30, 1606: ". . . delle cose di Moscovia ho poco che dirlo, poiche la speranza che si avea di ridurre quel Gran Ducato alla devotione della Sede Apostolica e svanita per morte de Demetrio, sebbene se dice ora che vive."
November 17, 1607: ". . . Li figlioli del Palatino di Sandomiria che sono qui hanno data per certa a N. S. la nuova della vita de Demetrio, e dicono di averla per lettere della Palatina lor madre. Stiamo in grandissa espettazione d'intendere la cetezza."

April 26, 1608: ". . . viviamo qui quasi sicuri della vita di Demetrio."

August 9, 1608: ". . . Demetrio vive anco qui in opinione di molti, e li piu increduli non contradicono ora, come facevano gia, assolutamente. La certezza della vita sua, e delle sue vittorie si aspetta con gran desiderio."

It was only after this date—two years after the murder of the alleged Demetrius—that suspicions begin to arise whether the Demetrius they are writing about is the same one who was crowned as Tsar in 1605 in Moscow.

From Cardinal Borghese to Mgr. Simonetta:

August 30, 1608: ". . . si è vero l'avviso della vittoria di Demetrio, si verifica necessariamente ch'egli sia Demetrio stesso e non altri."

An undated and unsigned communication to Nikolai Wolski, a Polish marshal: ". . . imposterum Demetrius ad Calugam collegit exercitus."

There is a message from Mgr. Simonetta to Cardinal Borghese, dated April 4, 1609, concerning the activities of Marina Mniszek who went "a Kaluga al suo Demetrio." It is well documented in historical literature that, after the murder of the first Demetrius, her husband, Marina Mniszek tricked Tsar Vasilij Šujskij and went over to the second Demetrius to maintain her claim to the throne of Moscow although she knew well that her husband had been murdered and the second Demetrius was a complete stranger to her.

Finally, according to the message which Cardinal Borghese sent to Mgr. Simonetta, dated June 13, 1609, the Roman Curia finally accepted the fact of the murder of the first Demetrius and is aware of the spurious origin of the second Demetrius. ". . . se il finto Demetrio è gli già entrato nella citta de Mosca," although it is not at all unconceivable that if the second Demetrius had been victorious, Rome would still have supported him in spite of his unquestionably false origin. Yet the second Demetrius, called the Brigand of Tušino in history, was murdered on December 12, 1610 by a converted Tatar prince. See A. I. Turgenev, *Historica Russiae Monumenta ex antiquis exterarum gentium archivis et bibliotecis deprompta* 2 vols. (St. Petersburg: v tip. Eduarda Pratsa, 1842-1848), 2:136, for the above exchange of messages. See Aleksander Hirschberg, *Maryna Mniszchówna,* (Lvov, 1927,) concerning the activities of the second Demetrius and Marina Mniszek after the murder of the first Demetrius. See also E. Šmurlo, "Le Saint Siège et l'Orient Orthodox Russe 1609-1654," *Publications des Archives du Ministère des Affaires Etrangères,* Premiere Série, 4 (Prague, 1928): 283.

52. Lope, III. 9.

53. "The Reporte of a Bloudie and terrible Massacre in the Citty of Mosco, with the fearfull and tragicall end of Demetrius the last Duke, before him raigning at this present," Howe, *The False,* trans. William Russel, pp. 27–68.

54. Castro, p. 279.

55. Milton A. Buchanan, "The Chronology of Lope de Vega's plays," *University of Toronto Studies* Philological Series 6 (Toronto: The University Library, 1922): 19; José F. Montesinos, "The Chronology of Lope De Vega's Plays," *Revista de Filologia Española* 10 (1923): 192; W. L. Fichter, "Notes on the Chronology of Lope de Vega's *Comedias,*" *Modern Language Notes* 39 (1924): 273.

56. Courtney Bruerton, "Lope's Belardo-Lucinda Plays," *Hispanic Review* 5 (1937): 310.

57. Morley and Bruerton, p. 39.

58. Bavía, Pt. 4, chap. 87, p. 329.

59. A. A. Parker, "The Approach to the Spanish Drama of the Golden Age," *Tulane Drama Review* 4, No. 1. (September, 1959) : 45.

60. Vossler, p. 282.

61. E. Plavskin, *Lope de Vega* (Moscow: Izd. Vses. knižnoj palaty, 1962), p. 5.

62. Mentioned by M. P. Alekseev, *Očerki istorii ispano-russkix literaturnyx otnošenij 16–19.* (Leningrad: Izd. Leningradskogo universiteta, 1964), p. 13. Yet Suvorin indicates that Lope's play was already staged in Russia in 1905. (*Tsar Dimitrij Samozvanec i Tsarevna Ksenija* [St. Petersburg, 1905], p. iii.) This survey is handicapped by the unavailability of much of the material and I am obliged to quote critical opinions from secondary sources. According to A. A. Čebyšev, "Tragedija Šillera iz russkoj istorii," *Žurn. Min. Nar. Prosv.*, No. 7 (1898), pp. 49–95, Lope did not know about Demetrius's death when he wrote his play. Had the Spanish playwright known about the bloody justice meted out to Demetrius, Lope would have included it for the sake of dramatic effects. Balašov mentions another article in the same year by A. N. Fedorov, *Lžedimitrij v ispanskoj drame XVII veka*. The next criticism of Lope's play was written by B. Varneke, *Lope de Vega "Dimitrij Samozvanec"* in 1903, followed by N. I. Nikolaev, "O tak nazyvaemom pervom Lžedimitrii v istorii i drame," *Efemeridy* (Kiev, 1912), pp. 467–69. Nikolaev erroneously indicates that Lope's source was Alexander Cilli's *Istoria di Moscovia*, written in 1627. In 1913 appeared S. G. Kovalevskaja's "Drama Lope de Vega 'Velikij Knjaz' Moskovskij'," *Minerva* (Kiev), pp. 87–138. In 1940 a short article by B. Rostockij and N. Čuškin in *Tsar Feodor Ivannovič na scene MXAT* discusses Teodoro's figure in Lope's play. A comment on Lope's drama was made by A. A. Smirnov in *Istorija zapadnoevropejskoj literatury* in 1947. In 1960 A. Pušnov wrote a brief study, "Lope de Vega o Rossii," *Teatral'naja Žizn'* (No. 15, August), p. 27. According to him Lope saw the events of the Time of Troubles through the crooked mirror of the Catholic chronicles. In the same year E. Plavskin compiled a useful bibliography, *Lope de Vega*.

63. M. P. Alekseev, "Boris Godunov i Dimitrij Samozvanec v zapadnoevropejskoj drame," *'Boris Godunov' A. S. Puškina*, ed. K. N. Deržavin (Leningrad, 1936), pp. 79–125.

64. N. I. Balašov, "Lope de Vega i problematika ispanskoj dramy XVII. veka na vostočnoslavjanskie temy," Izvestija, Ak. Nauk Otdel. Lit. i Jaz. 22 (Moscow, 1963) and "Renessansnaja problematika ispanskoj dramy 17. veka na vostočnoslavjanskie temy," *Slavjanskie Literatury, Doklady sovetskoj delegacii, V. Mežnarod. s"ezd slavistov* (Moscow, 1963), pp. 89–124.

65. Lope may have obtained some information from the two sons of Mniszek, who were in Spain at the time. Balašov also thinks that Lope's use of Cacuriso for the toponymic Zaporože reflects the Ukrainian dialect (i.e., the retention of the long vowel "ï" under stress) and may show Lope's familiarity with the Ukrainian language.

66. Lope, III. 18.

67. Rennert, p. 244.

68. Vossler, p. 233.

69. Amado Alonso, a Spanish literary historian, called Lope "el más grande poeta de la conformidad" in his "Lope de Vega y sus fuentes," *Thesaurus* 8 (Bogota: 1952) : 3. On Lope as a priest see Maximo Yurramendi, *Lope de Vega y la Teologia* (Madrid, 1935) ; Pedro M. G. Quijano, "Una vez más Lope y

Calderon," *Fénix* 5 (Madrid, October 27): 622, describes Lope's *auto La Santa Inquisición* and speaks of the "fervor mariano" and "el espiritu combativo" of Lope in his religion. Lope's lack of doubt and distrust, and his accord with the collective mentality of his people causes Vossler to find the reason for this "Entfernheit von revolutionaeren Gedanken," and Lope's conservatism in the spirit of the age. "Nicht nur bei ihm, im ganzen spanischen Schauspiel jener Zeit wird die menschliche Selbstbestimmung gelegentlich beschattet und verkuemmert durch eine religioes geheiligte Staatsraison." (Vossler, p. 236.) "Nichts liegt ihm ferner als die Auflehnung gegen Ordnung, Gesetz, Sitte und Glauben." (*Ibid.*, p. 73.)

70. Alekseev, *Ôcerki,* pp. 5–10.

71. Gerald Brenan, *Literature of the Spanish People* (New York: Meridian Books, 1957), p. 207.

72. Vossler, p. 332.

73. Lope, I. 6, 11; II. 16.

74. *Ibid.,* I. 8, 20.

75. Vossler, p. 236.

76. Possevino, f 4b.

77. Lope, I. 13, 14.

78. *Ibid.,* I. 13.

79. S. Griswald Morley and Tyler, *Los nombres de personajes en las comedias de Lope de Vega. Estudio de onomatologia* (Berkeley-Valencia: University of California Publications in Modern Philology, 1961), p. 390.

80. A. S. Suvorin, *O Dimitrii Samozvance* (St. Petersburg, 1905). pp. 73–90; Henry Richard Lord Holland, *Some Accounts of the Lives and Writings of Lope Felix de Vega Carpio and Guillén de Castro* (London, 1817), 1:153; Bavía, Pt. 4, chap. 86, p. 317.

81. Morley and Tyler, p. 390.

82. Grillparzer, p. 340.

83. Rennert, p. 382.

84. Mosquera, chap. 2, f 5a.

85. Barezzi, chap. 2, 3–4; Mosquera, chap. 2, f 4b; Possevino, f 36a.

86. R. D. Pring-Mill, ed., *Lope de Vega 5 Plays,* trans. Jill Booty (New York: Hill and Wang, 1961), p. xv.

87. Lope, II. 1.

88. *Ibid.,* II. 17.

89–93. *Ibid.,* II. 8.

94. Vossler, p. 288.

95. Quoted by Vossler, p. 321.

96. Emilio González-Lopez, *Historia de la literatura española, Edad media y Siglo de Oro* (New York: Las Americas Publishing Co., 1962), p. 395.

97. Vossler, p. 231.

98. H. Butler Clarke, *Spanish Literature* (London: Swan Sonnenschein & Co. Ltd., 1909), p. 96.

99–107. Lope, I. 12.

108. This is in accordance with Balašov's view that Lope, afraid to criticize Philip II directly, portrayed him as Basilio. The Soviet critic speaks of a "secret settling of accounts" between Philip II and Don Carlos in 1598. (Balašov, *Lope,* p. 9.) Yet modern historical evaluation of Philip II's character does not support

his view. See *The Character of Philip II. The Problem of Moral Judgments in History*. Ed. John C. Rule and John J. Te Paske (Boston: The Ohio State University, 1963). Concerning the development of the legend of the rivalry between Philip II and Don Carlos in history and literature see F. W. C. Lieder, "The Don Carlos Theme," *Harvard Studies and Notes in Philology and Literature* 12 (1930). Lessing's drama fragment *Das Horoskop* also treats a Slavic theme of father and son as rivals in love.

109. Rapp, p. 317.

Balašov refers to an edition of 1951 in Madrid of Altamira y Crevea's *Historia de España* 2: 89. Unfortunately this particular edition was not available for reference. However, in another edition the Spanish historian mentions that "No tiene valor ninguno al motivo alegado por algunos . . . de haber mantenido Carlos relaciones ilícitas con su madraste Isabel de Valois. La pasión política de los enemigos de Felipe II dió aire a estas y otras fantasías . . ." See Rafael Altamira y Crevea, *História de España y de la civilización española, Edad Moderna,* Tomo 3 (Barcelona: 1928): 114. For Lope's view of Philip II see also his play *Los españoles en Flandes* and *La tragedia del Rey Don Sebastian y bautismo del principe de Marruecos.*

110. Vossler, p. 243.

111. Lope, I. 1.

112. *Ibid.,* I. 12.

113. *Ibid.,* I. 13.

114. Frank G. Halstead, "The Attitude of Lope de Vega Toward Astrology," *Hispanic Review* 7 (1939): 205–20.

115. Quoted by Halstead, p. 205.

116. Richard H. Lawson, 'El Gran Duque de Moscovia . . . A Likely Source for Lessing," *Romance Notes* 4 (1952): 58–62.

117. Quoted by Lawson, p. 60.

118. Lope, I. 20.

119. *Ibid.,* II. 1.

120. *Ibid.,* II. 9.

121. *Ibid.,* III. 17.

122. Quoted by Halstead, p. 208. The quotation is taken from Lope's drama *El Duque de Viseo.*

123. Brenan, p. 203.

124. Vossler, p. 241.

125. *Ibid.,* p. 242.

126. Ricardo del Arco y Garai, "Lope de Vega", *Historia General de las Literaturas Hispánicas,* ed. G. Guillermo Diaz-Plaja (Barcelona: Editorial Barna; 1953), p. 222.

127. The recurring reference to the sun in the harvester's song of Lope's Demetrius drama and Pietrucha's plea to the sun in Szymon Szymonowicz's *Żeńcy* is of special interest. Lope (2:xvi): Blanca me era yo / Cuando entré en la siega; / Dióme el sol / Y ya soy morena. / Blanca solia yo ser / Antes que a segar viniese; / Mas no quiso el son que fuese / Blanca. . . ." II. 16. Szymonowicz: "Słoneczko, sliczne oko, dnia oko pieknego! Nie jesteś ty zwyczajów starosty naszego!" Lope's harvester regards the sun as an enemy, Szymonowicz's as a friend. See Mañfred Kridl, ed., *An Anthology of Polish Literature* (New York, 1957), p. 69.

128. J. H. Arsona, "La introducción del gracioso en el teatro de Lope de Vega," *Hispanic Review* 7 (January 1939) : 1.

129. Lope, I. 23.

130. *Ibid.*, II. 6.

131. *Ibid.*, II. 12.

132. *Ibid.*, II. 21.

133. *Ibid.*, II. 12.

134. Quoted by José F. Montesinos, *Estudios sobre Lope,* (El Colegio de México, n.d.), p. 16.

135. Ludwig Pfandl, *Geschichte der spanischen Nationalliteratur, in ihrer Bluetezeit* (Freiburg im Bresgau, 1929), p. 377.

136. Lope, II. 6.

137. *Ibid.*, II. 20.

138. Dr. Maria Heseler, *Studien zur Figur des gracioso bei Lope de Vega und Vorgaengers,* (Hildesheim, 1933), p. 78.

139. Rudolf Schewill, "The Dramatic Art of Lope de Vega," *Modern Philology* (Berkeley, University of California, 1918), p. 23.

140. Lope, II. 9.

141. Heseler, p. 75.

142. Montesinos, p. 19.

143. González-Lopez, p. 336.

144. Miguel Herrero, "Nueva interpretación de la novela picaresca," *Revista Filológía Española* 24 (1937) : 345.

145. Lope, II. 23.

146. Vossler, p. 233.

147. González-Lopez, p. 403.

148. James Fitzmaurice Kelly, *Lope de Vega and the Spanish Drama* (London, 1902), pp. 62–63.

149. Vossler, p. 231.

150. A. A. Parker, p. 55.

151. Quoted by Balašov, *Renessansnaja,* p. 104.

152. R. D. Pring-Mill, p. viii.

153. Lope, I. 25.

154. *Ibid.*, II. 4.

155. *Ibid.*, II. 8.

156. *Ibid.*, II. 10; III. 5.

157. *Ibid.*, III. 13.

158. *Ibid.*, II. 4.

159. *Ibid.*

160. *Ibid.*, II. 8.

161. *Ibid.*, II. 18.

162. *Ibid.*, III. 5.

163. *Ibid.*, III. 6, "fingido villano."

164. *Ibid.*, III. 6.

165. *Ibid.*, III. 9.

166. *Ibid.*, III. 10, "fingido o cierto." As an interesting historical co-incidence it may be mentioned that the historical Semon Godunov, Boris's chief of police, whose role is assigned to Rodulfo in the play, also became confused whether the Pretender was or was not the true son of Ivan the Terrible and told Basmanov

that he had dreamt that the Pretender was really Tsarevich Demetrius.

167. Marcelino Menéndez y Pelayo, *Estudios sobre el teatro de Lope de Vega,* Tomo 2 (Madrid, 1921) : 314.

168. Lope, I. 6; III. 2.

169. Margeret, p. 21.

170. Lope, I. 6. There is no historical proof of any attempt to poison Feodor. The legend of poisoning and its subsequent effect must be due to a hypothesis of some contemporaries in trying to find a satisfactory explanation for Feodor's feeble physical state in the robust and healthy family of Ivan the Terrible and in accusing with this imaginary deed someone who would have benefited from its consequences. The notorious activities of the *opričnina* may have given rise to such speculations. There is no mention of any poisoning attempt in Aleksej Konstantin Tolstoj's *Tsar Feodor,* the second of a dramatic trilogy, in which the characterization of the Russian Tsar shows certain distinct artistic affinities with Lope's Teodoro.

171. *Ibid.,* III. 6: "algun infame vasallo / Autor deste enredo fué."

172. *Ibid.,* I. 1. Karamzin's opinion is quoted by Ključevskij, 3 :10.

173. S. M. Solov'ev, *Istorija Rossii s drevnejšix vremen.* 11 bks. (Moscow: Izd. social'no-ekonom. lit., 1960). Bk. IV, p. 406.

174. Herman Skribanowitz, *Pseudo-Demetrius I.* Inaugural Dissertation, Fredrich Wilhelm Universitat (Berlin, 1913). p. 42.

175. Lope, III. 11.

176. From a letter of Paul Rangoni to the Vatican, dated March 20, 1604: ". . . Che in camera propia di quel gran Duca [Boris] fossessi trovata una lettera scritta da Demetrio." Quoted by Pierling, *Rome,* p. 181.

177. Lope, III. 19.

178. *Ibid.,* p. 276 n.

179. *Ibid.,* III. 16.

180. Mosquera, chap. 11, f 14a.

181. Lope, III. 9.

182. Bavía, Pt. 4, chap. 93, p. 325.

183. Rapp, p. 306.

184. Luis de Belmonte, Augustin Moreto, Antonio Martines, "El principe perseguido. Infeliz Juan Basilio," *El mejor de los mejores libros que han salido de comedias nuevas.* (Madrid, 1650).

185. Menéndez y Pelayo, "Observaciones . . ." 7 : 133 ; Ruth L. Kennedy, "The Dramatic Art of Moreto," *Smith College Studies in Modern Languages* 13 (Philadelphia, 1932).

186. This hitherto unknown Spanish drama is Balašov's discovery. "Hados y lados hacen dichosos y desdichosos. Parecido de Rusia," *Dramáticos posteriores a Lope de Vega,* por Ramón de Mesonero Romanos, Part 1, *Biblioteca de Autores Españoles,* vol. 47 (Madrid, 1858) : 49 and Part 2, *Biblioteca de Autores Españoles,* Vol. 49, p. xxxv. Also mentioned by H. C. Heaton, "Twelve 'Títulos de Comedias,'" *Revue Hispanique,* No. 7 (1933), pp. 81, 315. Also mentioned in La Barrera's catalogue under the title *El aparecido en Rusia* which, according to Balašov, is very likely the same as the subtitle of *Hados y lados* . . . (Catálogo de La Barrera, 3, No. 5: p. 305). See Balašov, *Renessansnaja,* p. 5.

187. Mentioned by Dr. Max Victor Depta, *Lope de Vega* (Breslau: Ostdeutsche Verlagsanstalt, 1927), p. 115.

3

John Fletcher's *The Loyal Subject*

Introduction

John Fletcher's play, *The Loyal Subject,*[1] was written in 1618. In this play, an unnamed Muscovite Duke dismisses Archas, the loyal general, because the latter has once corrected his mistakes in a military exercise. Yet at the time of a Tartar invasion the Duke must recall Archas because the army refuses to fight without its general. Boroskie, a wicked counsellor, reveals to the Duke that Archas holds a treasure, given to him by the Duke's father, to keep for the young Duke in case an emergency requires it. The Duke takes the treasure from Archas and orders him to send his two daughters to the Court. On Boroskie's false accusation that Archas aims at the throne, the latter is arrested and tortured. Theodore, Archas's son, storms the royal palace to free Archas and the repentant Duke apologizes to Archas and punishes Boroskie. The indignant soldiers revolt, and decide to join the Tartars to overthrow the Duke. However, the loyal Archas stops them and is ready even to punish by death Theodore, their leader and his own son, and spares him only on the Duke's plea. In the meantime Alinda, servant to Olympia, the Duke's sister, is revealed as Archas's younger son, disguised to save him from the Duke's wrath.

Unlike Lope and later dramatists, Fletcher used the Demetrius legend in an entirely unorthodox way. Demetrius himself is never mentioned by name in the play and his person is hidden behind a double mask. This disguised Demetrius hardly partipates in the main events, is relegated to the relative obscurity of a subplot and yet, from a historical point of view, represents one of the keys to a full understanding of the play. Only a few' fragments of the life of the historical Demetrius are developed in the play and these are so successfully concealed that, until now, commentators on Fletcher's plays—scholars and literary critics as well as historians, Westerners and Russians alike—have never noticed the presence of this baffling personality in *The Loyal Subject* and thus the hidden message and the real center of the play remained unsuspected. John Fletcher's Demetrius, alias Alinda, alias young Archas, has eluded not only the amorous advances of the Great Duke of Moscovia in the play, but also the interpreters of the adventures of this young Russian prince.

Traditionally accepted is the view that a tale by Matteo Bandello, the Italian Renaissance novelist is the source of the play; that the main idea is absolute loyalty to the monarch and an apology for his divine rights; and that the dramatic conflict is between a wicked king and a loyal subject. Yet, as this chapter will attempt to show, other interpretations are also possible. Finally, the presence of a hidden Demetrius theme and the composite portrait of the Great Duke of Moscovia will serve to prove that *The Loyal Subject* is not a tragicomedy set in an exotic and nebulous land, as it has been uncritically accepted up to this time, but a historical drama in that it incorporates many actual characters and elements of contemporary events drawn from the Russian Time of Troubles.

The Main Idea of the Play

After an initial controversy over whether Thomas Heywood's *The Royal King and the Loyal Subject*[2] influenced Fletcher's play or whether both plays were based on a common source, scholars came to regard Bandello's tale *Ariobarzane seniscalco del Re di Persia quello vuol vincer di cortesia ove vari accidenti intervengono* (1554)[3] as the source of *The Loyal Subject,* since it was asserted that Heywood's drama had been based on Bandello's tale and therefore this must also have served as the source for *The Loyal Subject.*

Bandello's is a story of the jealousy of Antaxerxes, king of Persia against his seneschal Ariobarzanes on the ground that the latter has tried to exceed him in acts of liberality and courtesy. The tale is introduced by the rhetorical question whether an "opera lodevole, o atto cortese e gentile" which the courtier accomplishes for his ruler should be called "liberalita e cortesia" or rather regarded as "obbligazione e debito."[4]

Antaxerxes accuses Ariobarzanes of three specific instances of utmost ambition, although veiled in the courtly sophistication of courtesy and generosity: 1) A chess game, in which the Seneschal, obviously winning, permitted the King to gain the upper hand, 2) A horse chase, in which Ariobarzane replaced the shoes lost by the King's horse with those taken from his own, and 3) A tournament, in which the Seneschal, in a commanding position, intentionally dropped his lance so that the King's son could win the honors.

On a state banquet the King degrades Ariobarzanes, banishes him, and appoints his enemy to his post. Later the King orders the Seneschal to send the more beautiful of his two daughters to the Court and gives his own daughter to Ariobarzanes to marry. The Seneschal again exceeds the King in generosity and the enraged King has him condemned to death. Yet at the last minute the King relents and restores the Seneschal to his former high office.

Motifs which Fletcher's play shares with Bandello's tale are the wrath of the sovereign, the dismissal of the high official, the appointment of the latter's greatest enemy to his office, the patience with which he endures all the successive wrongs, and, finally, the union between monarch and subject by marriage ties.

Scholars have been misled by this seemingly impressive list of parallels, which, on closer examination, turn out to be mere surface resemblances, coincidences rather than basic affinities. I believe that Fletcher's play has little or nothing to do with Bandello's tale. The spirit and atmosphere of Bandello's tale and those of *The Loyal Subject* are completely different. As R. Warwick Bond points out: "The subtlety of the Eastern tale, where generosity is seen passing into selfishness and humility into pride, is exchanged into a simple contrast between a half-spoiled young prince . . . and an extravagantly loyal subject."[5] Unnoticed by most critics is Fletcher's divergence from the initial relationship between ruler and subject shown by Bandello. The King who, in the Eastern tale, becomes envious of his high servant only gradually, is portrayed by Fletcher as a decided foe of Archas from the outset. Thus, the dismissal of the high servant and his replacement by his enemy are suddenly decided by the Persian King, while in Fletcher's play these acts are the logical consequence of the Duke's long-felt animosity. Finally, there is no textual similarity or verbal echo between these two works.

Heywood's *The Royal King and the Loyal Subject,* which

stands somewhere midway between Bandello's tale and Fletcher's play, has much more artistic affinity to *The Loyal Subject,* affinities which will be pointed out later.

The argument of Heywood's play is as follows: Returning from a war, an unnamed English king thanks his Marshal for having saved his life and promotes him to the highest office. Chester and Clinton, two envious courtiers, plot to eliminate the Marshal by overpraising his virtues to the King so that the Marshal's generosity would seem to exceed the King's. They choose three instances—a chess game, a horse hunt, and a tournament—to prove their charges that the Marshal tried to display an extraordinary generosity. On the occasion of a banquet the King humiliates the Marshal, commands him to transfer his staff to Chester, and banishes him from the Court. The affair of the ordering of the fairer daughter of the Marshal to the Court and the offering of the King's own daughter to the Marshal to marry is essentially similar to Bandello's tale. The intriguing Chester and Clinton again incite the King against the Marshal's proud conduct and the King decides to put the Marshal before his Council for judgment. Using an analogy in Persian history, in which a falcon was first crowned with laurels and then beheaded for having killed an eagle, the Council pronounces a similar sentence on the Marshal. Everyone clamors for the repeal of the sentence; only Chester insists that the Marshal be executed without delay. The hesitant King now realizes that Chester has been the real traitor and reinstates the Marshal to his dignified position.

According to F. E. Schelling, an American scholar, who reflects the opinion of the traditional school, which treats *The Loyal Subject* in a historical void, the main idea of the play is a "test of loyalty under extraordinary wanton royal inflictions."[6] But this school has consistently overlooked a number of important motifs of the play which do not derive from any of these sources:

1. The conflict is not so much between the Duke and Archas, as between a) Boroskie and Archas onstage, and b) Boroskie and Burris offstage. If it were not for Boroskie, intent on keeping the breach between the Duke and Archas open, the Duke would be completely reconciled to Archas at the time of the Tartar invasion. The conflict between Boroskie and Burris, if not so conspicuous as the one between Boroskie and Achas, far

surpasses the latter in importance, since its outcome determines the victory of good or evil influences on the Duke, and consequently on state policy. The unstated problem of the play is the restoration of social and political order.

2. In the Russian historical context of the play, Archas alone cannot be regarded as the main hero of the play. Boroskie, Theodore, the Duke, and Burris are not only equally important protagonists, but, as historical figures, they surpass Archas in significance. There are reasons to believe that Fletcher might have created Archas, the royalist, and changed the original title of the play as an afterthought for home consumption so that the rebellious spirit of the play might pass the censor unnoticed. A politically motivated change by Fletcher might explain the artificiality of Archas's character and the sudden reversal of the rebels' attitude at the end of the play. The ending is so obviously superimposed, and so contrary to the spirit of the play, that an intelligent audience might have easily disregarded it.

3. The play emphasizes the strong resentment and eventual rebellion of the army against the unjust treatment of its general.

4. The satire of the play is directed against the Duke, the Court, and especially Boroskie.

For a definition of the main idea of the play we have to look at the way in which the positive protagonists react to the arbitrary use of royal power. Out of the attitudes and actions of Archas, of Theodore and his group, and of Burris, the main idea of the play gradually emerges. It can best be stated as a question: How far should a good subject go in his attitude to a ruler swayed by bad influence?

To understand this definition the ideology of some of the protagonists must be explained in detail.

The loyal Archas: Unquestioning obedience based on the ethical concept of all-inclusive honor. This moral absolute creates such a paradox as love for a monarch who tries him sorely, and makes him willing even to sacrifice his own son.

The rebel Theodore: The right to resistance against unjust authority. There is more nobility in vigorous protest than in timid virtue. Honorable disgrace is preferable to disgraced honor.

In the practical solution of this problem various conflicts arise with a number of equivocal moral sympathies, and these place the heroes in typical Fletcherian dilemmas, reflecting the baroque texture of his dramas. While the basic contrast is between Archas's honor and Boroskie's greed, the active participation of Theodore creates additional conflicts.

Theodore and his friends, although basically allied with Archas, struggle simultaneously on two fronts. On Archas's side, they are opposed to the materialism of the Duke and Boroskie, but they are also opposed to Archas's servility to the Duke. When Archas, enraged at his boldness, asks Theodore whose son he is, the latter indignantly replies: "Yours, sir, I hope; but none of your disgraces."[7] The logic of Theodore's conviction inevitably leads him into an armed conflict with the Duke, and he finds himself branded as a rebel and traitor, and even threatened with death by Archas, the very man whose disgrace he wanted to revenge. Thus, we have the unusual spectacle of two men—father and son—equally honorable, but each trying a different way of solving moral problems, and each calling the other dishonorable. The play states the problem but does not give a definite answer as to the preferable course: a loyal subject but a false father, or a false subject but a loyal son.

Although Fletcher treasured the essential value of honor and most of his plays demonstrate variations on this value in a clash with dishonor, in *The Loyal Subject* there is a redefinition of values and a search for a third way out. While Eugene W. Waith, an American scholar, correctly states that "the pattern of Fletcher's situation is an issue towards which two characters assume diametrically opposed attitudes,"[8] he still disregards the third way out of the moral dilemma. This third way is represented in the play by Burris.

The statesman Burris: The middle way lies between absolute obedience and armed resistance. Not unaware of the fragility of moral order, he still believes that virtue gradually triumphs and wickedness is defeated. A man of practical statecraft, he prefers an imperfect king to chaos, civil war, and foreign intervention. Thus, the wise course is to temporize and to endure until reason reaffirms itself. This position is not spectacular and at times appears even ineffective. Yet it seems the preferable course for a statesman allied with the Duke and nominally in the same camp with Boroskie, to follow under the circumstances. Thus, Burris's position is not unlike Theodore's since he too fights on two fronts, but his tactics and weapons are different. He uses ruse while Theodore brandishes a sword; he is patient while Theodore cannot contain himself, and he often compromises in the zigzag course of his occasional strategic retreat, while Theodore, unskilled in the sophisticated labyrinth of practical politics, follows a straight road and prefers an open fight.

The uniqueness of the play is shown by Fletcher's apparent preference for this third way out of the moral dilemma. It is reinforced by the conduct of Honora, Viola, and Alinda in the subplot. These three children of Archas, like Burris, temporize, often even seem to yield, yet finally attain their purpose. This is the third way, for which Fletcher had hitherto been searching in vain. Although their dilemma is more extreme, neither Amintor in *The Maid's Tragedy,* nor Maximus in *Valentinian,* to mention just two of Fletcher's important plays, could find this third way out of their tragic impasse. Therefore, the remarkable figure of Burris, the artistic portrait of Boris Godunov, Russian statesman and later Tsar, can rightfully be regarded as one of Fletcher's main accomplishments in this play.

Source Investigation up to the Present Time

The problem of the sources of *The Loyal Subject* has not been definitely settled in spite of a long history of scholarly investigation. Nor have even accepted sources been analyzed carefully enough for their exact relation to the main idea, dramatic conflict, and character portrayal of the play. Conventional approach dimmed critical perspective sufficiently so that in the last fifty years no fresh attempt has been made to discover the source of the play. Thus, Fletcherian scholars, unable to cut the umbilical cord binding them to the past, merely rehashed previous hypotheses, hiding their inability to solve the problem under the unconvincing statement that the English playwright "made the widest departure" from his sources.[9]

THOMAS HEYWOOD'S *THE ROYAL KING AND THE LOYAL SUBJECT* AND MATTEO BANDELLO'S ARIOBARZANES TALE

There was little formal criticism in English literature until the Restoration and even in that period hardly any information concerning the source of *The Loyal Subject* has been recorded. Yet scholars must have been puzzled by the similarity in title and content between Fletcher's play and Thomas Heywood's *The Royal King and the Loyal Subject,* for the first reference to similarity can be found in the *Account of the English Dramatick Poets,* written in 1691 by Gerald Langbaine, an English scholar, who, after reading Heywood's play, pointed out that the argument of this play "extreamly resembles that of Fletcher's *The Loyal Subject.*"[10] Langbaine obviously felt that Heywood borrowed the plot from Fletcher.

This opinion survived for a long time, since during the neoclassic atmosphere of the eighteenth century when the reputation of Beaumont and Fletcher declined sharply, there was a dearth of critical opinion concerning their plays. Only the Romantic movement, which revived interest in the Elizabethan and Stuart drama, brought forth a different critical approach and showed interest in source material. Thus, in the nineteenth century a sustained effort can be witnessed in which English and German scholarship vie with each other to illuminate the great age of English playwrights.

In the introduction to his *Literature of Europe in the Fifteenth, Sixteenth and Seventeenth Centuries* (1837), Henry Hallan, an English scholar, reverses Langbaine's long-standing hypothesis and mentions that "the general idea of several circumstances of *The Loyal Subject* has been taken" from Heywood's play and points out

that Heywood's was the original, though the only edition of it is in 1637, while *The Loyal Subject* was represented in 1615 (1616) cannot bear a doubt. The former is expressly mentioned in the epilogue as an old play, belonging to a style gone out of date and not to be judged with rigour. Heywood has, therefore, the praise of having conceived the character of Earl Marshal, upon which Fletcher somewhat improved in Archas.[11]

The Reverend Alexander Dyce, in *Some Accounts of the Lives and Writings of Beaumont and Fletcher* in the 1843-46 edition of the works of Beaumont and Fletcher, endorses Hallan's opinion on the primacy of Heywood's play, but denies that it had anything to do with Fletcher's work. He suspects that there must have been a common source for both dramas.[12]

Agreeing with Dyce, Moritz Rapp, in his *Studien ueber das englische Theater* (1862) takes English literary criticism to task for accepting Heywood's play as a source for *The Loyal Subject* merely on the basis of some superficial similarities:

Was zu jener Vergleichung verfuehrt hat, ist wahrscheinlich der ausserliche Umstand, dass der gepruefte Vassal beidemal zwei Toechter hat, was in Heywood's Stuecke wesentlich, hier aber ganz zufaellig ist, da die zweite Tochter gar nicht in die Handlung tritt.[13]

This German literary critic, an expert on both the Spanish drama of the Golden Age and the Tudor and Stuart stage, must, in turn, be accused of superficial criticism, since he overlooked various important links between the two plays. Contrary to Rapp's analysis, Viola, Archas's second daughter, participates in the action, although, as her name indicates, she is the more timid of the two.

In his *History of English Dramatic Literature to the Death of Queen Anne* (1899) A. W. Ward joins forces with Dyce and Rapp for condemning a tendency which accepts similarity for fact and points out that "Fletcher's play owes no debt to Thomas Heywood. . . . The similarity in title is far more likely to be the result of accident than intention." Ward felt that both plays were based on the same story, but not knowing the right source, hazarded an incorrect guess:

Since the scene of Fletcher's play is laid in Moscovy while that of Heywood's is in England, the later dramatist on this had probably adhered to the authority, from which the earlier preferred to deviate.[14]

That both plays, instead of influencing each other, may have been based on a common source has thus been suggested by Dyce and Ward, but these scholars did not indicate any possible source. However, in his *Quellen-Studien zu den Dramen Ben Jonson's, John Marston's und Beaumont's und Fletcher's* (1895) Emil Koeppel, a German scholar, believed that he had found the source for the two dramas:

Wo Fletcher diesen extremen Loyalisten [Archas] und den tyrannisch veranlagten Fuersten gefunden hat, ist bis jetzt nicht festgestellt worden. . . . Es wird mir bei der Besprechung des Heywood'schen Werkes nicht schwer fallen, nachzuweisen, dass Heywood eine 1567 von Painter (II,4) aus Bandello uebersetzte Novelle dramatisiert hat.[15]

Scholars were divided in their opinion whether Heywood used Bandello's story in its Italian original or the story's recasting by William Painter in his *Palace of Pleasure*. Painter's version can be found as the fourth tale of the second volume of his book.[16]

Only slight changes can be noticed between Bandello's original and Painter's recasting. The English translator somewhat adorned and dramatized the tale. In the original, for example,

the King's servant tells Ariobarzane to hand over his insignias
to "Dario, tu nemico," while, increasing the tension, Painter
rephrased it to "Dario, your mortal enemy." He also elaborated
the description of the knights' tournament and gave a more detailed account of the verbal battle between the King and his
Seneschal, without, however, changing anything in the essence
of the story.

There are three important alterations between Bandello's
story and Heywood's drama: Heywood personified and emphasized the active role of the intriguers, who had remained unnamed and vague figures in the *novella*. The English dramatist's
second innovation consisted of enlisting the active support of the
Prince and Princess, wooden characters in Bandello's tale, for
the victimized Marshal. Another active change is the transfer
of the locale from Persia to England, which results in additional
modifications because of the different mores and conventions in
both countries. Thus, for instance, there is a different reason for
the arrangement of the banquet, which was an annual custom in
Persia, while in Heywood's play it was due to the successful end
of the war. Another example is the sentencing of the Seneschal
to death in Persia, based on a law according to which subjects
who incurred the emperor's wrath should be punished because
kings were regarded as divine in that country. Since there existed
no law in England that kings enjoyed divine rights, Heywood
had to motivate differently the sentencing of the marshal and
used the conventional method of intrigue.

Koeppel did not distinguish between Bandello's tale and Heywood's play as the direct source for Fletcher's drama, and
implies that, on the basis of the available information discovered
so far, it is not possible to establish definitely the direct influence:

Die Beantwortung der Frage ob Fletcher die Novelle oder das . . .
Drama im Auge hatte, ist kaum moeglich, da Fletcher dieser Quelle fast
nur den Hauptgedanken seines Stueckes verdankt, den Gedanken, Fuer-
stenlaune und Unterthanentreue gegeneinander auszuspielen. . . . Von
einem engeren Anschluss an die Quelle kann . . . nicht die Rede sein:
Fletcher hat dieselben Faeden verschieden gesponnen.[17]

Koeppel did not seem to have considered carefully enough
the relationship of the two plays, otherwise he would have modified his opinion of the main idea of *The Loyal Subject* and, in
addition, he would have discovered definite textual similarities
between them.

In her study *Die italianische Novelle im Englischen Drama von 1600 bis zur Restauration* (1904), Adele Ott, a Swiss scholar, gave stimulus to further scholarly investigation by the important statement that the plays of Heywood and Fletcher did not stem from the same sources and concluded that there may be another, as yet undiscovered, source:

> Fletcher kann also in der Haupthandlung seines Dramas . . .—sei es direkt oder indirekt durch Heywood, Painter, oder Bandello—nur im Hauptgedanken nicht aber in der Ausfuehrung und Veranschaulichung desselben, von Italien beeinflusst worden sein, es sei denn, dass noch eine neue, bis jetzt unbekannte Quelle aufgefunden werde.[18]

In spite of Ott's interesting speculation concerning the possibility of an undiscovered source, the majority of scholars have continued to regard the triumvirate of Bandello, Painter, and Heywood as Fletcher's direct source up to our days.

Thus, in *John Fletcher, A Study in Dramatic Method* (1905), Orie L. Hatcher, an American scholar, feels that Fletcher borrowed the main point from Bandello.[19] F. E. Schelling also believes that the origin of *The Loyal Subject* is to be found in Painter's version of Bandello.[20]

A more important work of scholarly investigation was done by Bond, who, after summarizing previous research, gave a detailed analysis of the play, correctly established the relationship of the sources discovered so far, discussed the date of composition, and considered the problems of authorship, sources, and the theatrical history of *The Loyal Subject*. Bond feels that it is more likely that Fletcher used Heywood's drama than the Italian tale:

> . . . whereas he employs no feature of the novel not found in the play [Heywood's] . . . he resembles the play in several features not found in the novel. . . . Though not printed [Heywood's play] he [Fletcher] may have witnessed or even read it; and it is difficult to believe he would have chosen his title save as a direct challenge of comparison with it, a comparison he had no reason to fear.[21]

Bond's critical acumen informs most of the contemporary studies which, however, do not throw any fresh light on the source investigation of *The Loyal Subject*.[22]

In summing up the relationship between Fletcher's *The Loyal Subject*, Bandello's *novella*, and Heywood's play, the reader notices a gradual transformation in the protagonists—the ruler, the high servant, and the courtiers—as the tale travels from Persia via England to Muscovy. While Heywood, in a home-spun English fashion, somewhat simplified Bandello's Monarch, Fletcher made him more complex. Bandello's ambitious Sene-schal, in emulating his King, appears in Heywood's play as a mixture of loyalty and ambition, while he is transformed by Fletcher into a paragon of submission and duty without a trace of ambition. Bandello's unnamed courtiers, individualized by Heywood, reach their zenith in the envy and cunning of Fletch-er's Boroskie.

Though different in spirit and simpler in execution, Heywood's play is unquestionably based on Bandello's tale. There are four identical episodes in both works. These episodes, centering around the courtesy and ambition of Bandello's Persian Seneschal and Heywood's English Marshal, are (1) a chess game, (2) a high servant's offer to a king of a horseshoe during a chase, (3) a deliberate loss by the high servant to his monarch's son during a lance tournament, and, finally, (4) the humiliation of the Seneschal and the Marshal by their respective monarchs. In addition, the story connected with the dispatch of the two daugh-ters to the court of the monarch is almost identical in both works. It can also be established from textual similarities that Heywood used William Painter's English recasting of Bandello's tale.

Although the main idea of Fletcher's play did not come from Heywood's work, there are striking resemblances between the two plays. The two intriguing courtiers Chester and Clinton, in Heywood's drama, may conceivably have served as prototypes for Boroskie, and Heywood's attractive Princess for Olympia, the Duke's sister.

From Heywood's play Fletcher presumably borrowed several episodes, details, and turns of phrase, of which the following may be mentioned.

Boroskie's cowardice in feigning illness in order not to fight the Tartars might have had its source in the cowardice of Chester and Clinton, who, in plotting against the Marshal, are afraid to fight him.

Boroskie's warning to the Duke concerning Archas's ambition to ascend the throne might have come from a similar statement by Chester, and the latter's suggestion to seize Heywood's Marshal "On the sudden ere provided . . ."[23] might be one of the sources for Archas's seizure at the banquet.

When the tribunal sentences Heywood's Marshal to die, he

tells the King: ". . . I have a life yet left / In which to show my bounty . . ." and Fletcher's Archas speaks with a similar accent "I have a life yet left to gain that love, sir."[24]

Heywood's King and Fletcher's Duke both decide to test the loyalty of their high servants:

> The King: A project we intend / To prove him
> faithless or a perfect friend.
> Duke: Through a few fears I mean to try his
> goodness
> That I may find him fit . . .[25]

LOPE DE VEGA'S *EL DUQUE DE VISEO*

Another source was suggested by J. K. Klein (1874), a German literary historian[26] who believed that Lope's *El Duque de Viseo*[27] might have influenced Fletcher's play. However, Ward and Bond refuse to admit that this play has sufficient resemblance to *The Loyal Subject*.[28] I disagree with these two scholars, since Lope's play reveals a great number of similarities with Fletcher's. While there is no counterpart to the Russian Burris in Lope's *comedia,* the main idea of *The Loyal Subject* is, in part, present in the Spanish play.

Don Juan, king of Portugal, reminds us of the Muscovite Duke because of his suspicious, credulous, and cruel nature, arbitrary actions, and fears for his throne as a result of his growing unpopularity. Absolute loyalty and the duty of passive obedience are represented by the two eldest of the four brothers and by the Duke of Viseo. All of them are sorely tried by the King, who finally orders the murder of the Duke of Guimarans, one of the brothers, and kills the Duke of Viseo with his own hand; yet, until the last minute, they keep their faith in the sovereign. In preferring active resistance the two younger brothers remind us of the Muscovite Theodore and his friends. Although his motive is different, Don Egas, the Machiavellian courtier, has a certain similarity to Boroskie. Don Egas falsely accuses the four brothers before the King and says that they are conspiring to put the Duke of Viseo on the throne. The popular Duke of Viseo does not have an exact counterpart in Fletcher's play, but the affection of the nobles and the people toward him, and his honesty and military valor reveal certain resemblances to Archas. Finally, the sympathetic figure of the unnamed Portuguese Queen, sister of Don Viseo, who listens with tenderness to the troubles of Doña Elvira, Don Viseo's fiancée, and intervenes with the King an favor of the young couple, although the King rudely rebuffs her, reminds us of Olympia, the Duke's sister, who also unsuccessfully intervenes with the Duke on Archas's behalf.

Some episodes and verbal echoes relate the two plays. Among others, Archas's acceptance of his humiliating dismissal and his silencing of Theodore's protest is an echo of Guimarans's surrender of his arms under similar conditions. In both plays the positive characters see the courtier's machination behind the king's arbitrary actions, and they praise the former ruler, father of the present monarch. Finally, the banishment of the three brothers and of the Duke of Viseo is paralleled by the humiliation of Archas.

PROCOPIUS'S *LIFE OF BELISARIUS*

E. Dietrich, in a German doctoral dissertation (1916), felt that Fletcher had used Procopius's Belisarius for the development of his theme,[29] but, aside from surface similarities and unessential generalities between the Roman and Russian military commander, he offers no factual evidence for his supposition. The long literary ancestry of the true vassal as a stock figure of the contemporary stage should have dissuaded Dietrich from presenting the events in Belisarius's life as the main source for Fletcher's play.

Presentation of the Writer's Theory

The foregoing represents the present stand of scholarship, to which I now add the following sources:

1. LOPE DE VEGA'S *EL GRAN DUQUE DE MOSCOVIA Y EMPERADOR PERSEGUIDO*

The main idea of *The Loyal Subject* can be found in Lope's play reflected in the reigns of both Emperors: Basilio (the his-

torical Ivan the Terrible) and Boris. At the beginning of the
play Teodoro and Juan protest against Basilio's conduct and
later the "great revolution" of the people is directed against
Boris's tyranny.

The strongest candidate for the prototype of Archas's loyalty
is Lope's Lamberto. There is a striking resemblance between
Lamberto's sacrifice of his son to save Demetrio, and Archas's
attempt to kill Theodore. A certain saintliness also links both
figures. Lope's Basilio has certain traits common with Fletcher's
Duke. Lope's Teodoro and Fletcher's Theodore are truthful,
blunt, and impatient characters. Rufino, Lamberto's servant and
Demetrio's companion, might have served as a prototype for
Fletcher's Ancient. Rufino's loyalty and comic traits as a Spanish
gracioso are paralleled by Ancient, "a stout, merry soldier."

In addition, the following episodes and textual similarities
may be pointed out:

In Lope's play Finea, who exposed Boris's plan to murder
Demetrio, proves her honor by refusing to accept Demetrio's
chain and ring as a present, while Fletcher's Alinda returns the
Duke's ring and saves her honor. Basilio wants Juan to succeed
him because Teodoro is unfit for governing, while Fletcher shows
the young Duke's unfitness to wear the crown by pointing out his
inability to handle the troops in the Muscovite military state.
Boris's visit to the monastery to learn the secret of whether or
not Demetrio is alive, may be regarded as one of the sources of
the motif of the Duke's visit to Archas's house to discover the
secret of the treasure. Demetrio's life among the harvesters in
Livonia might have induced Fletcher to use expressions in
Archas's speech related to harvesting. Also Lope's abbot, as
well as Fletcher's Theodore, shows the same sense of moral
integrity by refusing to obey an unjust ruler.

I have also to point out the important contribution of Lope's
play to the spirit, technique, and style of *The Loyal Subject*.
The baroque climate of Lope's *comedia* is evident in Fletcher's
play, especially in the sense of an almost morbid preoccupation
with fear, danger, and death, in the sudden contrast, and in the
hyperbolic language. The sentiment of harmony of the universe
is broken, a gradual tension between life and spirit overcomes
both plays, out of which most of the protagonists try to escape,
either in ascetic negation or in an ironic contemplation of life.[30]

2. DR. GILES FLETCHER'S *OF THE RUSSE COMMONWEALTH* AND SIR JEROME HORSEY'S *RELACION*

I now come to the most important historical sources of the play, which justify a more detailed treatment.

Most of the plays of Fletcher have been condemned by the critics for their improbable plots, unrealistic situations, and unlifelike characters. The critics have also pointed out that most of Fletcher's plays carry us into an imaginary and fantastic world with little or no relation to history or age.[31]

As far as the dramatic conflict and the characters of Fletcher's plays are concerned, Waith mentions in 1952 that "the conflict signifies nothing beyond itself" and "the characters are warped beyond recognition."[32] Singling out *The Loyal Subject* for his critical barb, Tucker Brooke, an American scholar (1945), rebukes Fletcher for having "replaced by costume dummies" Heywood's plain people and for having blown Heywood's plot into "phosphorescent froth by weird new motives: battle, invasion, mutiny, disguise . . . sex confusion and what not." Brooke's final verdict is that the play "is as hollow as a shell."[33]

Yet several scholars have also noticed a special quality about Fletcher's play. George Darley, editor of the works of Beaumont-Fletcher (1840), speaks of the "vigour" of *The Loyal Subject* and of its "singular anticipation" of the Moscow fire.[34] Rapp, the German scholar of European literatures stresses the liveliness of the play, and praises especially the truthful description of the milieu. "Der eigenthuemliche Werth dieses Stueckes beruht auf der lebendigen Darstellung des russischen Hofes im Jahrhundert des Dichters . . . bleibt das Localcostuem von ueberraschender Wahrheit."[35] Ward mentions the "vividness" of characterization and situations.[36] Parrott and Ball, two American scholars (1943), speak of a "firmer" characterization and of "more realistic situations,"[37] and William W. Appleton, an American critic, points out "a certain thematic unity."[38]

It is clear that the critics are divided about the artistic quality of *The Loyal Subject*. When I now present my view on the main sources of the play, it will become obvious that even the perceptive critics left the genesis of the remarkable realism of *The Loyal Subject* unexplored.

Against the vagueness and lack of historical, political, and geographical details in most of Fletcher's plays, *The Loyal*

Subject stands out in bold relief, with its great number of facts, events, and details relating to contemporary Russian actuality. This wealth of historical material, described with a vividness not encountered in any of the other plays of this dramatist, reveals Fletcher's close acquaintance with an immediate reality of a definite world. Thus, Fletcher must have based his play on sources which are the fruit of firsthand information and direct experience. Analyzing *The Loyal Subject,* Rapp accurately guessed that "Derselbe muss nicht unbedeutende Materialien aus dem Lande selbst gehabt haben."[39]

One of the immediate sources of the play is Dr. Giles Fletcher's *Of the Russe Commonwealth* (1591). Dr. Fletcher, John Fletcher's uncle, was Queen Elizabeth's ambassador to Tsar Feodor in 1588 to negotiate the restoration of trade between the two countries, and his pamphlet represents a systematic and comprehensive study and a penetrating analysis of the Russian government, administration, civil justice, military and social structure, religion, and manners of the Russian people at the end of the sixteenth century.

The connection between Dr. Fletcher's pamphlet and *The Loyal Subject* has been recognized only casually. In his Preface to the 1812 edition of the works of Beaumont and Fletcher, Henry Weber was the first to point out that Fletcher's transfer of the scene to Moscow may be attributed to the influence of the historical account by Dr. Fletcher. Yet scholars either ignored Dr. Fletcher's brochure as a questionable source of the play or, by their silence, minimized its importance.[40]

A comparison between the play and this source reveals that John Fletcher made several basic changes and even important reversals in the material collected by his uncle.

The most significant alteration occurred in the depiction of Burris—the historical Boris Godunov—in *The Loyal Subject.* According to Dr. Fletcher, Boris continued the wicked policy of Ivan the Terrible in destroying the power and the economic strength of the nobles by banishing them into remote places of Russia or forcing them into monasteries. The English diplomat gives his readers a list of the names of those nobles who were either killed or disappeared. He even mentions that the life of Demetrius, Ivan IV's youngest son, is in danger from some who aspire to the throne—an obvious reference to Boris.

We can only conjecture whether Dr. Fletcher's characterization of Boris was based on fact or rumor. Personally he had every reason to be resentful toward the powerful "Lord Protector," as all English accounts of the time called Boris. On his arrival Dr. Fletcher learned that the Russians were greatly angered by the improper conduct of some English traders in Russia and discovered that Boris had planned an anti-Turkish alliance with the Spain of Philip II, the mortal enemy of Protestant England at the time. Dr. Fletcher was not welcomed officially, or escorted to his lodging in Moscow, and during his stay he was treated with contempt, refused an audience, and kept like a prisoner; not unreasonably, he felt his personal safety to be constantly in danger. Yet the English victory over the Spanish Armada and his own diplomatic restraint and finesse finally changed the situation and he succeeded in obtaining important concessions for the Russia Company of English traders.

Why did John Fletcher reverse Boris's characterization as shown by his uncle and depict him as "an honest lord" who supports the innocent and fights the wicked? The usual explanation of reversal as a principle of his artistic convention should be overruled in this case on logical and emotional grounds, for why should he want to paint in bright colors the very man so hostile to his uncle, who became a second father to him when his father died in 1596?

I believe that the explanation for this reversal may be found in the combination of two important factors.

The first may be attributed to the fact that soon after its publication, Dr. Fletcher's pamphlet was suppressed through the intervention of the highly influential Russia Company, which felt that Dr. Fletcher's sarcastic criticism of Boris, of his aspiration to the throne, and of the general atmosphere of tyranny in Russia would hurt its present lucrative trade interest. Thus, it is logical to assume that John Fletcher, the politically sophisticated dramatist, saw the handwriting on the wall and, as a result, became considerably kinder to Russian history, the Russian people, Boris, and, at times, even Ivan.

The second factor may be due to the influence of other accounts of the Russian political events of the time. After "the discovery" of Russia by English travelers in the second half of the seventeenth century, Englishmen became interested in that distant and exotic land and, in order to satisfy that curiosity, a growing volume of travel literature about Russia began to appear. As a popular playwright in Court circles, Fletcher might have talked to English ambassadors, trade representatives, and travelers who visited Russia during the reigns of Tsars Ivan, Feodor, and Boris, and obtained additional information. He undoubtedly read the accounts of many of these diplomats and travelers and must have compared them with that of his uncle, and thus could not help seeing that Dr. Fletcher's interpretation of the events connected with Boris was subjective, one-sided, somewhat exaggerated, and based more on a personal grudge than on real facts.

There was also another important narrative of the period concerning the era of Ivan the Terrible, Tsar Feodor, and Boris, written by Sir Jerome Horsey, *A Relacion or Memoriall Abstratcted owt of Sir Jerom Horsey, His Travels, Imploiements and Negociaciones,* first mentioned in Hakluyt's *Voyages* (1589). This account is a curious mixture of historical information, personal reminiscence, rumor, gossip, and ideological theorizing. Horsey was an agent of the Russia Company who went to Moscow in 1573 for the first time, stayed in that country almost continuously until his expulsion in 1591, had friendly relations with, and at times even acted as the envoy of, the ruling personalities of the time, and learned Russian well enough to converse with Ivan, Feodor, Boris, and others at the Court. Horsey traveled with Dr. Fletcher when the latter returned to England in 1588, and, in his own account, indicates that he supplied Dr. Fletcher with much of the information contained in *Of the Russe Commonwealth.*[43]

Except for the last years of his stay in Russia, when he fell in disfavor, Horsey was very popular in that country and his success was achieved partly by the unusual favor he enjoyed with Boris, especially during the early years of Feodor's rule. There are a number of references to Boris in Horsey's account during that period, most of which describe him as a wise and skillful statesman. Even when Horsey was in disgrace with most Russian diplomats, Boris still continued to protect him, spoke to him "with tears" in his eyes, and, on one occasion, sent word to Horsey that he should not fear. The prototype of the Burris in Fletcher's play is clearly the Boris in Horsey's account.

An additional hint that John Fletcher followed Horsey rather than reversing his uncle's characterization of Boris may be found in the answer to the question as to why the dramatist named his hero "Burris" instead of Boris. A perusal of both accounts concerning the spelling of Godunov's first name shows that Dr. Fletcher alternately used the transcription of "Boris," "Borris," and "Borrise," but he never wrote it as "Burris." In Horsey's account, however, the reader also finds Boris's name transcribed as "Burris." It is interesting to note that, in the last case, Horsey adds the only explanation of a name in his entire account, mentioning that "we now come to the usurper called in their language Burris . . .," and even reproduces a facsimile of the latter's name in Slavonic script. In the Slavonic reproduction of Boris's name, Horsey, who was not quite familiar with the Slavonic alphabet of the period, made a mistake in writing the vowel "o" almost like the Greek omega which, at the time, was also used to denote the Russian vowel "u." This resulted in the English transcription of Burris instead of Boris.[44]

Since the accounts of Dr. Fletcher and Horsey mutually complement each other, I will treat them together as the main sources of *The Loyal Subject.*

A comparison of the two accounts reveals striking resemblances and distinct differences. Such events as the burning of Moscow, the attempt on Demetrius's life, and Boris's ambition to ascend the throne, i.e., the passages when both accounts treat the same subjects, are similar. The difference lies in the subjective evaluation of the two authors with regard to certain specific events. While for the most part Dr. Fletcher's account acquaints the reader with the manner of government, the institutions and society of the Muscovite state, Horsey's often ambiguous and imprecise reminiscences center around historical incidents, personal observations, and intimate anecdotes of his own adventures.

Arriving in Russia with the bias of a Western social milieu, Dr. Fletcher, an English patriot, a doctor of civil law, a man of progressive political views, and a proponent of parliamentary monarchy, looked for a Magna Charta in Muscovy and found none. A believer in written jurisprudence, Dr. Fletcher was dismayed that justice in Russia was administered arbitrarily by "speaking law," and, a pious Protestant, he felt that religious ignorance and superstition were appalling. He wanted to see the same relationship in Russia between ruler and ruled that characterized the more enlightened and progressive Elizabethan era in England, but he could see only the ruler's egoism. Disappointed in his expectations, his political evaluation became one-sided and, bitter and suspicious because of his painful personal experience, he tried to discover a calculated motive and ulterior purpose in each political measure of Ivan and Boris.

On the other hand, Horsey, lacking the education, social background, political conviction, and religious bias of his scholarly *confrère,* did not discriminate. He was a typical English traveler and merchant of the sixteenth century, impressed with the wealth of Muscovy, amused by her strange and exotic customs, scornful of the wickedness of her people, indignant at tyranny, but also an opportunist, willing to serve the masters of Russia when he could profit by it. Unlike Dr. Fletcher, he may have felt that the Russian "speaking law" was useful and practical, since, due to its ambiguity and vagueness, everybody could interpret it and plead his cause according to his own idiosyncrasy. Horsey was closer both in time and temper to Ivan's reign, to his *opričniks,* to the twilight period after Ivan's death, and the access he enjoyed to the palace of Feodor and Boris lends his account atmosphere, freshness, color, and immediacy, if not absolute truthfulness and accuracy.

The main idea of the play is the obvious result of the juxta-position of the two recurrent themes in the accounts of Dr. Fletcher and Horsey: the tyranny of the government and the resentment of the people. These themes provided John Fletcher with two clashing centers and constant dramatic tension for his play.

I must point out a shift of emphasis in the accounts of Dr. Fletcher and Horsey in describing the attitude of the people in face of the government's tyranny. Although Dr. Fletcher somewhat wistfully predicts a civil war, he still seems to stress the silent suffering of the people, who can do nothing to overthrow the government. But in Horsey's account the Russians are more active, participate in various plans to destroy Ivan, and, filled with treasonous activities, incite and encourage the Tartars to invade the country. This active disobedience, even rebellion, characterizes the play and establishes a close kinship between *The Loyal Subject* and Horsey's account.

In the play the tyranny of the government is shown by the public humiliation of Archas at the time of his dismissal, the refusal to welcome the victorious army, and the nefarious activities of the *opričnina.*

The discontent of the army is evident from the beginning of the play; it gradually gains intensity and finally erupts into open rebellion. Some of the more notable moments of this process may be enumerated as follows: Theodore's complaint about Archas's disgrace and his ominous reference to future actions; the soldiers' refusal to fight the Tartars in retaliation for the disgrace of their General, their cheering of the enemy attack, and their scorning of the Duke and Boroskie; the resentment of the soldiers because of the cold welcome after their victory; the storming of the royal palace to free Archas; and finally, the soldiers' decision to join the Tartars and together with them to "march straight against" the Duke.

Fletcher's two sources furnished him with information on the historical background of Russia, reflected in certain references to the old Duke in the play. They also supplied material for such contemporary political and military events as the elimination of the great boyars, a specific Tartar invasion, and the burning of Moscow in 1571, events which are illustrated in the play.

It is interesting to speculate on Fletcher's motive in giving a predominantly military cast to his play. One reason may be the news reaching England of almost continuous warfare in Russia, at one time against her Western neighbors and at others against the Tartars. Another reason may be that, since the play emphasizes vigorous resistance to the government, Fletcher needed active men and the logical place to go to was the army. The most convincing explanation, however, may be found in his sources. Dr. Fletcher believed that the army was the only hope to alter the Russian government's tyranny, if it were ever to break its allegiance to the Tsar. Even more specific is Horsey, who, at the time when Ivan laid new taxes on the high clergy, says

the chieff bishops . . . assembled . . . seeking and devising with discontended nobillitie how to turn head and make a warr of resistance: but there wanted such a head or generall that had currage sufficient to guide or lead such an army.[45]

As if to answer such a call by Horsey, John Fletcher created an army led by Theodore, who shows that resistance is possible and can even be successful. John Fletcher followed the idea that the army might become the potential liberator of Russia, and modeled his military organization on information obtained from Dr. Fletcher's brochure dealing with the Russian military forces.

The geographical information contained in the sources is reflected in Fletcher's reference to Moscow, the wooden buildings, churches, and inns of the city, to the Volga and the port of St. Nicholas. Fletcher also mentions the cold weather of the country. He found the name of an animal, "ollen" (Russian for "deer"), in his uncle's brochure, changed it to "Olin," and used it as the name of the Tartar chief. Perhaps he was thinking of the lightning speed with which the Tartars advanced in their military campaigns against the Russians.

We are also informed of certain customs of the Russian people such as their drinking, supersition, and vagrancy; the habits of the Russian women of painting themselves; and the Court custom of inviting girls from all over the country for the Tsar and his sons to select wives.

Dr. Fletcher devotes a whole chapter to a systematic description of the ten "means used to draw the wealth of the land into the emperours treasure," and we find various references to the revenues of the Duke in the play. Burris mentions that he often heard the Duke complain of lack of money, which he finds strange since the latter "has so many ways to raise it." In a conversation between the Duke and Boroskie, the courtier reports that the soldiers refused their pay "most confidently; 'tis not your revenues / Can feed them. . . ."[46]

There are many general references in the two sources to the great wealth of the Russian tsars, which may explain why Fletcher included in his play an episode concerning treasure. A specific reference may be found in Dr. Fletcher's study to the fact that Tsar Feodor was "left very rich . . . by his father," and Horsey also mentions that some treasure was hidden by Ivan and Boris in certain "unknowen and secreat places." This may be the origin of Archas's explanation of the treasure hidden in his house: "Your sire, before his death, knowing your temper . . . / . . . thriftily . . . / collected all his treasures."[47]

Of the great number of similar episodes and textual parallels we may mention Dr. Fletcher's meditation upon the "state of the vulgar people in Russia," which brings him to the conclusion that it is better for every Russian to keep his rank than "to advance any vertue," since there is no possibility of advancement "but rather procuring more danger to themselves the more they excell in any noble or principall qualitie." This thought is reflected in Theodore's reminiscences of his father's career:

> The memorable hazards he has run through . . .
> Had they been less, they had been safe(r) . . .[48]

Horsey mentions that Ivan planned to marry his brother's daughter to Duke Magnus of Denmark. Hence, Ivan sends for his brother, Andrew, who is popular among his people, and of whom Ivan is jealous.

When he [Prince Andrew] came to his [Ivan's] presence, he laied himself prostrate . . . he [Ivan] toke him up and kissed him. "O cruell brother" with tears, saies the storie, "this is a Judas kiss; thow has sent for me to noe good end. . . ." Died the next daie . . .

When Archas is invited to the feast and treacherously seized, he expresses himself in similar accent:

> Only the juggling way that toll'd me to it
> The Judas way, to kiss me, to bid me welcome
> And cut my throat . . .[49]

Dr. Fletcher mentions that "to drink drunke" is a common practice with the Russians. In introducing his sisters at the Court, Theodore mentions that the two girls, among other things, "Drink drunk . . ."[50]

Dr. Fletcher indicates that, in case of a crime (treason, murder, theft), the manner of examination is torture. The defendant is beaten with "whips," sometimes "one of his ribbes" is broken and his "flesh" is cut. He also points out that the people are often "racked." In the play, after Archas is freed from Boroskie's torture, Theodore exclaims: "He's rack'd and whipt." Later the soldiers murmur: "Our . . . general tortur'd and whipt." As the rebellious army is marching towards the border, Theodore tells his friends: "Your valiant old man's whipt. . . . That noble body, ribb'd in arms. . . ."[51]

Dr. Fletcher describes how Ivan created jealousy among the boyars "Wherein hee used to set on inferiours," so that these aspired to the rank of the higher nobles. This idea of inciting one group of people against another may also be found in the play but in a different context. The reader finds Boroskie complaining to the Duke about the behavior of the soldiers, who would not dare to do "these monstrous, most offensive things . . . / If not set on."[52]

THE ANONYMOUS *SIR THOMAS SMITH'S VOIAGE AND ENTERTAINMENT IN RUSHIA*

Another source which might have influenced Fletcher in his portrayal of Boris is the anonymous *Sir Thomas Smith's Voiage and Entertainment in Rushia* (1605),[53] in which Boris is shown as a fine statesman, popular ruler, and one of the best monarchs on earth.

The anonymous author also draws a sympathetic and tender portrait of the youthful Feodor, Tsar Boris's handsome son. There are several traits in young Feodor's characterization which make me believe that Fletcher might have, to some extent, relied on this source in creating his Alinda.

An important similarity between this source and the play is the atmosphere of fear and of impending doom which characterized the last days of Tsar Boris's rule as the alleged Demetrius's army was approaching Moscow. This corresponds to the fear and confusion created by the Tartar invasion in the play.

Since Horsey mentions this account, John Fletcher must have known it and may have read it.

THE REPORTE OF A BLOUDIE AND TERRIBLE MASSACRE IN THE CITTY OF MOSCO

Another source for *The Loyal Subject* may have been this anonymous report first published in Amsterdam in 1606. This account describes in a vivid and graphic manner the final days of Boris Godunov—the victorious entry of the alleged Demetrius, his overthrow, and the massacre of foreigners in Moscow.

This is a minor source, from which Fletcher may have used only one incident, the storming of the royal palace by the boyars and the population. The description of the Moscow mob running toward the Kremlin and shouting "to the fire, kill, kill . . ." may have contributed to the picturesque realism with which Fletcher depicts the attack on the palace by the army to free Archas.

TRAVELERS' REPORTS

John Fletcher may possible have read the accounts of several travelers to Russia in the sixteenth and seventeenth centuries, such as Chancellor, Killingworth, Jenkinson, and others in Hakluyt's *Voyages*. However, these accounts could not have given him anything he could not have obtained from his other sources.

CONCLUSION

To sum up the source investigation:

1. The main historical sources of the play are Dr. Fletcher's *Of the Russe Commonwealth*, Sir Jerome Horsey's *Relacion*, and the anonymous *Sir Thomas Smith's Voiage and Entertainment in Rushia*. A minor source may be *The Reporte of a Bloudie and Terrible Massacre in the Citty of Mosco*. Fletcher probably received some oral information from Horsey and others and he may also have read some travelers' reports.

2. The main literary sources of the play are Lope de Vega's *El Gran Duque* and *El Duque de Viseo*, and Thomas Heywood's *The Royal King and the Loyal Subject*.

Dramatis Personae

GENERAL OBSERVATIONS

According to the authoritative opinion of W. J. Courthope in his *A History of English Poetry*, the characters of Beaumont-Fletcher may be classified as follows: 1. voluptuous-tyrant type, like Valentinian in the play of the same name, 2. type of coward, like Bessus in *King and No King*, 3. plain blunt-soldier type, like Melantius in *The Maid's Tragedy*, and 4. innumerable varieties of courtier type, but particularly gay debauchee like Monsieur Thomas in the play of that name.[54]

In agreement with this general statement, Weber, the editor of the Beaumont-Fletcher works of 1812 said, that "there is no character in the play [*The Loyal Subject*] which is not extraordinarily one-sided."[55] Courthope (1903) calls the characters "invariably abstract . . . improbable . . . and . . . inconsistent."[56] In *The Age of Shakespeare* (1911), Thomas Seccombe and J. W. Allen, two English scholars, feel that Beaumont and Fletcher show "little or no sense of character. The result is lifeless when not absurd."[57] L. C. Knight, an English scholar, points out in his *Drama and Society in the Age of Jonson* (1937): "The reason for vagueness and generality, the commonplace figures . . . is that there is no informing emotion, no pressure from within."[58] According to Robert Ornstein, an American scholar: "After a while one grows slightly tired of interchangeable characters, . . . of pasteboard heroes and heroines who are suitable for all dramatic occasions because they have no inner reality or individuality."[59] Most recently, Waith, who devoted several essays to Beaumont and Fletcher, points to "Fletcher's calculated inconsistencies in characterization" in *The Loyal Subject.*[60]

In spite of this unanimous critical condemnation a more careful analysis of *The Loyal Subject* will prove that, although this action-filled drama hardly permitted a profound psychological characterization with the exception of Archas, all the other protagonists are convincingly drawn, realistic figures taken from the historical actuality of the Russian Time of Troubles.

THE GREAT DUKE OF MOSCOVIA

The correct solution to the puzzle of the historical personality hiding behind the unnamed Duke is the key to the proper interpretation of the period, events, and problems connected with the play. His identification is not easy and, even when all the available evidence is submitted, explained, and interpreted, the final answer still relies on a certain amount of guesswork because of missing links and conflicting information.

The Duke is a composite figure with a mixture of good and bad qualities. Under the influence of the evil Boroskie, he is suspicious, despotic, revengeful, sensuous, and deceitful. The general impression is that the Duke is a prisoner of his own passion who will destroy everybody who stands in his way and displeases him. His slogans, "that I will have, shall be" and "I am vex'd, and some shall find it," clearly reveal this monomania.[61]

Yet he can also be a good monarch when the prudent Burris's influence prevails. At such times he apologizes for his attitude to Archas, shows the wisdom to recognize and the eloquence to express his regrets for his mistakes. ("If men could live without their faults, they were gods.")[62] He rewards honesty, pardons the rebels, and even begs Archas to spare Theodore's life. Although Brooke maintains that the "king is a poor creature . . .

for whom Archas (or, in this play, any one else) never cared,"[63] the evidence shows that not only Archas, but Burris, Theodore, and Putskie think that he is noble. Some of his good qualities are introduced early and thus Fletcher makes us think that, even when the Duke is vicious, it may be only a temporary aberration in an otherwise dignified character, and does not let us forget even at the low point of the Duke's distasteful acts that he is still capable of tears and repentence.

The main historical sources provide us with all the information concerning the divided character of the Duke. Yet their treatment of the Muscovite rulers is different. Horsey, who came to Moscow in 1572, describes Ivan's rule separately from Feodor's, and Dr. Fletcher, who arrived in Moscow after Ivan's death, briefly depicts Feodor's rule with frequent and detailed flashbacks to Ivan's.

The reader hears Dr. Fletcher so often speak of "Iuan Vasilowich, father to this Emperour" that, after a while, he has the impression that the author speaks of two persons merged into one. Thus, to John Fletcher, the idea of blending these two monarchs must have come naturally. However, if Fletcher followed his uncle's structural approach, he seemed to rely more heavily on Horsey for information, since the latter's account is more detailed, firmer, and more dramatic concerning the character of these two Tsars. Horsey's description of the quizzical nature of Ivan the Terrible—his intolerance, suspicion, yet also his intellectual alertness—is especially successful in the episode about Elizabeth's navy.

Both Dr. Fletcher and Horsey indicate the physical and mental weakness of Tsar Feodor, and Dr. Fletcher has even left us an interesting description of the physical appearance of this Tsar. Yet, even in this case, Horsey succeeds better in his episodic and colorful narration of an unusual audience and brings this Tsar definitely closer to us as Feodor "began to crie . . . crossinge himself, saienge he never gave me cause of offense," and Horsey is rapidly hustled out of the room.[64]

Finally, these two sources also describe Boris, especially in connection with Feodor, which is natural since he governed for the weak Tsar. Thus, in Dr. Fletcher's pamphlet not only do the reigns of Ivan and Feodor seem to overlap, but also Boris is placed alongside them.

I can set up the following three hypotheses in a decreasing

degree of probability concerning the identity of the Great Duke in Fletcher's play.

1. He is most likely Ivan the Terrible. The strong, strange and enigmatic personality of this Tsar dominates all the historical sources which John Fletcher might have read. Two of the major events of the play, the Tartar invasion in 1571 and the establishment and fall of the *opričnina* (1565-1572), are clearly connected with his name in history. The greatest number of personal characteristics in the play can also be related to him. In addition there is a reference in Horsey's account which Fletcher retained with only a slight textual alteration. Horsey describes Ivan at one place as "comely in person" and at another a "goodlie man," and, in the play, Honora calls the Duke "the handsomest man I ever look'd on, / The goodliest gentleman."[65]

Yet we also find some evidence against this identification. We cannot explain the presence of Boris Godunov at the Court of the young Duke. In harmony with history, Fletcher's sources mention Boris only in the latter part of Ivan's reign.

The references in the play to the old Duke, father of the present Emperor, cannot be satisfactorily explained either. In this case the sources are contradictory. Dr. Fletcher describes Ivan's father, the historical Vasilij III (1505-1553), as a man who "atchieved his victories abroad" more by "civill dissentions and treasons . . . that by anie great policies . . . of his owne." Against this unflattering statement, which stands in contradiction to the sympathy with which John Fletcher describes the old Duke, we have a different characterization of Ivan's father by Horsey, who tells us "of Vazillie Andreowich his reigne . . . who inlarged his countries . . . and leaft . . . his people in great peace . . . strong and rich. . . ."[66] Although Horsey's description is closer to historical truth and better suited to the play, it still lacks the motif of the hidden treasure.

2. There are three reasons for regarding the Great Duke as the historical Tsar Feodor:

a. His inability "to draw up" troops, which, by extension, corresponds to Feodor's physical weakness and general unfitness for military life or for governmental duties, qualities which often coincide in a country on constant military alert against its aggressive neighbors. Horsey mentions that Feodor was of "no martiall disposition," and the Duke's acceptance of death rather than fight the Tartars in the play seems to justify this characterization.

b. The presence of Archas, Boroskie, and Burris at the Court as members of the historical council whom Ivan the Terrible, at his death-bed, appointed to help "the simple and slow-witted" Feodor govern the country.

c. Feodor's well-known inability in the practical matters of life, which could have suggested the old Duke's decision to leave part of his wealth to him in Archas's custody, to be used in an emergency. Historical literature mentions that Ivan often hid his treasures in secret places.

However, in this case, Ivan the Terrible would have to be identified as the good old Duke, which is an obvious impossibility. Nor could we explain the presence of the *opričniki,* because they had been disbanded before Feodor became the Tsar. Finally, the anticipated burning of Moscow by the Tartars would also remain unexplained.

3. The Great Duke could also be Tsar Boris. This would explain the Duke's insecurity and anxiety for the throne, qualities generally associated with Boris because of his low origin. This would also explain satisfactorily the hiding of young Archas alias Alinda as a potential victim of Boris's ambition or his concern, real or fancied, for his hold on an insecure throne. The reference to unemployed soldiers roaming the streets may hint at the economic disturbances in 1601-1603 and the great famine. The number of discontented people trying to escape to join the Cossacks or the Poles, reported by Horsey, may correspond to the soldiers' decision to make common cause with the Tartars in the play. The anonymous Smith account also describes a fire in Moscow during Boris's reign, which may perhaps resemble the anticipated burning of the Russian capital in the play. There were also Tartar raids at the time. Since Boris's father was not a ruler of Muscovy, the reference to the old Duke could not be explained on historical grounds. Yet Horsey offers a possible solution, since in his account we find references to Ivan's affection for Boris, whom he allegedly called his third son.

However, if Tsar Boris is regarded as the Great Duke in Fletcher's play, it would greatly increase the problem of trying to explain satisfactorily a number of historical events and facts. In the play the Tartar invasion is connected with the burning of Moscow; during Boris's reign Moscow was not burned by the invading Tartars. Also, it would be clearly impossible to explain the presence of Boris, the courtier, at the Court of Boris, the Tsar.

My conclusion is that Fletcher took some of the traits of the three rulers and, at the cost of historical truth, has neatly, although not always convincingly, welded them together according to his artistic needs. Thus, in one episode, the traits of Ivan the Terrible, in another those of Tsar Feodor, and, in a third, those of Tsar Boris, predominate. Therefore, while the characteristics of the overpowering Ivan the Terrible seem to prevail in general, as they do in all historical literature of the period and we do less damage, both artistically and historically, to the play if we conceive of the events as having taken place during his reign, we must still acknowledge in his characterization the presence of a few distinctive features of Feodor and Boris.

BURRIS

Aside from the fact that several researchers failed to identify the historical Boris Godunov in Burris, they were constantly baffled by the unique position that he occupies in the play.[67] Fletcher calls him "an honest lord, the duke's favorite."

In enumerating the features of the protagonists of the Beaumont-Fletcher tragicomedies, Waith emphasizes their "Protean characters," calling them "strange, unpredictable creatures . . . monsters and saints, living abstractions."[68] However, even to a superficial reader of *The Loyal Subject,* it will become immediately obvious that Burris's essential traits—wisdom, moderation, and skill—are not Protean at all and that he is anything but a strange and unpredictable character. Again, a general critical statement completely fails which brackets the characters of *The Loyal Subject* with those of the rest of the Beaumont-Fletcher dramas without considering the distinct features of the characters of the former.

While his position was not one to encourage impartiality in reporting events of the Court to the Duke, Burris, aside from the necessity of occasionally humoring the Duke, does not act slavishly at all. Undaunted by the Duke's anger and the possibility of political disgrace, he defends Archas and has enough courage, at the time of the Tartar invasion, to rebuke even the Duke for having foolishly dismissed the General. He warns the Duke against using violence when they are Archas's guests; sends a present to the disgraced General; shows his indignation at the banquet; and finally brings about Boroskie's downfall.

While the Mr. Hyde side of the Duke uses Boroskie to inflict wounds, the Jekyll in him employs Burris to heal them. Thus, whenever a national crisis develops, it is Burris's mission to effect a *rapprochement* among opposing forces, and reestablish unity between the Court and the army.

The authentic historical color with which Burris's activities are painted also reinforces my hypothesis that the Great Duke is probably Ivan the Terrible. In the play Burris merely advises the Duke and, as often as not, his advice is disregarded, while in Feodor's reign, as history tells us, Boris became the virtual head of the country and was hardly ever overruled. Also, his spectacular rise coincides with the dissolution of the *opričnina* in 1572, in which action he played an important part.

ARCHAS

The highly exaggerated loyalty, greatness of soul, and somewhat ostentatious generosity of Archas are obvious Spanish traits[69] which have no prototype in Russian history, and, in the world of the Great Duke, he moves as an abstract, colorless, and unconvincing figure, without a Muscovite passport. Fletcher was far from a Russian context when he used the "piece of Seneca" as the symbol of Archas's public Roman virtue and stoic philosophy. This reference may simply be attributed to a show of literary respect to Seneca who, of all the ancient writers, exercised the most profound influence on the Elizabethan intelligence. The "poor gown" found in the trunk was used to contrast Archas's asceticism to Boroskie's greed.[70]

Yet his Seneca symbol cracks, and his system of sententious maxims collapses when Archas wishes that they had "encouraged" him for "one knock more."[71] Nor is the "poor gown" so stoically worn when he expresses his preference for the Court. For this historical and literary analysis he is of interest only as a generic type symbolizing the class of the old Muscovite boyars which Ivan IV wanted to destroy.[72] His banishment from the Court clearly parallels the historical information about the predicament of the boyars whom, as John Fletcher could read in his uncle's account, Ivan IV exiled to the distant corners of Muscovy.

BOROSKIE

In discussing the characters of Fletcher, W. J. Courthope mentions Boroskie, together with Bessus in *King and No King* and Protaldy in *Thierry and Theodoret,* among the type of coward or impostor in higher places.[73] Yet this Russian courtier, far from being a mere coward or impostor, vividly recalls the sinister memory of Ivan's *opričniki.*

The name he carries is a misnomer. Fletcher created it from the Russian word *sinaboiarskie,* or sons of gentlemen, as indicated by Dr. Fletcher. Yet the sources also mention that the Russian "soldiers are called sinaboiarskie and every soldier in Russia is a gentleman."[74] Since in the play the soldiers are honest while Boroskie is the opposite, we wonder why Fletcher chose this name for the leading *opričnik.* If we could postulate the Great Duke as Tsar Boris—which, as pointed out before, is hardly possible—it would be tempting to see in Boroskie the historical Vasilij Šujskij, the notorious intriguer. An allegro pronunciation of Boyar Šujskij could produce a sound close to Boroskie with the hushing "sh" of the first syllable of the proper name accommodating itself to the hissing "s" of the second.[75]

In his wickedness and baseness, he is the villain of the play and Brooke aptly indicates that "the verse shrieks and hisses" at the mention of his name.[76] In intriguing against Archas, he obviously implies the necessity for a strong, centralized authority in an absolute Prince—a Machiavellian trait. In his gross materialism he epitomizes the ruthless economic and political opportunism of the age. Yet the critics have continually overlooked that Boroskie is also a Senecan villain who takes pleasure in the physical suffering of his victims.

THEODORE

Theodore, the leader of the rebellion, is another of the protagonists not understood by the scholars.

This hero had a curious literary birth. His first midwives—

Dr. Fletcher and Horsey—failed this time to supply John Fletcher with enough details to give his child Russian authenticity, color, or costume, and merely hinted at the regrettable absence of a resistance fighter against the tyranny of the government. In looking for a prototype, Fletcher apparently decided to borrow from Lope's treasure house, and he chose Teodoro from *El Gran Duque de Moscovia,* who came close to his imagination, transforming the latter's trait of passive resistance into the rebellious nature of his own hero. Thus, Fletcher combined English and Spanish material to create this Colonel in the Russian army, and Theodore appears to be a synthesis of literary and historical sources.

In spite of his eloquence and bravery, a certain existential pessimism characterizes Theodore. Of all the protagonists he is the only one with a tragic vision of life as he sees values disintegrate, values which are close to his heart and which he would like to defend. He doubts whether his father's stoicism is a satisfactory solution to the everyday manifold problems of life.

In his efforts Theodore is often frustrated and then finds escape in cynicism, sarcasm, and ribaldry. He is a mixture of noble sentiments and coarse language, whose words and deeds show all the uncertainties—both the tentativeness and the overstatement—of a man caught between two worlds, the Renaissance and the Baroque.

The Dramatic Art of John Fletcher

THE *OPRIČNINA* OF IVAN THE TERRIBLE

Many interesting episodes of the play are connected with the activities of the Duke's guards at the Court and in the country. The description of these activities stems from the information about the notorious *opričnina* which Fletcher found in his main sources.

Horsey and Dr. Fletcher describe the motive for the establishment and the activities of the *opričnina* in similar fashion. Horsey first narrates Ivan's cruelties and adds

This crueltie bread such a generall hatred, distreccion, fear and discontentement thorow his kyngdom, that there wear many practices and devises how to distroy this tirant; but he still did discover their plotts and treasons, by inoiblinge and countenancinge all the rascalest and desperatt souldiers.[78]

Later Horsey indicates that Ivan lived in "great danger and fear of treasons" and spent "much tyme in examinacion, torteringe." His suspicion was directed especially against those "of his nobillitie of best credit and most beloved."[79]

Dr. Fletcher mentions that the Russian nobles were powerful before, but Ivan "beganne to clip of their greatness and to bring it downe to a lesser proportion" and

Hee deuided his subjectes into two partes. . . . The one part hee called the *Oppressini* [*opričniki*] or select men. These were such of the Nobilitie . . . as he tooke to his own part to protect . . . them as his faithful subjects. The other he called *Zemskey* or the commons. [They] conteyned . . . such Noblemen . . . as he meant to cut off as suspected to mislike his gouernment and . . . practice against him. Wherin he provided that the *Oppressini* for number and qualitie of valure, money, armour farre exceedeth . . . the *Zemskeys* whom he put . . . from under his protection; so that if any . . . were spoiled or killed by . . . the *Oppressini* . . . there was no amendes to be sought for by way of publike justice or by complaint to the Emperour.[80]

The reflection of this information is found in various scenes scattered through the play, and I will reproduce them under the following headings: 1. The presence of the *opričniki* at the Court, 2. The Duke's fear and the *opričniki's* spying, 3. Their false accusations, 4. Their robberies, and 5. Their cruelty.

1. Theodore tells Putskie, Archas's disguised brother that the political situation has changed (". . . hours are strangely alter'd") since the new men [*opričniki*] were installed at the Court. ("So many new-born flies his [the Duke's] light gave life to / Buzz in his beams, flesh flies and butterflies, / Hornets and humming scarabs . . ."). Using the swarm of flies as symbols of the *opričniki,* Fletcher hints at their irritating and vulture-like nature ("it must be very stinking flesh they will not seize on"), their insignificance to which only the Duke's favor gives importance, and their obscure origin such as the "scarabs" which come from the dung-heap. Let us notice that Fletcher again selected Horsey's information in preference to his uncle's in regard to the low origin of the *opričniki.*[81]

2. We hear Theodore tell Putskie of the Duke's fears of disloyalty in Archas and that he therefore "has too many eyes upon him . . . maintains too many instruments." Boroskie is such an instrument "ever in the duke's ear," as Theodore ironically comments to Archas "for your good." Later the Duke asks Boroskie, "Do you fear me for your enemy?" meaning Archas.[82] Thus, in

Boroskie and Archas we have the typical representatives of the *Oppressini* and *Zemskeys* of Fletcher's sources, and regard their clash as a reflection of the historical struggle between the old boyar class and the rising service gentry—the "new flies" in the play—created by Ivan the Terrible.

3. That the *opričniki* are informers and do not tell the truth we learn from Theodore's outburst to the Duke: ". . . I dare speak to ye / And dare speak truth, which none of their ambitions / That be informers to you, dare once think of." Archas refers to Boroskie as a worm "who crept into ye [the Duke] has abused ye." In a conversation with Boroskie, Theodore sarcastically tells him "I bring no tales nor flatteries; in my tongue, sir / I carry no fork'd stings . . . my tongue was never oil'd. . . ." Throughout the play Boroskie insinuates that Archas cannot be trusted and that he aims at the throne.[83]

What happens to a nobleman who falls into disgrace because of such false accusations? In Dr. Fletcher's account we find a description of one of the several means with which Ivan tried to destroy the nobles:

Some are put into Abbeys, and shire themselves Friers by pretence of a vow to be made voluntary, and of their owne accord, but indeede forced vnto it by feare vpon some pretended crime.[84]

In this play this is the origin of Archas's vow to retire and to become "devotion's souldier." We also find the explanation of the involuntary nature of Archas's vow at the time when Theodore, angry at the slight given to his father, declares that it will be repaid. Although Archas tells him "Understand . . . voluntary I sit down," Theodore remains unconvinced: "You are forced, sir, / Forced for your safety."[85]

4. Two scenes—the Duke's visit to Archas and the comments by Theodore and his friends on this visit—have to be read together since the latter, in the role of a Greek chorus, explain the significance of the former.

Thus, Theodore and his friends discuss the activities of the new men, still using insect imagery: they mention that ". . . not one honeybee, / That's loaden with true labour, and brings home / Increase and credit, can 'scape rifling; / And what she sucks for sweet, they turn to bitterness."[86]

The juxtaposition of the two scenes is helpful in understanding that what on the surface looks like a harmless visit to Archas's country house is, in reality, the reflection of an *oprič-*

nik's nocturnal raid, which was the favorite method of Ivan the Terrible to destroy his unwanted nobles. That the Duke is no mere guest paying a social visit to one of his nobles is revealed by his abrupt order to break into one of the rooms and disarm Archas. Also, the ordering of Archas's two daughters to the Court is a form of violent abduction of maids practiced by Ivan's *opričniki*. As pointed out before, Fletcher has been kinder to history than his sources and almost consistently tamed, veiled, and civilized the original material.

5. The invitation of Archas to a royal feast is, in reality, a peremptory order which cannot be disobeyed. That it is not a regular social invitation to the high officials of the state becomes evident when Putskie tells Theodore that the Duke "bids for guests all his . . . counsellors and . . . favorites," and Theodore realizes that something is wrong since his disgraced father is "neither in council nor in favour." Putskie's rejoinder only reinforces his suspicion: "That's it . . . they mean him no good."[87]

The reason for this "invitation" is Boroskie's accusation that Archas's aim is the throne. The Duke apparently believes the accusation, wants to punish Archas, asks Boroskie whether the old General "is sent for?" and, after the guests have assembled, in a sinister "aside" implying some impending evil act, inquires whether "all things are ready," to be then informed by Boroskie that "All the guards are set, / The court-gates shut." This state feast finds its prototype in Ivan's occasional orgies, to which he used to invite, along with his favorites, some of the nobles whom he wanted to punish.[88]

After the initial merriment at the banquet, the Duke distributes robes to let his guests "look nobly" and Archas is given "the robe of death," is seized by a guard, and dragged away to torture.[89]

Bond feels that the source for the black robe is Bandello's tale, in which the black cover of a scaffold is mentioned. However, there are more logical explanations. Bishop Fletcher, the playwright's father, officiated at the execution of Mary of Scotland in 1587, and, without any doubt, he spoke to his family about the solemn moment when Mary, dressed in black, ascended the sombre scaffold. Fletcher could also have found indications of the black color in his uncle's work, in which the latter describes the Muscovite Tsar's black guard and the black hood of the clergy. Most likely he learned about Ivan's ritual of distributing robes to his guests from oral sources. There were a number of diplomats, travelers, and merchants who visited Russia at the time, and Fletcher, curious to know more of the customs of this strange country, presumably discussed with these people various aspects of Russian life and found out this particular detail. I believe that Horsey may have been the oral source.

From whatever source Fletcher received his information, this incident reflects historical truth, since a later account by the German historian Samuel Treuer states that "Gebrauch in Russland, Kleider in Festlichkeiten auszutheilen. Basilides [Ivan IV] laesst denen, die er zum Tode bestimmt, schwartzsamtne Roecke geben."[90]

We have noticed Archas's initial shock to see, and reluctance to accept, the black gown. It is quite possible that Fletcher was acquainted with Ivan's custom of dancing in masks with his friends and distributing jester's kaftans to his invited guests. According to historical literature Prince Mixail Repnin, a conservative old boyar, refused to wear such a mask at one of Ivan's orgies and was later killed on the Tsar's order.[91] It seems that Fletcher was well acquainted with these details and that the picturesque realism with which the entire ritual of the royal banquet is described is due to this familiarity.

What artistic method did Fletcher use in describing the *opričniki*? He partly followed and partly reversed his sources. He followed them in the description of the *opričniki*'s activities, but changed their motivation. In his sources the *opričnina* is the result of the Machiavellian Ivan's hatred and mistrust of the traitorous nobility, while in the play the Duke appears innocent and the blame is put entirely on the *opričniki,* who "like a devil . . . possess the duke."[92]

That Fletcher had access to oral information is suggested by the ending of the banquet scene, in which we learn that Boroskie tortured Archas in spite of the Duke's order. There is nothing in his sources about the *opričniki*'s exceeding Ivan's command, yet later historical literature confirms this fact.[93]

Another interesting reversal occurs in the play relative to the use of the broom. One of the symbols of the *opričniki* was a broom, tied to the saddle of their horses as they were riding through the land, to show that they would sweep out treason from Russia. We would expect this symbol to be displayed by Boroskie or the guard to whom it naturally belongs. Yet the broom is mentioned and used rather by the band of unemployed soldiers of Theodore's group, the antagonists of Boroskie's *opričniki.* The broom is first indicated when the soldiers, slighted after the Tartar invasion, refuse their pay. Later the soldiers are selling the broom, but its symbolism is still reflected in the song of a soldier, "Will ye buy any honesty?" Thus, Fletcher did not change the allegorical meaning of the broom, but rather the hands that carry it. Obviously it did not make sense to him that the very people who ruin the land and the old nobility should carry an object associated, literally, with cleaning, and, figuratively, with honesty, and he logically transferred the symbol to the men who stood for traditional values and fought dishonesty. Nor is the presence of the *opričnik* Boroskie and his group on the stage incidental to this ritual. It is just to Boroskie and his followers that the Ancient wants to sell his broom, symbolically, to change their dishonesty, and the soldier's invitation to buy honesty is also addressed to them. Thus, when the perplexed Boroskie asks the Ancient why he sells brooms, the latter, acting as Fletcher's spokesman, answers: "The only reason is, / To sweep your lordship's conscience." The soldier also asks Boroskie: "Will your lordship buy any honesty?" and his reference to sell honesty "openly, by day" rather than by "forced light," or by "candle" may allude to the night raids of the *opričniki.*[94]

A final reference to the broom occurs when the Ancient meets Theodore at the Court and tells him that he left his "brooms at the gate here" and "the porter has stole 'em, to sweep out rascals." Then the Ancient goes on to explain that he has been "crying brooms all the town over," and he has made "such a mart . . . there's no trade near it." The sense of cleaning the whole country of the "many new-born flies" who are everywhere, and the enthusiastic response of the Russian population to participate in this purge, is clear.[95]

There are two more puzzling allusions in the play which may be related to the *opričniki.* The Ancient speaks about being "cramm'd up into favour like the worshipful," for the reason:

> That we may enjoy our lechery without grudging,
> And *mine* or *thine* be nothing, all things equal,
> And *catch* as *catch may* be proclaimed; that when we
>   borrow,
> And have no will to pay again, no law
> Lay hold upon us, nor no court control us.[96]

While in the second part of this passage John Fletcher clearly refers to the impunity of the *opričniki,* with which they may commit any unlawful act indicated by his uncle's pamphlet, I am not sure what he meant by the first. Could John Fletcher have had in mind the occasional religious fervor of Ivan the Terrible when, obsessed by the fear of God, he decided to turn his palace into a monastery and the savage *opričniki* into meek monks? Could the English playwright have meant the rituals of this strange brotherhood of the Tsar, which practiced religion?

Another allusion concerns Theodoro's satirical remark about the Duke's gift for Boroskie's "turning handsomely o' th' toe."[97] This may refer to Ivan's frequent orgies, in which handsome males entertained the terrible Tsar by dancing for him. Aleksej K. Tolstoj's historical novel *Knjaz' Serebrjanij* (translated as *A Prince of Outlaws*) describes Feodor Basmanov, an effeminate *opričnik* of great beauty, who danced in girls' costumes for Ivan the Terrible. These two allusions again point to the possibility of oral sources.

Let us finally add that the play is almost accurate in time regarding the fall of the *opričniki.* Because of the traits of three different Tsars blended into one, we cannot tell the exact date when the play takes place. However, there is one definite event in the play which is historically attested, i.e., the Tartar attack and the "anticipated" burning of Moscow in 1571. Boroskie's feigned illness in the play implies his incompetence to defend Moscow from the Tartars, and in historical literature it is assumed that one of the reasons for the dissolution of the *opričnina* was its obvious failure to ward off the Tartar invasion. In my historical interpretation, Boroskie's disgrace symbolizes the disintegration of the *opričnina,* which began about a year before, since already in 1570 such leading *opričniki* as Feodor and Aleksej Basmanov and Prince Afanasi Vjazemskij were executed.[98]

The play shows that the fall of Boroskie—the hated *opričnik* —created an entirely different emotional climate at the Court. It is as if the people around the Duke had been delivered from a nightmare and a long period of suffering has finally come to an end. We are witnessing an upsurge of national consciousness and pride, and an urgent patriotic sense of participation to help to restore social order. Burris tells the Duke that the whole Court is in arms, a curious phenomenon which contrasts strikingly with their previous indifferent and lewd attitude, and the people are ready to confront the rebels:

> Every man mad to go now: inspired strangely,[99]
> As if they were to force the enemy.

THE TARTAR INVASION

The description of the Tartar invasion stands out as an unforgettable picture of savage ruthlessness, with its merciless attack of burning and killing everything in its path. It is so fearful that not only man and beast, but also nature—rivers and forests—tremble and even cities sweat at its wild frenzy.

Fletcher's art did not invent, only improved, the vivid picture which his sources transmitted to him of the attack of Devlet Girei, Khan of the Crimean Tartars, on Moscow. Dr. Fletcher mentions that the Tartars

came as farre as the citie of Mosko. . . . The cities he took not but fired the suburbs which by reason of the buildinges (which is all of wood . . .) kindled so quickly and went on with such rage as that it consumed the greatest part of the citie . . . the huge and mightly flame of the citie all on light fire, people burning in their houses and streates. The Chrin [Crimean] thus having fired the citie and fedde his eyes with sight of it.[100]

Horsey dwells a little longer on the fate of the people, stressing "infinite thowsands men . . . burnt and smothered to death by the fierie eyre. People loaden with gold . . . verie fewe escapinge."[101]

Fletcher stresses the terror and force of the Tartars, who suddenly overrun the light garrisons at the border and swiftly advance, spreading panic all over Russia. We hear the Second Post report

> Fire and sword, gentlemen;
> The Tartar's up, and with a mighty force
> Comes forward, like a tempest; all before him
> Burning and killing.[102]

The nouns "fire and sword" and their verbal equivalents "to

burn and to kill" become the symbol of the Tartars and Fletcher uses them throughout the play. He occasionally complements them with the words "famine" and "wants" which are natural consequences of such a savage warfare. Horsey's "Crym was onward" and his description of the Tartar campaign "by sword, fier and famen" were obvious sources.

In referring to Tartars' violence in the past Burris refers to the "dangers . . . the wants and famines . . . the fires of heaven . . . death," while the Ancient warns Boroskie that the Tartars "burn and kill."[103]

The news of the wild Tartar attack spreads and Olympia's attendants run away with the cry, "The Tartar comes." Olympia's report further heightens the approaching danger: "The posts come hourly in, and bring new danger; / The enemy is past the Volga and bears hither, / With all the blood, and cruelty he carries." Fletcher, like Lope before him, made curious mistakes in geography. In order to accomplish their blitzkrieg against Moscovy, the Crimean Tartars obviously chose the most direct route and never crossed the Volga. Fletcher probably used Volga because both his uncle and Horsey mention it several times and call it a famous river. From the Duke's conversation with the Second Post we learn that the Tartars have already destroyed the forces of the Duke's lieutenant, and a feeling of immediate disaster hangs in the air. The Court can already smell the burning city and the chastised Duke, in a mellow, philosophical mood now, accepts that "we must die."[104]

Yet, in a curious reversal of his sources, Fletcher succeeds in bringing back Archas just in time to defeat the Tartars before they can reach Moscow. However, this is only a partial reversal, because, in a scene between Theodore and Boroskie, the former describes what would have happened if the Tartars had taken the city. "His [the Duke's] enemy that would have burnt his city . . . drunk dry your butteries . . . purloined your . . . plate . . . trimmed your virgins . . . your wife too . . . would have killed you too, and roasted ye, and eaten ye."[105]

It is interesting to point out that, in the description of the burning of Moscow, Fletcher's sources say nothing about murdering of people, plundering of the city, and raping of women, but the playwright has nevertheless included these "unhistorical" details in Theodore's imaginary flashback. Yet Fletcher had a source, although not that of the Tartars' burning of Moscow. I refer to Horsey's description of the pillage of Novgorod by

Ivan the Terrible, which reports "cruell slaughters," "ravizinge of weomen and mayeds, strippinge them naked," and the plunder of "goodlie persons cladd in velvett . . . with jewelles, gold and perell."[106] Why did Fletcher prefer this passage to the historical details of the burning of Moscow? The logical hypothesis would be that Fletcher found more cruelty in Ivan's sack of Novgorod and this detail artistically suited more his baroque taste.

In Archas's speeches we also find reflections of the Tartar warfare. He speaks of "fire and famine" when depositing his arms; later he refers to "grim Olin's . . . attack," which "made the city sweat" and drove before him "as a storm drives hail . . . showers of frosted fears" so that even "the Volga trembled at the terror." In saying farewell to his troops, Archas mentions "flame and fury" in obvious reference to previous wars with the Tartars.[107]

To indicate their fury, Fletcher models the army's assault against the palace on the Tartars' savagery and their "fire and sword" tactics. Having broken into the palace they demand the freeing of the General or they will "fire the court," . . . "smoke," . . . "and fry" the people at the Court. Theodore tells the Duke: "Ye see those torches; All shall to ashes," and Putskie shouts "Burn, kill, burn." The Ancient's phrase "We'll light you such a bonfire else" links this scene with the impending Tartar attack early in the play when he made a similar statement about the burning of Moscow.[108]

The ruthlessness of the Tartar attack is further stressed by the bloodshed it causes. Olympia refers to "all the blood . . ." the Tartars carry, and later in the play a Gentleman mentions that the rebels want to join "the bloody enemy."[109]

In Dr. Fletcher's description the Tartars look "fearse" and Archas refers to the "fierce" Tartar blood. To Horsey the Tartar ambassador seemed "grimly" and Fletcher logically portrayed Olin, the Tartar chieftain, after his ambassador, as "grim."[110]

The Demetrius Theme

The reflection of the Demetrius saga—hidden, but still probably recognizable in embryonic shape in the romantic subplot—seems the most fascinating aspect of the play.

That Fletcher knew of Demetrius in his double aspect, as the son of Ivan the Terrible and as the alleged Demetrius who appeared in Poland to claim the Russian crown, cannot be doubted. His main historical sources contain specific references to this historical figure. Fletcher also knew Lope's *El Gran Duque,* though in that play Demetrio appears as Teodoro's son and Basilio's (the historical Ivan the Terrible's) grandson. In addition, Fletcher must have heard of the fate of the alleged Demetrius from other sources as well, since this extraordinary figure was widely discussed in the capitals of Europe at the time. His exploits were published in numerous pamphlets. He was often compared to such similar historical personalities as Perkin Warbeck (1474-1499), whom the adherents of the York party had persuaded to pretend to the English throne, as well as to the several claimants who pretended to be Sebastian, King of Portugal, presumably killed in a battle against the Moors in Africa.

Moreover, the discussion of the political events in Russia, events which Dr. Fletcher witnessed personally, followed by others which involved the same historical figures, must have formed an almost daily concern of the Fletcher household, of which John Fletcher became a member after his father's death.

John Fletcher included in *The Loyal Subject* a simplified version of the initial phase of the Demetrius legend—the danger to the life of the young Prince and the measures taken to thwart such an attempt—and centered it around the figures of Alinda and Putskie. The masked figures of these two protagonists, the only two with an alias in the play, proved a stumbling block for all the critics, and the latter, unable to explain the presence of these two protagonists in the play, judged it an unnecessary and unartistic device by Fletcher to complicate the story.[111]

That the authentic Russian background was completely overlooked at first can best be seen by an adaptation of Fletcher's play, *The Faithful General,* written by a "young lady" in 1706.[112] The anonymous author wanted to improve Fletcher's drama, yet she left a great part of the play intact, except for the Russian material, which she mistook for Fletcher's otherwise customary pseudo-historical device, and dropped, as entirely unessential to the higher theme of honor, loyalty, and love. Thus, Fletcher's play is emasculated of its Muscovite reality, historical events, and personalities; the locale is transferred to a nebulous Byzantium, and the Duke becomes a nonexistent, nonhistorical Galerius, Emperor of an abstract "East." History entirely disappears to make room for composite love affairs. The Russian Burris, in Fletcher's play still recognizable to anyone with a minimum knowledge of Muscovite history, is sacrificed, and the realism of the savage Tartar attack is transmuted into an anemic Thracian invasion. Needless to say, the main protagonists of the Demetrius theme, Alinda and Putskie, are completely dropped, for the author, entirely unfamiliar with Russian history of the period, did not know what to do with them.

Unanimous critical condemnation of Fletcher's use of Alinda and Putskie once more underlines the inadequacy and superficiality of criticism of *The Loyal Subject,* which is perhaps Fletcher's most misunderstood play. Unfortunately, no critic has ever read this play with a history book in his hand, though without a sense of history it is unlikely that a correct solution of the identity of these two figures and their role in the play can be successfully achieved.

One of the most characteristic elements in Fletcher's plays is his fondness for mystification, with which he strives through disguise and mistaken identity to create a surprise ending. The key to the Demetrius theme is to be found in the unusual dénouement of the play, when it turns out that Alinda, who has served as Olympia's maid, is in reality Archas's younger son. As to the reason for young Archas's disguise, the reader must listen to Putskie's revelation; when asked by the astonished Duke, "Why was this boy conceal'd thus?" he replies

> Your grace's pardon: / Fearing the vow you made
>   against my brother
> And that your anger would not only light
> On him, but find out all his family
> This young boy, to preserve from after-danger,
> Like a young wench, hither I brought . . .
> The boy your grace took, nobly entertain'd him,
> But thought a girl—Alinda, madam.[113]

I believe that the direct source of this motif of disguise was Dr. Fletcher's pamphlet (although Demetrius is not mentioned by name in it), in which John Fletcher found the following reference to the danger surrounding the young Demetrius:

The Emperours younger brother of sixe or seuen years old . . . is kept in *a remote place* from Mosko vnder the tuition of his mother and hir kindred of the house of the Nagaies [Nagojs]: yet not safe (as I haue heard) from attempts of making away by practice of some that aspire to succession if this Emperour die without issue. The nurse that tasted before him of certaine meat (as I haue heard) died presently.[114]

Dr. Fletcher's statement is weakened by the introduction of hearsay evidence, but he followed Horsey, who also has a reference to this effect:

A prectice was discovered to poison and make away the yonge prince, the old Emperors third sonn, Demetreus, his mother and all his alliances, frendes, and famillies, narrowly guarded in *a remote place* at Ougletts.[115]

The italicized words show that Dr. Fletcher may have obtained the information from Horsey. A collation of historical sources proves that Demetrius became the subject of important discussions in Moscow during Tsar Feodor's reign, when it seemed that this weak ruler would not have any offspring and that Boris Godunov, as early as 1588-89, was suspected of attempting to poison Demetrius.

Fletcher transformed the information obtained from his sources, so that it is not a royal person whose life is in jeopardy but the son of the highest ranking officer in the country; he made it logical by justifying the device of disguise for reasons of safety. Although it is unthinkable that Archas, the loyal subject, would ever have aspired to the throne, it is quite possible that the army, resenting the evil influence of the new men at the Court, might have overthrown the weak Duke, put the popular Archas on the throne, or in case of his refusal, his universally liked "nobler" son. The possibility of such a revolt is clearly indicated in Dr. Fletcher's treatise

And this wicked pollicy (though now it be ceased) hath so troubled that countrey and filled it so full of grudge and mortall hatred euer since, that it wil not be quenched (as it seemeth now) till it burne againe into a ciuill flame.[116]

Presumably Fletcher discussed various aspects of the Demetrius affair with his uncle in the "fireside chat" of their family, with Horsey, and with other English travelers to Russia, and learned that the entire family of the Nagojs, the uncles and cousins of Prince Demetrius, were uprooted and punished. Thus, as a reflection of such information, we find in *The Loyal Subject* that every member of the Archas family, which in Fletcher's play corresponds vaguely to the Nagojs, is in constant danger.[117]

In his book *Fletcher, Beaumont and Company*, Lawrence B.

Wallis mentions that "our playwrights . . . normally avoided 'whole meaning,' that is, full illustration of a theme in the structure and characterization of a play."[118] In *The Loyal Subject* Fletcher unquestionably mystified the spectators and misled the critics. He concentrated on young Archas's disguise, and made him the axis of the subplot as well as the important connection between the main plot and the subplot. Only a careful critical approach could have discovered that there was a more profound hidden meaning in the device of disguise than a mere romance between the general's son and the duke's sister.

It must be admitted that the correct identification of Alinda is a difficult task since it is complicated by a double mask, which the English dramatist made his hero wear. The outer mask is the somewhat usual male-female disguise, but the inner mask, it seems to me, is the entirely unique young Archas-Demetrius disguise. Accordingly there are two sets of hints and innuendoes concerning the double puzzle, and it is quite obvious that Fletcher has consciously provided suggestions for the solution of the outer mask as he did, for example, in *A King and No King,* another of his plays. Yet how about the inner mask? Can we attribute to the selective contemporary audience of courtiers, lawyers, bankers and rich merchants—prepared to solve riddles and disguises by Boccaccio, Bandello, and Painter—the ability to perceive the presence of hidden allegories and vague clues concerning an episode from the complex history of a foreign nation which was recently discovered by England? Yet several scholars think highly of the intelligence of the Stuart audience. According to Swinburne this audience was capable of enjoying the "subtlest and most sustained allusions of ethical or political symbolism," and Ornstein credits the sophisticated Jacobeans "with an ability to discern obscure allegories and allusions."[119] Unfortunately, there is no evidence that anyone in the audience of the time plumbed this hidden device. I cannot even be sure whether Fletcher intended the inclusion of this Demetrius fragment to excite the curiosity of his spectators, or whether this episode was only the unconscious reflex of a sensitive dramatist, who, accustomed to listening so often to the events of Russian history at the end of the sixteenth century, could not help utilizing motifs from this fascinating tale. The presence of the Demetrius episode in *The Loyal Subject* might even owe its origin to the appeal by George Wilkins, Fletcher's fellow dramatist, who, comparing the tragic fate of the Godunovs to Hamlet's, asked the poets of his age to dramatize the Godunov-Demetrius subject.[120]

One set of suggestions in *The Loyal Subject* concerns the sex disguise. Although Fletcher carefully conceals the identity of Alinda, there are enough indications for the alert spectator to feel, if not actually to know, that there is something hidden from him, that he must not accept everything at face value and must be sensitive to possible revelations.

We have no reason to suspect Alinda's identity when she is first introduced. Her modesty and loyalty win Olympia's approval, and her beauty arouses the Duke's sensuousness. Yet Petesca and the Gentlewoman, the envious attendants of the Princess, are quick to point out that she has "a manly body" and looks as "though she would pitch the bar." Later, amazed at her courage, Olympia asks, "How com'st thou by this spirit? Our sex tremble." Grateful for Alinda's advice to call Archas to fight the Tartars, Olympia wishes that Alinda "wert a man," another of Fletcher's curious anticipations of the truth.[121]

Another suggestion may be found in the Duke's attempt to seduce Alinda. It is a boisterously comic interlude, and those in the audience who by this time understood the sex disguise must have enjoyed the scene enormously. Rebuffing the Duke's advances, Alinda innocently asks him: "What would ye do?" and, upon the answer of the Duke, who is surprised at the naïveté of this question, "Why, I would lie with ye," she retorts with perfect aplomb: "I do not think ye would."[122]

Still another suggestion is contained in the pivotal second scene of the fifth act, which is really a prologue to the final revelation, when young Archas, for the first time "in his own dress," visits the Princess pretending to inquire about his sister, and Olympia, in an aside, remarks that "two silver drops of dew were never liker," and tries to detain him in order "to read that face again . . . Alinda in that shape." Thus, for the intelligent spectator who understood some of these hints, the final revelation that Alinda is young Archas might not have come as a complete surprise.[123]

It is much more difficult, however, to unravel the inner riddle, since the set of innuendoes appears to be vague and inconclusive. Yet, if the interpreter of this play applies the right analytical tools—i.e., the proper sources of the play, a detailed study of the life of the alleged Demetrius, and a sense of history—the seemingly pointless innuendoes and suggestions may be con-

structively filled with meaning. In addition to the accounts of
Dr. Fletcher and Horsey, I find the first and second acts of
Lope's *El Gran Duque* to be an ideal key for this decoding oper-
ation. These two acts, as we recall, treat in detail the danger
to Demetrio's life, the assassination attempt, and the wandering
and hiding of this Russian Prince. Especially important is that
Lope and Fletcher both stress the danger not only to Demetrio
but also to Demetrio's father.

Like Demetrio in the Palatine's castle in Lope's *comedia,*
Alinda is also a servant in the Duke's palace. Like Margarita,
who, impressed with Demetrio, does not know whether to stay
or to go, Olympia is also impressed with Alinda at first sight:
"Something there was, when I first look'd upon thee, / Made
me both like and love thee."[124] Eager to discover her identity,
Olympia asks Alinda several questions, and this episode appears
to be in some respects a counterpart of the confrontation between Boris and the monk Demetrio in Lope's play.

One of the first questions Olympia asks Alinda is whether
she ever served in a "place of worth." We recall that Boris,
equally struck by the dignified appearance of Demetrio among
the monks, asks him whether he is a nobleman. The equivalence
of the English "value" and the Spanish "valor" in both their
literal and figurative sense needs no further comment.[125]

Asked about her age, Alinda, instead of answering directly,
gives a poetic description of her origin, linking it with Olympia's
birth:

> My mother oft has told me,
> That very day and hour this land was bless'd
> With your most happy birth, I first saluted
> This world's fair light. Nature was then so busy,
> And all the Graces, to adorn your goodness,
> I stole into the world poor and neglected.[126]

We must note the contrast between the happiness with which
Russia has been blessed at the Princess's birth and the lack of
fanfare which accompanied Alinda's modest beginning, since a
comparison between this passage and Demetrio's reply to Boris's
question in Lope's play reveals interesting resemblances. Aside
from references to the mother of Demetrio-Alinda in both plays,
Demetrio's answer is essentially a contrast between his life and
that of Boris similar to the contrast in Fletcher's play between

the births of Alinda and the Princess. The endings of the respective scenes in both plays are also similar.

Even more revealing is a conversation between the Duke and Alinda, in the course of which she speaks of herself as "a thing of no regard, no name, no lustre."[127] The idea conveyed by the monk Demetrio's cryptic answer to Boris in Lope's play is similar. Furthermore, Alinda's quizzical answer to Olympia's questions and her manifest reticence at the time of her introduction recalls Lamberto's warning to Demetrio to be cautious in the world and not to reveal himself.

Alinda often mentions that she is a "stranger," and speaks of her "grief," "fear," and "woful experience." In the general context of the Demetrius legend all these words are meaningful and can be creatively related to exactly that phase of Demetrius's life which we are seeking to reconstruct in Fletcher's play, i.e., his wandering and his hiding. The fugitive Demetrius, wandering over unknown lands, is obviously a stranger. In Lope's play we see him in the monastery, the Livonian countryside, and the Palatine kitchen. In each of these he is a stranger, hiding most of the time in disguise. In Lope's play Demetrio complains of "grief" and "pain" which he must endure in this "fugitive life," and these expressions may also be related to Alinda's description of her life. The "fear" and "woful experience" might find their source in the catastrophe at Uglič, which Lope described at the end of the first act of his play.[128]

At the time of her introduction we also find out that Alinda's father is a "good gentleman, but far off dwelling." The indication that he lives far away from the Court is an obvious paraphrase of the "remote place," Uglič, which occurs in the accounts of both Dr. Fletcher and Horsey. The reference to a "good gentleman," clearly the opposite of the "bold bad men" with which Archas characterizes the *opričniki,* may point to a victim of the latter, since these nobles were dislodged from their places near Moscow and resettled in distant regions of the country.[129]

In her statement to Olympia, at the time of the Tartar invasion, that she is "not unacquainted with these dangers"[130] we have a double-entendre, neither meaning of which is easy of interpretation. If and when we know that Alinda is a boy and Archas's son, we can understand that, in spite of his youth, Archas might have taken him along on one of his campaigns against the Tartars. In the context of the Demetrius legend, however, the hint of dangers would obviously refer to the numerous attempts to assassinate him.

Alinda refers to her "truth" twice in the play. In the first instance she uses the word in connection with her defense of the Princess at the time of the Tartar invasion ("you shall know my truth"), suggesting her courage, loyalty and constancy, all of which are qualities of a noble knight to his lady in danger. I believe that, in this case, Fletcher translated the Spanish "verdad" (truth) and used it in the sense of an ideal Platonic truth, i.e., something which is hidden from the eye of a superficial observer. This is exactly how Lope uses the term when Demetrio assures Lamberto and his family that he wants "to honor his truth" ("honrar mi verdad"), i.e., to doff his disguise and to become what he really is: the legitimate emperor of Russia. To reinforce this argument I mention that when Olympia dismisses Alinda, the latter rebukes the Duke for having "kill'd my truth," suggesting that now that "she" is dismissed, "she" will not be able to prove her identity to Olympia.[131]

This last episode connects Fletcher's Alinda to Lope's Demetrio in still another way. After her dismissal Alinda tells Olympia that she has "no being now, no friends, no country," and that she will now "wander Heaven knows whither, Heaven knows how," for she has "no life." Later she asks the Duke, "Oh, whither shall I go?" and calls herself "poor and lost." This mood of despair at the ebb of her fortune is an exact parallel of Demetrio's life when the latter, at the death of Lamberto, finds himself abandoned, and does not know what to do or where to go.[132]

The jealousy of Olympia's attendants and the Princess's doubts about Alinda's honesty in *The Loyal Subject* conform, in the scale of a different moral sensibility, to the envy with which the possibility of Demetrio's accession to the throne was regarded as well as to the doubts concerning his true identity.[133]

With the introduction and interpretation of the role of Putskie, I will finally be able to remove the inner mask from Fletcher's Alinda alias young Archas. Obviously, the mysterious Putskie with his manifold roles in the play, captain in the army in disguise, protector of Alinda, fomentor of revolts, and Archas's brother, is a key personage, and his identification in the sources of the play, in history, and in the play itself is imperative. Putskie is never mentioned in any of Fletcher's sources. However, we find numerous references in the accounts of Horsey and Smithe to a certain "Bodan Baelscoie," who, under his correct name—Bogdan Jakovlevič Belskij—is an important historical figure during the reigns of Ivan the Terrible, Tsar Feodor, and Tsar Boris. He even plays a significant role at the inauguration of the alleged Demetrius in 1605.

On the birth of Tsarevich Demetrius in 1583 Belskij became his guardian. According to Horsey's testimony, when Sir Jerome Bowes, Elizabeth's ambassador to Ivan the Terrible in 1583, demanded that in case of Ivan's marriage with an English noblewoman, the future children of this union should inherit the Muscovite throne in preference to Feodor and Demetrius, the English diplomat clashed with Belskij, who sought to uphold Demetrius's right to the throne.

After the death of Ivan the Terrible, Horsey narrates that

Bodan Belskoie, the chieff favorett and mynion to the old Emperour was now sent to a castell and town remott Cazan in displeasur as a man feared to be a conspirator and sower of sedicion between the nobillitie and this tyme of discontentment.[134]

Belskij's banishment was owing to his attempt, after Ivan's death, to put young Demetrius on the throne in defiance of Feodor's claim, since in case young Demetrius should become the Tsar, he would rule as the latter's guardian. Horsey also informs us that, before Feodor's coronation, there was "some tumult . . . among some of the nobilitie and communaltie," and later that "Charewich Demetrie . . . of one yeres age" was banished to "a Towne called Owglets." There is evidently some connection between these events and Boris Godunov's confidential information to Horsey "of many strainge accidents and alteracions . . . praectices between the Emporis mother to Chariwich Demetrius, her kyndred."[135]

Our next information about Belskij's activities after his banishment comes from the Smith account, which tells us that Andrej Ščelkalov and Andrej Klešnin, two friends of Belskij, remained in touch with Belskij after the latter had been banished, and kept him informed about Boris Godunov's movement.

Bodan (knowing the ambitious-thirst of Borris to extirpate the race of Evan Vassilewich) took deliberation with the old Empresse (mother to Demetre) for the preservation of the child. And seeing a farre off arrowes aimed at his life, which could very hardly be kept off, it was devised to

exchange Demetre for the child of a churchman (in yeares and proportion somewhat resembling him) might live safe though obscure.[136]

Shortly afterward, this "counterfet churchmans sonne being then
taken for the lauful prince" was killed. Yet, as the account adds,

. . . heaven protected the lawfull. . . . Obscurely lived this wronged
prince, the changing of him being made private to none but his own
mother . . . and to Bodan Belskey.[137]

After Tsar Feodor's death and the coronation of Tsar Boris,
we again hear of Belskij. The sources do not indicate, but obviously he made an unauthorized return to Moscow. Horsey
now relates his importance and Godunov's fear of him, which
may be related to Godunov's suspicion that Belskij had saved
Demetrius and was hiding him somewhere.

Bodan Baelscoie, the great favorett . . . to that great Emperour Ivan.
. . . Noen so famillier nor inward, noen so powerfull nor better able
to achive or bringe to pass the subverscion of his greatest enimies. . . .
This Emperor [Boris Godunov] stode in fear of his suttel worckinge
will; found means and many fained occasions to be ridd of his presenc;
placed him and his confederates farr off and saffe enough, as they
thought. . . . Yet the infinit treasur and mass of monyes which he had
gotten . . . served him in such good stead [that he] now escaped joininge
with many discontented nobles . . . [in Poland].[138]

Horsey goes on to relate how Belskij succeeded in stirring up
the Polish King, the great Palatines, and the Princes of Lithu-
ania on Demetrius's behalf and, returning to Russia, Belskij

gave out that they brought the pleasinge tidings unto them for their
redempcion, the right and true heir to the crown and kingdom, Demetrius . . . whoe miraculously . . . was preserved alive.[139]

In *The Loyal Subject* the role of Bielskij is assumed by Putskie, whose real name is Briskie. There is a definite resemblance
between the two names in view of the similar-sounding liquid
consonants of "l" and "r." It is interesting that in the Demetrius
drama of Aleksandr N. Ostrovskij, whose faithful reproduction
of the contemporary local color and idiom was admired by the
historian Kostomarov, the word "ryčarstvo" (knighthood) is
pronounced as "lyčarstvo" and in Aleksej S. Suvorin's Demetrius play one of the protagonists mentions that, while in London, he saw a play entitled King "Ličard."[140] We may thus

assume that in substandard Russian of the sixteenth and seventeenth centuries the two liquids were easily interchanged. Therefore, a rapid pronunciation of Belskij with metathesis of the
liquid "l" could have produced Briskie, which name, in certain
editions of Fletcher's works, is also spelled as Briski. In the
first act we hear of Putskie (alias Briskie), who recently arrived
in Moscow and joined the army. Theodore calls him a "stranger," not recognizing him in this disguise. Putskie presumably
assumed this mask for safety's sake, since he felt himself in
danger. This may well correspond to the secret movements of
the historical Belskij, who was banished but escaped from his
exile. Theodore assures him that the Princess has accepted his
protegée, who turns out to be Alinda. In the meantime Putskie
serves in the army to remain near "her," and the play supplies
us with proof of their close contact when we see them together
discussing the coming of Honora and Viola to the Court. The
final revelation of his protecting role over Alinda—now called
young Archas—comes in the surprise ending of the play when
Archas, ready to kill Theodore, silences the Duke's protest that
Archas has no more son to inherit his name:

> Yes, sir, I have another and a nobler; . . . Young Archas,
> A boy as sweet as young; my brother breeds him,
> My noble brother Briskie breeds him nobly:
> Let him your favour find, give him your honour.[141]

At this point Briskie appears, for the first time without disguise, and tells the story of hiding the young boy under the
disguise of a maid while he himself stayed near by to be "still
. . . ready to all fortunes," presumably to continue to protect
young Archas in case of further danger.[142]

Horsey stresses the close ties between Belskij and Demetrius
and, in one passage in the Smith account, their names are even
mixed up. According to the Smith account, "There appeared a
certain person who called himself Dmitrij Ivanovič Belij, son of
the former Tsar Ivan Vasilevič, believed to have died in Uglič."
Boldakov, the translator of this work, mentions the name in the
original English spelling as Demetre Evanowich Beola and, over-
looking the fact that Beola is a corruption of Belskij's name,
assumes that it is mistakenly used for Demetrius and adds in a
footnote that "there is no evidence that Tsarevich Demetrius
had such a name."[143]

Why does Putskie appear as Alinda's uncle in *The Loyal Subject,* when the historical Belskij was not a relative of Tsarevich Demetrius?

In a letter to Lord Burghley on June 10, 1591, Horsey wrote from Jaroslavl that on May 19

a most unfortunate chaunce befell the younge prince of ix yers adge, son unto the old Emperor. . . . [He] was cruelly . . . murdered his throate cutt in the presence of his dere mother . . . ; with other such lyke prodigious matter which I dare not wryte of.[144]

Horsey received the information from his friend Afanasij Nagoj, who visited him on the night of May 20 and asked for "some good things" to heal Maria Nagoj, Demetrius's mother, who was poisoned at the time of the murder. After Horsey gave him some kind of medicine, Afanasij Nagoj hurried away.

We know that Demetrius was "killed" on May 15 and not on May 19, 1591. Afanasij Nagoj was in Uglič on May 15, yet when the Šujskij commission arrived a few days later to investigate the catastrophe, he was no longer there. Since the distance between Uglič and Jaroslavl is about seventy miles, Nagoj could have reached Jaroslavl in several hours after the alleged murder of Tsarevich Demetrius. Yet he only arrived in Jaroslavl on the night of May 20, although he must have been in great haste to ask Horsey for the medicine. Thus, we must ask where this uncle of Tsarevich Demetrius was between May 15 and May 20.

At this point it is appropriate to recall, and elaborate on, the hypothesis of A. S. Suvorin, editor of the newspaper *Novoe Vremja* and a dilettante historian and playwright, concerning the events which took place in Uglič.[145]

In Suvorin's hypothesis Demetrius had an epileptic fit in Uglič on May 15, 1591. He cut himself on the knife he was playing with, lay motionless, and appeared to be dead, but was not really dead. His uncles took advantage of the occasion to settle accounts with the Bitjagovskij clique, and the enraged population killed the enemies of their beloved Tsarevich. Demetrius regained consciousness, and the Nagojs were faced with their responsibility for having incited a massacre. They could not admit that Demetrius did not die and therefore decided to spirit him away. Afanasij Nagoj took Demetrius to Yaroslavl in a boat on the Volga and hid him somewhere. Suvorin believes that it took Nagoj several days to reach Jaroslavl because he was traveling with the utmost caution in order to find a hiding place for the Tsarevich, and his nocturnal visit must also have been due to his desire to maintain secrecy about his movements. In addition, Suvorin holds that the medicine Nagoj requested from Horsey was not intended for Demetrius's mother, but for Demetrius himself.

According to Suvorin, Horsey knew the truth about the events in Uglič, but was afraid to tell the whole story at the time, and his letter to Burghley was deceiving. In Suvorin's view, Horsey was familiar with Boris's plan to eliminate Demetrius and with his frustration because of the events in Uglič and of the possibility of Demetrius's escape from his clutches. Why, Suvorin asks, did Boris punish the people of Uglič so severely? If Demetrius had died, Boris's purpose was attained, and he could have afforded to be generous to the inhabitants of Uglič, who killed Bitjagovskij and his companions. The reason for the unusual severity of the punishment was that Boris suspected that Demetrius had escaped and that many people of Uglič might have known about his escape, and he wanted to get rid of such potentially dangerous witnesses. Suvorin feels that Horsey was also, in one way or another, involved in the Uglič affair, and the strange contradictions concerning his departure from Moscow seem to reinforce this hypothesis. On the one hand, in the letter which Horsey carried from Tsar Feodor to Queen Elizabeth, he was called a rascal and criminal who would deserve death for his deeds, yet there is no indication in the letter what those deeds were. Suvorin thinks that this letter was written to discredit the trustworthiness of Horsey in London and Moscow. On the other hand, Boris offered the departing Horsey a large sum of money and exerted his influence in favor of a trade treaty with England. Thus, Suvorin comes to the conclusion that, since Horsey was an undesirable witness of the Uglič affair, the Russian government resolved to buy his silence and, at the same time, to declare him a *persona non grata* by blackening his reputation, in case Horsey decided to tell his story. Suvorin ends his speculation with the presumption that Horsey never revealed his indirect participation in the events of Uglič and took some important secrets of his time into the grave.

I wish to add to Suvorin's interesting hypothesis that it is most probable that Horsey did not take his secret into the grave. I believe that Horsey gave John Fletcher the information about the *opričniki* of Ivan the Terrible and other details relative to the Russian Time of Troubles. It is difficult to believe that in his conversation with Horsey, the curious John Fletcher, so sensitive to the temper of his time, would not have asked what those "other . . . lyke prodigious matters" were that Horsey did not care to "wryte about." In my opinion Horsey told John Fletcher the story of the Uglič affair and consequently the playwright must have known more of this particular phase of Russian history than most are willing to assume.

John Fletcher used Horsey's information in the same cautious or even unconscious manner which characterized his treatment of much of the Russian material in *The Loyal Subject*. In the person of Putskie, the English playwright synthesized two distinct historical personalities, Bogdan Belskij, Demetrius's guardian, and Afanasij Nagoj, Demetrius's uncle, both of whom were supposed, according to tradition and speculation, to have played an important part in the saving of Tsarevich Demetrius. Hence it is clear why in the play Putskie turns out to be young Archas's uncle.

This apparent use of the Demetrius theme in Fletcher's *The Loyal Subject,* together with the interpretation of the historical figures, would justify my claim that it is not a tragicomedy, but a historical play. Fletcher's treatment is rather brief and the allusions are vague, robbing the theme of much of its vitality and historical reference. However, even if *The Loyal Subject* gives us only a skeleton of the Demetrius legend, it still draws for us the essential life of the period, not because of what it describes but because of what it incorporates.

Can we explain the relative thinness, looseness, and vagueness of the Demetrius theme in the play and the reasons that Fletcher could not write a Demetrius drama à la Lope? It is possible to suppose that Fletcher originally and much earlier—perhaps even during the ephemeral reign of Demetrius—had a fuller treatment in mind; then such unclarified expressions of Alinda as her "grief," "pain," and "woful experience," as well as her cryptic answers, were previously better motivated and explained. Yet as time went on and the events began to lose their romantic glow, it must have become apparent to Fletcher, the son of a Protestant minister, that the Pretender to the Russian throne was an impostor. Therefore, while Lope had a powerful religious reason to exalt his Demetrio, the Protestant Fletcher, who came to dislike the Catholic Gondomar, the Spanish ambassador, and his clique at James's Court,[146] could have no desire to glorify the protegé of the Catholic world. Thus, he may have changed his original intention and declined to produce a play in which a guilty Godunov and an impostor Demetrius would have shared the dramatic spotlight. Even more important, a play which would have included the murder of the lawful sovereign might have been interpreted in England as an attack on the legitimacy of the reigning king, James I, who was becoming more and more unpopular at the time. Thus, Fletcher may have changed his initial project completely and lopped off the foliage of his tree so that only a few sturdy bare branches survived. The original manuscript of *The Loyal Subject* was lost and the play was first published in the so-called First Folio of the Works of Beaumont and Fletcher only in 1647, twenty-two years after Fletcher's death, and it is impossible to tell how true this edition was. That *The Loyal Subject* may have included some politically dangerous material in its first performance is quite possible since, at its revival in 1633, the play was licensed only after "some reformation," according to Sir Henry Herbert's Office Book. What the extent of the revision was is not known, but it is possible to assume from this veiled allusion that by purifying the play from some topical references the cautious Herbert wanted to render it more palatable to royal taste. Indeed, when the play was revived "it was well likt" by the King and the Queen, according to Malone.[147] This King, Charles I (1625-49), actually concerned himself with censorship of dramas, and it was Herbert's view that old plays should be resubmitted to him "since they may be full of offensive things against church and state; ye rather that in former time the poetts tooke greater liberty than is allowed them by mee."[148]

Even the temper of the period may have contributed to this surgical intervention. There was a flurry of political and diplomatic events and trade interests between the two countries at the time.[149] England helped Russia in her internal and external difficulties. English and Scottish mercenaries fought on Russia's side against foreign intervention and, in 1617, England arranged a peace between Russia and Sweden. The Russia Company of English merchants was still doing a lucrative trade, although the Dutch were beginning to oust them from their privileged position and, in 1618, the year when *The Loyal Subject* was first performed, a Russian embassy came to London to negotiate a loan for Russia. This was hardly the atmosphere in which the highly unflattering events of the recent history of a friendly nation—a gruesome story of political murder, Machiavellian intrigue for succession, and the coronation of an impostor—could be displayed on the stage.

The general impression that a reader gets from *The Loyal Subject* is that Fletcher has made a conscious effort to avoid being involved in the rapidly changing currents of contemporary history. It is true that he disregarded this maxim in the case of *The Tragedy of Sir John Van Olden Barnavelt* (1619), but the result was disastrous, and the extent of Fletcher's share in that venture is still not known. Thus, Fletcher, like the historical Burris in his play, was prudent enough to temporize and to wait for a more promising and calmer political climate, which, however, did not come in his lifetime.

That Fletcher, well acquainted with various details of Russian history and of Demetrius's life, was planning to write a play with a Russian subject, and most likely on the Demetrius theme which was so popular at the time, may be seen by a review of his plays. The title of his *A King and No King* (1611) may owe its origin to Fletcher's interest in the dual role of the Russian Demetrius. The protagonist of the play, Arbaces, is a figure, like the Muscovite Duke in *The Loyal Subject,* composed of contradictory elements: he is generous and corrupt, glorious and humble, and wise and foolish. In his Prologue to *The Faithful Shepherdess* (1608) Fletcher mentions a "Poor mountain Muscovite, congeal'd with cold"; in *Valentinian* (1610-1614) he refers to the Volga; and in *The Humorous Lieutenant* (1619) he speaks of "arrows from a Tartar's bow" and "weapon hatch'd in blood." It would seem as if Fletcher were unconsciously trying out a chord of a future, yet unfinished, theme to hear how it would sound. A curious example of this artistic practice may be seen in a geographical reference in *The Loyal Subject* to the Moluccas Islands. What possible connection can this tropical island, recently discovered by the Portuguese in East Indonesia, have with a Russian theme? Can it be believed that Fletcher used this reference constructively, within the framework of the play, assuming that people of the Russian Court in the sixteenth century knew of the richness of the far-away, exotic Moluccas? A possible explanation is that even while writing *The Loyal Subject*, Fletcher was already looking ahead toward a future play, for in a year or two he indeed wrote *The Island Princess,* which takes place in those very islands.

Another indication may be found in Fletcher's leaving the

main personalities in *The Loyal Subject* without proper identification and historical names. A Demetrius play usually pits an alleged Demetrius and a wicked Godunov against each other. Would this have been possible for Fletcher in a future Demetrius drama, after he had depicted Boris as a paragon of honesty in *The Loyal Subject?* In addition to reversing Boris's character —an artistic suicide—he would have had to make another *volteface* in the portrayal of Ivan the Terrible. In a historical play he could not have completely ignored the information of his sources and disregarded Ivan's cruelty. However, if this hypothesis is correct, Fletcher obviously sidestepped the issue by leaving the Great Duke unnamed. Finally, he may have masked the historical Demetrius under a double alias precisely in order to prevent the proper identification of his hero.

In connection with *The Humorous Lieutenant,* one of Fletcher's tragicomedies, F. E. Schelling mentions that "A tragedy called *Demetrius and Marsina or The Imperial Impostor and the Unhappy Heroine* was among the manuscripts of Warburton, but not destroyed. What has become of it I do not know, nor whether it concerns any historical Demetrius."[150] Since one of the heroes of *The Humorous Lieutenant* is Demetrius (c. 337-283 B.C.), king of ancient Macedon, Schelling presumably thought that the title hero of the manuscript might be identified with the Macedonian Demetrius. Schelling may be forgiven for his ignorance of Russian history, but the manuscript he is referring to is undoubtedly a dramatic representation of the Demetrius legend. Marsina is obviously the historical Marina Mniszek, wife of the alleged Demetrius, and the title description of the respective roles of the heroes makes the assumption completely clear. The title recalls a popular historical pamphlet, *The Russian Impostor; or The history of Muscovie, under the Usurpation of Boris and the Imposture of Demetrius, the late Emperors of Muscovy,* written by Sir Roger Manley in 1674.

Unfortunately, the manuscript cannot be found. According to W. W. Gregg, an English scholar, a certain J. Haslewood appended an extract from the catalogue of the Warburton's sales in November, 1759, to Bridges's *Censura Literaria,* in which Massinger's *The Tyrant* was included, but another manuscript entitled *Demetrius and Marina (or Marsina) or the Imperial Impostor and the Unhappy Heroine* was not. Concerning this manuscript Fr. G. Fleay, a biographer of English drama, states: "One of Warburton's manuscripts not destroyed." E. H. Oliphant, a researcher in the authorship of Elizabethan dramas, declares that he is ignorant whether the play is extant or destroyed. Finally, Gertrude M. Sibley, an American scholar, mentions that "apparently it is lost."[151]

I have no idea who wrote this tragedy and, to my knowledge, no one has ever made any conjecture about the author, the subject matter, or the date of the manuscript. I may only hazard the guess that the tragedy remained in manuscript because of the political intolerance of the time. It is revealing to note the fate of some of the dramas on foreign political subjects which were written and performed during this period. *The Tragedy of Sir John Van Olden Barnavelt* (1619), describing the trial and execution of the great Dutch statesman who played a leading part in the joint struggle of England and the Netherlands against Spain, had great difficulty in passing the censorship. A number of long passages were eliminated and many words and phrases were altered, including what seemed like an allusion to the recent execution of Sir Walter Raleigh. The play had a great success on the stage, but it was soon forbidden and remained in manuscript until 1883 when it was discovered. Fletcher wrote this play with Philip Massinger, who was always keenly interested in the foreign policy of the Stuarts. Thomas Middleton's *A Game of Chesse* (1624), an allegorical play concerning the Spanish political intrigue in England and lampooning the nefarious role of Gondomar, was suppressed and the actors jailed. Massinger's *Believe as You List* (1630), treating the story of Sebastian and the pretenders to the throne of Portugal, was refused license because "it did contain dangerous matters, as the deposing of Sebastian, King of Portugal, by Philip II, and there being a peace sworn 'twixt the Kings of England and Spain."[152] The story of the Portuguese pretenders was quite old in 1630, but it was precisely the kind of political dynamite which the cautious Charles I would not want to display prominently on the stage at the time when he had achieved a highly unpopular peace with Spain. Massinger had to rewrite the play completely in order to appease the royal censor, and, in Schelling's words, the new play presents a "striking example of the practice of a transfer of events from the scene to which they actually refer to one in which reference is unmistakable but the disguise is sufficient to relieve the poet and players of attendant pains and penalties."[153] Still another play of Massinger's, *The King and Subject,* incurred the wrath of the English monarch. Charles I was outraged when he read the manuscript of the play and, according to W. Gifford, an English scholar, he "set his marke upon the place with his own hands, and in these words: 'This is too insolent, and to bee changed!" The offensive passage concerns raising money for King Pedro of Spain.[154] Massinger had to rework this play, too, under the new title of *The Tyrant.*

Thus, Massinger may be considered as a candidate for the authorship of the anonymous Demetrius manuscript because of his intense interest in extraordinary foreign statesmen, pretenders, and tyrants, and Fletcher too, because of his intimate familiarity with the Russian events of the time. Nor is the possibility of a joint venture of these two playwrights excluded. The presence of Massinger's *The Tyrant,* a recasting of his previous play *The King and Subject*—which, as its title indicates, may have been ideologically linked with Fletcher's *The Loyal Subject*—on Warburton's list together with the anonymous Demetrius manuscript, may be more than a simple coincidence. Yet this is still only a conjecture, and a conjecture it must remain at the present stage of scholarship until, if ever, the manuscript is found.

The Jacobean World of John Fletcher

In spite of Waith's statement that the theme is vague, that it is "a series of spectacular variations," and that "the novelty of the display is all that counts,"[155] the Russian historical theme of *The Loyal Subject* has, by this time, been made sufficiently obvious.

At the same time, the curious reader becomes aware of the presence of another theme, that of the English world of John Fletcher, in the play. Allusions to this world are, at times more, at other times less, manifest, as if the playwright intended both to invite and to confuse his audience in a way similar to his treatment of the Demetrius theme. There are unmistakable signs of a simultaneous double dialogue in the play, and the reader is often left with the impression that while Fletcher speaks of Russian history, he is, in reality, using some of these historical events as an allegory or a protective coloring in addressing himself to his English audience through the actors of the King's Men's Company in London. This hypothesis of the Aesopian character of the play requires that the reader look at the life of John Fletcher amid the political, social, and economic events of his formative years in relation to his environment in order to be convinced that, beyond its literary and historical sources discussed before, *The Loyal Subject* is also a genuine product of the temper of the playwright's English homeland.

The early years of John Fletcher were filled with the echo of England's greatest military glories. The English navy won its most successful battle in history against a powerful Spanish armada in 1588, when the playwright was only nine years old. The daring exploits of Drake and Raleigh, and the discoveries of new lands all around the world, filled Englishmen with pride and patriotism, and the expansion of English trade and commerce ushered in a new era of wealth and prosperity. These achievements were connected with the name of Queen Elizabeth, who symbolized the power, wealth, and national unity of England. In the more advanced years of John Fletcher, however, this bright picture gradually changed as anxiety gripped England in the uncertainty of the succession. Although the reign of James I brought temporary relief, it also brought profound changes. The relation of the new king to Englishmen was often strained, his repeatedly pronounced doctrine of the monarch's divine right met with disbelief and hostility, and his peaceful policy toward Catholic Spain was highly unpopular. The great number of Court favorites, sophisticated and pleasure loving, whom he imported from Scotland, created a center of intrigue. The national temper changed, the tightly knit social structure of the Elizabethan era gradually disintegrated, James I constantly quarreled with Parliament over money, and his imprisonment and execution of Raleigh, the last Elizabethan hero, further alienated him from the nation. Thus, before long, James I found himself surrounded by a disunited nation and a Court in which the *nouveaux riches* replaced the old landed aristocracy.

As a playwright connected with the Court by birth, training, and affiliation, John Fletcher informed his plays with, and catered to, the taste of the Court. They echo the political excitements, intrigues, amorality, and sophisticated life of the court as well as the strong undercurrent of unrest and disaffection of the population. Let us review some of the most distinct elements in his dramas which concern the king and his divine right, foreign policy, and the Court and society.

Ever since Coleridge coined the phrase about Beaumont and Fletcher as "the most servile *jure divino* royalists,"[156] a literary battle has raged to determine whether these playrights justified or condemned the attitude of the kings in their plays. It is customary to point to such plays as *Valentinian, The Maid's Tragedy, Thierry and Theodoret,* and *Wife for a Month,* as well as *The Loyal Subject,* to analyze the charges. While it is undeniable that Aëcius in *Valentinian* and Amintor in *The Maid's Tragedy*—just to mention the two most striking examples—are abject apologists for the king's divine right, the subsequent fate of these kings in the two plays, both of whom are murdered, supplies a proper rebuttal to the charge of the servile royalism of the authors.

I do not know whether Fletcher used *The Loyal Subject* for a variation on this subject, but we can see that the Great Duke who, at times, utters such commands "that I will have, shall be," is repeatedly frustrated in his designs. Although Theodore respects him, and refuses the Duke's challenge to fight with him, saying that "I dare not; / You are my prince," he still retains his independence to "dare speak truth." Translated in the rough climate of the English political situation of the period, this incident may well indicate a desire of the King's subjects for a parliamentary dialogue which was often denied them. The conversation between the gentlemen of the Court and Burris in the first scene of the second act, in which we learn that the Duke "oft complain[s] for money"; the Duke's anxious question, "But where's the money?" to pay his army; and his subsequent treasure hunt may point to King James's tight pecuniary situation. The efforts of Boroskie, and of the "new-born flies" at the Court, whose "rifling" of "true labour" is pointed out, may be read as so many illegal attempts to raise money by taxation without due parliamentary procedure. On the other hand, James's extravagance may be seen in Boroskie's wealth, in the "plate the duke bestowed on" him, and in the Duke's lavish gift to Burris.[157]

When we read about James's life, we are impressed with some distinct similarities between it and the Great Duke's in the play. Obviously these similarities should not be stretched too far, since it is a matter of conjecture how much conscious use Fletcher made of his material. James I (1566-1625) was treated as being incapable of taking any real part in public affairs until 1578 because of a physical weakness which obliged him to lean on the shoulder of an attendant when walking, and this feebleness contributed to certain deficiencies in his character. James's immediate guardian, the Earl of Morton, an honorable man, was driven from the regency when James was 12 years old, and for some time James was a mere puppet in the hands of intriguers and party leaders. Can it be a mere coincidence that Archas—who was obviously the young Duke's guardian, suggested by the fact that the old Duke has left the treasure for his son in the General's custody—is dismissed at a similar time in the Duke's life?

I have pointed out before the duality of the Duke's character in *The Loyal Subject,* and Appleton mentions the double aspect of James's character, which created a divided court. This author also shows the distrust and fear of James I of his subjects and we recall the Duke's distrust of Archas and his fear of the soldiers.[158]

The negative qualities of the Great Duke in the play should not lead us to believe that Fletcher was not sympathetic to monarchy. Like his friend Massinger, he favored a constitutional monarchy and censured absolutist tendencies. Let us also remember that Fletcher did not write for the King, but rather for the gentlemen commoners of the House of Commons, who disliked James.

As indicated before, James's peaceful foreign policy was unpopular. There was a continuous demand for warfare against Spain, and James's obsequious attitude to Gondomar, the Spanish ambassador, and his plans for a Spanish match for Prince Charles, his second son, enraged Englishmen. Thus, there is a recurring echo of anti-Spanish sentiment in Fletcher's plays, and wars and military virtues are usually described by him in an attractive light, as we can read in *Valentinian, Bonduca, The Knight of Malta, The Humorous Lieutenant,* and *The Loyal Subject.* In *The Mad Lover* even women use military expressions in describing their clashes with their admirers. In *The Loyal Subject* Archas glorifies war, calling it "glorious," "a child of honour," and "a golden danger." He personifies his weapons, addressing them as "noble arms," "good sword," and "bird of honour." In this play soldiers are called "faithful and honest," even "saints," who should be "canonized for their services."[159] When Fletcher reversed his sources in eulogizing the Russian army and showing their bravery and honesty against the cowardice and greed of the court favorites, he unquestionably had one eye on current English political conditions. Rapp correctly noticed that to these soldiers "[hat] der Dichter all' Energie und den Humor englischer Krieger seiner Tage verliehen."[160]

The first performance of *The Loyal Subject* was in 1618 and, after a long imprisonment, Sir Walter Raleigh was executed in

that year. Appleton tries to see a political allegory in *The Loyal
Subject,* which concerns this last Elizabethan adventurer.

Without question *The Loyal Subject* contains some explicit political
comment, and certain details lead one to suspect that in creating Archas,
Fletcher once more had Raleigh in mind. Act III scene 5 makes little
sense read otherwise. A mysterious Ancient, with the function of a chorus,
cries out for brooms. A second soldier cries potatoes—a commodity associated with Raleigh. Elsewhere in the play we come across mention of
Virginia. The Duke's seizure of Archas' treasure may also have called
to mind James' seizure of Raleigh's estate at Sherborne. Archas . . .
chafes against a stagnant peace as Raleigh pleaded for more vigorous
anti-Spanish policy.[161]

Also the Ancient's reference to "I' th' wars we have no more
rooms," and the song of the First Soldier, "The wars are done
and gone / And soldiers, now neglected, pedlars are"[162] bring
the Russian and English theme of the play close together for
the number of demobilized soldiers swelled the ranks of unemployed in both countries. In this English allegory, Theodore's
defense of Archas and his satirical comments on Boroskie might
be interpreted as a plea for Raleigh and against Gondomar,
Raleigh's great enemy, who demanded the latter's execution.

A reading of the play as a political commentary on the fate
of Raleigh might explain some allusions which I have interpreted
so far only in terms of Russian historical events. The reference
to "hours . . . strangely altered" may mean the changed atmosphere between the reigns of James I and Elizabeth, an interpretation which may be reinforced by a later hint of the thrift
of the latter and the prodigality of the former. The allusion to
the former ruler who "loved [Archas] dearly"[163] may be associated with Raleigh's early popularity with Elizabeth. The suggestion that if Archas's services had been less conspicuous he would
have been less an object of envy, might again well be linked with
the intrigue against Raleigh. The allusion to gold and treasure
may hint at his attempts to discover the famed El Dorado in
America and later his voyage to Orinoco in search of gold. Archas's unfair treatment at the banquet and Boroskie's unjust
accusation may be construed as the trial of Raleigh, the unfair-
ness of which shocked English public opinion of the time. Raleigh's gallant behavior in face of the brutality of Attorney
General Sir Edward Coke might be the source for Archas's
dignified conduct at the royal feast.

The corrupt Court is an almost indispensable element in any

pseudo-historical plays of Fletcher, and there is usually also a comparison between this Court and a demoralized army which objects to the lewdness of the Court. We have such a situation in *Valentinian,* in regard to which Wallis mentions that its resemblance to James's Court is not coincidental, and he also emphasizes the boldness of the attack of *The Loyal Subject* on the "unworthy favorites" of James I.[164]

Boroskie's great wealth and power as well as the swarm of "flies" in *The Loyal Subject* call to mind such ignoble courtiers as Carr and Buckingham and a great number of new nobles at James's Court. In view of this English King's preference for handsome male favorites, it is worth while to recall Theodore's satirical comment on Boroskie's merit "for turning handsomely o' th' toe" to have deserved the Duke's rich gifts. Homosexuality in *The Humorous Lieutenant* and lesbianism in *Philaster* may also be regarded as veiled allusions to James I's liking of males. The Russian and English themes coincide once more, as they do in another of Theodore's satirical remarks in referring to Boroskie's "ancestors and all their battles / Their silk and golden battles,"[165] which points out the sudden rise and cowardice of the court parvenus, called "new flies" in the play.

The Duke's vacillation between the charms of Alinda on the one hand, and those of Honora and Viola on the other, may reflect James's indecision between a French and Spanish match for Prince Charles. A similar, but more open allusion to the possibility of Charles's marriage with the Spanish infanta may be found in *The Scornful Lady,* a play Fletcher revised between 1613 and 1615.

The message of the political allegory of the play may be interpreted as a warning against abuse of royal power and court intrigue, since these conditions lead to rebellion and civil war. Coming events in England were to prove Fletcher right.

The Success and Influence of *The Loyal Subject*

The Loyal Subject was one of Fletcher's most successful plays. There is no information concerning the reception of its first performance in 1618, but it was well received when it was performed in a revised edition before Charles I in 1633. The play continued to find favor with theatergoers for nearly a hundred years. A "Young Lady" rewrote it under the title *The Faithful General* in 1706, but she was called a "Puny Poetaster, disguis'd under Coverture of a Petticoat" for her poor artistic efforts.[166] About this time an alteration of the play by the elder Sheridan was played, but not printed.[167] In view of the great number of literary and political allusions in the play, it would be of interest to learn what those alterations were.

Certain definite verbal echoes connect *The Loyal Subject* to *The Tragedy of Sir John Van Olden Barnavelt.* The sharp political satire of Middleton's *A Game of Chesse* may have received some indirect inspiration from the veiled anti-Gondomar allusions in Fletcher's play. The hidden Demetrius theme in the play may also have influenced in choice of subject matter Massinger's *Believe as You List* and John Ford's *Perkin Warbeck* (1634), both of which deal with political pretenders. The title of Massinger's suppressed *The King and Subject* seems to indicate ideological kinship with Fletcher's play.

The strong influence of *The Loyal Subject* on Grillparzer's *Ein treuer Diener seines Herrn* serves to show both the intricate and essential relationship between Fletcher's play and Lope's *El Gran Duque,* since the Spanish *comedia* also influenced Grillparzer's drama. Bancbanus, the Hungarian hero of *Ein treuer Diener seines Herrn,* a historical figure in the thirteenth century, combines the characteristics of both Fletcher's Archas and Lope's Lamberto.

It is worth while pointing to another interesting coincidence. The manner of saving the young Tsarevich Demetrius in Lope's play influenced La Rochelle's popular historical novel, *Le Czar Demetrius,* and the French author disguises his Demetrius as a girl for safety's sake. There is even an incipient love affair between Demetrius and the daughter of Boris Godunov, his avowed enemy, although, unlike Fletcher's play, this youthful romance never blossoms into a marriage. However, there is no evidence that La Rochelle read *The Loyal Subject* and he probably arrived at his own artistic solution independently.

There is, finally, a remarkable similarity in the historical background, some of the events, and the characterization of Boris Godunov between *The Loyal Subject* and Aleksej K. Tolstoj's historical novel *Knjaz' Serebrjanij* (translated as *A Prince of Outlaws*), written in 1863. Tolstoj, author of three historical dramas about the personalities of the Russian Time of Troubles, read Dr. Fletcher's *Of the Russe Commonwealth,* but it is highly doubtful whether he was familiar with John Fletcher's play, which was not translated into Russian. The parallel is rather due to the artistic affinity of two writers who, although separated by time and place, arrived at a similar artistic conclusion on the basis of the same source material.

NOTES

1. John Fletcher, "The Loyal Subject," ed. John Masefield. With an introduction by R. Warwick Bond. *The Works of Francis Beaumont and John Fletcher,* ed. A. H. Bullen, 4 vols. (London: George Bell & Sons and A. H. Bullen Variorum Edition, 1908), 3:221-357.

2. Thomas Heywood, *The Royal King and Loyal Subject,* ed. J. Payne Collier, Esq. (London: Printed for the Shakespeare Society, 1850), p. vi.

3. Matteo Bandello, "Ariobarzane seniscalco del Re di Persia quello vuol vincer de cortesia ove vari accidenti intervengono," *Novelle,* 2 vols. (Milano, 1813), 1:27-83.

4. "Praiseworthy deeds, or courteous and gentle acts," "liberality and courtesy," "obligation and duty." Bandello, pp. 26-27.

5. R. Warwick Bond, Introduction to John Fletcher, "The Loyal Subject," p. 225.

6. F. E. Schelling, *Elizabethan Drama 1558-1642, a history of the drama in England from the accession of Queen Elizabeth to the closing of the theaters, to which is prefixed a résumé of the earlier drama from its beginning,* 2 vols. (Boston and New York: Houghton, Mifflin & Co., 1908), 2:223.

7. John Fletcher, 2:i, 272.

8. Eugene W. Waith, "The Pattern of Tragicomedy in Beaumont and Fletcher," *Yale Studies* (1952) No. 120, p. 148.

9. Bond, p. 226.

10. Gerald Langbaine, *Account of the English Dramatick Poets,* (London, 1691), p. 268.

11. Henry Hallam, *Literature of Europe in the Fifteenth, Sixteenth and Seventeenth Centuries,* 3 vols. (London: J. Murray, 1843), 3:103.

12. Rev. Alexander Dyce, "Some Account of the Lives and Writings of Beaumont and Fletcher," *The Works of Beaumont and Fletcher,* 11 vols. (London: E. Moxon, 1843-1846), 1:60.

13. Moritz Rapp, *Studien ueber das englische Theater* (Tuebingen, 1862), p. 73.

14. A. W. Ward, *A History of English Dramatic Literature to the Death of Queen Anne,* 3 vols. (London: McMillan & Co., 1899), 2:699.

15. Emil Koeppel, *Quellen-Studien zu den Dramen Ben Jonson's, John Marston's und Beaumont's und Fletcher's* (Erlangen und Leipzig, 1895), p. 76.

16. William Painter, *Palace of Pleasure* (London, 1890), pp. 176-209. The original edition is dated 1566-67, and the tale is entitled: *Ariobarzanes, great steward to Antaxerxes, king of Persia, goeth about to exceede his souveraigne lord and maister in curtesie: where in be conteyned many notable and pleasaunt chaunces, besides the great patience and loyaltie naturally planted in the sayd Ariobarzanes.*

17. Koeppel, pp. 76-77.

18. Adele Ott, *Die italienische Novelle im Englischen Drama vom 1600 bis zur Restauration,* (Zuerich: Universitaet, 1904), pp. 52-53.

19. Orie L. Hatcher, *John Fletcher. A Study in Dramatic Method* (University of Chicago: 1905), p. 43.

20. Schelling, 2:223.

21. Bond, pp. 223–29.

22. Frederick S. Boas, *An Introduction to Stuart Drama* (London: Oxford University Press, 1946), p. 279; Waith, p. 143; William W. Appleton, *Beaumont and Fletcher. A Critical Study* (London, 1956), p. 62. The only dissenter is Gerald E. Bentley, who, in his *The Jacobean and Caroline Stage* (Oxford: Clarendon Press, 1956), p. 373, doubts whether the source is either Bandello or Heywood since "neither . . . seems to be used in a typical Fletcherian fashion." However, he does not suggest any other source.

23. Heywood, 5:v.

24. *Ibid.,* V. 5; John Fletcher, IV. 7.

25. *Ibid.,* I. 1.; Fletcher IV. 6.

26. J. K. Klein, *Geschichte des Dramas,* 12 Bks. (Leipzig: 1874), 10:490.

27. Lope de Vega, "El Duque de Viseo," *Obras Escogidas,* 4 vols. (Madrid: Aguilar, 1955), 3:1066–1111.

28. Ward, 2:701; Bond, p. 226.

29. E. Dietrich, *Th. Heywoods "The Royal King and the Loyal Subject" und J. Fletcher's "The Loyal Subject" in ihren Beziehungen zu einander und zu ihren Quellen* (Koenigsberg i. Pr., 1916).

30. Concerning the influence of the Spanish drama of the Golden Age—especially that of Lope—on Fletcher, Charles Dibdin states that Fletcher "copied Lope badly, adding to the extravagance of the Spaniard wild and eccentric wit of his own." *A Complete History of the Stage* (London, 1800), pp. 204–5. According to Coleridge: "An accurate and familiar acquaintance with all the production of the Spanish stage previously to 1620 is an indispensable qualification for an editor of Beaumont and Fletcher." *Lectures and Notes on Shakespear and Other English Poets* (London, 1914), p. 437. First edition in London, 1818. After these pioneers a growing number of scholars stress the Spanish influence on Fletcher. Rapp names nine plays of Fletcher based on Spanish sources. (pp. 86–87); Koeppel enumerates eleven (pp. 34–132); and Schelling seventeen (p. 215). According to recent scholars Fletcher knew Spanish and could have read Spanish plays in the original. See E. M. Wilson, "Did John Fletcher read Spanish?" *Philological Quarterly* 27 (1948) pp. 187–90; E. M. Wilson, "Rule a Wife and Have a Wife and El sagaz Estacio," *Review of English Studies* 24 (1948), pp. 189–94; Oscar M. Villarejo, *Lope de Vega and Elizabethan and Jacobean Drama* (Ph. D. diss., Columbia University, 1953), p. 370. Since *El Gran Duque* was first printed in 1617 and *The Loyal Subject* in 1618, we have to assume that Fletcher read the Spanish play shortly after it had been printed or somehow obtained a *suelta* edition from the Netherlands, where many of Lope's plays were printed at the time. I am greatly indebted to Prof. Emilio González-Lopez, who, having read the original draft of this chapter, expressed the opinion that Diego de Sarmiento de Acuña, Conde de Gondomar, the Spanish ambassador to James I between 1613 and 1618, who strongly influenced the literary taste of the English Court, may have taken a copy of the play with him to England. We recall that there was also a copy of the Spanish play as early as 1613.

31. *Philaster* takes place in a Sicily which no one can recognize; *Wild-Goose*

Chase in a France which is not French; Naples is called an island in *Wife for a Month;* although it deals with Roman history, *Bonduca* transfers the events from Italy to Britain and from the fifth to the first century. Even in such historical plays as *Thierry and Theodoret* and *The Bloody Brother* contemporary reality is slight.

32. Waith, p. 42.

33. Tucker Brooke, "The Royal Fletcher and the Loyal Heywood," *Elizabethan Studies and Other Essays in Honor of George F. Reynolds* (Boulder; University of Colorado Studies, 1945) 2, No. 4, p. 193.

34. *The Works of Beaumont and Fletcher,* ed. George Darley, 2 vols. (London-New York: Routledge, 1851), 1:50.

35. Rapp, p. 73.

36. Ward, pp. 700–701.

37. Thomas M. Parrott and Robert H. Ball, *A Short View of the Elizabethan Drama together with some accounts of the principal playwrights and the conditions under which it was produced* (New York: Scribner, 1943), p. 192.

38. Appleton, p. 62.

39. Rapp, p. 73.

40. It is worth while mentioning the comments of M. P. Alekseev, the Soviet Puškinist who, without reference to any source or mention of Dr. Fletcher's brochure, correctly connects various episodes of the play with the historical events of the Russian Time of Troubles. "The activities occur in Moscow, the name of one of the main characters is Burris . . . as the practical ruler of Russia at the Court of the young and inexperienced Great Duke [he] reveals his identity as the historical Boris Godunov. . . . There are excited crowds on the streets . . . groups of soldiers standing up for the defense of their commanders, stern and unjust monarchs surrounded by a crowd of flatterers. . . . In the reflection of internal political struggles, forgotten only when the nation faces a foreign invasion, we hear a clear echo of the troubles in Moscow of the seventeenth century." Although this résumé contains some mistakes—Burris is not the practical ruler at the country at all, the Duke is not so much Feodor as Ivan the Terrible and there is only one monarch in the play—this scholar still succeeds, where many of other commentators failed, in summing up the essence of *The Loyal Subject.* Yet he also overlooked the presence of the hidden Demetrius theme (see chapter *The Demetrius Theme*) and stated that this English drama did not touch the Demetrius legend. See Alekseev, *Boris Godunov,* p. 16. Janko Lavrin, an English scholar of Russian literature, mentions that Dr. Fletcher's book was written to acquaint Englishmen with Russia and adds that John Fletcher "must have been familiar with it when writing his play." Yet Janko is also a traditionalist since he believes that John Fletcher derived the plot of *The Loyal Subject* from Bandello's tale and merely transferred the locale from Persia to Moscow. See Janko Lavrin, *Puškin and Russian Literature* (London, 1947), p. 149.

41. In Fletcher's early play, *The Faithful Shepherdess* (1608), partly based on Giovani B. Guarini's *Il Pastor Fido,* the English playwright changed the role of Amarillis, the faithful lover of Silvio in the Italian pastoral, and made his own Amarillis a wanton shepherdess. He also reversed the character of the lustful satyr, "an old gotish fellow" in Guarini's play, and his own Satyr appears as a good person who honors Clorin, the faithful shepherdess. See

Giovanni B. Guarini, *Il Pastor Fido* (Londra, 1812), p. 22. Also Walter F. Staton, Jr. and William E. Simeone, *A Critical Edition of Sir Richard Fanshawe's 1647 Translation of Giovani B. Guarini's Il Pastor Fido* (Oxford, 1964).

42. Dr. Fletcher's pamphlet was first mentioned by Hakluyt in his *Voyages* (1589) under the title of "The late ambassage of Master Giles Fletcher" and contained only twenty-one chapters of the twenty-eight of the first edition. That Dr. Fletcher felt a storm coming is shown by Hakluyt's comment concerning *Of the Russe Commonwealth*: "The booke it selfe he [Dr. Fletcher] thought not goo, for diuers considerations to make publike at this time." The full first edition was published in 1591. After the suppression of Dr. Fletcher's study, the next edition of Hakluyt omitted all the unflattering references to Russia and its government. See Hakluyt, *Voyages,* vol. 1 (London, 1598). Even more characteristic is the way Samuel Purchas handled Dr. Fletcher's treatise. He explained the considerable revisions of the original as follows: "I haue in some places contracted, in other mollified the biting or more bitter stile which the Author vseth of the Russian Gouerment; that I might doe good at home, without harme abroad." See Samuel Purchas, *Hakluytus Posthumus or Purchas His Pilgrimes,* vol. 3 (London, 1625).

43. The extent of Horsey's contribution to Dr. Fletcher's pamphlet varies with scholars. Joseph Hamel feels that Dr. Fletcher's treatise "was collected almost entirely from Horsey's notes." See Joseph Hamel, *England and Russia* (London, 1854), p. 225. J. M. Seredonin thinks that Dr. Fletcher owes Horsey his information for the chapters on the nobility, government, the Tsar's council, the revenues, the military forces, and the Tsar's private life. In the author's opinion "the most interesting and realistic part of Dr. Fletcher's work is a retelling of Horsey's information." See S. M. Seredonin, *Sočinenie Džilsa Fletčera kak istoričeskij istočnik* (St. Petersburg, 1891), p. 67. In the most recent edition of Dr. Fletcher's work, Berry comes to his defense by mentioning that the latter knew some Russian, could have collected some information of his own, and Horsey's contribution is more limited. See Berry, p. 147.

44. The last part of Horsey's information—after he left for England and did not return to Russia—is historically the weakest, since it was based on rumors and added later. Completely contrary to the spirit of the previous part of his memoirs he now calls Boris, his former friend and protector in Russia, a "usurper," a "tyrant."

45. Jerome Horsey, "A Relacion of Memoriall Abstracted of Sir Jerome Horsey, His Travels," *Russia at the Close of the Sixteenth Century,* ed. Edward A. Bond (London: Hakluyt Society, 1857), pp. 177–78.

46. John Fletcher, II. 1; II. 9.

47. Dr. Fletcher, chap. 12, pp. 214, 218; Horsey, p. 84; John Fletcher, II. 7.

48. Dr. Fletcher, chap. 13, p. 228; John Fletcher, I. 1.

49. Horsey, p. 170; John Fletcher, 4: v, 95–98.

50. Dr. Fletcher, chap. 28, p. 301; John Fletcher, III. 4.

51. Dr. Fletcher, chap. 14, p. 231; John Fletcher, IV. 7; V. 4.

52. Dr. Fletcher, chap. 9, p. 199; John Fletcher, IV. 3.

53. The English original, published in London in 1604, is not available. The Russian translation, *Sera Tomasa Smita putešestvie i prebyvanie v Rossii,* perevod, vvedenie I. M. Bolkalov (St. Petersburg, 1893) was used instead. Robert Boyle, a scholar of the Elizabethan stage, attributes this anonymous work to George

Wilkins, a minor contemporary English dramatist, author of *The Miseries of Inforst Mariage* (London, 1607) and a collaborator with John Day and W. Roley on a historical play, *The Travels of Three English Brothers* (London, 1607).

54. W. J. Courthope, *A History of English Poetry*, 6 vols. (London: McMillan and Co., 1904–1925), 4:304–47.

55. Quoted by Eugene M. Waith, "A Tragi-Comedy of Humors: Fletcher's *The Loyal Subject*," *Modern Language Quarterly* (September, 1945), p. 299.

56. Courthope, pp. 322–23.

57. Thomas Seccombe and J. W. Allen, *The Age of Shakespeare*, 2 vols. (London: G. Bell and Sons Ltd., 1911) 2:158.

58. L. C. Knight, *Drama and Society in the Age of Jonson* (London: 1937), p. 294.

59. Robert Orstein, *The Moral Vision of Jacobean Tragedy* (Madison: The University of Wisconsin Press; 1960), p. 163.

60. Waith, "A Tragi-Comedy . . . ," p. 311.

61. John Fletcher, I. 2.

62. *Ibid.*, I. 5.

63. Brooke, p. 194.

64. Horsey, p. 253.

65. *Ibid.*, p. 209; John Fletcher, IV. 3.

66. Dr. Fletcher, chap. 5, p. 189; Horsey, p. 157.

67. "The critics could not explain Burris' role . . ." Waith, "The pattern . . . ," p. 146.

68. *Ibid.*, p. 38.

69. It is presumably Archas's presence in the play which made Robert Proells, a German scholar, exclaim: "Spanischen Ursprung ist es" adding ". . . in der Behandlung fast noch spanischer als spanisch geworden." Robert Proells, *Geschichte des neueren Dramas*, vol. 2 Part 2 (Leipzig, 1882): 192.

70. John Fletcher, II. 5.

71. *Ibid.*, I. 3.

72. It is possible to believe that John Fletcher may have had his uncle, Dr. Giles Fletcher and his father, Bishop Fletcher, in mind when he portrayed Archas. Phineas Fletcher, Dr. Fletcher's son and John Fletcher's cousin, a well-known poet, often refers to "the arrows of outrageous Fortune" which marked Dr. Fletcher's life. John Fletcher, a member of the household of Dr. Giles Fletcher's family after his father's death (1596), must have been well aware of the ups and downs of his uncle's fortune and the stoical reserve with which Dr. Fletcher bore it. Hence his reference to Archas's statement "Fortune ne'er raz'ed this fort yet." John Fletcher, 4:v, 92. See Rev. Alexander B. Grosart, *The Poems of Phineas Fletcher* (London, 1896), 2:110. Archas's love for the life of the Court may well have found its inspiration in the life of Bishop Fletcher, whose "whole mind was centered in the court. Away from the influence of the sovereign's smile he pined . . ." See *The Knight of the Burning Pestle*, ed. Herbert S. Murch (New York, 1908), p. xv.

73. Courthope, p. 322.

74. Dr. Fletcher, chap. 15, p. 234.

75. "The reader will be sometimes puzzled by the variety in the spelling of the names, especially in that of Šujskij, but Russian names have evidently always proved a stumbling-block to the British—and these authors lived in the days of

perfect liberty as to spelling." Some of the ways in which this name is reproduced in contemporary English accounts are as follows: Shoskey, Sviskey, Suiskey, Cinskie, Shooskee, Vansusces (obviously the corruption of Ivan Šujskij), Kneseuansusce (the corruption of Knjaz's Ivan Šujskij). p. vii. Sonia E. Howe, *The False Dmitri* (London: Williams and Norgate, 1916), p. XVI.

76. Brooke, p. 195.

77. In borrowing Lope's Teodoro, Fletcher obviously was not thinking of the Spanish Teodoro's historical prototype—Tsar Feodor. As discussed before, Tsar Feodor is part of the composite portrait of the Great Duke.

78. Horsey, p. 163.

79. *Ibid.*, p. 164.

80. Dr. Fletcher, chap. 9. p. 200.

81. John Fletcher, I. 1; II. 5; III. 4.

82. *Ibid.*, I. 1; II. 1.

83. *Ibid.*, I. 3; II. 6; II. 1.

84. Dr. Fletcher, chap. 9, p. 201.

85. John Fletcher, I. 3.

86. *Ibid.*, II. 5.

87. *Ibid.*, IV. 2.

88. *Ibid.*, IV. 3; IV. 4.

89. *Ibid.*, IV. 5.

90. Quoted by Gustav Kettner, "Schillers Demetrius," *Schriften der Goethe Gesellschaft* (Weimar, 1894), p. 244.

91. In refusing to comply with Ivan's demand to wear a mask Prince Repnin said: "The sauverain can play the buffoon, but I . . . will not play the fool." Stephen Graham, *Ivan the Terrible* (New Haven: Yale University Press, 1933), pp. 158–59.

92. John Fletcher, I. 3.

93. "Another function of the new court [established by Ivan the Terrible through his *opričnina*] was to seek out and punish treason. *Opričniki*'s ensuing license was a perversion of Ivan's original idea."

S. V. Veselovskij, *Issledovanija po istorii opričniny* (Moskva: Akad. Nauk, 1963), p. 245.

94. John Fletcher, II. 1; III. 5.

95. *Ibid.*, IV. 2.

96. *Ibid.*, II. 1.

97. *Ibid.*, II. 6.

98. A. A. Zimin, *Opričnina Ivana Groznogo* (Moskva: Mysl', 1964), chap. 10, pp. 430–81.

99. John Fletcher, V. 3.

100. Dr. Fletcher, chap. 19, p. 247.

101. Horsey, pp. 163–65.

102. John Fletcher, I. 3.

103. *Ibid.*, I. 2; I. 3.

104. *Ibid.*, I. 4; I. 5.

105. *Ibid.*, II. 1.

106. Horsey, pp. 160–62.

107. John Fletcher, 1: iii, 11; 4, v, 65–69; 1: iii, 164.

108. *Ibid.*, 4: vii, 1, 4–5; 13, 17, 26–27, 31.

109. *Ibid.,* 1: iv, 12; 5: i, 25.

110. Dr. Fletcher, chap. 19, p. 254; John Fletcher, I. 4; IV. 5, IV. 6.

111. Rapp, p. 73; Ward, 2: 699: Bond, p. 227.

112. *The Faithful General. A Tragedy.* Written by a Young Lady M. N. (London, 1706).

113. John Fletcher, 5: vii, 70–80.

114. Dr. Fletcher, chap. 5, 190.

115. Horsey, p. 226.

116. Dr. Fletcher, chap. 9, p. 201.

117. John Fletcher, I. 1; III. 2.

118. Lawrence B. Wallis, *Fletcher, Beaumont and Company, Entertainers to the Jacobean Gentry* (New York: King's Crown Press, 1947), p. 217.

119. Algernon Charles Swinburne, "Thomas Middleton," *The Age of* Shakespeare (New York and London: Harper Brothers Publishers, 1908), p. 170; Ornstein, p. 21.

120. Sera Tomasa Smita, p. 72. Appleton pointed out that this is one of the earliest references to *Hamlet*.

121. John Fletcher, I. 2; I. 4.

122. *Ibid.,* III. 3.

123. *Ibid,* V. 2.

124. *Ibid.,* I. 1.

125. *Ibid.,* I. 2.

126. *Ibid.*

129. *Ibid.,* I. 2; IV. 5.

130. *Ibid.,* I. 4.

131. *Ibid.,* I. 4; IV. 3.

132. *Ibid.,* IV. 1; IV. 3.

133. To see clearly the basic artistic yardstick of Fletcher's fundamental values concerning chastity and valor we must compare the almost similar tone of Lucina, ravished by Valentinian and Poenius, disgraced in war. (*Valentinian,* 3: i, *Bonduca,* 4: iii.)

134. Horsey, 3: 217–18.

135. *Ibid.*

136. Quoted by N. I. Kostomarov, *Kto byl pervij Lžedimitry* (St. Petersburg, 1864), p. 37.

137. *Ibid.,* p. 39.

138. Horsey, p. 259.

139. *Ibid.*

140. Aleksandr N. Ostrovskij "Dmitrij Samozvanec i Vasilij Šujskij," *Sobranie sočinenij* (10 vols.; Gosizdatel' xudožest. lit., 1960), 5: 1, ii; Aleksej S. Suvorin, *Car Dmitrij Samozvanec i Carevna Ksenija* (St. Petersburg, 1905) 1: ii.

141. John Fletcher, V. 7.

142. *Ibid.*

143. Sera Tomasa Smita, p. 39, 118 n. 36.

144. Horsey, p. 257.

145. Suvorin, *O Dimitrii, Samozvance* (St. Petersburg, 1906) pp. 1–114.

146. For an unflattering remark on Gondomar see Fletcher's play *The Scornful Lady,* 3: ii, 11–24. Boas (p. 272) mentions that the references to the Spanish ambassador suggest a revision.

147. Edmond Malone, *The Plays and Poems of William Shakespeare,* (21 vols. (London, 1821), 3: 234.

148. Robert C. Bald, *Bibliographical Studies in Beaumont and Fletcher Folio of 1647* (New York: Oxford University Press, 1938), p. 66.

149. S. Konovalov recently published a batch of royal letters between James I and Tsar Mixail Romanovič. See *Oxford Slavonic Papers,* 2 (1951): 142-44; 4 (1953): 103-4, 124-27; 7 (1957): 118-34, etc.

150. Schelling, 2: 39n.

151. W. W. Gregg, "The Bakings of Betsy," *The Library* 2, Third Series, No. 7, July 1911, 225-28; Fr. G. Fleay, *Biographical Chronicle of the English Drama, 1559-1642,* (2 vols. (London: Reeves and Turner, 1890-1891), 1:300; E. H. Oliphant, "Problems of Authorship in Elizabethan Dramatic Literature," *Modern Philology* 8 (1910-1911): 413; Gertrude M. Sibley, *The Lost Plays and Masques, 1500-1642* (Ithaca, N. Y.: Cornell University Press, 1933), p. 40.

152. Boas, p. 314.

153. Schelling, 2: 430.

154. The passage is as follows: "Monies! We'll raise supplies what way we please / And force you to subscribe to blanks, in which / We'll mulct you as wee shall think fit. The Caesars / In Rome were wise, acknowledging no laws / But what their swords did ratify, the wives / And daughters of the senators bowing to / Their will, as deities . . . " This is all that survives of the play. *The Plays of Philip Massinger,* ed. W. Gifford (London, 1813), Introduction, pp. 81-82. It is interesting to note that *The Loyal Subject* also has some passages dealing with the king's revenues but perhaps their milder tone may have saved the play from royal wrath or, possibly, these may have been the "reformed" passages. Let us also note the different tone of the two plays concerning royal divinity. Don Pedro of Spain proclaims his divine rights in a prohibitive military fashion, while the Great Duke of Moscovia never goes so far and there is no indication of his divine rights in the entire play.

155. Waith, "The Pattern . . .", pp. 143.

156. Quoted by Leo Strachey, *The Works of Beaumont and Fletcher* (London, 1887), Introduction, p. xxv.
Samuel Taylor Coleridge, *Shakespeare's Criticism,* ed. Thomas Middleton, 2 vols. (London: Raysor; 1930), 1:136, 147.

157. John Fletcher, I. 3; II. 1; II. 1; III. 3.

158. Appleton, pp. 27-28.

159. John Fletcher, I. 3; II. 1.

160. Rapp, p. 73.

161. Appleton, p. 63.

162. John Fletcher, III. 5.

163. *Ibid.,* I. 1.

164. Wallis, p. 208.

165. John Fletcher, II. 1.

166. Bond, p. 229.

167. *Ibid.,* p. 228.

4

The German and Russian Demetrius Dramas

A General Survey of the Period After the Baroque

Lope de Vega's Demetrius *comedia* influenced the development of the Demetrius dramas in the Catholic countries, Spain, Italy and France in the seventeenth and eighteenth centuries. As we have seen, Lope was convinced of the legitimate claim of his Demetrio, and his belief was shared by the dramatists of the above-named countries, who, however, did not give any new artistic treatment to the theme. Thus, in the South of Europe the conflict between an innocent Demetrius and a guilty Boris continued to dominate the Demetrius dramas.[1]

I do not know whether John Fletcher created a new school of Demetrius plays in the North of Europe, since, aside from the anonymous manuscript which was lost, no dramatic representation of the Demetrius legend has come down, although, as the appeal by George Wilkins, Fletcher's fellow dramatist shows, the theme was well known in England and the tragic grandeur of Boris Godunov was found worthy to be compared with that of Shakespeare's *Hamlet*. The "Young Lady" who wanted to improve *The Loyal Subject* and wrote her own drama, *The Faithful General,* based on this play, completely overlooked the hidden Demetrius theme and, unable to use young Archas outside of his authentic habitat in the state of Muscovy, simply eliminated him from the cast. However, the existence of an anonymous and nonextant manuscript *Demetrius and Marina or the Imperial Impostor and the Unhappy Heroine* has ideological importance since its title illustrates the fact that Demetrius was regarded as an impostor in the Protestant countries. Thus, the Demetrius dramas gained a new dimension, for the main idea, which had previously been that of retaliation against a guilty

Boris in the best tradition of the Elizabethan revenge tragedies was now broadened to include also retaliation against an impostor Demetrius.[2]

In the literature of the eighteenth century little attention was paid to the dramatic representation of this episode of the Russian Time of Troubles. Perhaps the overwhelming influence of French neoclassicism on literary trends was to blame for this hiatus, since it frowned on topics of recent history and on romantic treatment, and preferred to treat antique themes against a classical background.

Yet the vitality of the subject exerted such an attraction for the playwrights of Europe that the extraordinary adventures of this Russian Pretender have never been quite forgotten. Indeed, just the opposite happened and, after a partial eclipse, the Demetrius legend has almost attained the popularity of such perennial themes as the legends of Faust and Don Juan, since its thematic richness continued to lend itself to constantly fresh artistic reinterpretations according to the changing social and intellectual trends of the time.

The end of the eighteenth and the entire nineteenth century constitute a renaissance of the Demetrius theme because of renewed and heightened interest in this fascinating personality. It is worthy of note that, while in the seventeenth century this subject was treated almost exclusively by playwrights of the Catholic countries, it has now become, by a curious ideological, intellectual, and geographical shift, almost entirely the private property of German and Russian dramatists. The reason may partly be found in the changed attitude of Spain and Italy, the two militant Catholic countries of the South, which were finally convinced that the conversion of Demetrius and his promise to eradicate the Greek schism in Russia were politically motivated and that the Pretender was actually indifferent to religion.[3]

The German Demetrius Dramas

The dramatic conflict of the Demetrius theme received a new treatment in Germany, where two giants, Schiller in the concluding phase of the *Sturm und Drang* period and later Hebbel, as well as a multitude of epigones, wrestled with the riddle of the Russian Pretender. On the one hand, the German dramatists were so fascinated with the problem of the mysterious origin, puzzling character, and sudden fall of Demetrius that they assigned to Boris, his great adversary, a secondary and, at times, unimportant role, and, on the other hand, in contrast to the previous concept of an external drama, they saw the conflict as occurring within the personality of Demetrius himself.

Conscious of the turbulent intellectual heritage of their rebellious past, the intellectuals and playwrights of Young Germany regarded Demetrius as the ideal rebel, expressing man's yearning for his dignity and wholeness, a liberator of serfs, a kind of Napoleon shorn of his inflated personal ambition, who, sensing the malaise of the age and defining its problems, wants justice and freedom, not only for the downtrodden masses of Russia but for all mankind. Through the universality of his purpose, nobility of his ideas, purity of his emotion, and youthful enthusiasm, Demetrius has become a kind of unofficial literary spokesman for these romantics, who, rallying to his revolutionary flag, welcomed him as a reaffirmation of their own beliefs and celebrated in him their own spiritual echo of the intoxicating political and social currents of the French revolution. The dynamism of Demetrius aroused in them a long-felt desire for political commitment and social change, and a strong sense of self-fulfillment. Thus, the enormous artistic potential of this modern Prometheus, at the same time innocent and guilty, pure and compromised, creative and destructive, has continued to exert an extraordinary fascination on the literary intelligence and sensibility of the German dramatists, even after the death of Schiller and Hebbel.

Yet the idea of the eternal rebel has injected a certain measure of neoclassical rigidity into the artistic brush of the playwrights of Young Germany. While the towering genius of Schiller and Hebbel enabled these two writers to save the man Demetrius in spite of their lofty conception and idealization of him, in the interpretation of their intellectual and scholarly followers, the man Demetrius has largely been lost and, instead, often a lifeless abstraction created. These romantics preferred to play with the idea of Demetrius as the symbol of the eternal rebel rather than with the ambiguities, vacillations, and imperfections of the living man. They removed Demetrius from the actuality of his struggles, from the sound, heat, and smell of the Russian countryside, and clamped a mask of universality on him. Thus, for the majority of the German playwrights of the period, the Demetrius of their dramas is not really a vital and historical rebel of the seventeenth-century Russian Time of Troubles, with a delicate heartbeat of his own, but rather a rebel of all times and places. Consequently the shouting mob, carrying the red banner of revolution to the Russian capital and later storming the gates of the Kremlin, loses its specific Russian coloration and becomes a faceless, amorphous cluster of surging humanity without any definite place and time in history.

In spite of their artistic tendency to create abstractions, the viewpoint of the German dramatists is, in general, more objective than that of the Russian playwrights. Not being directly involved in the vital issues of the Russian political and social scene, the German dramatists were able to remain relatively free to examine the Demetrius saga from a calmer historical perspective and, not affected by the controversy about the changing current of political opinion concerning the role of the protagonists in Russian historiography, they could form their judgment more independently. This political and social aloofness also gave the German dramatists a much wider scope for artistic experimentation.

KOTZEBUE'S *DEMETRIUS IWANOWITCH. CZAR VON MOSKAU*

The first German play on the subject is August Friedrich Ferdinand Kotzebue's *Demetrius Iwanowitch. Czar von Moskau,* written in St. Petersburg in 1782. The play had difficulty in passing the censorship and reaching the German theatre in Petersburg. The police demanded that part of the title ("Czar von Moskau") be eliminated and Kotzebue had to declare solemnly that his play was merely a fantasy and that he agreed with the official view, according to which Demetrius was a defrocked, runaway monk of the čudov monastery.

Kotzebue depicts Demetrius not as an impostor but as Ivan's son and, although some researchers have attempted to read in this play a great and bold new idea, there is, in reality, nothing in its conception to justify such a claim and the play may better be regarded as a step backward rather than forward in its dramatic use of the historical material. Kotzebue was not interested in historical research or in a fresh evaluation of the motives and facts of the Time of Troubles. As his whole literary production reveals, Kotzebue was a typical representative of the contemporary European movement of sentimentalism, and his Demetrius recovers the throne not so much because he is the legitimate Tsar but as a reward for his noble instincts and good deeds. The play is mediocre, without any real dramatic conflict or artistic merit.

SCHILLER'S *DEMETRIUS*

Although Schiller's *Demetrius* remained a fragment, its powerful treatment of the theme, psychological depth, and passionate characters destined his drama to be the finest and most distinguished poetic representation of the Demetrius legend.[5] First published in the *Morgenblatt* in 1815, the torso of Schiller's play is, according to Gustav Kettner, the German literary critic, "one of the greatest dramas of all times and nations."[6]

Schiller had always been attracted by unusual historical personalities who participated in conspiracies, liberation of peoples, or in governmental coups for the sake of freedom and progress. He liked to treat conflicts between historical and natural rights, the old order and the new, the ruler's right and the people's freedom, and the sanctity of inherited rule and the claims of exceptional men for power, and to see the triumph of democratic principles. The revolutionary ideas of the young Schiller gradually yielded to a belief in the importance of legitimate succession, especially after the final events of the French revolution, which greatly disappointed him.

Schiller left behind two important dramatic fragments, *Perkin Warbeck* and *Demetrius,* which had engaged his attention toward the end of his life. These two fragments closely resemble each other since, in both, the central character is a claimant to the throne.

Warbeck treats the impostor who disputed Henry VII's title to the crown. He posed as Richard, Duke of York, son of Edward IV and the legitimate king of England. According to his story, he miraculously escaped the assassin sent to murder him. Yet Schiller abandoned this project because he felt that it lacked dramatic action and proper ending. Thus, when he began to work on *Demetrius,* he drew up a balance sheet, showing the positive and negative aspects of this drama as compared to *Warbeck,* and his comment on the latter was that fraud as a basis for a drama is repugnant.

Schiller chose *Demetrius* for "the greatness of its subject and scope."[7] While Warbeck's attempt to conquer the throne failed, the Russian claimant was successful. To the German playwright, Demetrius's triumph, accompanied by the claimant's subsequent awareness that his pretensions were without foundation, presented itself as the climax of a tragic action.

Schiller's historical sources were Mueller, Levesque, Treuer, and Rochelle. He asked Goethe for a translation of Nestor's old Russian *Chronicle,* although this *Chronicle* has nothing to do with Demetrius. Presumably Schiller was interested in the early history of Russia to gain a proper perspective of contemporary events for the plot of his drama. In addition the reader learns from a letter of Wolzogen, Schiller's brother-in-law, that the latter promised to bring the poet Sumarokov's Demetrius play and Ščerbatov's *Kratkaja povest' o byvšix v Rossii samozvancax* (*A Brief Story of Former Pretenders in Russia*),[8] although one cannot tell how Schiller was going to read the play and the history which were not translated into German.

The hero of the German playwright is a new creation in the history of the Demetrius dramas, since he is neither the impostor that tradition made him, nor the legitimate heir to the Muscovite throne, yet he is completely innocent because he genuinely believes, at least at the beginning of his career, in his royal birth. He is both the hero and the victim of an ethical idea. He feels God's guiding hand in his destiny, that hand which saves him from danger and carries him on to victory. Schiller felt that his Demetrius is not unlike his maid of Orleans in this respect, for both regard themselves as saviors of their native land, fired by a divine spark.

Schiller conceived his Demetrius in terms of both an antique and modern tragedy. The Demetrius of the first two acts is modeled on Oedipus, who, found at an early age before knowing of his origin, is suddenly catapulted by fate into a position where a whole nation obeys him and, when at the summit of his power, just as suddenly by another twist of fate, learns his true origin. At this stage Demetrius is transformed into a hero of a modern tragedy, for, instead of resigning himself to his fate, he asserts his free will and chooses to become a usurper.

Demetrius has much in common with the heroes of Schiller's early tragedies. Like Karl Moor and Fiesco, Demetrius is also a defeated idealist. Like the idealism of these two protagonists, Demetrius's idealism is tainted with egoism and, when frustrated in his ambition, he scorns morality to gain his purpose. Thus, in *Demetrius,* Schiller again shows the downfall of a misguided idealist unable to sustain his "schoene Seele" at the height of integrity. Yet, *Demetrius* really belongs, both in time and in drama conception, to Schiller's later dramas. In his philosophical essay *Ueber das Pathetische* (1793) Schiller stated that tragic action is compounded of the twofold influences of character and circumstance and that the protagonist's conduct is determined both by the situation in which he finds himself and by his own personality. Although in his plays external circumstances trigger the dramatic action, they are not the essence of the drama. In his later tragedies Schiller placed greater responsibility on the hero by making him primarily responsible for his own plight. Thus, the fundamental conflict is in the struggle within Demetrius which his combat against outside forces evokes and heightens but does not replace. The essence of the tragedy lies in Demetrius's moral degeneracy and, at the end of this unfinished drama, the hero stands before us as a deceiver, no longer a deceived. The play reveals the disintegration of the hero's character through deceit and his transformation from a republican idealist with his humanist fervor into a monarchic despot.

In the *Vorgeschichte*—which Schiller later dropped—the reader sees an obscure Russian youth at the estate of George Mniszek, Palatine of Sandomierz, accidentally kill the admirer of Marina, Mniszek's daughter. Sentenced to die, he kisses his cross as he is awaiting his execution. The precious cross attracts attention and causes an inquiry into the man's origin. In his psalter a Greek inscription is found which explains that this young man is the son of Ivan the Terrible. In the meantime Russian refugees arrive who identify the cross as given by Prince Mstislavskij to Tsarevich Demetrius at the latter's baptism, and they also recognize in the Russian youth Tsarevich Demetrius, who was believed to have died in Uglič sixteen years before.

The first act of the actual play, into which Schiller later incorporated the *Vorgeschichte,* takes place in the Polish Senate (Sejm), to which Demetrius is now invited to prove his origin to the Polish King and Senators, and to state his plea. In a majestic speech, relentless in its tempo and fierce in its intensity, Demetrius shows himself a progressive humanist preoccupied with freedom, who wants to rule justly for the good of mankind, and to turn slaves into free people. Thus, Demetrius becomes one of the New Men who preach a kind of democracy that would do away with class distinction. Similar to the sentiments expressed in Schiller's *Ode to Youth,* Demetrius's plea is for a universal brotherhood and, as a deeply thinking statesman, he establishes a set of ethical principles. In this powerful scene Schiller has Demetrius proclaim:

> Es ist die grosse Sache aller Staaten
> Und Thronen, dass gescheh' was rechtens ist,
> Und jedem auf der Welt das seine werde.
> Denn da, wo die Gerechtigkeit regiert,
> Da freut sich jeder sicher seines Erbs
> . . . .
> Ich will aus Sklaven   Menschen machen.[9]

Yet the duality of Demetrius's nature, with a hint of his dormant demonic character, is also shown in this episode. In his plea to Sigismund, he reminds the Polish King of the latter's birth in prison, and of his subsequent support by others who helped to put him on the throne. In his address to the Senators he pictures their glorious role as transformers of Russia, their eternal enemy, into a friendly neighbor. However, at the same time he also appeals to the greedy nature of the lower gentry in promising them war booty from the great wealth of Moscow if they lift their swords in his cause.

Most of the Senators vote for him, but Sapieha, who recently signed a peace treaty with Tsar Boris, opposes the war and his *liberum veto* dooms the prospect of open conflict with Muscovy. However, Sigismund assures Demetrius that he gives his magnates free hand to support him, and advises him to respect Russian traditions ("Zeuget euch als Moskaus wahrer Sohn / Indem ihr Achtung tragt vor seinen Sitten") and not to imitate Polish customs ("Der Arm, der euch einfuehrte, kann euch stuerzen"),[10] and thus he will be able to maintain himself on the Russian throne in spite of the foreign help which opened the gates of Muscovy for him.

In the second act we meet Marfa, Demetrius's mother, who, after the presumed death of her son, has been forced by Boris to take the veil in a remote cloister where she has spent sixteen long and painful years. Suddenly a fisher-boy, their only occasional contact with the outside world, brings startling news: Tsarevich Demetrius escaped from the nocturnal fire at Uglič, later hid in various monasteries, and now came back to conquer his throne. Shortly after this scene Archimandrite Hiob (Jov) comes and asks Marfa, on Boris's behalf, to repudiate the impostor who, abusing the name of her dead son, is fomenting civil war in Russia. In a magnificent display of motherly affection Marfa refuses to comply with Boris's request, since from the latter's fear she had concluded that the "impostor" may be her son. ("Er ist mein Sohn. An diesem Zeichen allein / Erkenn ich ihn. An deines Czaren Furcht / Erkenn ich in. Er ists. Er lebt. Er naht . . .") Her main impulse is revenge on Boris, whom she hates, and even if this Demetrius were not the son of her heart, he would still be the son of her revenge. Yet, when Hiob leaves, her confidence begins to ebb, and she has to assure herself that this Demetrius must be her son, because she wills it. ("Er ist mein Sohn, ich glaub an ihn, ich wills.")[11]

One more scene of the second act, in which Russian peasants listen to Demetrius's proclamation and the majority decides for him, completes the fragment. Yet Schiller left a great number of notes which permit us to follow the probable line of events, though it is impossible to tell what specific episodes he would have chosen from this material for the completion of the tragedy. Out of the multitude of events which he outlined for his drama, let us look at the two most important moments, consisting of two confrontations of Demetrius, one with the person who made him the Tsarevich and the other with Marfa.

Schiller thinks that there is an intrigue behind the appearance of the Pretender. He assigns this role to "einem rachsuechtigen und intriganten Geistlichen, welchen Boris schwer beleidigt."[12] Along with many of the chief boyars coming to the camp of Demetrius, the virtual ruler of Russia after Boris's suicide, this man, called alternately X and Andrei in the notes, also comes to greet the Pretender. Demetrius remembers that this man helped him in his youth and is happy to express his gratitude; but it is from him that Demetrius learns his true origin. Boris had hired the man to kill the real Demetrius, but, instead of rewarding him after he had fulfilled his order, planned to have him killed in turn so that he might not reveal the crime. To revenge himself for Boris's ingratitude, of which he learned only after having committed the crime, this assassin decided to bring up in secrecy a boy similar in age and appearance to Tsarevich Demetrius, and gave him the cross which he had stolen from the dead Demetrius. He manipulated the Greek inscription in the boy's psalter, helped him to escape to Poland and, at the same time, spread the news that Demetrius was alive. In his conversation with Demetrius, this man proudly describes himself as the king-maker of Russia and demands his due reward.

Thus, the hero discovers that he is not Ivan's son, that he is not what the world and he himself believed he was, and that from the summit of his noble dreams he will fall into insignificance. Overcome with rage and indignation Demetrius kills the man, and thus the only person who could have betrayed his secret is now dead. But what shall Demetrius do now? Shall he accept this degradation, give up the crown, and let anarchy rule in the land, or shall he defy fate and maintain his ambiguous position? The decision lies with him alone; the choice is his, and so is the terrible responsibility. But the duality of his character, at which Schiller hinted in the Senate scene, and the force of events determine his behavior: he must go ahead regardless of the consequences.

From this moment a complete metamorphosis takes place in Demetrius; his calm confidence disappears and demonic traits begin to rule. It is interesting to compare two of Schiller's notes, one before and the other after this fateful confrontation:

Before:

Er ist mild und liebenswuerdig, zeigt eine edle Ruehrung bei der Nachricht vom Tode des Boris, begnadigt einen entdeckten Anschlag gegen seinen Leben.

After:

Die Abgeordneten des Stadt Moskau kommen und unterwerfen sich dem Demetrius. Sie werden finster und mit drohenden Anstalten empfangen. Unter ihnen ist der Patriarch. Demetrius entsetzt ihn seiner Wuerde und verurteilt darauf einen vornehmen Russen, der an seiner Echtheit gezweifelt hat.[13]

This juxtaposition shows that, while the former Demetrius in his innocence and confidence could pardon the greater crime, the new Demetrius, burdened with guilt, feels so insecure that he must punish the smaller crime in order to maintain himself. It is a superb instance of Schiller's dramatic irony to raise Demetrius into the position of becoming Boris's adversary, to contrast them as representatives of idealism and despotism, and then to show how similar Demetrius is to the tyrant whom he has just supplanted.

To a certain extent the second confrontation, that between Demetrius and Marfa, comes as an anticlimax after this scene. Both of these protagonists have undergone a marked change since we last saw them. As the hour of their meeting approaches, doubts whether this Demetrius is really her son overcome Marfa, and, when she is led into Demetrius's tent, she sees a stranger before her. Demetrius's feeling of guilt and loss of confidence further reinforce Marfa's doubts. Yet, if Demetrius knows that he must play a comedy, he can still speak with the accent of a man who, deeply wounded, seeks a safe anchor to which to tie his sinking ship. He asks Marfa to be his mother: "Wirf das Vergangene von Dir, ergreife das Gegenwaertige. . . . Scheine nicht meine Mutter! sei es!" and reminds her that her dead child cannot give her anything, but he will give her everything: "Der, welcher in Grabe liegt, ist Staub; er hat kein Herz, Dich zu lieben, ich aber gib Dir alles."[14] When Marfa is moved to tears, Demetrius opens the entrance to the tent and lets the people see this melodramatic sight, and they interpret her tears as evidence that the mother has indeed recognized her child. It is important to note at this point that if Marfa's tears help Demetrius become the Tsar, her silence at the end of the play, when she is asked by Šujskij to swear that Demetrius is her son, dooms him to death.

Schiller's *Demetrius* is not really a political drama, though a certain social criticism is definitely implied by the hero's social commitment. Schiller's idea of tragedy rested more on an analysis of man's nature than on the observation of social conditions. However, the German playwright was not primarily concerned with the creation of individual characters and preferred to depict types and symbols. True rather than real was Schiller's credo concerning the purpose of art and in his characters he wanted to reproduce the essence of universality.

Of the earlier Demetrius plays, Schiller had heard of Sumarokov's and may well have known of Kotzebue's, but both of these were completely alien to his aesthetic view. He did not know Lope's *comedia,* yet, in spite of their different spirit, there is a certain artistic affinity between the Spanish and German plays in the characterization of Boris, the decisive role of the *vox populis,* and the motif of the presence of Russian refugees at Mniszek's estate in Poland.

Although Schiller did not treat Boris in such detail as Lope had, the reader still finds a historically correct estimate of this monarch in the warning of Schiller's Sigismund: "Czar Boris herrscht mit Ansehn und mit Kraft / Mit keinem Weichling geht ihr in den Streit."[15] Lope did not attribute Boris's fall to the murder of Demetrio's double, but to the legitimate claim of the Tsarevich, and Schiller thinks similarly:

Der Mann, der mit allen Anlagen zum Herrscher ausgeruestet, alle Pflichten seines Amtes erfuellt hat, sieht den ganzen Einsatz seines "ernsten muehevollen Lebens" verloren sobald ein Juengling gegen ihn den Anspruch des Rechts auf den Thron erhebt.[16]

In Lope's play public opinion supports Demetrio, and Schiller's Sigismund assures the Pretender that the Russians will come to his help. Lope attributes Boris's fall to the changed attitude of the people, and Schiller interprets it similarly: "[Boris] sieht die Meinung des Volks umgewendet, die Armee treulos, die Grossen verratherisch, die Gluecksgottin falsch, das Schicksal feindselig."[17]

In Lope's play Russian refugees spread the news that Demetrio is alive and the people hate Boris, and Schiller writes in a similar vein: "Ein ausgewanderter . . . Russe bringt die Nachricht mit, dass Demetrius noch lebe; dass Boris verhasst sey."[18] In harmony with Lope's play, Schiller's Demetrius is recognized by Russian refugees.

Did Schiller think of contemporary history while writing *Demetrius?* The great German playwright became interested in Russian history when, at the time of composing his *The Robbers,* he saw the Russian Crown Prince Paul Petrovič, later Tsar Paul I, visit Dresden. The murder of this Tsar in 1801, in which members of the royal family also participated, interested Schiller because it strongly reminded him of the similar murder of Albrecht of Hapsburg by his nephew. This similarity became so striking in his artistic imagination that, when Paul's daughter married the Crown Prince of Weimar, Schiller felt obliged, in order to avoid undesirable comments, to change somewhat the fifth act of his *Wilhelm Tell,* in which the subject of regicide is treated.[19] Thus, the close Russo-German ties at Weimar and the actuality of the *coup d'état* in Russia obviously influenced Schiller in his choice of a Russian subject. In addition, the theme of usurpers who seize power by a crime was a political reality in various parts of Europe in the beginning of the nineteenth century. It is not impossible to assume that Schiller, disllusioned over the events in France, had Napoleon in mind.

CONTINUATORS OF SCHILLER'S DRAMA FRAGMENT

Schiller's genius gave a new treatment to the Demetrius theme and paved the way for an infinite number of new interpretations, possibilities, and recastings. His dramatic torso proved to be an irresistible attraction for a great number of German playwrights who eagerly sought to complete it.

As we have seen, the kernel of Schiller's tragedy lies in the motivation of the transformation of the hero from an unconscious cheater into a conscious one, and the tragic events which follow such a transformation. The efforts of those dramatists who attempted to finish Schiller's *Demetrius* consisted in trying to discover Schiller's intention by finding the most truthful and convincing artistic motivation for such a transformation.

Goethe, who took a creative part in the composition of Schiller's *Demetrius,* was the first to plan the completion of the dramatic fragment. A famous passage in Goethe's *Tag-und Jahreshefte* (1805) eloquently depicts the sense of sadness and frustration which overwhelmed this greatest of German poets when he felt that he had to abandon this plan.[20]

Most of the other writers who sought to finish Schiller's fragment were intellectuals, scholars, and dilettantes rather than real dramatists. None of them rose to the unusual artistic challenge of being worthy of the legacy of their great master. One can truthfully quote Martin Greif, one of the continuators of Schiller's *Demetrius,* to the effect that only Schiller himself could have convincingly finished his fragment. Of the great numbers of epigones, perhaps Otto Sievers (1888) deserves to be mentioned for, although he departed from Schiller's original design, he still succeeded in bringing Schiller's *Demetrius* beneath a temporary roof.

In Otto Sievers's play, at the discovery of his origin, Demetrius tries to hide it from everybody and attempts to ennoble his fraud. If he must become a cheater, let it be for human and altruistic purpose: "If the blood which flows in my veins is not royal, let my deeds be princely. . . ." Demetrius exclaims, ". . . come to me you tired, hungry . . . serfs . . . my brethren. I will take you to freedom's light. . . ." He falls because Russia is not ripe enough for his reforms.[21]

While I will treat some of the interesting aspects of Schiller's continuators in this century in the conclusion, two somewhat more independent works are worthy of note because of their relation to the Russian Demetrius dramas.

Friedrich Bodenstedt's *Demetrius* (1856) was definitely influenced by the author's translation of Puškin's *Boris Godunov* and his own familiarity with the Slavic world. While his Demetrius reveals traits of Puškin's clever impostor before his fall, he also utters words reminiscent of Puškin's Boris about the ingratitude of people. ("Man glaubt nicht an das Gute / Und Feindschaft ernt' ich, wo ich Liebe saete.") The reference to further disturbances and the regicide at the end of the play is again characteristic of Puškin's drama. ("Ich sehe Zeiten schweren Ungluecks kommen. . . . Gott straft den Koenigsmord.")[22]

Adolf I. Wilhelmi's *Dmitri Iwanowitsch* (1869) shows certain similarities to Aleksandr N. Ostrovskij's drama in its structure, plot, and conflict. Yet more striking is the German dramatist's unconcern about his hero's origin and tragedy. This play ends with an unexpected twist: Demetrius becomes the victim of his passion for Ksenija Godunova.[23]

INFLUENCE OF SCHILLER'S *DEMETRIUS* IN FRANCE

With its unswerving concern for human rights and noble ideas Schiller's *Demetrius* fructified not only the literature of his own country but also the dramas of his French neighbors. Although the baroque spirit of the Demetrius dramas was not congenial to the classical concept of French dramatists, the success of Leon Halevy's *Czar Demetrius* (1829) is due to his clever imitation of Schiller's fragment. The plea of Schiller's Demetrius that Russia transform her hostility into a friendship with Poland underlies the anonymous drama *Un moment de toute-puissance* (1873), presumably written by a Polish emigrant.[24]

HEBBEL'S *DEMETRIUS*

Friedrich Hebbel's *Demetrius* (1864) is one of the finest dramas on this subject in world literature.[25] His dramatic plan was to create a "historical picture of the enormous Slavic world" rather than to imitate "Schiller's firework."

Hebbel's drama is both similar to, and different from, Schiller's. The similarity lies in the main idea, that of an innocent hero who believes that he is the legitimate ruler until he discovers that he is not. The difference is the result of the dissimilar philosophy of both poets and their distinct psychological motivation. If Schiller can be called freedom's bard, Hebbel is obviously the more prosaic singer of necessity. If Schiller's hero is relatively free in his choice at the decisive moment, Hebbel's Demetrius finds himself a captive in an existential trap and must submit to the plea of his supporters.

Following Schopenhauer's pessimistic philosophy, Hebbel sees a tragic dichotomy between the individual and society. The individual's tragedy begins when, driven by the logic of necessity, he faces a hostile world. Most of Hebbel's historical dramas represent a variation on this theme, in which the rights of the individual clash with the greater rights of society. In Hebbel's view the tragic hero must be different from society, and is invariably characterized by his inflated pride. Thus, most of his heroes are superlatives: Holofernes is the quintessence of the ruling nature, Siegfried of sunny heroism, Agnes Bernauer of beauty, and Demetrius of moral conscience. All these figures have something in common: they are out of tune with the world and, although persecuted for nonconformism, they are unable to compromise. We hear an echo of the Kantian imperative when Hebbel declares that we are responsible before God not only for our actual deeds, but for what we would have done in all possible situations. There is no final harmony in Hebbel's dramas, but perhaps only the discovery of a wound with which the hero must live, yet more often die, while the basic dissonance remains. Thus, in Hebbel's dramas a modern existential pathos is clearly discernible.

The above explains why Hebbel, originally interested in the continuation of Schiller's fragment, finally had to give up his plan. He admired Schiller's dramatic torso and regarded it as one of Schiller's best works, yet he "could not use even a single line of it." In Hebbel's opinion the main difference between their methods was that "er [Schiller] laesst den Sturm elementarisch in seine Welt hineinbrausen, ich suche ihn aus Athemzuegen enstehen zu lassen."[26] The Demetrius drama of Schiller was conditioned by his philosophical and aesthetic conviction, Hebbel's by history and reality.

Hebbel's *Vorspiel,* set in the Mniszek estate in Poland, is

similar to Schiller's *Vorgeschichte,* but is much more important
as a key to Demetrius's personality. Demetrius's mysterious
origin and enormous pride is stressed throughout this dramatic
introduction. Asked by the monk Gregory who this young man
is, the two Polish noblemen, admirers of Marina, who hate Demetrius because of his proud conduct, explain that Demetrius
came on a stormy night, smuggled in by a monk, who had found
him somewhere "in the mist" near "starvation." Yet, even when
the two Poles refer to Demetrius as the "Junker mit der Feder-
hut," they grudgingly admire him. ("Er hat die Art, die man-
chem Koenig fehlt.")[27] Demetrius's words to Marina are clearly
a self-portrait, an exercise in egocentrism:

> Ich setzt' mich lieber auf die nackte Erde,
> Als auf dem Stuhl des Bauern, trinke lieber
> Aus hohler Hand, als aus dem Napf des Knechts,
> Und such' mir lieber Beeren fuer den Hunger,
> Als dass ich schwelge, wo der Bettler zecht.[28]

Demetrius's killing of the Polish noble in an angry outburst
is, in reality, a suicide attempt, since he feels that the division
between him and the world will gradually choke him, and, as
he implies, it is better to die as a result of some wild action than
to live ignobly. The sudden revelation of his "origin" raises
him above the law, and his words to the Cardinal in Poland,
the concluding part of his self-portrait, reveal how he has felt
persecuted by a society which he did his best to antagonize:

> Das Recht zu sein, wie ich nun einmal bin!
> Ich ward, so lang' ich diese Erde trete,
> Gescholten und gehasst, und einen Jeden
> Habe ich beleidigt oder hoch gekraenkt,
> Und sagt' ich auch nur guten Tag zu ihm.
> Man ist mit meinem Augen nicht zufrieden,
> Man moegte, dass ich anders Athem holte,
> Man tadelt meine Mienen, meine Stimme,
> Und es ist wahr, ich red' ein wenig laut.
> Herr Kardinal, bin ich der Czarevich,
> So setzen meine Fehler Kronen auf,
> Und huellen sich in Purpurmaentel ein . . .
> Wer nennt mich uebermuethig oder stolz?[29]

This remarkable psychological self-analysis of Demetrius shows Hebbel's fine sense of history and makes his Demetrius a highly believable royal figure in whom Hebbel infused some of the characteristic traits of Ivan the Terrible. The reader understands why both the Cardinal and Marfa are inclined to compare him to the terrible Tsar.

While the killing of the Polish nobleman is similar to Schiller's, the motivation of the intrigue is different. The intriguers are the Cardinal and Gregory, his assistant, and their plan is both more historical and logical than Schiller's. The reader learns from the Cardinal that, at the time of Demetrius's birth, the young Prince was replaced by a peasant boy in order to frustrate Boris's plans, for his desire for the throne and determination to eliminate a potential rival were known. Thus, while Boris's henchmen killed the peasant boy, the Cardinal saved the true Demetrius and had him brought to Poland incognito; since that time he himself has been waiting for the right psychological moment to reveal the boy's identity. This moment has now come, and, in front of the Palatine and his household assembled to sentence Demetrius to death, the Cardinal now solemnly declares the young man to be the son of Ivan the Terrible who miraculously escaped Boris's assassins.

The Cardinal's ulterior motive is to use Demetrius for the eradication of the Greek schism in Russia. ("Es gilt / Das heil'ge Werk, das tausend Mal misslungen / Doch aber tausend Mal mit frischen Kraeften / Begonnen und vollendet werden muss. . . . Der Czarewitsch ist unser, seinen Raub / Setzt' ich als Preis der Absolution / Fuer einen Mord, der eingebeichtet ward."[30] Even stronger is the Cardinal's egoistic motive. If he can accomplish the great deed of healing the schism and bring the Russians back to the fold of the Catholic Church, he will be deemed worthy to sit in Peter's chair in Rome.

The scene with Marfa is different from Schiller's. Although Hebbel's Marfa hates Boris, she is convinced that her son is dead, and comes to unmask an impostor hiding under her son's name. Yet Hebbel's Demetrius, unlike Schiller's, still believes in himself at this stage and therefore he is able to disperse her doubts, at least temporarily, with his noble behavior, greatness of heart, and physical resemblance to Ivan. However, after her meeting with Demetrius, doubts again overcome Marfa, and she cannot answer the question of her friend from the cloister "Nun hat das Mutterherz in Dir gesprochen?"[31]

Entering Moscow in triumph, Demetrius notices an old woman, Barbara, faint in the welcoming crowd as she tries to touch his garment. Lifting up the old peasant woman, he invites her to the royal palace and, in his highly emotional state, promises to fulfil any wish she may have. Gregory, who visits Demetrius at the same time, tells him that this was the same woman who, at his [Demetrius's] birth, replaced him with another child. However, from his conversation with Barbara, Demetrius learns to his utter dismay that she is his real mother. The explanation of this mystery is that both Barbara, who used to work at the Court of Ivan the Terrible and Marfa bore their children by Ivan at the same time, and when Gregory asked Barbara to replace Demetrius with her own child, she promised to do so at first but later she did not have the heart to sacrifice her own son, and consequently she did not change the children.

This is the second traumatic experience in Demetrius's life, and true to himself and unlike Schiller's hero, he now wants to give up his aspirations and accept punishment for his unjustified claim. Thus, he immediately declares to Mniszek that he is no longer the Tsar, and wants to assume his previous role as the latter's servant.[32]

Yet Mniszek reminds him of his obligation to those who, like himself and Marina, believe in him and will be ruined by his decision. ("Was wird mit uns? Soll ich mit meiner Tochter / Am Bettelstab zurueck nach Polen wandern? / Ich in den Thurm zu Ratten. . . . / Sie auf den Markt als Karten-Koenigin.") When Demetrius replies that he has no legitimate right to be the Tsar since he is not Ivan's lawful son, Mniszek tells him:

> . . . Bist Du nicht
> Der letzte Traeger eines grossen Stammes,
> So sei der erste eines groesseren. . . .
> Erwerben ist unendlich mehr als Erben.[33]

Demetrius's tragic conflict is whether to violate his ethical principle or let his friends suffer. He realizes that, to save Mniszek and Marina, he must continue to play the role of the person he previously thought himself to be and, after some soul-searching, decides on a temporary compromise:

> Ich bin der Kapitain von einem Schiff,

Das scheitert; rasch in's sich're Boot mit Euch
Dann zuende ich die Pulverkammer an.[34]

To illustrate the difference between the attitudes of the hero
of Schiller and Hebbel after he learns his origin, it should be
mentioned that while Schiller's Demetrius becomes a tyrant,
Hebbel's hero continues to act just as humanely as before. He
even pardons Šujskij, sentenced to death for a conspiracy, since
he feels that Šujskij could not have committed a juridical crime
against him who is no longer the real Tsar, and, indeed, never
was the Tsar.

In the fifth act we see Šujskij prepare another revolt against
Demetrius, but we do not know the result, since the play was
never finished, although it is at least probable that Demetrius
would be overthrown as he was in history. Thus, by a strange
coincidence, the two great Demetrius dramas of nineteenth-
century Germany remained incomplete.

Except for some specific distortions for obvious stage effects,
Hebbel has the best historical motivations of any Demetrius
play in German literature. His sources, Karamzin, Mérimée the
French novelist, and Margeret, gave him a firm grip of the
characters and events. If his Demetrius shares many common
traits with Schiller's, such as his desire to rule justly ("Doch
wird gescheh'n, was recht und billig ist") and to undo his father's
wicked deeds ("Hat mein Vater / So furchtbar hier gehaus't—
Nun, ich will segnen / Wie er geflucht"), Hebbel, unlike Schiller,
brought his hero down to earth and depicted a human being.[35]

Hebbel's Boris shows certain traits similar to those of Schiller's, but Hebbel went beyond Schiller's portrayal both historically and psychologically. His monarch attained his position
through personal skill and wisdom and, although he does not
have a "right" to the throne, he accepts the sceptre because
circumstances force him. His Boris is no political Tartuffe who
only pretends that he does not want the crown. He is genuinely
afraid of assuming power, for he has seen how Ivan has consistently abused it. Boris does not brush Demetrius aside as an
impostor, but he mistrusts Demetrius's supporters, the Jesuits
and the Poles, Russia's traditional enemies. Demetrius does not
abuse Boris either; on the contrary, he thinks highly of the
latter. ("Es ist nicht Alles schlecht / Was Boris that, und Nichts
bloss darum schlecht, / Weil er es that. Wer sich vom Stall
heraus / Den Weg zum Czaren-Thron bahnen weiss, / Der ist

kein Thor!")[36] It is a subtle feature of Hebbel's play that his Demetrius unconsciously respects in Boris his own tenuous position, for it soon appears how closely his fate parallels that of Boris.

Was Hebbel influenced by any previous Demetrius dramas other than Schiller's? He does not seem to have used any of the dramas by Schiller's continuators for the obvious reason of their inferior dramatic quality.

There is no reference in Hebbel's notes to Lope's Demetrius *comedia,* translated by Rapp only in 1868, and therefore it could hardly have had any direct influence on his own drama. Yet it is worth while pointing out certain artistic affinities between the two plays and especially the distinct baroque spirit of Hebbel's *Demetrius.* The possibility of replacing Demetrius with the child of the peasant woman is an indirect echo from Lope. The opinion of Lope's Teodoro on the evil influence of the throne is echoed by Hebbel's Marfa. ("Die Krone macht die Teufel, die den Menschen / Zu allen Boesen reizen, doppelt stark.") The description of the battle is similar in both plays. In Hebbel's fragment Demetrius's army seems to lose the encounter when he, by personal courage and leadership, turns the fortunes of the battle. ("Reisst er Alles / Unwiderstehlich hin; Ein Wort von ihm / Wirkt wie ein Schluck.")[37]

That the Demetrius legend had a personal significance for the German dramatist, we learn from Richard M. Werner, who points out that Hebbel gave Demetrius many traits from his own character and experience.

The events of 1848, a time of revolutionary movements in many countries of Europe, when civil wars thundered, pretenders arose, legitimate rulers were deposed by revolutions and reinstated by force, obviously gave occasion to Hebbel for a dialogue with his epoch to point out the duality of the universe, a theme with which he was constantly preoccupied.

Although not so numerous as Schiller's, Hebbel's remarkable play also had its continuators, but their efforts were mediocre and without any real artistic merit.

The Russian Demetrius Dramas

It is tempting to make a general comparison of the German and Russian Demetrius dramas. We have seen that the German dramas were dominated by the puzzling, noble, rebellious, and tragic personality of Demetrius. On the other hand, a sympathetic or even objective portrayal of Demetrius on the Russian stage was impossible since, according to the Orthodox Church, he was under anathema, and until the second half of the nineteenth century, Russian historians, following the principles of orthodoxy and autocracy which governed contemporary Russian policy and sharing the passionately antagonistic view of the Church, considered him to be Grigorij Otrep'ev, runaway monk and impostor, an agent of the Poles and Jesuits, who invaded Russia with a foreign army, caused a civil war, devastated the country, tried to introduce foreign customs and religion, and won his way to the throne by false means. Presumably Kotzebue's play, which was almost suppressed by the authorities in St. Petersburg, remained in manuscript because no Russian publisher wanted or dared to print a drama which showed Demetrius as Ivan's son and the rightful Tsar. Some Russian playwrights (Sumarokov and Lobanov) who were interested in the dramatic representation of this period of the Time of Troubles must have felt that it would have been a slur on their national pride to make a hero out of a man whose activities, in their partisan opinion, were hostile to the Russian state and Orthodox Church. This attitude gradually changed only after Puškin's sympathetic portrait of the Pretender, when, simultaneously with a new look at the past, a new period of dramatic reappraisal could begin.

Boris Godunov, clearly a secondary character in German dramas in general, is more prominently displayed on the Russian stage. Although almost invariably portrayed as the man who ordered Tsarevich Demetrius's murder, he was still regarded, in spite of his Tartar origin, as a Russian national type who was a progressive ruler and acted in the spirit of the time. Some Russian dramatists (e.g., Aleksej K. Tolstoj, Mixail E. Lobanov) preferred to treat Boris's problem as their main theme and created a *Seelendrama* of this introspective, guilt-ridden, brooding personality, while others (e.g., Aleksej S. Xomjakov, Alexandr N. Ostrovskij) chose Demetrius as their central hero. Puškin's drama stands somewhere between these two groups, since it gives the two main heroes almost equal treatment.

Although not so obviously as the German continuators of the fragments of Schiller and Hebbel, the Russian dramas also have their own line of continuity. Following Puškin's open-ended

Boris Godunov, almost each successive Russian Demetrius play may be viewed as an attempt to carry on or to reinterpret artistically Puškin's central idea. In contrast to the German dramas, which, especially in the twentieth century, become more and more abstract and less and less historical, the Russian Demetrius plays, always patriotic and passionate in spirit, were concerned with a more detailed and more convincing portrayal of history, striving to give a realistic illumination to a complex period of their past. Thus, each successive Russian play is an attempt to improve and to refine some details or character portrayals of its predecessor in accordance with the latest historical research on the subject and the artistic sensibility, convention, and *Weltanschauung* of the playwright. In general, the Russian dramas—more passionate, vigorous, and concrete than the German—seem to show a preference for historical heat and color and for a realistic representation of the disturbance of the age rather than for a universal human truth.

It is worth pointing out that, while in most German plays the people's participation in the decisive events is rarely acted out on the stage, in those German works which are influenced by the Russian Demetrius dramas, the people generally play an important role.

If Schiller, and perhaps Hebbel too, fructified the Russian tradition of Demetrius dramas, the German-Russian literary relationship with regard to this subject was not completely one-sided, since Puškin's play has enjoyed a great literary prestige in Germany, has been translated several times, and has influenced the Demetrius dramas of Friedrich Bodenstedt and Paul Ernst, while Aleksej K. Tolstoj's *Tsar Boris* clearly inspired Henri von Heiseler's sensitive drama *Die Kinder Godunofs.*[38]

SUMAROKOV'S *DIMITRIJ SAMOZVANEC* (THE FALSE DEMETRIUS)

The first Russian Demetrius drama, Aleksandr P. Sumarokov's *Dimitrij Samozvanec* (The False Demetrius), written in 1771,[39] has little to commend it. History became a casualty when Sumarokov forced the Demetrius legend into the straitjacket of French neoclassicism, while the happy ending of the play reminds us of his travesty of *Hamlet.* Sumarokov may have based his play on the early seventeenth-century chronicle *Inoe Skazanie* (Another Narration), an obviously politically inspired pamphlet, in which the anonymous annalist highly praises Tsar Vasilij (Vasilij Šujskij) for his efforts to overthrow the False Demetrius.

In the meager plot, the tyrant and sadist Demetrius, who has come to power with the help of the Poles and the Pope, falls in love with Ksenija, Šujskij's daughter (!), although he is already married to Marina. Ksenija and her lover choose to die rather than to submit, but Šujskij, depicted as a wise statesman, suggests that they heed the urgency of time, dissemble and even lie if necessary, and in the meantime he prepares the uprising which finally topples Demetrius.

Although it has some patriotic overtones, this unhistorical play, like most of his other dramas, shows that Sumarokov was little interested in the actual events of this episode of the Time of Troubles and used his play as a convenient vehicle to express his artistic beliefs and social views. Imitating the strict canons and rigid forms of the seventeenth-century French tragedy, in long monologues Sumarokov contrasts social duty with individual passion and condemns those who cannot make sacrifices for the good of the nation as unworthy of the higher code of his ethical concept. As a follower of the enlightened absolutism of his age, Sumarokov held that people should be ruled by wise monarchs and not vice versa, but monarchs should rule according to the law, be "fathers of the people," and never become tyrants.

In the rarefied air of classicism Sumarokov's symmetrically divided and wooden black-and-white characters, moving more as abstract ideas than real persons, dutifully but unconvincingly preach, as in all his other tragedies, their tube-tested clinical truth. Sumarokov's Demetrius reminds us of a mixture of Nero and Caligula, and Parmen, Demetrius's confidant, seems to parrot Voltaire's favorite dictum of reason against faith.

The theme of an unpopular ruler and a Court-inspired revolt may represent a topical allusion to the palace revolutions in Russia of the time and serve as a justification of such uprisings. The author's well-known dissatisfaction with the German academic community's monopolizing Russian intellectual life of the period may help to account for the play's xenophobia.

PUŠKIN'S *BORIS GODUNOV*

"Une tragédie sans amour sourioit à mon imagination," wrote

Puškin in his letters[40] and this idea marked the beginning of work on his *Boris Godunov,* the finest Demetrius drama in Russian literature, written in 1825, printed in 1831, but staged only in an expurgated version in 1870.

Puškin describes the events connected with the coronation and fall of Boris and the triumph of Demetrius, whom he regards as Grigorij Otrep'ev, a young monk in the čudov monastery. His historical sources were the tenth and eleventh volume of Karamzin's history, along with old Russian chronicles, while his literary sources were some of Shakespeare's chronicle plays and Ryleev's *Dumy.*

Before pointing out Karamzin's influence, it is important to mention Puškin's familiarity with old Russian chronicles. A study of these chronicles gave Puškin the possibility of seeing how Karamzin wrote his history and helped him to reinvoke the language, temper, and color of the period. Gorodeckij, the Soviet literary critic, is of the opinion that, had Puškin used only Karamzin's history, he would not have been able to create so convincingly his *Boris Godunov.*[41] The remarkably truthful invention of Pimen, the old Russian chronicler, is obviously indebted to Puškin's acquaintance with the annals. Some specific details in the play also indicate that Puškin knew the Russian chronicles. The inclusion of an unhistorical young Kurbskij may be due to Puškin's sympathy with the plight of Andrej Kurbskij, statesman, soldier, and writer, who fled to Poland to escape the wrath of Ivan the Terrible.

Puškin borrowed from Karamzin almost all the factual material, almost all his protagonists, and the general flow of historical events. In addition Puškin composed the following scenes of his drama exclusively on Karamzin's account: Red Square, Public Square, and Šujskij's conversation with Vorotynskij, another of the great boyars antagonistic to Boris. Occasionally Puškin even borrowed words and phrases from Karamzin, the dramatic character of whose style must have helped him considerably.

Yet in spite of his reliance on Karamzin, Puškin, due to his remarkable sense of history, intuition, and emotion, was far from following the historian's account slavishly, and, liberating the protagonists of his drama from the straitjacket of tradition, he occasionally changed his source. Karamzin, for example, while describing Boris's apparent reluctance to accept the crown, in order to show the genuine desire of the Russians to see this statesman on the throne, wrote: "Mothers threw their little babies down to earth and did not listen to their cries."[42] Puškin, however, slightly altered this episode through the individual behavior of a peasant woman and her child in the following scene:

Peasant Woman (with child.): Now what's this? Just when it ought to cry, the child stops crying. I'll show you! Here comes the bogie-man! Cry, cry, you spoilt one! (Throws it on the ground; the child screams.) That's right, that's right![43]

Karamzin sees the crowd as a homogeneous group and a "frozen" amorphous mass with no difference among its particular members; a kind of synthetic world, from which the sentiments and emotions of daily living and the sense of small human conflicts are momentarily—and conveniently for his self-enclosed black-and-white brush—eliminated, while the sensitive Puškin individualizes them and shows distinct personal traits in their complex humanity according to their subjective motives, desires, and beliefs. They live and move, speak and act differently from one another. With this dramatic approach Puškin also shows indirectly that, although the crowd usually functions as a result of spontaneous emotional impulses and not from studied and standardized conviction, a certain fear and anxiety of the moment may still drive them to conformity. Bringing this artistic approach to the stage, Puškin implies a lack of unanimity in Boris's election, concerning which Karamzin is completely silent. Thus, Puškin dramatizes the historical controversy regarding the genuineness of the people's demonstration by isolating some people in the crowd who simply imitate and follow what others do without sharing the sentiments of the latter and without the slightest understanding of the reason that they are required to go through this ritual. While Karamzin mentions that the sincerity of the people's feelings overcame their pretense and inspiration triumphed over the indifferent and hypocritical in the great act of Boris's election, Puškin reverses his source and in the following scene shows the complex psychology of human beings who, under pressure, often act contrary to their instincts:

1st Person: As everyone is crying
             We also, brother, will begin to cry.
2nd Person: Brother, I try my best, but can't.

1st Person: Nor I.
                    Have you got an onion?
2nd Person: No; I'll wet
                    My eye with spittle. What's up there now?[44]

It is interesting to point out that the above scene was originally taken by Karamzin from the *Xronograf* (*Chronicle*), an
early seventeenth-century account concerning the events of the
Time of Troubles. Yet, while Karamzin revised the original
source to suit the refined taste of the Russian Court, Puškin
characteristically preferred the immediacy and vivacity conveyed
by the local color of the early chronicle to Karamzin's official
but, in the aesthetic judgment of the poet, somewhat denatural-
ized history.

Who is the hero of the play? In his *Tvorčeskij put' Puškina*,
Blagoj, a Soviet literary scholar, holds that there is no individual
hero, and, in another place, mentions that the collective hero
of the play is the historical epoch.[45] The German critic Flex
feels that the Russian people are the real hero of the tragedy.[46]
It is perfectly true that both the important role of the people
and the significance of the epoch are clearly reflected in the
play, yet the majority of commentators still regard either Boris
or Demetrius as the hero.

According to Karamzin, Boris is a wild mixture of piety and
criminal passion, and he sees in Boris's tragedy heaven's punishment for Demetrius's murder and usurpation of power.

Puškin, however, sees Boris differently. For him the Tsar is
not only a public, but also a private figure. So the poet enters
Boris's household, listens to his ideas and motives, reveals his
forbidden thoughts, and shows the microcosm of his inner life.
In the various portraits which he draws of Boris, who is for
him no Richard III or Cromwell, the Monarch appears at times
ambitious, majestic, and powerful, and, at other times, appre-
hensive, suspicious, tired, and unhappy. He is not only a criminal,
but also an enlightened ruler, a clever and progressive governor,
and a tender and anxious father. The carrier of the main idea
and the title of the play, Boris is a tragic hero because his
expectations concerning the high position he had bought with
his enormous crime prove illusory. He genuinely wants to bring
prosperity and happiness to his people, but they gradually turn
against him. Boris's tragedy is completed, *post mortem*, when

his son, for whom he had labored so hard and for whom he had so much hope, is innocently murdered for his father's crime, of which he knew nothing at all.

Even greater is the difference between the poet's and the historian's characterizations of Demetrius. Karamzin called the False Demetrius a "defrocked monk" who favored the Jesuits, "a villain," "an abominable sensualist," and, denying him any positive role, saw in him merely the weapon of providential punishment for Boris's crime.[47]

Puškin looked at the Pretender-Impostor with unmistakable sympathy. He regarded him a dreamer who was clever, ambitious, and determined to fulfill his purpose. A simple Russian soldier, speaking as a chorus, calls him a fine fellow ("molodec"),[48] and Kurbskij's son fights and dies for his cause. The two Puškins in the play are on his side, and the elder Puškin describes him as wise, affable, cunning, and popular with all men. To the poet's obvious delight, Demetrius leads the Polish King, the Pope, and the Jesuits by the nose and uses them only as temporary and expendable allies in his campaign to gain the Muscovite crown. He is heroic on the battlefield, gentle to his men and even to his horse, and courageously attacks Boris's large army with his small force.

In addition, Demetrius seems to express Puškin's own poetic views. In looking at Pimen, he expresses Puškin's affectionate opinion of the annalists: "I love the peaceful sight, / When, with his soul deep in the past immersed, / He keeps his chronicle." Through him Puškin proclaims the poet's prophetic mission: "I believe / The prophecies of singers. Not in vain / The ecstasy boils in their flaming breast." His magnanimity in victory ("Spare Russian blood") corresponds to many Puškinian statements on the subject of humane treatment of the defeated.[49]

The greater number of scenes allotted to Demetrius (out of twenty-two Demetrius appears in eight and Boris only in six), and a certain, perhaps unconscious, idealization of his character would create the impression that Puškin wanted to make him the hero of the play in spite of its title. Yet in two important scenes —Grigorij's dream in the monastery and the terror-stricken silence of the people at the end of the drama—Puškin predicts the eventual doom of Demetrius and manages to balance his two heroes.

The *Dumy* of Ryleev, the poet and Decembrist leader, may

be regarded as a predecessor of Puškin's tragedy, and the mono-
logue of Ryleev's Boris and Puškin's show unmistakable similarity:

Ryleev	Puškin
I thought I would be on the throne and, from its height, pour a river of good to the people.	I thought To satisfy my people in contentment, In glory, gain their love by generous gifts.[50]

Yet Ryleev's influence on *Boris Godunov* should not be
stressed too much. Puškin's Boris is infinitely more complex
and aesthetically a much more convincing human portrait than
Ryleev's. Ryleev concentrates only on Boris's ambition, on his
projects and crimes and their consequences, but does not show
us this monarch among his family, boyars, patriarch, and people, nor Boris's preoccupation with the war against Demetrius.
Ryleev's portrait of Demetrius is almost a carbon copy of Sumarokov's one-sided tyrant and has nothing to do with Puškin's
clever adventurer. Nor did Ryleev contribute anything to the
creation of secondary characters and events, in which *Boris
Godunov* is so rich.

The form, style, and ideological content of *Boris Godunov*
are largely derivative from Shakespeare's historical dramas.
Especially close to Puškin's drama were such of Shakespeare's
plays as describe the fate of usurpers on the throne (*Richard
III, Henry IV*).

The rulers in *Richard III* and *Boris Godunov* both murder a
young child, the legitimate heir, to attain power. The conduct
of both rulers at the time of their coronation, and their first
political pronouncements, show a partial resemblance. Both are
tormented by a guilty conscience, although Richard III only at
the very end of the play. The behavior of the people at the end
of Puškin's tragedy is almost identical with that of the city folk
at the time of Richard III's coronation.

There is a similarity between the rulers in Puškin's play and
in *Henry IV*, and further Shakespearean echoes may be found
in such mass scenes of *Boris Godunov* as the Red Square, Virgin's Field, and Public Square in Moscow. Perhaps an episode
of a mass scene in *Julius Caesar*, which Puškin probably read in
French or in Karamzin's translation first, may have influenced
him.

When he wrote *Boris Godunov,* was Puškin familiar with any
of the previous Demetrius dramas? There is no evidence that
he was acquainted with any of the Spanish, Italian, French, or
English Demetrius plays, and therefore it is generally assumed
that *El Gran Duque* was not known to him. Yet a juxtaposition
of both plays admits unquestionable similarities. Some of these
similarities reveal a remarkable degree of artistic kinship, in
spite of diametrically opposite sources from the point of view
of religious ideology.

In Lope's *comedia* Cristina urges Demetrio to study "armas
y letras," while in Puškin's play the Pretender stresses the relationship of the sword and the Muse: "Musa gloriam coronat,
gloriaque musam."[51] Both Puškin's Pimen and Lope's Lamberto
are elderly and saintly figures, narrate Boris's crimes, reveal the
past, prophesy the future, and bless their young disciples as
they are about to die.

When news reaches Puškin's Boris about Demetrius's appearance in Poland, he asks Šujskij, as Lope's Boris asks Rodulfo,
whether he has recognized the dead Prince Demetrius. Even
the answers of Šujskij and Rodulfo reveal distinct echoes.

Lope	Puškin
(Boris to Rodulfo:)	(Boris to Šujskij:)
¿Murió Demetrio?	Declare to me . . .
(Rodulfo to Boris:)	Didst recognize the slaughtered
Por Dios	boy; was't not
Que entre estas manos le vi	A substitute? Reply!
Rendir el alma del pecho.	(Šujskij to Boris:)
Que me digas me maravillo	. . . Could I deceive myself?
De lo que estas satisfecho.	So blindly as not recognize
Ni una piedra se descubre. . . .	Dimitry?
	. . . .
	No, my liege,
	There is no doubt; Dimitry
	sleeps in the grave.[52]

When definite news arrives concerning the Pretender's existence, both Lope's Rodulfo and Puškin's Šujskij console the
Tsar by putting the blame on the mob, which accepts blindly
any news.[53] In both plays Russian noblemen, political refugees
in Poland, recognize the Pretender as their rightful Tsar. In
both plays the people's opinion is decisive: in Poland Lope's

Demetrio hears of a "grande revolucion" against Boris, while Puškin's Šujskij speaks of a "mighty tempest" against the same monarch.[54] In Lope's play some noblemen talk of executions and tortures which Boris introduced against those who dare speak about Demetrio, and in Puškin's play a Russian prisoner describes the same conditions. Finally, there are some similarities in Boris's character. His essentially peaceful nature and his progressive ideas are stressed in both plays.

Puškin might have heard of Schiller's fragment from Žukovskij, a preromantic poet and translator who, as late as 1816-1817, planned to translate it. Puškin did not know German well enough at the time to have read Schiller's play in the original, and Žukovskij translated only the beginning of this fragment. The similarity must rather be due to artistic temper, with one basic difference. While Schiller is aloof from the masses and his heroes incarnate abstract ideas, Puškin shows great interest in the attitude of the people and in concrete situations.

The strongest resemblance between the two plays is in the scene at the Russian border. Schiller's Demetrius feels elated at the peaceful sight of the smiling spring landscape, as he is leading his troops toward the promised land, yet a reflective mood overwhelms him at the thought of bringing enemies into his beloved fatherland:

Der Czar . . . sei ganz nachdenkend geworden. . . . "Noch kann ich umkehren! Kein Schwerdt ist noch aus der Scheide! Kein Blut ist geflossen."[55]

At the crossing of the Polish-Russian border Puškin's Pretender feels a momentary sadness too because he regrets that "Russian blood . . . first must flow" before the way to "beauteous Moscow" is covered.[56]

Highly revealing is the contrasting attitude of the Pretender's companions in this scene. In Schiller's play even Odowalsky, the Polish mercenary, seems at first moved by the beauty, expanse, and fertility of nature.

> Doch ist ein kleiner Anfang nur, o Herr,
> Des grossen Russenreichs, denn unabsehbar,
> Streckt es der Morgensonne sich entgegen,
> Und keine Grenzen hat es nach dem Nord,
> Als die lebendige Zeugungskraft der Erde,[57]

Yet, as Marina's agent, he is essentially hostile to Russia and regards the land as booty which he can plunder at will. Thus, when the noble Demetrius feels depressed to have come to conquer his native country "mit des Krieges furchtbarem Geraeth,"[58] he contemptuously retorts that Demetrius should think about this aspect of his campaign later. In one of Schiller's most majestic poetical statements, Demetrius rebukes Odowalsky and states his own position:

> Du fuehlst als Pohle, ich bin Moskaus Sohn,
> Es ist das Land, das mir das Leben gab!
> Vergieb mir theurer Boden, heimische Erde,
> Du heiliger Grenzpfeiler, den ich fasse,
> Auf den mein Vater seinen Adler grub,
> Dass ich, dein Sohn, mit fremden Feindeswaffen
> In deines Friedens ruhigen Tempel falle.
> Mein Erb zurueck zu fordern komm ich her
> Und den geraubten edeln Vaternahmen. . . .[59]

How different all this sounds in Puškin's play! The roles have been completely changed and, instead of the indifferent Odowalsky, we have the highly patriotic young Kurbskij, much closer in spirit to Schiller's Demetrius than to Puškin's Pretender. As Kurbskij, unable to contain himself, is galloping at the head of the Russian troops toward his beloved native land, he exclaims in a passionate outburst:

> There, there it is: there is the Russian frontier!
> Fatherland! Holy Russia! I am thine!
> With scorn from off my clothing now I shake
> The foreign dust, and greedily I drink
> New air; it is my native air.[60]

Even the references to the fathers of both protagonists have similar overtones. Schiller's Demetrius claims the land "in the noble name of his father" and Puškin's Kurbskij is exultant that his father's name will be vindicated:

>   O father,
> Thy soul hath now been solaced; in the grave
> Thy bones, disgraced, thrill with a sudden joy!
> Again doth flash our old ancestral sword,

This glorious sword—the dread of dark Kazan!
This good sword—servant of the tsars of Moscow![61]

Still another contrast can be made. Odowalsky does not want
to serve the Muscovite Tsar, and merely accompanies him on
behalf of Marina who, as we learn later from Schiller's notes,
does not believe in Demetrius's true origin. Kurbskij, on the
other hand, in his childish innocence never doubts the impostor
and wants wholeheartedly to serve him. It is characteristic of
Puškin's sensitive art that he makes his Pretender follow Kurbskij "with bowed head,"[62] obviously ashamed of himself, both
admiring and envying him: "Brave knight, I envy thee. . . .
Righteous art thou."[63] Puškin's Pretender feels guilty in the
presence of such innocence and this is clearly shown by his repeated reference to Kurbskij's "stainless soul."[64] He understands
Kurbskij's desire to fight and to shed blood for his father's
honor, but what are his motives?

> . . . Thou for the tsar
> Hast drawn the sword . . . but I lead you
> Against your brothers; I am summoning
> Lithuania against Russia. . . .[65]

Finally, as if in reply to the reflection of Schiller's Demetrius
that "Kein Blut ist geflossen," Puškin's Pretender stops the
fight against Boris's army at Novgorod Seversk: "Enough!
Spare Russian blood."[66]

Another similarity may be found in the people's attitude
toward Demetrius. Schiller's Sigismund, the wise Polish king,
predicts to Demetrius:

> Die besten Waffen wird dir Russland geben
> Dein bester Schirm ist deines Volkes Herz
> Russland wird nur durch Russland ueberwunden.[67]

In *Boris Godunov,* the younger Puškin sways the vacillating
Basmanov to the Pretender's side:

> Our army is mere trash, the Cossacks only
> Rob villages, the Poles but drag and drink. . . .
> Wherein our strength lies? . . .
> In popular opinion. Dost remember

The triumph of Dimitry, dost remember
His peaceful conquests when, without a blow
The docile towns surrendered, and the mob
Bound the recalcitrant leaders? Thou thyself
Saw'st it; was it of their free-will our troops
Fought with him?[68]

Puškin might have heard of Kotzebue's play, but its spirit must have been completely contrary to his artistic concept. He certainly knew Sumarokov's tragedy, but he preferred Shakespeare's full-blooded romantic tragedies to the abstract neoclassicism of Corneille and Racine on which Sumarokov had based his play. The assurance of Sumarokov's Šujskij ("the mob's noise is not important, it is an empty sound, the wind disperses their bark, it disappears.")[69] with the intent of deceiving Demetrius finds a distant echo in the Boris-Šujskij confrontation in Puškin's play.

Despite Puškin's assertion that the dramatist "can completely separate himself from his own subjective thoughts in order to transfer himself fully to the century which he depicts,"[70] he himself could not avoid bringing personal experiences into his drama. The very theme of *Boris Godunov,* the usurpation of power through murder of the lawful heir, not only occurred in the eighteenth century, but also in Puškin's own time when Aleksandr I came to the throne after the assassination of Paul I, an assassination in which he to some extent participated. In reading Karamzin's history, Puškin saw the reflection of modern times, and wrote to Žukovskij: "C'est palpitant comme la gazette d'hier."[71] Having finished his drama, Puškin hinted at its hidden political thought: "Elle est remplie de bonnes plaisanteries et d'allusions fines à l'hist. de ce temps."[72] He also refers to "ears" which "jut out" from the tragedy.[73] In his study, "Boris Godunov i dramaturgija 20-x godov" ("Boris Godunov and the Drama of the Twenties"), A. L. Slonimskij, a Russian literary scholar, points out that in Demetrius's role there are some autobiographical moments such as Pimen's "writer's" cell, in which the thoughts of a person bored with the "monk's captive life" are born, and relates it to Puškin's own exile in Mixailovskoe.[74] The author mentions that *Boris Godunov,* completed five weeks before the Decembrist revolt (December 14, 1825), was the fruit of a definite political moment, and the optimistic description of Demetrius's triumphal campaign may be construed as a perhaps unconscious reflection of the Decembrist temper on the eve of the uprising.[75] I may complement Slonim-skij's comments by noting the important role of the two Puškins —uncle and nephew—in the play. While the nephew sends the electrifying news about the Pretender's appearance and his social and political success in Cracow, the uncle triggers the play's final resolution by his nocturnal visit to the tent of Basmanov, convincing the commander of Boris's army of the hopelessness of the fight against the determined attitude of the Russian peo-ple who regard Demetrius as their rightful ruler. Boris's angry comment, "I like not the seditious race of Puškins,"[76] when Semen Godunov, his brother, informs him of the secret conver-sation between Šujskij and the elder Puškin, reinforces this im-pression.

XOMJAKOV'S *DIMITRIJ SAMOZVANEC* (THE FALSE DEMETRIUS)

In Puškin's giant shadow Aleksej S. Xomjakov's excellent play, *Dimitrij Samozvanec* (The False Demetrius), written in 1833,[77] did not receive its undoubtedly well-deserved critical acclaim. Although it lacks the epic calm and sustained lyrical quality of Xomjakov's drama *Ermak,* this play is an extraor-dinary and moving manifesto of the author's special brand of Slavophilism. A romantic nationalist, Xomjakov idealized Rus-sia's past and wanted to become a prophet of national conscious-ness by documenting and glorifying the unique characteristics, inherent strength, and historical mission of Russia.

The play begins after Demetrius's coronation, shows his clash with the Poles, Jesuits, and boyars, and ends with his fall engi-neered by the Šujskij group. The tragedy is partly within Deme-trius himself. He is basically a Russian and a heroic figure, but by accepting Polish and Jesuit aid he compromises the purity of his position and opens the way to a tragic ethical resolution.

In this drama Xomjakov convincingly shows the basic oppo-sition and inevitable struggle in a world historical perspective between two civilizations, the Catholic West and the Orthodox East, and points out that true friendship cannot exist between the intellectually arrogant, aristocratic Poles and the more sim-ple Russians because of the Poles' animosity, feeling of superior-ity, and contempt, incited by the Popes of Rome. The existence of the Muscovite state is threatened by Western emissaries who humiliate the people, trying to force their religion and social ideas on them, and when the Russians refuse to accept these foreign concepts as inimical to their own ideals, the combined forces of Rome and Cracow prepare to crush the Muscovites. This disciplinarian and intolerant Roman heresy is for Xomjakov more political and imperialistic than religious in nature since it seeks to destroy Christian fellowship through the Jesuits, its *avant-garde* who foster rivalries in their drive for power, offering the Russians the choice of baptism or death. Yet in Xomjakov's view, this Western Catholic scholasticism is doomed, and the end of the play must be interpreted not so much as Demetrius's fall, but as the fall of those opportunists who, hiding behind his shield, are only waiting for the proper psychological moment to grab the power for themselves.

Although richly sprinkled with Xomjakov's philosophical and theological thought, *The False Demetrius* is neither a rigid drama *à thèse,* nor a reactionary attachment to a sterile past of Russian history. It is one of the most enlightened Demetrius dramas in world literature and worthy of being juxtaposed with the great fragments of Schiller and Hebbel with their double *Leitmotifs* of justice and civilization in a new era for mankind. In his play Xomjakov looks forward to a better and more glorious Russia as he charts out an intelligent progress for the destiny of his beloved country based on unity and freedom.

Xomjakov relied heavily on Karamzin for most of his historical material. The positive evaluation which he gives to Boris Godunov suggests that he was also acquainted with the defense of this statesman by Pogodin, the first Russian historian who seriously doubted Boris's complicity in Demetrius's death. As for the roles of Jesuits and Poles in his play, Xomjakov may have read Metropolitan Platon's *History of the Church* and Pogodin's study about Otrep'ev. Xomjakov was also familiar with *The Reporte of a Bloudie and Terrible Massacre in the Citty of Mosco,* an anonymous contemporary account concerning the revolt against the alleged Demetrius, and in a preface to his play he quotes the opinion of the anonymous author that Demetrius's fall was mainly owing to the machinations of the Pope and the Jesuits.

The author continues Puškin's innocent idealization and moral rehabilitation of Demetrius and carries it one step further. Although set on the throne by Poles and Jesuits, Demetrius is not their tool. Xomjakov's hero is eloquent, brave, passionate, generous, and intelligent, perhaps the messenger of a new age. He loves glory, is willing to fight for it, and has both the physical and intellectual faculties for attaining it. Although he believes that culture will come to Russia from the West, he is a Russian and not a Westerner, a Puškinian dreamer who wants to bring enlightenment to make Russia great, and to unite Russians and Poles in a friendly family. He is ready to embrace his Russian brothers, but finds a great many obstacles in his way. Carried away by the fashions of Europe, he likes to dress elegantly and to display his physical strength and gallantry, forgetting that in tradition-bound Russia the tsar is a saint and that he should avoid such external manifestations of West-European civilization. Demetrius of Xomjakov's drama is not a tyrant maintaining his throne by violence, nor a sovereign upheld by confidence. When threatened by an uprising he does not compromise or seek to save his life at the cost of innocent victims. He does not like the Poles' haughtiness and denounces the Jesuits' intrigues. He knows that he is not Ivan's son, but feels that by his courageous actions he has justly immortalized Demetrius's name and given it fame and glory. As if in delirium this visionary Demetrius outlines his great plan for the future of Russia in the last scene of the play and, as Basmanov, his faithful disciple, listens in fascination, he promises to help Russia, in harmony with her great past, accomplish her sacred mission for the good of mankind so that the whole world will revere her. This is the only Russian Demetrius play in which Demetrius pays a warm tribute to Boris's virtues as a great statesman.

The boyars are at times paralyzed, at other times divided among themselves, and Šujskij, the hypocrite, utilizes their vacillation to have Demetrius murdered and himself elevated to the throne. Yet Xomjakov hints at further trouble when one of the important boyars, Skopin-Šujskij, accuses Vasilij Šujskij of "having turned a just tribunal into a criminal act." Another boyar, Ljapunov, originally Demetrius's enemy, repents the death of "this fallen leader" who had "so many noble thoughts," promising that "the day of revenge" will come against "this wicked old man" (Šujskij), and now that "the lion is dead, we will get even with the fox."[78]

The Jesuit Kvickij is a sinister figure who prepares a blood bath for the boyars and people of Moscow when he sees that his plans for the establishment of Catholic churches in the Kremlin are frustrated. The Polish ambassadors are arrogant, regard

Demetrius as their inferior, and openly insult him. Yet the confident and strong Demetrius not only puts the Polish diplomats to shame, but even goes so far as to challenge Poland to war. Such a war would have been the only way to stop political and social dissent in Russia, to satisfy national pride badly hurt by the unwelcome visitors, and to rally most of the vacillating boyars to Demetrius's sinking flag. However, Marina, *the femme fatale* who dominates the passionate Demetrius, intervenes and, coached by her Jesuit confessor, deceives him and prevents the war. This seals Demetrius's fate, since the disappointed boyars abandon him, and the cunning Šujskij gains a free hand for his conspiracy.

The main hero of the play is the Russian people and the idea of Russian nationality. The Russians are shown as childlike, simple, and unaffected, if backward and gullible. If the people's conceptions are traditional, rude, and imperfect, they are still sincere, and it is the people who retain the idea of national consciousness. They are truthful, but the Šujskij clique betrays them, and they become confused and lose their unity. This is perhaps the most patriotic Russian Demetrius drama and the occasional lyric tone, the poetic description of the Kremlin at night, and the recurring folklore elements movingly reveal the author's love for his native land.

In contrast to Karamzin, Xomjakov conceived of Basmanov as a good Russian and patriot who shares Demetrius's dream of a better and greater Russia, although he knows that the Pretender is not Ivan's son.

Xomjakov presumably read Sumarokov's play and, although their Demetriuses are diametrically opposite, the anti-Popist and anti-Polish sentiments of Sumarokov must have found his approval. Puškin's play was an important literary source for Xomjakov, and he continued the events of the Time of Troubles at the point where Puškin left them at the end of *Boris Godunov*.

Although it is possible that Xomjakov, who spoke several languages, read Schiller's *Demetrius* in German, there is no definite evidence of it in his drama. Demetrius's noble dreams, the Marfa theme, Marina's egoism, and the Jesuits' intrigues are, as pointed out before, motifs dear to the German dramatist and therefore we can speak of general similarities rather than distinct borrowings. The objective evaluation of Tsar Boris may also have been borrowed from Schiller. However, specific instances of Schiller's influence on Xomjakov cannot be found, and it is difficult to believe that a playwright who had read Schiller's majestic fragment would not have succumbed to the temptation of imitating, subconsciously at least, a situation, introducing an idea, or reproducing a verbal image from the German drama in his own play.

Xomjakov's entire drama is a passionate dialogue with the ideas of his time, the Slavophile and Westernizer controversy, and the Polish uprising of 1830. His personal participation and experience in the Crimean war against the Turks (1828-1829) may also account for the sharpness of his topical references.

LOBANOV'S *BORIS GODUNOV*

I mention Mixail E. Lobanov's *Boris Godunov* (1835)[79] as an extreme example of a play which idealizes the ruler's legitimacy. Dissatisfied with Puškin's divergence from Karamzin's monarchism, Lobanov apparently decided to correct "this mistake," and to set the record straight. The hero of the play is Nikita Romanov, Ivan the Terrible's brother-in-law by his first marriage, and the events deal mainly with his exile and martyrdom. Boris, the villain of the play, is overthrown by Šujskij's machinations; the latter, although an intriguer, is viewed with sympathy since he is related to the House of Rjurik. Demetrius, regarded as an impostor, never appears in the play, but his influence is manifested indirectly and his threatening shadow looms large in the background.

The playwright was obviously influenced by the numerous palace revolutions, the fall of legitimate rulers, and the chaotic conditions in Russia of the eighteenth century.

OSTROVSKIJ'S *DIMITRIJ SAMOZVANEC I VASILIJ ŠUJSKIJ* (THE FALSE DEMETRIUS AND VASILIJ ŠUJSKIJ)

For my historical-literary study of the Demetrius legend Aleksandr N. Ostrovskij's tragedy *Dimitrij Samozvanec i Vasilij Šujskij* (The False Demetrius and Vasilij Šujskij), written in 1867,[80] plays an important role, since this is the first Russian drama which shows Demetrius as a completely innocent man who does not know his origin.

Ostrovskij's drama is "the fruit of fifteen years of experience and a long study of sources."[81] Although Karamzin still figures prominently among Ostrovskij's sources, by this time his unique position in Russian historiography was broken, and the author relied also on the history of Solov'ev, who had already indicated that the Pretender was not necessarily a conscious fraud. The playwright was most significantly influenced, however, by Kostomarov's brochure, *Who Was the First False Demetrius?* Ostrovskij adopted and dramatized all the main postulates of Kostomarov's new thesis: 1) The Pretender was not Otrep'ev; 2) Neither Boris nor Šujskij knew who the Pretender was; 3) Although the Pretender was helped by the Poles and the Jesuits, he was basically the tool of boyars hostile to Boris; 4) The Pretender was not a conscious fraud; 5) Marfa's recognition of the Pretender as her son was due to her emotional condition; 6) The circumstances surrounding the Pretender's appearance invalidate the claim that he was Ivan's true son. In addition, Ostrovskij accepted Kostomarov's phrase, the "alleged" Demetrius, and used it to indicate that the Pretender was neither Ivan's son nor a conscious impostor.

Ostrovskij cast the historical information obtained from his sources into a realistic and vivid drama. If the construction is loose, the background, plot, and characters are highly dramatic. Ostrovskij was especially successful in capturing the spirit and color, and reproducing the idiom, of the period. The playwright liked to deal with vices such as lust, greed, and fraud, and in the Demetrius legend he found these on a national scale. In addition, this chronicle play gave him an opportunity to display once more the characteristic trait of *samodurstvo* (blind obduracy), a favorite theme in most of his social dramas, in the tyrannical power and backwardness of the boyars. It is interesting to note that he highlights the role of merchants among Šujskij's followers, which role, while historically attested, permits him to expose the superstition and barbaric atmosphere of merchant life and so reminds the reader of his "Kingdom of Darkness," the world of his great play, *Groza* (The Thunderstorm), to use the phrase of the contemporary Russian critic Dobroljubov.

Ostrovskij's drama shows the struggle of a progressive Demetrius with a cunning Šujskij and his final defeat by him. It follows Kostomarov's historical theory: the boyars, having become tired of Boris's haughty treatment, raise an unknown waif in secrecy, similar in age and appearance to Prince Demetrius, in order to put him forward as Pretender for the throne.

This Demetrius is brought up in Poland, where he secures the help of the Jesuits and the Poles in exchange for his promise to convert the Russians to Catholicism and to award some Russian lands to Poland. The boyars become desperate when Demetrius, already Tsar of Russia, instead of serving as their obedient instrument, turns out to be a highly imaginative and enlightened, though at times foolishly romantic, monarch who has his own ideas as to how to govern the land. The tension lies between the reform government of Demetrius, which, while incorporating the constructive elements of the past, stands for progress, enlightenment, and Western culture, and the egoism and unscrupulousness of the great boyars who, appealing to xenophobia, religious tradition, and coarseness of their followers among the Muscovites, engineer the fall of the hero.

Ostrovskij's play appears as a kind of continuation of Puškin's *Boris Godunov,* and relates the subsequent events of the Time of Troubles. Puškin's play ends with the murder of Boris's son and wife as Demetrius approaches Moscow, while Ostrovskij's chronicle drama begins in the early days of the entry of Demetrius into Moscow (June 19, 1605).

As a direct continuation of a scene in Puškin's play in which Demetrius admires the German mercenaries in Boris's army who have distinguished themselves in one of the battles in Russia and consequently decides to hire them to be his bodyguards, in Ostrovskij's play they already act in that capacity. Ostrovskij's Demetrius recalls the high opinion of Puškin's Demetrius as to the military valor of the German mercenaries at the battle of Dobryna, and congratulates Captain Margeret, their French leader.

There are many echoes of Puškin's play in Ostrovskij's, such as the egoism and ambition of Marina, who does not really love the Pretender, and the frequent reference to the crown of Monomax, the famous Russian ruler at the end of the eleventh and the beginning of the twelfth century. At the end of Puškin's drama the boyar Mosalskij falsely informs the people that Boris's son and wife have poisoned themselves, while at the end of Ostrovskij's play Šujskij misinforms the people that Demetrius has confessed his crime when just the opposite has, in fact, happened and the dying Demetrius asked to be taken to the people to tell them the truth about himself. It is interesting to note that when Ostrovskij had a choice of using an almost equivalent phrase coined by Karamzin and Puškin, he consistently preferred Puškin's dramatic version to Karamzin's historical treatment.[82]

Since Ostrovskij belonged vaguely to the Slavophile camp, it is not surprising that his play reveals a striking resemblance to that of Xomjakov. These resemblances are not necessarily influences and may be due to a similar reinterpretation of the events of the Time of Troubles on the part of both writers, their ideological kinship, artistic preference, and the *Zeitgeist* of the period. Another link between both writers is their obvious intention to use Puškin's tragedy as a common denominator and a point of departure for their own plays.

Ostrovskij, whose play has almost the same plot as Xomjakov's, sees in Demetrius much the same dreamer as does his Slavophile predecessor. His hero is good, brave, intelligent, and eloquent. He wants to introduce Western ideas and civilization and to bring glory to Russia. He has no need for a bodyguard "among his own children." A just and honest ruler, he does not want to spill one drop of Russian blood. Though helped by the Jesuits, and flattered by them as a new Constantin, leader of religious schism, he does not listen to their demands, and regards both Latins and Turks in the same light, as enemies of his Russia. The Russians like him as their father, and when they hear of the conspiracy, they rush to save him. Especially strong is the similarity of the two plays in the last scene when Ostrovskij's Demetrius, like Xomjakov's hero, already wounded and in a coma, dreams of a great crusade against the Turks and calls "his spirited steed" to take him to "Tsargrad," the old Russian name for Constantinople in Byzantium, so that he can "hang Oleg's shield on its gate."[83] The reference to the daring conquest of Constantinople by the Varangian Rus' tribe under the leadership of the legendary Oleg in 907 (mentioned by the old Russian *Nestor Chronicle*) is meant to show Russia's great past, to link the two figures together, and to emphasize the Russian nationality of the Pretender.

As in Xomjakov's play, the boyars are disunited. The great boyars, followers of Vasilij Šujskij, are against Demetrius, while the smaller nobles, who dislike the machinations of Šujskij and his clique, are ready to die for him. As in Xomjakov's play, Šujskij is shown to be a liar and a hypocrite who wants to become Tsar even at the cost of a crime. At the end, when he makes himself a self-proclaimed Tsar, two boyars, Golicyn and Kurakin, are as much outraged at his duplicity as Skopin-Šujskij and Ljapunov were in observing Šujskij's dishonesty in Xomjakov's tragedy.

Ostrovskij also continues the human portrait of Basmanov drawn by Xomjakov. He is not the Karamzinian traitor, an opportunist, who sells his services to the highest bidder, but a true patriot who sincerely loves his country and admires the wisdom of the young Pretender. Basmanov shares the high ideals of Demetrius and repeatedly, although unsuccessfully, warns him of the boyars' intrigue.

The role of the people, originally sketched by Puškin in the tradition of Shakespeare and developed by Xomjakov, has been further intensified by Ostrovskij. Since Ostrovskij was an admirer of Shakespeare, the two influences converged, leading him to allot seven scenes out of fourteen of his play to show the decisive importance of the people's participation in the historical events during the reign of Demetrius.

Finally, it is interesting to note that both Ostrovskij's and Xomjakov's are open-end plays and invite continuation. This is obviously a device of Puškin, who, taking Shakespeare as a model, at the end of his play used the eloquent silence of the people to predict the ultimate fall of the Pretender. Although less artistic in that they leave no room for the reader's imagination, both Ostrovskij and Xomjakov end their plays with the denunciation of Šujskij, the apparent winner of this political scramble, and prophesy further trouble to come. Indeed, the next drama Xomjakov planned was to be entitled *Prokopij Ljapunov,* the name of a historical person and a character in his Demetrius drama, who in the latter play rings down the curtain with the prophetic vow that now that "the lion is dead, we will get even with the fox." Presumably in this projected drama, which remained a fragment, Ljapunov, in the camp of the second Demetrius, was to fight against Šujskij. Similarly, Ostrovskij's next historical play *Tušino* dealt with Šujskij's downfall against the background of the second Demetrius's siege of Moscow.

Ostrovskij, the most prolific Russian playwright, followed with interest the development of drama abroad and undoubtedly knew Schiller's fragment; certain definite influences of the German drama on his own play can be pointed out.

The desire of Ostrovskij's Demetrius to be a just ruler and his refusal to tyrannize his people is a motif similar to that of the German play. In his notebook Ostrovskij described the political program of Demetrius "to give freedom to all these serfs," which parallels Schiller's "Ich will aus Sklaven Menschen machen."[84]

Almost every German Demetrius play has exploited the highly dramatic and emotional encounter between Demetrius and Marfa. Of the Russian dramas available to us, only Ostrovskij's treats their first confrontation. Schiller's influence may already be seen in the physical arrangement and décor of the scene, which takes place inside a tent, the sides of which are raised at an appropriate psychological moment so that the Russians, who come to witness the meeting of the royal mother with her miraculously saved son, may see the weeping mother in her son's arms and be fully convinced, in spite of whispers and doubts spread by the Šujskijites, that Demetrius is Ivan's son. As in Schiller's fragment, Ostrovskij's Marfa at first refuses to recognize her son in Demetrius, yet the latter's moving plea and noble conduct impresses Marfa so strongly that a certain *modus vivendi* is established between them. Of several passages in which the verbal echo is unmistakable, I quote the following two examples:

Schiller
Ich zerriss den traurigen Nonnenschleier, der dich von der Welt getrennt. . . . Ich habe dich geraecht an deinem Feind, dich und dein Blut, ich habe aus dem Elend, aus der Gruft in der du lebendig begraben warst, dich gezogen und auf den Fuerstenstuhl zurueckgefuehrt.

Ich will dich als Mutter behandeln. Du sollst einen ehrerbietigen Sohn in mir sehen.

Ostrovskij
While you lived in captivity among the old, lifeless, and quarrelsome . . . I prepared a throne for you. I destroyed your torturers. I liberated your family and relatives. . . . I cleared a wide road for you to your capital.

My soul burns with childlike love for you. . . . I will try to be such a son to you that you will forget your own.[85]

Schiller describes Demetrius: "Er hat alle ritterliche Geschicklichkeiten inne, weiss die wildesten Pferde zu baendigen, feuert Kanonen ab," and Ostrovskij's Šujskij depicts him thus: "He loves wars, he is bold. . . . He jumps on a horse, like a Tartar, without a saddle and handles his sword especially well."[86]

As far as I can ascertain, the similarity between Hebbel's

Demetrius and Ostrovskij's play has never been investigated. Although the dates of the publication of the two dramas are uncomfortably close, 1864 and 1867, Ostrovskij still could have obtained and read Hebbel's play. Common sources of simple coincidences do not give a satisfactory answer and the number of similarities justify a more thorough investigation of this problem.

Ostrovskij skillfully shows the mysterious origin of his enigmatic hero, who feels himself a stranger and interloper on the throne of Ivan the Terrible. It seems to Demetrius that Ivan's ghost addresses him from the empty throne and calls him "a tramp without a beard," wafted aross Russia "by criminal hands."[87] Demetrius asks himself who he can be if he is not Ivan's son, when everybody calls him Tsar Demetrius and he looks like Ivan. Perhaps, Demetrius muses, he is the product of Ivan's sensuousness, an incidental fruit of his passing fancy. The physical similarity between Demetrius and Ivan was also stressed by Hebbel.

If Ostrovskij read Hebbel's fragment, he might have been influenced by the German playwright's solution of presenting Demetrius as Ivan's illegitimate son. This assumption may be reinforced by a reference which Ostrovskij's Marfa makes in her conversation with Demetrius concerning the latter's mother, who "may be hiding somewhere in the crowd."[88] In Hebbel's play Barbara, Demetrius's mother, is actually hiding in the crowd during Demetrius's triumphant entry into Moscow.

In Ostrovskij's play Demetrius also recalls his passionate youth, quite similar to his "father's," while Hebbel shows Demetrius's passionate temper in an early scene when he kills Odowalsky, the Polish nobleman, on a slight provocation. After reporting this event to the Cardinal, Gregory tells him "Ich weiss nicht wie es kam," and the Cardinal replies, "Das wusste man auch nie bei seinem Vater."[89] His grandiose dreams for glory and heroism convince Ostrovskij's Demetrius that no common blood flows in his veins, and the reader recalls in Hebbel's *Vorspiel* the allusion to his "koenigliche Eigenschaften."[90]

There are some references in connection with Marfa common to both plays. Marfa's recollection, in Ostrovskij's play, of her conduct in Uglič when she stirred people to a "bloody uprising" may find its prototype in a similar passage in Hebbel's fragment.[91] The complaint of Ostrovskij's Marfa that she was forced to come to the camp of the alleged Demetrius finds its parallel in the German play.

There is an important parallel dealing with the abortive attempt to introduce Catholicism in Russia in both plays. Ostrovskij's Demetrius refuses to pay attention to the Jesuits' request in this matter and in Hebbel's play Demetrius turns down a similar plea, "Nein, nein, mein Volk soll beten wie es will."[92]

The Polish uprising of 1863-1864 may have been instrumental in the sharp anti-Polish tone of Ostrovskij's play. His Basmanov remarks that there can be no true friendship between Poles and Russians and that Demetrius should throw the Poles out of the country. Ostrovskij obviously used his Demetrius as his mouthpiece for outlining his social philosophy, developed in many of his plays: to do away with fear, to give women rights, and to end the yoke of patriarchal customs.

ALEKSEJ K. TOLSTOJ'S *TSAR BORIS*

In his trilogy Aleksej K. Tolstoj dramatized a great part of the Time of Troubles. In the second drama of the trilogy he produced a remarkable human portrait of Tsar Feodor, a portrait which, as we have seen, resembles Lope's Teodoro. But his real hero is Boris Godunov, who serves as the link connecting his three dramas. Tolstoj traces Boris's rise on the political ladder at Ivan's court in the first part of his trilogy, his *de facto* rule during the reign of the weak Feodor, his crushing of the boyar opposition, and his engineering of Tsarevich Demetrius's murder in the second, and finally, in the concluding part, his coronation and fall.

In *Tsar Boris* (1870)[93] we see Boris crowned amid general jubilation. The land, left desolate and torn after Ivan's death, has prospered anew and grown strong under his able leadership during Feodor's nominal reign. His fame even spreads abroad so that foreign ambassadors vie with one another in heaping gifts on him. Boris rules as an enlightened monarch, suppresses pangs of conscience, refuses to listen to his nun-sister who suggests that he do penance for his past, and feels that the general happiness of the people absolves his original sin—his criminal past, and justifies his conduct. Yet when news of Demetrius's appearance arrives and the Muscovites begin to spread the word, he loses his confidence, becomes a tyrant, and punishes anyone who dares to speak of his adversary. Thus, he gradually loses everyone's sympathy, people flock to the camp of Demetrius, and political and social crises envelop Russia. Trouble develops even in Boris's own family as Kristian, the young Danish prince, Ksenija Godunova's bridegroom, is senselessly poisoned by Boris's wife, who is opposed to their match because of her religious intolerance and superstition. Boris sees the ghost of Tsarevich Demetrius, realizes that his crime was a grievous mistake, loses control of himself, feels death near and, just before dying, names his son as the new tsar.

Tolstoj was well acquainted with the old Russian chronicles and historical literature, and was himself a folklorist and writer of historical ballads. His two important historical sources were Karamzin and Kostomarov. Karamzin's influence may be seen, among many other details, in Boris's activities and in the reception of foreign envoys. In addition, Tolstoj borrowed several verbal images and phrases from the historian.

The influence of Kostomarov's thesis is shown in Boris's feverish efforts in the play to give a name to the mysterious Pretender, who, so long as he is not named properly, may well pass for Tsarevich Demetrius for the people; in the play Semen Godunov, Boris's brother and police chief, suggests that they identify the Pretender with the runaway monk Griška Otrep'ev. The inclusion of a scene, in which we see Otrep'ev, a hungry and cowardly monk speaking stilted Church Slavonic, is an obvious echo of Kostomarov's opinion that Demetrius was not Otrep'ev.

Tolstoj also used Isaac Massa's contemporary account for the episode in which Boris's wife, the daughter of the *opričnik* Maljuta Skuratov, throws a burning candle in Marfa's face when the latter refuses Boris's request to disavow the Pretender as her son.

Finally, Tolstoj also read some Danish accounts of the background of Kristian, the Danish prince and fiancé of Ksenija, Boris's lovely daughter. He correctly reversed Karamzin's unhistoric statement that Kristian fought for Spain and showed him among the Protestant insurgents in the battle of Flanders against the Catholic army of Philip II of Spain.

Tolstoj did not know Lope's *El Gran Duque,* but we find some similarities between the two plays. Of these the most arresting is Boris's reference in Tolstoj's drama to Tsarevich Demetrius when he says that "he is killed, but [is] alive,"[94] revealing his doubt as to Demetrius's identity. This reference recalls the famous encounter of Boris with the monk Demetrio in Lope's *comedia,* when Boris saw, or believed that he saw, the "murdered" Demetrio "alive" in front of himself.

The author unquestionably knew all the previous Demetrius dramas in Russian literature. A comparison of Tolstoj's *Tsar Boris* with Puškin's *Boris Godunov* creates the impression that Tolstoj broadened the psychological portrait of Puškin's Boris, created a full-fledged *Seelendrama,* and left out all the material not closely connected with Boris. Among several similarities the most important are the following: Boris's displeasure at the people's ingratitude, the people's calling him a new Tsar Ivan because of his cruelty, and his assuring his son Feodor, of the latter's innocence of his crime. A continuation of a Puškinian idea may be seen in the frequent references to St. George's Day ("Jur'ev den'") with its tying of serfs to one estate in Tolstoj's play. In *Boris Godunov* Šujskij offers to go to the people to unmask Otrep'ev's lies, while in *Tsar Boris* he is already telling the people that Demetrius died in Uglič and therefore the Pretender cannot be Demetrius.

One verbal echo will suffice to show Tolstoj's indebtedness to Puškin. In Puškin's play when the Pretender asks a Russian prisoner what the people in Moscow think of him, the latter answers "Even if you may be a criminal, you are still a fine fellow" ("ty . . . i vor, a molodec"). Speaking of the Pretender in Tolstoj's play, Basmanov mentions, "Although he is a criminal, he is still a brave fellow" ("xot' on i vor, a udal").[95]

It is interesting to speculate on the reason for a missing link in Tolstoj's chronicle plays. Why did he not write a play on Demetrius, create a tetralogy and complete the history of the epoch? Why did he avoid the subject which most of the Russian and German dramatists found so fascinating?

"They way to the False Demetrius has been prepared by my first dramas," Tolstoj wrote in 1870, "but this theme has been quite mishandled."[96] Since, in the same letter, Tolstoj polemicizes Xomjakov, stating that the latter's Slavophilism disgusts him, we can conclude that he was dissatisfied with Demetrius's portrait as painted by Xomjakov. In spite of Tolstoj's statement that he planned to write a drama on the subject, the absence of the Demetrius theme among his works may also be due to his religious views and national consciousness, which presumably clashed with the interpretation of most of the other playwrights of Demetrius's role. Tolstoj obviously regarded the Pretender as an impostor, an agent of the Poles and Jesuits, and not a Russian type, and had no desire to immortalize an enemy of the Russian state in his historical dramas.

It should be pointed out in this connection that, while Tolstoj followed the main line of Puškin's play in general, he almost completely disregarded the Puškinian portrait of the Pretender. We find only such occasional references to Demetrius as the general movement of the drama requires. This impression may be reinforced by a curious shift of ideological emphasis in the introduction of Western ideas in Tolstoj's play. We have seen that, in the Demetrius plays of Puškin, Xomjakov, and Ostrovskij, it is the Pretender who dreams of bringing culture and civilization into Russia, while in *Tsar Boris,* Tolstoj, the most Western-minded of these playwrights, credits Boris with all these progressive plans.

In a conversation with a poet, Puškin's Pretender mentions that "I was born beneath / A northern sky, but yet the Latin muse / To me is a familiar voice; I love / The blossoms of Parnassus," while Tolstoj's Boris, who is called "the friend of knowledge and art," tells the envoy of Florence that "Our Russian land is severe, / God did not bless us, as He did you, / To rejoice our eyes with art's beauty / Under a free sky,"[97] as he accepts the offer of Prince Ferdinand of Medici to send artists, painters, and architects to Russia.

Ostrovskij's Pretender defends the girls' freedom to marry without being forced; Tolstoj's Boris represents the same idea. The Demetrius of Xomjakov and Ostrovskij feels that enlightenment will come from the West, and in Tolstoj's drama Feodor, Boris's son, explains to Kristian that Boris wants to rebuild what the Tartars destroyed with help from the West; the choice of this Danish Prince as Ksenija's husband is regarded as an obvious link with the rest of Europe and an end to Russia's isolation.

In the plays of Puškin, Xomjakov, and Ostrovskij, the Pretender is shown as mild, liberal, and generous, reluctant to punish even criminals, and anxious not to spill Russian blood. This is the portrait Tolstoj draws of Boris through the entire drama up to the point when, threatened by loss of power, he turns into a tyrant.

Boris's unfriendly conduct toward the Polish ambassadors and his desire to lead a Crusade against the Turks are reminiscent of Demetrius's attitude and plans in the plays of Xom-jakov and Ostrovskij. In Puškin's play the dissatisfied boyars expect the Pretender to abolish the custom of St. George's Day in order to stop the flow of fugitive serfs, while in Tolstoj's drama it is Boris who promises that this will be done.

One can even extract the Slavophile ideology from Deme-trius's portrait in the plays of Xomjakov and Ostrovskij and that of the Westerners from the portrait of Tolstoj's Boris. The former stresses the legendary strength of the Russian earth and Russia's ties with the East in Demetrius's imaginary foray against Byzantium, while Tolstoj emphasizes the wisdom and intelligence of the early leaders of the Rus' of Kiev and Nov-gorod in having established peaceful political and commercial connections with the West.

Finally, Schiller's important literary influence on the character construction of Tolstoj's art must be pointed out. In his project for *Tsar Feodor,* Tolstoj revealed his preference for the analyti-cal German school by quoting a passage from Schiller's *Wallen-stein.* We find that Tolstoj analyzes Boris not from a historical and political but from a moral and psychological viewpoint. Thus, both playwrights make their heroes bearers of an ethical idea, human truth prevailed for both over historical actuality, and both used psychological realism in depicting their protag-onists. Tolstoj stresses that art, without denying reality, should choose the typical traits and essence of characters, and he illus-trates his thesis by contrasting painting to photography. The rigid employment of this thesis, however, leads Tolstoj to a certain abstraction in Boris's portrait. Compared to the vivid and idiomatic speech of the other protagonists in his dramatic trilogy, Boris at times speaks not unlike an eighteenth century *raisonneur* and reminds the reader of Starodum, the hero of *The Minor,* a comedy by Denis Fonvizin, a pioneer of Rus-sian satirical drama.

SUVORIN'S *CAR DMITRIJ SAMOZVANEC I CAREVNA KSENIJA* (TSAR DMITRIJ THE IMPOSTOR AND PRINCESS KSENIJA.)

The key to the main idea of the last Russian Demetrius drama, Aleksej S. Suvorin's *Car Dmitrij Samozvanec i Car-evna Ksenija* (Tsar Dmitrij the Impostor and Princess Ksen-ija),[98] written in 1905, can be found in the author's own essay

On the False Demetrius, containing several of his articles on the subject. The point of these articles is the bold new idea that the alleged Demetrius could have been the son of Ivan the Terrible, and that the leaders of the *coup d'état* in Moscow were aware that they had killed the last offspring of the Rjurik dynasty and not a runaway monk. Yet, as the title of the play reveals, in spite of his new thesis Suvorin is not sure of his conclusion, since he still calls his Demetrius, who is haunted by reverie, memory, and dreamlike associations, an impostor.

A dilettante historian and occasional playwright, Suvorin was a conservative intellectual who possessed considerable historical and literary knowledge. He had discussed the Demetrius problem with Kostomarov, Ključevskij and Father Pierling, and had read most of the previous Demetrius dramas in Russian and world literature, including Lope's *comedia.*

Suvorin's rich historical fund of knowledge should be noted. In addition to Karamzin, Solov'ev, and Kostomarov, several other sources influenced his drama. For example, the reflection of the account of Captain Margeret, the bodyguard of the alleged Demetrius, is shown in Otrep'ev's presence in Demetrius's own camp, a fact which Margeret recorded, so that anyone can be convinced of the falsity of Boris's charge that the Pretender is Otrep'ev. Suvorin's familiarity with contemporary Polish sources, also, is reflected in a conversation between Lisjanskij, the Polish nobleman, and Bučinskij, Demetrius's secretary, in which the former asserts that Demetrius's escape from the murderers at Uglič sounds "like a comedy by Plautus or Terence."[99] This statement was originally made by Jan Zamojski, the influential Polish chancellor, who expressed his doubts about Demetrius's identity in reply to King Sigismund's inquiry.

Suvorin's acquaintance with Rochelle's popular history may have prompted the statement of Demetrius that he has been in Moscow with Sapiega, the Polish ambassador to Boris, and is familiar with the atmosphere of the Russian Court. Rochelle's treatment of a spurious early romance of the young Demetrius with Ksenija Godunov may also have influenced the scene between the alleged Demetrius and Ksenija in the play. The possibility of convergence of such various sources as Baer, Margeret, Karamzin, and Mérimée may be seen as authority for the admiration of Suvorin's Demetrius for Stephen Bathory, the Polish king of Transylvanian-Hungarian origin. According to these sources, many distinguished Polish diplomats suggested that Demetrius was Bathory's illegitimate son.

In a religious polemic against Kostomarov, Father Pierling, the Russian Jesuit, in his *Rome et Démétrius,* tried to prove that Demetrius had accepted Catholicism. Suvorin took Kostomarov's side in the controversy and when in his play Stadnickij, the Jesuit confessor of Marina, tells Bučinskij that the Pretender has become a Catholic, the Protestant secretary replies: "It is a lie. The Tsar was born in the Orthodox faith and his Catholicism is just a political move."[100]

Having searched the Vatican for historical correspondence between Demetrius and Rome, Father Pierling published, for the first time in history, the Pretender's letter to Clement VIII, in which Demetrius asks the Pope's help for his campaign against Boris and concludes, "I kiss the feet of your Holiness as if they were those of Christ Himself. . . ." The Orthodox Suvorin ridicules this statement, and his Demetrius, poking fun at the Pope, asks Stadnickij which of the Pope's feet is to be kissed, the right or the left?[101]

Suvorin must also have read the accounts of English eyewitnesses of this episode of the Russian Time of Troubles. Captain Gilbert, one of the bodyguards of Demetrius, reported the following incident:

Lying on his bed not long before his death . . . an aged man came to the Tsar, which sight caused him to . . . come to me and his guard . . . but none . . . had seene any thing. . . . [The Tsar] sent for Buchinskie: telling him that . . . [this] aged man . . . told him that though for his owne person he was a good Prince, yet the injustice . . . of his . . . Ministers must bee punished, and his Empire . . . taken from him.[102]

This incident was dramatized by Suvorin in a conversation between Demetrius and Ksenija. Unheard by Ksenija, a voice from somewhere tells Demetrius: "You are a good Prince, but your Empire will be taken away from you because of your unjust servants."[103]

Suvorin's play is a literary potpourri continuing the events of the Time of Troubles at the point at which Tolstoj's *Tsar Boris* breaks off. The play opens in the twilight interregnum of young Feodor, Boris's son; depicts Demetrius's triumph; treats in detail the latter's complex relation with Ksenija; and ends with his fall.

Suvorin mentions that Lope's dramatic device of saving Demetrius from Boris's henchmen was interesting, and Lopean echoes may be found in his use of the astrologer episode and in his reference to Alexander the Great.

The conversation between Stadnickij and Bučinskij, the two Polish protagonists, in Suvorin's play, in which Bučinskij reminds Stadnickij that Luther played a trick on the Jesuits, may find its source in Sumarokov's Demetrius drama, in which Parmen mentions the victory of Protestantism in England, Holland, and Germany. The conviction of Suvorin's Demetrius regarding his noble descent, and his desire to rule justly are traits common to Schiller and Hebbel, both of whose dramas Suvorin had read.

While it cannot be proved that Suvorin had read Cumberland's picaresque fragment, at least the similarity of the dramatic treatment of both writers regarding the relationship between Demetrius and Ksenija can be pointed out. In both plays Ksenija, after initial hesitation, becomes convinced that Demetrius is Ivan's son and, overcoming her fear and hatred, begins to admire him. Similarly, in both plays, Demetrius is attracted to Ksenija, understands her fate, and wants to help her.

Suvorin's Feodor, Boris's young son who followed his father on the throne, wants to convince everybody that Demetrius is an impostor, but his efforts fail to move the Latin priests, the Polish king, and the Pope, who exploit Demetrius's claim to the throne as a pretext to conquer Moscow. The source is Puškin, whose Pretender tells Marina ". . . Neither king, nor pope, nor nobles trouble / whether I be / Dimitri or another. . . . / But I provide a pretext for revolt and war."[104]

Among several borrowings from Ostrovskij's tragedy should be mentioned the Jesuit Lavitskij's reference to Demetrius "as a new Constantin, defender of Christianity," the dispute over the hero's royal title, Demetrius's visionary dream of conquering Tsargrad as Oleg, his great predecessor, had done, and his reference to his mysterious childhood.

A Tolstojan motif can be seen in the preoccupation of Boris's children with the identity of Demetrius.

There is also a reference to Shakespeare: Mikulin, Boris's ambassador to Elizabeth, tells Xvorostinin, a Russian noble, that when he was in England, he saw a play about King Ličard (!), in which a man killed his king, had the king's son murdered, and became the king himself until a young prince came who cut off his head. Xvorostinin drily comments, "Just like our Godunov."[105]

Considering his heterogeneous elements, Suvorin accomplished a veritable tour de force of consolidation, integration, and synthesis in blending these various elements into an informative and entertaining drama whose principal merit lies in his new concept of the elusive Demetrius as the probable son of Ivan the Terrible.

However, if Suvorin's drama is reviewed within the corpus of the Demetrius plays of world literature, the evaluation will be different. Suvorin's literary image of Demetrius suffers from an inferiority complex due to too much midwifery from Lope, Schiller, Puškin, etc. Thus, his self-conscious, but not self-confident hero shows that he is too obviously aware of an overburdening literary heritage from his great predecessors, and he makes painful and awkward efforts to avoid the pitfalls of his elders in the previous Demetrius plays. Suvorin's Demetrius is unhappy because he knows that his origin is not believed, though he tries hard to convince people of his noble birth. Expecting the charges of the Muscovite government against him, Demetrius obligingly displays an Otrep'ev in his camp and triumphs over the combined lies of Boris and Jov, the Metropolitan of Moscow. He anticipates Šujskij's intrigues and does not listen to his flatteries. He even tells Šujskij what a bad boy he has been in perjuring himself concerning his [Demetrius's] identity and asks him such an embarrassing question as how he could have buried Tsarevich Demetrius in Uglič when the latter, alive, stands in front of him. Understandably, Šujskij becomes confused and even forgets to intrigue for a while. On the other hand, Suvorin's Demetrius seems to have known and learned from the mistakes of the heroes of Xomjakov and Ostrovskij and dutifully, although too mechanically and unconvincingly, listens to Basmanov and Bučinskij, the two positive heroes of the play who, as often happens in the previous Demetrius plays, do their best to save him.

In his attempt to profit from the great Demetrius dramas of the past, Suvorin went a little too far and produced a logical and intellectual, rather than an artistic, drama. His prefabricated, enigmatic dream-play lacks the fascination of Schiller's fragment, the freshness of Xomjakov's production, or the spontaneity of Ostrovskij's tragedy. In its geometrical construction, the play seems to explain almost everything, leaves little to the imagination of the sensitive reader, and creates the impression of a corrected version of previous Demetrius dramas. His robot-like heroes often move with the clay feet of an abstraction in this computer-fed play.

Yet, it would be unfair to call Suvorin's play a completely cliché-ridden pastiche. Often we come upon singing birds and live flowers in his artificial garden. There is movement, force, and color in his description of the Pretender's camp as Demetrius is about to start his triumphal entry into Moscow. The folk-lore elements are tender and charming and their "visual" poetry and lyrical mood soften the heaviness of Suvorin's didacticism.

Was Suvorin's drama the answer of a conservative to the dilemma of the *mal du siècle?* Was his Demetrius's royal origin the polemic of a monarchist against the nihilism of his times? Suvorin may have been influenced by the views of the Jesuit Pierling, the Polish-French historian Waliszewski, the Russian Šeremetev who, from different points of view, believed that Demetrius could have been Ivan's son. In trying to create a Russo-Polish *rapprochement* Suvorin may have listened to the Panslav idea of the anonymous French-Polish Demetrius play and the call of Bučinskij to Basmanov, "Let us work together for our two countries," may reflect a belated echo of Polish political positivism.[106]

NOTES

1. For Italian and French Demetrius dramas see M. P. Alekseev, "Boris Godunov i Dimitrij Samozvanec v zapadnoevropejskoj drama," *"Boris Godunov" A. S. Puškina,* K. N. Deržavin, ed. (Leningrad, 1936), pp. 96–99.

2. The only English play written after the restoration is Mary Pix, *The Czar of Moscow* (London, 1701), which was unavailable. Mentioned by Alekseev, p. 86.

3. There were two English plays on the subject in the nineteenth century: One is Richard Cumberland's fragment *The False Demetrius* (London, 1813). In this picaresque play Demetrius changes into an enlightened monarch and his noble conduct wins Ksenija Godunov's love. Yet the hero is described with inconsistency and his final fate remains in doubt. The other—G. G. Alexander's *Dmitri* (London, 1827)—continues the events of the Time of Troubles after the murder of Boris's wife and son.

4. This play remained in MS and was later discovered by Herman Kienzle. See "Der erste deutsche Demetrius," *Deutsche Rundschau* 181 (1916): 417.

5. *Schillers Demetrius,* Gustav Kettner, ed. (Weimar: Schriften der Goethe Gesellschaft, 1894).

6. Alekseev, p. 108.

7. *Schillers,* p. 115.

8. Alekseev, p. 108.

9. *Schillers,* I, p. 26.

10. *Ibid.,* I, p. 27.

11. *Ibid.,* I, pp. 49, 50, 53.

12. *Ibid.,* p. 214.

13. Walter Flex, *Die Entwicklung des tragischen Problems in den deutschen Demetriusdramen von Schiller bis auf die Gegenwart* (Dissertation, Friedrich Alexander Universitaet, Erlangen Hofbuchdruckerei, Eisenach H. Kahle, 1912), p. 23.

14. *Schillers,* pp. 158–59.

15. *Ibid.,* I, p. 148.

16. *Ibid.,* p. 148.

17. *Ibid.*

18. *Ibid.,* p. 210.

19. R. Boxberger, "Ueber Schillers Demetrius," *Zeitschrift fuer vergleichende Literaturgeschichte* 5 (1892) : 56.

20. *Schillers,* p. viii.

21. Otto Sievers, *Demetrius* (Leipzig, 1888).

22. Friedrich Bodenstedt, *Demetrius* (Berlin, 1856).

23. Adolf I. Wilhelmi, *Dmitri Iwanowitsch* (Leipzig, 1869). Comments based on Flex, p. 56.

24. Alekseev, p. 117.

25. Friedrich Hebbel, *Saemtliche Werke,* Richard M. Werner, ed., 9 vols. (Berlin: B. Behr's Verlag, 1904), 6: 5–140.

26. *Ibid.,* 6 :xxi.

27. *Ibid., Vorspiel,* 1.

28. *Ibid., Vorspiel,* 6.

29. *Ibid., Vorspiel,* 12.

30. *Ibid., Vorspiel,* 10.

31. *Ibid.,* II. 14.

32. *Ibid.,* IV. 10, 12.

33. *Ibid.*

34. *Ibid.,* IV. 12.

35. *Ibid.,* II. 9; II. 11.

36. *Ibid.,* II. 9.

37. *Ibid.,* I. 6; II. 1. I could not find any study devoted to the possibility of Puškin's influence on Hebbel. The lack of scholarly investigation on this interesting problem may be due to the superiority complex of German literary critics of the nineteenth century, who presumably felt that the Demetrius dramas of Schiller and Hebbel were superior to any other in the world. But how about Russian scholars, who certainly did not share this opinion? It is quite possible that Hebbel read one of the many German translations of Puškin's drama.

38. The following Russian Demetrius-Godunov dramas were not available: V. S. Narežnij, *Dimitrij Samozvanec* (1804) ; M. Pogodin, *Istorija v licax o Dimitrii Samozvanec* (1835) ; G. R. Novgorod, *"Lžedimitrij" Tragedija v 10 bylinax* (1854) ; N. Polozov, *Dimitrij Samozvanec* (1858) ; L. A. Čaev, *Dimitrij Samozvanec* (1864) ; M. Pogodin, *Istorija v licax o Care Borise Godunove* (1868) :

Endogurov, *Pravitel' Boris Godunov* (1870) ; N. Lwov, *Zar Dimitry, Historisches Trauerspiel* (St. Petersburg, 1896). The last is a combination of the plays of Schiller and Puškin.

39. Aleksandr P. Sumarokov, "Dimitrij Samozvanec," *Xrestomatija po russkoj literature XVIII veka*, A. V. Kokorev, ed., 3rd ed. (Moscow: Gos. Učeb. pedag. izdat. min. prosv. RSFSR, 1961), pp. 164–91.

40. Quoted by V. P. Gorodeckij, "Boris Godunov v tvorčestve Puškina," *"Boris Godunov" A. S. Puškina*, K. N. Deržavin, ed. (Leningrad, 1936), p. 22.

41. *Ibid.*, p. 28.

42. N. M. Karamzin, *Istorija Gosudarstva Rossijskago*. 11 vols., 5th ed. (St. Petersburg, 1845), 10: iii, 134.

43. *Boris Godunov;* a drama in verse by A. S. Puškin. Rendered into English verse by Alfred Hayes. (London: K. Paul, Trench, Trubner, 1918), *The Virgin Field*.

44. A. S. Puškin, "Boris Godunov," *Sočinenija*. 3 vols. (Moscow: Gosizdat. xudožestv. literatury, 1954), p. 273.

45. D. D. Blagoj, *Tvorčeskij put' Puškina* (Moscow-Leningrad: Izd. Akademii Nauk SSSR, 1950), pp. 422, 423.

46. Flex, p. 124.

47. Karamzin, 11:76, 80.

48. Puškin, p. 329.

49. *Boris Godunov*, trans. Hayes. Scenes: *Night; Cracow, House of Višnevetsky; A Plain Near Novgorod-Seversk*.

50. Quoted by Gorodeckij, p. 26.

51. Lope Felix de Vega Carpio, "El Gran Duque de Moscovia y emperador perseguido," Tomo Cuarto de las Comedias Escogidas, *Biblioteca de Autores Españoles* 52 (Madrid: Edición Atlas, 1952): I. 8 ; *Boris Godunov*, trans. Hayes, *House of Višnevetsky*.

52. *Ibid.*, II. 4 ; *Palace of the Tsar*.

53. *Boris Godunov*, trans. Hayes, *Palace of the Tsar;* Lope, II. 18.

54. Lope, II. 21. *Boris Godunov*, trans. Hayes, *Moscow: Shuisky's House*.

55. *Schillers*, p. 143.

56–65. *Schillers*, II, p. 143. *Boris Godunov*, trans. Hayes, *The Lithuanian Frontier*.

66. *Ibid.*, p. 143 ; *A Plain near Novgorod Seversk*.

67. *Schillers*, I, p. 169.

68. *Boris Godunov*, trans. Hayes, *A Tent*.

69. Sumarokov, 1. 4.

70. Gorodeckij, p. 19.

71. *Ibid.*, p. 22.

72. *Ibid.*, p. 37.

73. *Ibid.*

74. A. L. Slonimskij, "Boris Godunov i dramaturgija 20-x godov," ("Boris Godunov and the Drama of the Twenties"), *"Boris Godunov" A. S. Puškina* (Leningrad, 1936), pp. 73, 75, 76.

75. *Ibid.*, pp. 75–76.

76. *Boris Godunov*, trans. Hayes, *Palace of the Tsar*.

77. Aleksej S. Xomjakov, "Dimitrij Samozvanec," *Polnoe sobranie sočinenij*, 6 vols. (Moscow: Univers. tipograf., 1900), 4:1–173.

78. *Ibid.,* V. 5.

79. Mixail E. Lobanov, *Boris Godunov* (Moscow, 1835).

80. Aleksandr N. Ostrovskij, "Dmitrij Samozvanec i Vasilij Šujskij," *Sobranie sočinenij,* 10 vols. (Moscow, Gosizdatel xudožestv. lit., 1960), 5: 7–155. Also mentioned in chapter 3, n. 140.

81. *Ibid.,* p. 515.

82. Demetrius to Šujskij: "Don't you dare to lay bare your soul to the people?" (Ostrovskij, II. 6.) Karamzin (10:132) uses "heart," while Puškin has "soul." (*Boris,* p. 274.)

83. Ostrovskij, II. 6.

84. *Ibid.,* p. 516. ("Vsem etim rabam dat' svobodu.")

85. *Schillers,* pp. 157, 158, 159; Ostrovskij, I. 5.

86. *Ibid.,* p. 89; I. 1.

87. Ostrovskij, I. 3.

88. *Ibid.,* I. 5.

89. Ostrovskij, I. 5; Hebbel, *Vorspiel,* 9.

90. *Ibid.,* I. 5; I. 4.

91. *Ibid.,* I. 5; I. 4.

92. *Ibid.,* I. 3; IV. 7.

93. Aleksej K. Tolstoj, "Car Boris," *Dramatičeskaja Trilogija* (St. Petersburg: Tip. M. M. Stasjulevica, 1898), pp. 330–510.

94. *Ibid.,* V, p. 481.

95. Puškin, p. 329; Tolstoj, V, p. 498.

96. *Polnoe sobranie sočinenij Gr. A. K. Tolstogo,* 6 vols. (St. Petersburg: Izdanie T–va A. F. Marks, 1908), 4: 233.

97. *Boris Godunov,* trans. Hayes, *Cracow:* House of Visnevetsky; *Tolstoj,* I, p. 345–46.

98. Aleksej S. Suvorin, *Car Dmitrij Samozvanec i Carevna Ksenija* (St. Petersburg, 1905). Also mentioned in chapter 3, n. 140.

99. *Ibid.,* III, p. 84.

100. P. D. Pierling, *Rome et Démétrius* (Paris: E. Leroux, 1878), pp. 20–37; Suvorin, V, p. 147.

101. *Ibid.,* p. 158. ("Osculor pedes Stis Vrae Tanquam ipsius Christi . . ."), V, p. 155.

102. Quoted by Sonia E. Howe, *Some Russian Heroes, Saints and Sinners* (London: Williams and Norgate, 1913), pp. 271–72.

103. Suvorin, V, p. 177.

104. Suvorin, I, p. 20; Puškin, *Sočinenija,* p. 315.

105. Suvorin, III, p. 89.

106. Jules F . . . , *Un moment de toute puissance.* (See p. 308.) Suvorin, V, p. 149.

5

Conclusion

It is difficult to imagine a more suitable and effective theme for dramatic representation than the strange and stormy life of the alleged Demetrius, whose adventures contain so many miraculous elements that at times he seems more of a legendary hero than a historical person.

Thus, it is not surprising that the anonymous author of *Sir Thomas Smith's Voiage and Entertainment in Rushia,* a witness of Boris's death and Demetrius's triumph, already felt that these events deserved to be brought to the stage by some great writer who could sing the fates of these heroes with the poetic inspiration of a Sidney and a Ben Jonson. Later the German literary critic Gottschall mentioned that Shakespeare's genius would have been required to depict the origin and rise of Demetrius.[1] Lope, the greatest writer of the Golden Age of Spanish literature, attained one of his notable successes with the representation of this hero on the stage, and later Schiller and Goethe, the two most distinguished literary figures of Germany, cooperate in an attempt to give a truly human portrait to this unusual personality.

The life of Demetrius, with its continuous action, with its sudden changes of fortune, intrigue, and confusion, with its sharp clashes against such formidable opponents as the strong-willed Boris and the cunning Šujskij, and with its inevitable doom, proved to be an irresistible attraction for playwrights of various lands and ages. The immense volume of dramatic production is due to the mystery surrounding Demetrius's origin, the possibility of his being a hero or a villain—or both—which openness and looseness permitted almost complete freedom to the creative imagination of playwrights. In addition, the Demetrius dramas were used by a number of playwrights as vehicles through which eras and cultures established a dialogue, and the events of the past were cited as illustrations and examples for the interpretation of the present.

In the above analysis of the alleged Demetrius as he is represented in dramas of world literature, we have seen that these literary portraits do not depict him with the same basic traits, but reflect a wide range of variety, depending on the diverse natures of the playwrights, the Zeitgeist of the age, and the social ideals of the country where they were created. The various portrayals can be classified as follows:

1. The prince of royal descent, a pure hero *sans peur et sans reproche,* an almost superhuman being who fights against incredible odds. This is the Lopean school, the model for subsequent Spanish, Italian, and French dramas and operas.

2. The impostor and runaway monk who usurps the throne and becomes a tyrant. This is Sumarokov's interpretation of Demetrius.

3. The cheated cheater. Demetrius is neither the son of Ivan the Terrible nor an impostor *per se,* but is made to believe that he is the offspring of this Tsar and is convinced of his royal blood until he learns the truth of his origin. This is the school of Schiller and his epigones.

4. A refinement of the preceding school: Demetrius is Ivan IV's illegitimate son, but this fact is not revealed to him until his triumph over Boris; as in Schiller's portrayal, he acts the Tsarevich with full conviction. This is the school of Hebbel and his followers.

5. The clever adventurer who, in spite of his conscious fraud, is basically a good Russian. Having outwitted the Jesuits and Poles he repudiates them and wants to use his high office for the welfare, and his culture acquired in the West for the progress, of his native land. This is Puškin's hero, whom Xomjakov refined.

6. The clever adventurer who is not a conscious cheater and does not know his origin. In other respects he is like Puškin's hero. Ostrovskij's play belongs here.

7. The man who believes in his royal origin and could be Ivan's son. In all other respects he is similar to the heroes of the two preceding groups. This is Suvorin's protagonist.

8. The hero is depicted with inconsistency so that the reader is left to speculate over his real character and ultimate fate. This is Cumberland's *Demetrius.*[2]

9. Demetrius is disguised as a girl, his true identity being a

matter of guesswork. The reader cannot decide whether this is the result of a conscious effort by the playwright or of his habitual reflex. This is Fletcher's masked Alinda.

10. Demetrius is not the hero; he may not even appear on the stage, though his influence is felt in the drama. The real hero is either Godunov, as in Tolstoj's *Tsar Boris,* or some other historical person or persons connected with the events of the Time of Troubles, as in Heiseler's *Die Kinder Godunofs.*

Since the two main selections were taken from the age of the baroque it is appropriate to consider at this time what is characteristic of the baroque in them.[3] The central baroque situation in most of these dramas is, of course, the obvious fact that the alleged Demetrius is not what he appears, claims, or is claimed, to be.

The depiction of heroes as victims of external forces and circumstances is a baroque theme *par excellence.* Baroque is the atmosphere of the Demetrius dramas with their pretenders, Machiavellian schemes, and political tyranny. It was in this age that the stories of such notorious claimants as Perkin Warbeck in England and the batch of false Sebastians in Portugal were also brought to the stage.

El Gran Duque and *The Loyal Subject* reflect the climate of baroque sensibility. In the apparent dilemma between true kings who are tyrants, or weak, false kings who are nevertheless progressive rulers and outstanding personalities whom the *vox populis* would like to see on the throne, the baroque disparity and fusion of reality and appearance are shown. The second—the Lancastrian—tetralogy of Shakespeare's historical plays, *Richard II* and the two parts of *Henry IV* and *Henry V* illustrate this point. In the apparent disorder of royal succession of these plays, the central political issue is the deposition of the lawful king (Richard II), who is incompetent to rule and may even bring destruction to his country, in favor of a usurper (Bolingbroke) who, although morally tainted, paves the way through his political virtues for the ideal king in the person of Hal, the future Henry V. In the conflict between Richard II and Bolingbroke, the conflict between the idealism of the Christian Middle Ages and the skeptical materialism of the Renaissance *Weltanschauung* may be seen.

The problem of time—the fleetingness of earthly existence and therefore man's insignificance—is illustrated in Teodoro's conversation with the tailor in Lope's play. This Russian prince

orders a simple suit instead of a luxurious royal garment that
would need the assistance of several servants and take away
precious time on earth. (". . . se nos lleva / La mitad del
tiempo breve / Que pasa, y no ha de volver.")[4] It is this existential awareness of his brief sojourn on earth that makes Teodoro
completely indifferent to royal title and riches. Archas in Fletcher's drama represents the same philosophy, although not so
convincingly, when he retires and wants to become devotion's
soldier. His stoicism and the Seneca emblem are indicative of
this attitude.

Both plays, the Spanish and the English, emphasize the transitoriness of life and the lack of security in man's attempts to
fortify himself against his fate. Doubts and temptations over-
whelm the protagonists; a climate of anguish is created; confidence in man and in his reason crumbles. This lack of belief is
closely connected with the theme of death.

The theme of death is not in itself baroque, but becomes
characteristically baroque when concern with death is distorted
to the extent of obsession and a taste of the macabre permeates
the atmosphere. Violence, danger, and death are omnipresent
in Lope's play. Basilio threatens Teodoro, kills Juan, and men-
aces Isabela. Boris is suspected of having killed Cristina and
Teodoro. Saved once from almost sure death, Demetrio has to
face constant threats of death throughout the *comedia*. In
Fletcher's drama, Archas's whole family is in constant danger:
Alinda and Putskie must wear disguises to escape persecution;
Archas is on the point of death in Boroskie's torture chamber.
The drama is staged against the background of savage Tartar
raids; the Tartar slogan "burn and kill" resounds through this
play of military baroque.

Violent and sudden transformations and contrasts dominate
both works. In Lope's drama, Demetrio, the heir to the throne,
becomes a persecuted vagabond, a poor monk, a wretched la-
borer, and a kitchen help. Then, just as suddenly, he is transformed into a victorious hero and the emperor of Russia. From
the bare walls of the monastery and the smoky kitchen of the
Palatine, he is unexpectedly transferred to the splendor and
pomp of the palace of the Polish king. Boris also undergoes
unexpected transformations: from a mere courtier he becomes
tsar and, at the end of the play, defeated in battle, commits
suicide. Teodoro wants to retire to a monastery, and instead, by
a change of fortune, is pushed onto the throne. In Fletcher's

drama, Archas, the famous military hero, is suddenly dismissed, becomes a solitary old man contemplating death, and then is suddenly recalled to reach the height of his glory. Alinda, a fugitive from assassins, becomes the husband of the Duke's sister. From the brink of death, Teodore is elevated to the rank of general, the most important person after the Duke in Russia.

One example will serve to compare the technique with which Lope and Fletcher work out the sudden contrast of situations. The most moving episode in Lope's *comedia* is the innocent, childish game between César and Demetrio, followed by the wanton murder of the former. We are warmed and chilled in turn without transition. We can witness a similar situation in Fletcher's play when preparations are made for the royal banquet, to which Archas has been invited. The servants freely express their delight in having the old general back, since "that joy will make half the court drunk."[5] All, outwardly, is happiness and mirth. The Duke hides his guilt beneath a manner of gracious, regal, almost paternal beneficence. Amid this universal gaiety "the robe of death" is suddenly given to Archas and he is dragged away to the torture chamber.

The clash of spiritual and sensual elements characteristic of baroque is reflected in Lope's Demetrio. He seeks refuge in a monastery, knowing that man is born to die, but after Lope's introduction of Renaissance elements, he is suddenly transformed and wants to enjoy life fully. If in Demetrio's case the earthly elements triumph, the mystique of the Catholic Middle Ages is reflected in Lamberto's sacrifice. His roots are in heaven and there he would like to return. Since he cannot sacrifice himself, which would be his greatest joy, he sacrifices his son in a gesture, as he asserts, reminiscent of the biblical Abraham. Perhaps the example of the Count Palatine best illustrates the unity of these clashing elements. Against a background of a smiling landscape in the midst of deer hunting, he recalls life's transitoriness. ("Asi contemplo / Nuestra vida veloz que va corriendo / Al mar de nuestra muerte.")[6] The theme of *memento mori* is sounded several times by Archas in Fletcher's play.

Yet the baroque contrast prevails even at the most serious moments. When life is too oppressive at the monastery, Rufino is suddenly transformed into a *gracioso* and his jokes disperse the clouds. At other times he dreams of a *picaro*'s carefree existence. When the universe seems to fall apart in Fletcher's play, Theodore becomes ironic and the Ancient follows Rufino in his jokes.

Both dramas display extravagant, unbalanced, and bizarre men characteristic of the baroque. Driven by violent impulses Basilio is a typical *Zerrbild* of the age, reminding us of Gongora's huge cyclops in their monstrosity. Lamberto's inhuman sacrifice and Teodoro's grotesque behavior are also typical traits of the baroque. Archas's incredible loyalty and revolting attempt to kill his own son are symptomatic of the duality of the baroque atmosphere. Fletcher's Duke is a split personality wavering among uninhibited sensuality, despotic cruelty, and noble instincts.

The baroque exaggeration tending toward hyperbole is no less in evidence. Demetrio is called a new Alexander and his ambition is to become a new Caesar. At the sight of Demetrio in rags, Sigismundo is more moved than if he saw the suffering of the greatest men in history. Boris is the greatest, the cruelest, and the most powerful tyrant who ever lived on earth. Fletcher does not lag behind Lope in this use of hyperbole. Such statements by Archas and Putskie as "the Volga trembled," "call back the sun," "prescribe a law to death," etc., are equally characteristic of the baroque exaggeration.[7] Superlatives abound everywhere. The march of Archas's army is the "heaviest," Alinda feels it is her "greatest and happiest" hour to serve Olympia, and so on.[8]

Neither Lope nor Fletcher is content to count in singles or tens. It must be at least a hundred. Yet most of the time a hundred will no longer do. Thus, in Lope's play there are a thousand Demetriuses, and a thousand other pretenders are ready to appear. In Fletcher's play we hear that death has a thousand doors and Theodore asks his father to give him a thousand blows rather than disown him. At times even a thousand will not suffice. Boris must send to the German Emperor sables worth a million golden pieces to assure himself of the latter's friendship against Demetrius's claim. Fletcher's Duke asks Burris to take ten thousand crowns and when he feels that it may not be enough, he raises it to twenty thousand.

The problem of illusion and identity is reflected in Lope's play by the abundance of such cerebral and playful verbs as "parecer" ("to appear"), "engañar" ("to deceive"), "encubrir" ("to conceal"), and "fingir" ("to pretend"), etc., and by the masked figures, the aliases, and the use of disguise in Fletcher's drama. Lope's baroque art is conceived to deceive with the truth, yet the signs are there to distinguish reality from appearance. We have seen that Boris was unable to interpret the *double entendre* of the baroque language of Demetrio, and Marina came only halfway to the truth. But the Count Palatine, a man of baroque sensibility, can read the signs correctly; in reply to Sigismundo's question whether he is sure of Demetrius's claim, he assures the King: Las señas, la majestad / Del rostro, la autoridad / Aunque en un roto vestido / Muestran bien que no es fingido.[9]

Fletcher stresses the disparity between the apparently real and the real, and his baroque style deceives with the disguise of appearance. Yet as the reader has seen in the Demetrius theme, the English playwright also provides allusions and clues to enable the sensitive spectator to detect, or at least to search for, the truth.

The paradox and the contrast are shown in Lope's play by Basilio's killing the son whom he loves and thereby unintentionally elevating to the throne the son he dislikes and wants to disinherit. In his letter to the Count, Sigismundo mentions that Boris calls the innocent Demetrio the impostor, while the impostor is clearly Boris. In Fletcher's play the coward Boroskie becomes the general of the Muscovite army and Archas, the general who "never was acquainted but with conquest," is dismissed.[10] The Duke falls in love with Alinda, whom he is suspected of attempting to kill. Archas wants to kill Teodoro, his son, who just saved his life. The virtuous Honora undertakes to teach the sensuous Duke how to kiss and encourages her sister to do the same. Archas is sentenced to death for using the sword with which he saved his country. The device of oxymoron, so frequently used in baroque literary art, is evident in such phrases in the play as "golden danger" and the "dear master (who is) crooked yet."[11]

Perhaps the differences separating Lope and Fletcher as baroque writers are even more striking than their similarities. These arise from divergent outlooks, dependent on the social, religious, and political climate in which the Spanish Lope and the English Fletcher lived.

There is no bourgeois type in Lope's community. The sense of a comfortable and sedentary life, improvement of material conditions of existence, the spirit of economy and savings, the instinct of foresight—all these traits which bourgeois civilization created are almost entirely absent in the Spanish play. For Lope the ideal life is in the open fields, gardens, and hills of the country, is ruled by innocent idealism, adventure, and chance, and is subject to the enjoyment of that spiritual and earthly happiness which only the passing moment can produce. Lope's *comedia* is a typical product of the mystique of the Spanish Catholic baroque, which brings several senses into play almost simultaneously. Miraculous elements in the rich religious garb of his *autos sacramentales* are superimposed on the apparent austerity of the communal existence of his heroes and are, occasionally, complemented by the joyous *hic et nunc* of the spirit of the Renaissance.

The sensuous decoration and the symbolic metaphor derive from the aesthetic-religious creed of the Counter-Reformation, with the physical suffering of Christ and the raptures of the Saints as its focal point. Thus, Lope's *comedia* emphasizes the traditional Catholic use of the visual art and makes a direct emotional appeal to the senses through pictorial and ornamental elements. The use of brilliant colors, light, sun, stars, the aurora, richly decorated flags, and even luxurious attire are suggestive of sensuousness. The visual effect is further heightened by the addition of precious stones—gold, diamonds, and jewels. Yet this ritual—this veritable orgy of colors—invites not only our eyes, to contemplate various objects, but also our ears, to hear soft and insinuating songs, sweet and gratifying voices, and even pleasurable metaphors. The contrasting shrill sounds of war remind us of the martial spirit of the Counter-Reformation. Even tears are made use of to symbolize the blessing of the actions of heroes fighting in this religious crusade.

The importance of the individual, the significance of personal experience, the emphasis on individual freedom as well as the abuse of freedom, and a new dignity of man—all these motifs are encountered in Fletcher's play. Struggle for power, and competition with its multifold viewpoint predominate in the Protestant baroque climate of *The Loyal Subject,* which is devoid of religious miracles. Although we are apparently in Moscow, we may still catch a few rare glimpses of the decadent atmosphere, lewd courtiers, swarm of new titles, and bawdy servants of James I's court with noisy and dissatisfied soldiers, enterprising merchants, and reckless adventurers of London in the background. Thus, it is natural that some of Fletcher's protagonists are preoccupied with money, payment to soldiers and departing servants, problems of unemployment, with search for riches, and with discoveries of distant lands and new products. In the orchestration of Fletcher's nervous rhythms, in the mixture of his tragic, skeptical, and vulgar voices, both the bizarre ornamentation and the pomposity of his baroque art can be found.

Lope's enchanting rural setting almost entirely disappears, and Fletcher takes his spectators to the streets, buildings, and rooms of a growing big city. In this mundane locale the court occupies a central and magnetic position, providing power, office, pleasure, and wealth, often corrupting and degenerating the office-holders. The confusion and lack of discipline of his baroque art may suggest the passing of the full-blooded Elizabethan age and predict the coming of the civil war. Unlike Lope, Fletcher is much concerned with leisurely life, material comfort, and social amusements. Lope hardly leads us inside a house, while Fletcher takes great delight in escorting us to the great chambers and the galleries, and showing us the handsome rooms, the well-contrived structure, and the other conveniences of his hero's house. Fletcher does not forget to point out the fountains in the garden and such decorations as paintings, strange clocks, and even a broken bust of Seneca. The fashionable coach of his hero is conveniently waiting nearby to transport him to his neighbors for a social call.

As its inheritance from the Renaissance, the social milieu of the Jacobean age demands good breeding, entertainment, and music. Good manners and courtly behavior conveniently replace good morals and convictions. While Lope's peasant Lucinda is envious of the well-dressed Margarita, all of Fletcher's women seem to be elegantly dressed. They wear bracelets, caps, feathers, scarves, and silk stockings. At the court of the Russian-English Duke of his Demetrius play, Fletcher's outspoken, erotic, and militant females have crowded out Lope's religious women.

Religion thus is pushed into the background. The simplicity of the pagan rite at the temple has little religious motivation. Fletcher pokes fun at the strictness of the Puritans at the Court. The metaphors have military and not religious connotation. Even death becomes a "grim soldier."[12] Precious metals—rings, jewels, pearls—are also present in Fletcher's play, but they are used as material objects for presents, often as baits, to seduce pretty women, and to reward honest courtiers. They are not religious symbols. Perhaps their use underlines the fundamental difference between the Calvinistic belief that the senses are enemies of the spirit and the Catholic affirmation that the senses are an integral part of man, and can, therefore, be made to contribute to God's glory. Similarly, Fletcher does not summon us to taste the salt of the tears, and when his heroes weep, they do it for emotional and not for religious reasons.

Schiller and Hebbel did not work in the age of the baroque, yet their Demetrius plays are actually baroque in spirit. The roots of Schiller's drama lie in the seventeenth century, and as the protagonists of his most characteristic historical plays illustrate, the great German playwright was an adherent of the baroque tragedy. Schiller was presumably acquainted with John Fletcher's tragicomedy *A King and No King* and refers to it in his letters. Thus, it is not unreasonable to assume that the original idea of creating his *Demetrius* may have stemmed partly from the central situation of Fletcher's hero who discovers, when he learns his true origin, that he has no right to the throne. Schiller's drama is a typical product of baroque sensibility as it reflects the ethical dilemma of the awakened dreamer. The typical baroque themes of persecution, political tyranny, and intriguing politicians are prominently displayed in Schiller's drama. But perhaps Hebbel's fragment is even more characteristic of the baroque and carries the audience back to Calderón's Sigismund, in *Life Is a Dream*. "What is life if not a dream?" the Demetrius of Hebbel's drama must ask himself when his anaesthetic wears off. In the brief span of Demetrius's life, reality is replaced by illusion and, after a rich moment of fairy-tale existence, reality again takes over and the hero must return to the existential prison of his former self. No better poetic illustration of this strange metamorphosis can be found than in the language of the painful and resigned cry of Hebbel's existential hero at the time of his second awakening, when he rhetorically addresses Mniszek, his father-in-law:

> Herr Woiwod, wen sucht
> Ihr hier? Doch nicht den Czaren aller Reussen?
> Den blies ein Hauch in's leere Nichts zurueck,
> Und euer Jaeger wartet Euren Winks.[13]

When the Polish nobleman, highly disturbed at this sudden turn of events, asks for an explanation, Demetrius tells him:

> Der Morgen brach herein,
> Die alte Frau dort stiess die Laden auf,
> Und meine Maske leg' ich wieder ab.[14]

If, in our subject, illusion begins at the nocturnal catastrophe in Uglič, in the general confusion of which Demetrius was presumably saved, harsh reality breaks in with the ruthlessly penetrating light of morning when the old woman, representing both Demetrius's mother and an impersonal fate, opens up his past and the hero must doff his mask.

It is the mask worn by the dreaming hero which, more than anything else, becomes the symbol of the baroque art of these plays. While the heroes of Puškin and Xomjakov put on this mask consciously at first, the mask becomes a reality, and, like a magic wand, transforms them into the very person whom they wish to impersonate. The dreamers of the Demetrius dramas of Ostrovskij and Suvorin are only partly conscious of the fact that they may be wearing masks, and, in an almost Proustian manner, hark back to the mystery of their half-forgotten youths in order to understand whether or not they live in reality or illusion.

We find the use of the mask in a new interpretation in one of the last German plays written on the subject. In Wilhelm Heinitz's *Demetrius* (1937)[15] a mysterious "Maskenschneider" appears, who knows everybody in the play. He even recognizes the man whom Demetrius killed for revealing him his past, since he had also made a mask for this man. When Demetrius does not know which way to turn after this murder, the "Maskenschneider" assures Demetrius's friend:

Wenn unser Dimitri eine Maske braucht, schickt Ihn zu mir.
Ich schneide, was er braucht: Die Maske des Tyrannen.[16]

Yet after Demetrius is killed and chaos threatens the land, it is the "Maskenschneider" who jumps on the vacant throne:

> Wenn ich nun seine Maske mir gewaenne? . . .
> Wie solche Maske doch belebt! Ich glaube,
> Ich bin es schon. . . . Sie haben keinen Zaren. . . .
> Ein guter Zufall! Hier! Des Zaren Siegel,
> Ein Stueck Papier mit diesem Wappen darauf . . . ?
> Ich waere nicht der Zar? Wer will's beweisen?[17]

While Heinitz may have used the theme of the second Pretender and blended it with the story of the first Demetrius, his "Maskenschneider" is a highly original figure who, acting in the baroque spirit of the Demetrius saga, confounds illusion with reality in his factory of masks.

Thus, the whole corpus of the Demetrius dramas may be held to reflect, to a greater or smaller degree, the baroque sensibility, regardless of age, country, or predominant artistic temper.

In addition to the baroque, the apparent timelessness of the Demetrius legend permits us to follow the development of other literary currents which have given birth to ever-new versions of the theme. Sumarokov reflects neoclassicism, Kotzebue sentimentalism, most of the German dramas of the last century, Puškin and Xomjakov romanticism, Hebbel a kind of preexistentialism, and Heiseler symbolism.

This study has been directed not so much to a literary analysis but rather to a consideration of the works in relation to the *Zeitgeist* of the period. This historical-literary approach to the connection between the avatar of Demetrius in the dramas considered and the specific ideological, political, social, and cultural atmosphere of the age has made it possible to see the changing psychological portrait of the hero as a mirror in which the historical events peculiar to the epoch and country of their origin are reflected.

Except for Fletcher's play, the writing of which was partly influenced by the political and trade interests of England and the atmosphere of the Court of James I, the seventeenth century saw the first Demetrius portraits in a religious light. Although Lope curtailed the religious fanaticism of his sources, his hero's invasion of Russia with the support of the representatives of the Catholic world resembles the exploits of many of Lope's other Catholic crusaders. Sumarokov's play, written in the next century, may be regarded as a statement of the fundamental Orthodox viewpoint of the Russian Church. It is noteworthy that the sources of these two plays, the Jesuits Barrezzi-Mosquera and the old Russian annalists, speak with the same accent and invoke the same supernatural forces, but, because of their different religious motivation and ideological bias, they reach exactly opposite results. If the Jesuits regard Demetrius as God's messenger on earth to bring the stray lambs back to the fold, for the Russian chroniclers he is Satan's instrument intent on destroying the purity of their faith. The man Demetrius, with his likes and dislikes, joys and sorrows, victories and defeats, grandeur and simplicity, is obviously lost in this medieval theological dispute and in his place a lifeless abstraction is created.

In his drama Hebbel incorporated these two opposing forces in the persons of Hiob (Jov) and the Cardinal (Legate).

So stehen sich, in Hiob und im Legaten verkoerpert, zwei Maechte gegenueber, die uns zeigen, wie das Leben "als einzige Welle sich in das grosse Meer unendlicher Wirkung verliert," wie die Schicksale des Einzelnen mit dem Ganzen des Weltgetriebes zusammenhaengen. Hiob erscheint "wie die Zeit": "er giebt und nimmt und bleibt, als waer' er nicht auch ein Mensch, in allem Wechsel, was er ist," wie eine Verkoerperung des unbarmherzig waltenden Schicksals. Der Legat erscheint wie die immer streibende Kraft, die tausendmal mit frischem Antrieb versucht, was tausendmal misslungen. . . ."[18]

Patriotic motifs come to be added to the religious portrayal of Demetrius in Spain. In the war of independence against Napoleonic France, the Demetrius theme in *El principe perseguido* by Belmonte, Moreto, and Martines, along with Cervantes's *Numancia,* is prominently displayed on the Spanish stage. The story of the innocently persecuted Russian prince and the oppression of Muscovy by a tyrant was used in the same way as was, in Cervantes's patriotic drama, the heroic resistance of the legendary Spanish defenders of Numancia to the Roman invaders: as an allegory of the predicament of Spain under French occupation and as an inspiration to honor and glory. The fact that Russia had to fight her own war of independence against the French invaders at the same time further increased the interest of the Spanish theatergoers in *El principe perseguido* and even implied the common struggle of the two countries, situated at the opposite ends of Europe, against the same tyranny.

The religious controversy disappears in the nineteenth century and the genius of the age demands social and cultural values from its heroes. The German admirers of Demetrius present him as the universal ideal of a just monarch and an enlightened human being indifferent to religion, while his Russian interpreters also stress his epic dreams, legendary military valor, and physical strength through a magic mirror of poetic myth woven by the century-old strands of memory, illusion, and nostalgia for a common past. Although Demetrius tries to pacify the impatient Jesuits and Poles with the promise of a war against the Turks, he will wear no biretta on this campaign. We are reminded more of an adventurous Varangian raid on Byzantium than of a religious crusade, and the romantic hero dreams of nailing Oleg's shield on the iron gate of Tsargrad (Constantinople) rather than of presenting the infidel Mohammedans a symbolic crucifix. The folkloric elements woven around Demetrius suggest a sense of national consciousness and patriotic pride, the might of the Russian earth, the rustle of the medieval Scythian forests, and the rebirth of an Ilja Muromec, the legendary Russian warrior of Herculean strength. Yet simultaneously Demetrius also appears as a forerunner of the progressive reforms of Peter the Great, the Russian Renaissance emperor, in advocating such cultural and social measures as the building of universities, increased contact with the West, new modes of dress, shaving of beards, and more enlightened treatment of women. He is also similar to Peter in his relative indifference to religion.

In the twentieth century the subject has become practically monopolized by German playwrights and, especially between the two world wars, reflects at times as much the delirium, agitation, and confusion of the political and social climate of their own country as their artistic concern with the historical exploits of the Russian Pretender. Except for *Die Kinder Godunofs* (1923),[19] Henry von Heiseler's symbolist play of great psychological strength—which, based on the dramas of Puškin and, especially, Tolstoj, in an entirely Russian spirit sensitively depicts Boris's crime and atonement, and his complex relationship with his children—the other German dramatists consciously or unconsciously often address themselves to the temper and mood of their times. Paul Ernst's *Demetrios* (1910),[20] influenced by what he conceived to be the pessimistic ending of Puškin's *Boris Godunov* when the people's ominous silence predicts further troubles, reenacts the Demetrius legend in a classical Greek setting and creates a tragic fall of the once-proud aristocratic Spartan state. Boris appears in the complex role of Orestes and seems to carry on his shoulder the curse of the House of Atreus.

However, in his study *Der Tragiker Paul Ernst in der Reihe seiner Dramen "Demetrios" bis Brunhild. Versuch einer Wuerdigung vom Standort national-sozialistischer Weltanschauung,* Hans Schneider, a literary theoretician of the *neue Ordnung* and a propagandist of a twentieth-century Nordic ethos, regards the work as a sociopolitical document of the time concerning the inevitable destruction of a decadent society which expects its historical regeneration and high position among the nations of the world from the rule of a new and supreme race.[21]

After the First World War, Ernst's drama was followed by a discordant chorus of expressionistic, futuristic, and grotesque plays. Is it difficult to see in the symbolism of Lernet-Holenia's *Demetrius* (1926),[22] describing the pathetic attempts of the hero, an alienated orphan of history, to find his primitive roots, present identity, and future destiny in a spiritual wasteland, the road to Golgotha of the short-lived, unfortunate Weimar Republic? In this modern *Goetterdaemmerung* the distinction between yes and no, truth and untruth, good and bad, right and wrong becomes blurred and meaningless. The cynical and vulgar voices occasionally remind us of the "underground" language of the *Bierstube* of Muenich, the licentiousness of the smoke-filled cabarets, and the destructive hysteria of the *Parteiversammlungen*. The once pure and beautiful Ksenija, the daughter of Boris Godunov, turns into a heavily powdered, sickly courtesan, a faded flower of the street who is ready to sell her favors to anybody although she still professes her love for Demetrius. The typical slogans, menacing gestures, and political shenanigans of Nazi Germany find their distinct echoes in the shrill, irrational, and unrestrained voices of some of these plays. In the fragmented world of Wilhelm von Spaun's *Demetrius* (1936),[23] the hero is greeted with "Sieg, Heil!"[24] and referred to as the "Mehrer des Reichs."[25] In an attempt to prolong his crumbling reign Boris calls the alleged Demetrius "Volksverraeter"[26] and tells Hiob (Patriarch Jov) that he had Demetrius murdered for "Staatsraison." Hiob feels that, in the interest of the people, murder is permitted and ". . . des Volkes Feind vernichtet werden [muss]."[27] The reader must ask himself whether he is listening to a scene of the universal Demetrius saga or to a topical allusion to the almost contemporary bloody liquidation by Hitler of the infamous stormtroopers of Ernst Roehm in Germany. It is tempting to discern the reflection of the cunning efforts of the Nazi propaganda machine to hypnotize its future victims to helplessness in such statements in the play as, "Herrenvolk ist generoes auch mit Gefangenen,"[28] a curious coincidence with the ideology and phraseology of the times. Yet the ethic of absolute obedience even to inhuman commands by superiors has been formulated and the sinister shadows of the Nazi prison camps are already in the air. Ksenija is captured by an officer who, hoping for a great reward, decides to drag her to the rapist Demetrius. The officer refuses to listen to the desperate plea of Ksenija to let her escape and defends his action by the excuse, later used so often at the war-crime trials in Germany, that, as a soldier, he must obey orders: "Es tut mir leid; hab' meine Order! Soldaten sein heisst . . . dem Befehl zu folgen."[29] The anti-Semitic sentiments of the Nueremberg Law are clearly reflected in Basmanov's exclamation in the play: "Man glaubhaft luegt als wie der Jud!' "[30] Is this the voice of the patriotic Russian guardian of Demetrius or that of the editorial of the *Voelkischer Beobachter,* the official mouthpiece of the Nazi party? And yet Spaun, an Austrian playwright who composed his play while he was hospitalized, claims to have received his poetic inspiration from Schiller and to have followed the great German poet in his dramatic design; he even dedicated his play to the immortal genius of the Master. This is a striking example of how uncritical infatuation with the mesmerizing appeal and sly blandishments of the half-baked theory of a destructive political system may doom even a talented writer to artistic sterility. In Wilhelm Heinitz's manuscript *Demetrius,* we witness a meeting of the hero with Marfa, at the end of which Demetrius meditates: "Ein Volk! Ein Herr! Ein Reich! . . ." which appears to be a perfect imitation of the Nazi party slogan of contemporary application or perhaps a habitual reflex of a playwright who was exposed too long to the corrosive effect of the daily trumpeting of the political jargons of this new jingoism.

The lack of religious motifs in some of these plays, the excessive use of them in others, the appearance of a Messiah who is expected to go mad, the desire to create an exclusively military state, and the instigation to a bloody nocturnal pogrom in this hallucinating atmosphere reveal the enormous distance to which the dramatic treatment of the Demetrius legend in this period departed from the original purity and lofty artistic conception of Schiller and Hebbel.

The few available Demetrius plays of the period do not permit a definite conclusion about the curious attraction of the subject for the German playwrights. Yet there are certain similar elements between the era of Boris Godunov and Demetrius in Russia and Germany's own Time of Troubles between the twilight period of the two world wars and the rise of Hitler's Third Reich. In Russia the extinction of the seven-hundred-year-old Rjurik dynasty (1598) and, similarly, in Germany the end of the House of the strong Hohenzollern (1918) created a dangerous power vacuum. The political and social insecurity during the latter years of Boris's rule and the ephemeral reign of Feodor, his son, and the civil war which preceded and followed Demetrius's brief rule find their modern German counterpart in the tottering edifice of the Weimar Republic, the abortive Nazi *Putsch* of 1923, the continuous internal strife, the daily street fights between Brownshirts and Communists, and the fall of one cabinet after the other.

The struggle between the historical Godunov and Demetrius gave the German dramatists a convenient vehicle to mirror the tension between conservative and extreme, between legal but hated, and illegal but popular, elements in their own country. In their occasional positive portrayal of some of the personalities of the Demetrius dramas, the German playwrights may have incorporated certain traits of their own political figures. Bluth's depiction of a Messianic Demetrius who would bring salvation to the downtrodden mass of Russian peasants may have been influenced by the German writer's apocalyptic vision of Hitler's mission in Germany.[31]

The increasingly vitriolic anti-Soviet tone of the Nazi press doubtless contributed to the unflattering representation of the Soviet political personalities and events of the period within the framework of the Demetrius dramas. In depicting a degenerate Boris and an insane Demetrius in his play of Kafkaesque mood, Spaun may have had Stalin in mind. Heinitz's reference to the conflict between plebeians and aristocrats may have predicted the forthcoming war between Russia's ignorant masses and the German military *Herrenvolk*. It may be more than a coincidence that three German Demetrius plays were written in 1937, period of the great Soviet purge, in which the victims were accused of having plotted against Stalin with the aid of Nazi Germany. The strong denunciation of political tyranny in Klefisch's drama, and the trial scene in Schreyvogel's play, in which the accused confesses his crime and pleads guilty, may also have been inspired by the Soviet purges, the show trials, and the enforced recantations in the late thirties.

The conscious or unconscious exploitation for political and chauvinistic purposes of a theme which the most revered names in world literature have cherished throughout the centuries can be seen symbolically as a break with traditional culture in favor of the shallow, emotional, and obvious propaganda campaign of a new society whose spirit harks back to the barbarism of a pagan era. In some of the pages of the few available Demetrius dramas of Nazi Germany a new darkness is revealed—the prostitution of knowledge and the debasement of civilization. The deeper meaning of the degeneration of the Demetrius theme by the playwrights of the Third Reich can be found in its own tortured transformation as the spiritual chronicle of the new Dark Ages in German history.[33]

This overworking of the Demetrius legend in Germany also serves to emphasize indirectly another curious phenomenon in world literature, that is, an almost complete silence of Russian and Soviet playwrights with regard to new creations of Demetrius dramas in the last sixty years.

The puzzling lack in the Soviet Union of Demetrius dramas, which so much fascinated important Russian dramatists in the previous century, cannot be explained satisfactorily by the two world wars and the great social upheaval which swept Russia after the Revolution of 1917. Indeed, in a combined artistic and ideological effort to link the present to the past in order to find in the lives and activities of their distinguished ancestors and rulers parallels and justification for their own revolution, Soviet playwrights have shown an increasing concern for historical themes. As a result, historical dramas have always occupied a prominent place on the Soviet stage. One possible explanation may be found in the choice of subject matter. The Soviet literary imagination was understandably fired with the representation of the Civil War, the documentation of the new life under Communism, and the feverish search for positive heroes. Presumably this new assortment of literary fare, concerned mainly with current realities of Soviet life, and the past in its creative relationship with the present, must have pushed into the background the dramatization of what Soviet dramatists considered to be the unsavory adventures of a seventeenth-century Russian anti-hero, a skeleton in the closet of their history, a closet which they had reserved for their respectable forefathers.

The rigid application of socialist realism to works of literature in the Soviet Union is another conjecture. Since this critical approach demands of Soviet writers an optimistic point of view, a cheerful and capable leader, and an almost complete lack of doubt respecting a rosy future, it is not difficult to understand that a complex, self-questioning, and occasionally vacillating Demetrius would not qualify. Finally, the current Soviet historical opinion that Demetrius was a puppet-adventurer, manipulated by his Polish and Jesuit masters, made him a *persona non grata* for the contemporary stage.

The playwrights of the world also used the Demetrius theme as an expression of their views on various forms of government, and consequently their plays became a political manifesto of royal dignity or a harbinger of republican freedom. The monarchic tendency is unmistakable in the plays of Lope, Kotzebue, Lobanov and even Tolstoj, although the latter was a constitutional democrat, while most of the dramas of the others, less simply catalogued, have to be judged individually. Although monarchic in spirit, Fletcher's play warns of royal abuse and hints at the possibility of an eventual overthrow of the king. There is an echo of Voltaire's empiricism in the statement of Sumarokov's Parmen that it is not birth but merit which counts, and it does not matter to the people whether their ruler is Demetrius or not as long as he rules justly. In Schiller's play no final judgment is reached, since his demonic hero incorporates both noble and tyrannical traits. While Hebbel is a monarchist who judges his hero juridically, he still permits Mniszek to voice his protest that it is an incomparably greater achievement to establish a new ruling dynasty than to inherit an already existing one. Although Puškin's statement that the Pretender is a "fine fellow" and his sympathetic treatment of the false Demetrius may be interpreted as an endorsement of the playwright's republicanism, Boris's fate and the end of the play more than offset this view. With some slight reservations, Ostrovskij and Xomjakov would vote the alleged Demetrius into his high office over Šujskij's claim of descendancy. It is interesting to see how the reactionary Suvorin managed to get out of his apparently unsolvable dilemma. He admired the brave adventurer of Puškin, Xomjakov, and Ostrovskij, yet, unable to shed his royalist views, he clothed his hero, dreaming in a land of phantasy, in the king's purple to make him eligible for the throne.

From a purely Russian point of view the slow but persistent

development of a Panslavic idea in the theme is of special interest. The ridicule of Poles by Sumarokov and Puškin is an expression of their obvious rejection of Panslavism. Xomjakov disliked the militant and haughty Poles and Germans, but his Demetrius is happy to see "how Poles and Russians were sitting in a friendly group."[34] Ostrovskij follows Sumarokov and Puškin in ridiculing the Poles, yet from his Mniszek's remark to Marina we can conclude that if the Poles behaved better and respected Russian customs, Ostrovskij might have judged them more favorably. Tolstoj's dignified Boris has little use for the proud Poles, but in Suvorin's play we see the Panslav idea in full bloom. Demetrius's two closest collaborators, the Polish Lutheran Bučinskij and the Russian Orthodox Basmanov are seen in amicable cooperation in spite of religious and national differences and Bučinskij invites Basmanov "to work together for the good of our two countries."[35]

It is appropriate to conclude this study with a brief review of the relationship between source material and final artistic product.

The historical sources which Lope used in the early seventeenth century were superficial, incomplete, and biased. While these sources do reflect a certain reality of Russian customs and mores of the age, their authors were obviously handicapped by their imperfect understanding of the Muscovite state, by a lack of historical material about Russia in general, and mainly by their own preconceived religious opinions and ideological bias, and they were content to form their judgments of Russia on the basis of the culture-bound tradition of the West. Thus, the lack of precision and certain vagueness of these sources made Demetrio appear as Teodoro's son in *El Gran Duque,* and caused a certain vacillation in various historical details, notably concerning the murderer of Demetrio's double in Lope's drama.

In the modern age, however, this vagueness and inaccuracy tend to disappear, and it is chiefly due to the remarkable development of Russian historiography in the second half of the nineteenth century that a play like Ostrovskij's, for example, is distinguished by an unusual richness of historical details, by clarity and truth of episodes as well as firmness of characterization. Thus, the stand of historiography may justifiably be regarded as the cornerstone for the ideological content, historical truth, and characterization of the Demetrius dramas, and each successive Russian Demetrius play reflects the most recent trend in historical research and ideological evaluation, not merely in the ever-changing portrait of the alleged Demetrius and in the greater measure of understanding Boris's complex character, but even in the characterization of such secondary figures as, for example, Basmanov, Demetrius's bodyguard. It was owing to his excellent historical preparation that Hebbel, who criticized Schiller for his disregard or misconception of contemporary reality, could say: "[Mir] ist . . . das ganze Stueck schon so klar wie eine wohlbelauchtete Gebirgslandschaft: ich sehe alle Umrisse und kann nicht mehr fehl gehen."[36] Yet the relationship between historical source and artistic product is by far not so one-sided as Hebbel implied in his rebuke of Schiller's "firework."

Refusing to let the events of history restrain the free play of his poetic imagination and artistic purpose, Schiller, in a letter to his friend Koerner, described briefly his method of creating his passionate *Demetrius:* "Es kommt alles auf die Art an, wie ich den Stoff nehme, und nich wie es wirklich ist."[37] Thus, the German poet pleaded for an imaginative rather than restrictive treatment of history and, as an illustration of this thesis, it may be pointed out that, contrary to all historical sources, his Joan dies on the battlefield in *The Maid of Orleans.* Indeed, in the process of reading the historical literature and the Demetrius dramas, we become aware of a curious relationship between the poet and his source, often characterized by an independent and even disrespectful attitude of the former toward the latter.

Obviously the sources supplied the raw material for the playwright, and so Lope had to rely to a great extent on Mosquera and Bavía, Fletcher on his uncle and Horsey, and Puškin on Karamzin. But the Demetrio whom Lope drew, the Boris whom Fletcher portrayed, and the two heroes in Puškin's drama are clearly not those of their sources only. Thus, while Ostrovskij relied mainly on Kostomarov's account of the events and characters of the Time of Troubles, his portrait of Vasilij Šujskij was so masterly that, after reading Ostrovskij's Demetrius drama, Kostomarov himself felt that the poet had definitely surpassed the historian in his understanding and interpretation of this crafty old boyar,[38] and, by extension, of the entire period of the Russian Time of Troubles. Dr. Fletcher left an interesting and

truthful description of Tsar Feodor in his historical account of the time. Yet Tolstoj, whose method of character construction closely parallels Schiller's, in referring to Dr. Fletcher's portrait of this Russian Tsar, wrote: "This is clearly not my Feodor."[39] Indeed, Tolstoj's own characterization of this saintly Tsar was so excellent and, in Ključevskij's words "approximates so closely . . . its ancient Russian model,"[40] that this historian, a fine stylist himself, used excerpts from Tolstoj's *Tsar Feodor* to illustrate better the human portrait of the Russian monarch. Thus, the relationship between historian and poet is not always completely one-sided and, in some cases, the roles are completely reversed and it is the historian who follows the poet, admires his fine perception and intuition, and even borrows from him for a mimesis of reality.

While maintaining most of the historical facts, the artistic sensitivity and poetic insight of the playwrights motivated them differently, and brought the protagonists of their dramas closer to a universal human truth. Also, their intuition often predicted future trends and changed traditional interpretations, which historical literature perceived only decades and even centuries later. That the poets were often ahead of their times can easily be illustrated. In illuminating Demetrius's mask as the innocent tool of an intriguer, Schiller's genius anticipated the similar idea of Solov'ev and Kostomarov by half a century. Although Fletcher relied on Horsey for Boris's portrait, he completely discounted the unreliable information at the end of the latter's account, and his characterization of Boris as an honest, loyal, and humane statesman in *The Loyal Subject* was followed by Pogodin and Platonov, defense attorneys for the integrity of that monarch some two hundred years later. The hint of Lope, elaborated by Schiller and Hebbel and echoed by Xomjakov, that Boris was not a bloodthirsty and cunning Richard III at all, but a wise statesman who acted out of sincere conviction to save his country from internal chaos at a time of great danger, is now historically certified by Vernadsky's recent study. It is worthy of note that the moral rehabilitation of Boris in Russia first began after Puškin had drawn a sympathetic human portrait of that much-maligned monarch in spite of his historical source.

Although his history was dramatically colored and was at times even episodic in nature, Karamzin, nurtured on the tastes and emotions of the regime, still remained a Court interpreter of political events and, reflecting the rigid absolutist view of the government of Alexander I in his self-enclosed private world, he reduced almost everything to the obviousness of black and and white. With an infinitely greater variety of colors in his artistic brush, the independent and sensitive Puškin, closer to the people and more intimately connected with their mores and customs, characterized both the protagonists and the people differently. Because of his official attitude and evident desire to cater to the contemporary aesthetic mood at the Emperor's palace in writing his monumental history, how dated, stale, and sanctimonious Karamzin now reads! In comparison to him— defying official truth, age, and changing currents of taste, and retaining a sense of wonder and mystery, to which only the poet and his dreaming heroes have a key—how fresh Puškin still remains in our time!

Without forsaking historical reality Puškin depicts Boris in the storm center of the moral disturbance of this monarch's age and, at the same time, revealing the secrets of his heart, renders him more inwardly dramatic. Without sacrificing the vital historical information he received from Karamzin, Puškin parts company with the historian's stern and puritanical view of *ne rien pardonner* and, by synthesizing the elements and rhythm of art and life, sensibility and vitality in the human portrait of his Boris, he creates his own artistic credo of *tout comprendre*. Because he himself is an accomplished dreamer, Puškin understands well the dreams of his Demetrius in spite of the one-sided interpretation by the official historian of the Russian establishment of the early nineteenth century. Hence the boldness, concreteness, and truthfulness of passion of the Pretender, symbol of the restlessness and popular aspiration in the critical turning-point of Muscovite history and reflection of the energy and excitement of the Decembrist uprising in the poet's own time.

The portrait of that remarkable old Russian chronicler Pimen, whom Puškin described in his *Boris Godunov,* was presumably the fruit of the poet's speculation on an objective search for historical truth. Although the exiled poet often heard the cascade of angry shouts from St. Petersburg, once he entered Pimen's quiet cell, all the noises became muted and lost their sting, and he regained a sense of measure, balance, and values.

In the fifth scene of this drama we hear old Pimen—who has

just related to the young monk, Gregorij Otrep'ev, the gruesome details of Demetrius's murder—exhort the novice to carry
on his chronicle:

> To thee I hand my task. In hours exempt,
> From the soul's exercise, do thou record,
> Not subtly reasoning, all things whereto
> Thou shalt in life be witness.[41]

Can "subtly reasoning" be read as an implied criticism of historians who, in their eager obsequiousness to temporal powers
and the fashions of the moment, sacrificed a higher truth? Can
it be the reaction of a modern man, imbued with the national
consciousness of Russia's new age as well as with the liberating
currents of European enlightenment, to the superstitions, myths,
and legends which characterized the historiography of the past?

The historian is one instrument. The poet is a whole orches-
tra. Thus, Puškin's statement that "the history of a nation belongs to the poet" finds its consummate artistic justification.

NOTES

1. Rudolf von Gottschall, "Die Demetrius Dramen," *Studien zur Neuen
Deutschen Literatur* (Berlin: 1892), pp. 95–133.

2. This play is briefly described in chapter 4, n. 3.

3. In recent years a great volume of studies has been written on the baroque
in literature. Especially interesting are M. Mincoff, "Baroque Literature in
English," *Annuaire de l'Université de Sofia*, Faculté Hist. Philol. (1947); A.
A. Parker, "Reflections on a New Definition of Baroque Drama," *Bulletin of
Hispanic Studies* 30 (1953).

4. Lope Felix de Vega Carpio, "El Gran Duque de Moscovia y emperador
perseguido," Tomo Cuarto de las Comedias Escogidas, *Biblioteca de Autores
Españoles* (Madrid: Edición Atlas, 1952), I: 4.

5. John Fletcher, "The Loyal Subject," ed. John Masefield. With an introduction by R. Warwick Bond. *The Works of Francis Beaumont and John Fletcher*,
ed. A. H. Bullen. Variorum ed. 4 vols. (London: George Bell & Sons and A. H.
Bullen, 1908), IV. 5. 4.

6. Lope, II. 13.

7. Fletcher, IV. 5. 69: V. 4. 20–21.

8. *Ibid.*, I. 3. 1; I. 2. 45.

9. Lope, III. 1.

10. Fletcher, II. 1. 5.

11. *Ibid.*, I. 3. 10; IV. 3. 156.

12. *Ibid.*, I. 3. 154.

13. Friedrich Hebbel, "Demetrius," *Saemtliche Werke,* Richard M. Werner, ed. 9 vols. (Berlin: B. Behr's Verlag, 1904), 4: 10.

14. *Ibid.*

15. Wilhelm Heinitz, *Demetrius von Friedrich von Schiller.* Nach den Schillerschen Entwuerfen zu Ende gefuehrt. In MS. (Hamburg, 1937). Quotations are from Salgaller's study, p. 159.

16. *Ibid.,* p. 66.

17. *Ibid.,* p. 96.

18. Hebbel, p. xxxii.

19. Henry von Heiseler, *Die Kinder Godunofs* (Berlin, 1923). First performed in Regensburg in 1930. The author left behind two brief fragments on a projected drama, *The False Demetrius.*

20. Paul Ernst, *Demetrios* (Berlin, 1910).

21. The author speaks about the liberalism of the nineteenth century, which, in his opinion, was "kulturzerstoerend," caused a serious "Verarmung und Erstarrung des Lebens," and finally led to a "geistliche Sterilitaet." Hans Schneider, *Der Tragiker Paul Ernst in der Reihe seiner Dramen "Demetrios" bis "Brunhild." Versuch einer Wuerdigung vom Standort nationalsozialistischer Weltanschauung.* (Dissertation Wilhelms Universitaet, Muenster, Essen, 1935).

22. Alexander Lernet-Holenia, *Demetrius, Haupt-und Staatsaktion* (Berlin: S. Fischer Verlag, 1926).

23. Wilhelm Anton von Spaun, *Demetrius, Vollendung des Schillerschen Fragments* (Wien-Leipzig: Europaeischer Verlag, 1936).

24. *Ibid.,* p. 55.

25. *Ibid.,* p. 57.

26. *Ibid.,* p. 56.

27. *Ibid.,* p. 61.

28. *Ibid.,* p. 75.

29. *Ibid.,* p. 78.

30. *Ibid.,* p. 74.

31. Karl Theodor Bluth, *Die Nacht auf dem Kreml* (Berlin, 1930). Mentioned by Salgaller, p. 353.

32. Friedrich Schreyvogel, *Der Gott in Kreml* (Berlin-Wien, 1937); Johann Wilhelm Klefisch, *Demetrius,* in MS (Berlin, 1937); Hofmann von Guenther, *Der falsche Zar,* in MS (Berlin, 1937). Mentioned by Salgaller, p. 328 and *passim.*

33. A list of the German Demetrius dramas—other than Schiller's and Hebbel's —in chronological order follows: Franz von Maltitz, *Demetrius* (Karlsruhe, 1817). Rev. ed 1835; Hermann Grimm, *Demetrius* (Leipzig, 1854); Friedrich Bodenstedt, *Demetrius.* Historische Tragoedie in 5 Aufzuegen. (Berlin, 1856); Gustav Kuehne, *Demetrius.* Fuer die Buehne bearbeitet. First performed in Leipzig in January, 1857 (Dresden: Verlag und Druck der National Lotterie, Blockmann und Ernst, 1860); Otto Friedrich Gruppe, *Demetrius.* Schillers Fragment fuer die Buehne bearbeitet und fortgefuehrt, nebst einer literarhistorischen Abhandlung. (Berlin, 1861); Ludwig Goldhann, *Demetrius,* in MS (Berlin, 1869); Karl Hardt, *Demetrius* (Hamburg: Hoffmann und Sampe, 1869); Adolf Wilhelmi, *Dmitri Iwanowitsch* (Leipzig, 1869): Heinrich Laube, *Demetrius.* Historisches Trauerspiel in fuenf Akten. Mit Benutzung des Schillerschen Fragments. First performed in Leipzig on February 1, 1869. (Leipzig, 1872); Heinrich von Zimmermann, *Demetrius.* Trauerspiel in fuenf Aufzuegen als freie Vollendung des gleichlauten-

den Schillerschen Fragmentes (Prag, 1885); Otto Sievers, *Demetrius. Geschicht-liches Trauerspiel in vier Aufzuegen. Mit Benutzung des Schillerschen Bruch-stueckes bis zur Verwandlung in zweiten Aufzug.* (Braunschweig, 1888); Heinrich Teweles, *Demetrius. Trauerspiel in fuenf Aufzuegen und einem Vor-spiel von Friedrich Hebbel. Ergaenzt und fuer die Buehne bearbeitet.* (Leipzig: Reclam Universalbibliothek, 1895); Auguste Goetze Weimar, *Demetrius. Trauer-spiel in fuenf Akten nach Schillers Entwurf mit Benutzung von Scenen der Gustav Kuehneschen Bearbeitung.* First performed in Weimar 1893. (Dresden and Leipzig, 1897); Martin Greif, *Demetrius. Das Fragment, dazu ein Nach-spiel mit Prolog und rhapsodischem, von vier lebenden Bildern begleitetem Epilog* (Leipzig, 1902); Franz Kaibel, *Demetrius. Eine Tragoedie in einem Vorspiel und vier Akten. Das Schillersche Fragment fuer die deutsche Buehne bearbeitet und ergaenzt.* (Dresden, 1905); Karl E. Schaarschmidt, *Demetrius. Trauerspiel in fuenf Akten unter Benutzung des Schillerschen Fragments. Zur 150. Wiederkehr des 10. November 1759–1909.* (Leipzig: Verlag von Hermann Zieger, 1909); Walter Flex, *Demetrius. Ein Trauerspiel.* (Berlin, 1909); Otto Harnack, *Friedrich Hebbels Demetrius. Vollendet.* (Stuttgart und Berlin, 1910); Paul Ernst, *Demetrios* (Berlin, 1910); Max Martersteig, *Demetrius* (Muenchen und Leipzig, 1911); Albert Schaeffer, *Demetrius* (Berlin: Ernst Rohwolt Verlag, 1923); Henry von Heiseler, *Die Kinder Godunofs* (Berlin: Karl Rauch Verlag, 1923); Alexander Lernet-Holenia, *Demetrius* (Berlin: S. Fischer Verlag, 1926); Otto Erler, *Marfa* (Berlin: H. Haessel Verlag, 1930); Karl Theodor Bluth, *Die Nacht auf dem Kreml* (Berlin; Arkadia Verlag, 1930); Wilhelm von Spaun, *Demetrius* (Wien-Leipzig: Europaeischer Verlag, 1936); Wilhelm Heinitz, *De-metrius* in MS (Hamburg, 1937); Friedrich Schreyvogel, *Der Gott in Kreml* (Berlin-Wien-Leipzig: Paul Zsolnay Verlag, 1937); Johann W. Klefisch, *De-metrius* (Berlin: S. Fischer Verlag, 1937); Theodor von Guenther, *Der falsche Zar* in MS. (Berlin: Drei Masken Verlag, 1937). There may be some other Demetrius dramas which remained in manuscript, and still others which were either lost or destroyed during the war. See Flex and Salgaller for content and criticism.

34. Aleksej S. Xomjakov, "Dimitrij Samozvanec," *Sobranie sočinenij,* 6 vols. (Moscow: Univ. tipogr., 1900), 4: 3.

35. Aleksej S. Suvorin, *Car Dimitrij Samozvanec i Carevna Ksenija* (St. Petersburg, 1905), V, p. 148.

36. Hebbel, 6:20.

37. Eduard Castle, "Der falsche Demetrius in der Auffassung Schillers und Hebbels," *Jahrbuch des Freien Deutschen Hochstifts* (Frankfurt-am-Mein, 1930), p. 237.

38. Aleksandr N. Ostrovskij, "Dmitrij Samozvanec i Vasilij šujskij," *Sobranie sočinenij,* 10 vols. (Moscow: Gosizdat. xudož. lit., 1960), p. 521.

39. Aleksej K. Tolstoj, "Car Boris," *Dramatičeskaja Trilogija* (St. Petersburg: Tip. M. M. Stasjuleviča, 1898), p. 526.

40. Vasilij O. Klučevskij, *A History of Russia,* trans. C. J. Hogarth. 5 vols. (New York: Russel and Russel, 1960), 3:16. Originally published in the U.S. by E. P. Dutton & Co. inc.

41. A. S. Puškin, *Boris Godunov,* a drama in verse. Rendered into English verse by Alfred Hayes. (London: K. Paul, Trench, Trubner & Co., Ltd., 1918), *Night. Cell in the Čudov Monastery.*

Bibliography

A. Primary Sources

Alexander, G. G. *Dimitri. A Dramatic Sketch from Russian History*. London, 1827.

Belmonte, de Luis, Moreto, Augustin, Martines, Antonio, "El principe perseguido. Infeliz Juan Basilio," *El mejor de los mejores libros*. Madrid, 1650.

Bianchi, Bianco. *Demetrio*. Luche, 1645.

Bisaccioni, Conte Mayolino. *Demetrio di Russia*. Venezia, 1643.

———. *Storia Tragica di Demetrio*. Venezia, 1649.

Bluth, Karl Theodor. *Die Nacht auf dem Kreml*. Berlin: Arkadia Verlag, 1930.

Boccabodatti. *Arlequin Demetrius*. No date. Probably late seventeenth century in Italy.

Bodenstedt, Friedrich. *Demetrius*. Historische Tragoedie in 5 Aufzuegen. Berlin, 1856.

Čaev, L. A. *Boris Godunov*. Moscow, 1864.

Camerino, Conte A. Varano di. *Demetrio*. Venice, 1799.

Carrières, Aubry de. *Demetrius*. Paris, 1689.

Circourt, Compte Adolph de. *Boris Godunov*. No date. In France. (Mentioned by Emile Haumant, *Pouchkine*. Paris, 1911, p. 226.)

Cumberland, Richard. *The False Demetrius*. Fragment. London, 1813.

Delrieu, Etienne Joseph Bernard. *Demetrius*. A novel. Paris, 1823.

Endogurov. *Pravitel' Boris Godunov*. Moscow, 1870.

Erler, Otto. *Marfa*. Leipzig: H. Haessel Verlag, 1930.

Ernst, Paul. *Demetrios*. Berlin: Inselverlag, 1910.

Fletcher, John. "The Loyal Subject," ed. John Masefield. With an introduction by R. Warwick Bond. *The Works of Francis Beaumont and John Fletcher,* ed. A. H. Bullen. Variorum ed. 4 vols. London: George Bell & Sons and A. H. Bullen, 1908.

Flex, Walter. *Demetrius*. Ein Trauerspiel. Berlin, 1909.

Goldhann, Ludwig. *Demetrius*. Berlin, 1869.

Greif, Martin. *Schillers Demetrius*. Leipzig, 1902.

Grimm, Hermann. *Demetrius*. Leipzig, 1854.

Gruppe, Otto Friedrich. *Demetrius*. Berlin, 1861.

Guenther, Hoffman von. *Der falsche Zar*. Berlin: Drei Masken Verlag, 1937.

Halevy, Leon. *Czar Demetrius*. Paris, 1829.

Hardt, Karl. *Demetrius*. Hamburg: Hoffman und Sampe, 1869.

Harnack, Otto. *Friedrich Hebbels Demetrius*. Vollendet Coltasche Handbibliothek 761. Stuttgart und Berlin, 1910.

Hebbel, Friedrich. "Demetrius," *Saemliche Werke*, Richard M. Werner, ed. 9 vols. Berlin: B. Behr's Verlag, 1904.

Heinitz, Wilhelm. *Demetrius von Friedrich von Schiller. nach den Schillerschen Entwuerfen zu Ende gefuehrt*. In MS. Hamburg, 1937.

Heiseler, Henry von. *Die Kinder Godunofs*. Berlin: Karl Rauch Verlag, 1923.

Hilman, Johs. *Demetrius. Ketzer von Russland*. A novel. Amsterdam, 1867.

Jeanser, Victoren. *Dimitri*. (Opera) Libretto by Henry Borne and Arman Sylvester. Paris, 1876.

Kaibel, Franz. *Demetrius*. Dresden, 1905.

Klefisch, Johann Wilhelm. *Demetrius*. MS. Berlin: S. Fischer Verlag, 1937.

Koetzebue, August von. *Demetrius Ivanovitsch. Czar von Moskau*. Ungedruckt. (First performed in St. Petersburg, 1782).

Kuehne, Gustav. *Demetrius*. Dresden: Verlag und Druck der National Lotterie, Blockmann und Ernst, 1860.

Laube, Heinrich. *Demetrius*. Leipzig, 1872.

Lernet-Holenia, Alexander. *Demetrius, Haupt-und Staatsaktion*, Berlin: S. Fischer Verlag, 1926.

Lobanov, Mixail E. *Boris Godunov*. Moscow, 1835.

Lope, Felix de Vega Carpio. "El Gran Duque de Moscovia y emperador perseguido," Tomo Cuarto de las Comedias Escogidas, *Biblioteca de Autores Españoles* 52. Madrid, Edicion Atlas 1952.

Lwov, N. *Zar Dimitry*. St. Petersburg, 1896.

Maltitz, Franz von. *Demetrius*. Karlsruhe, 1817.

Martersteig, Max. *Demetrius*. Muenchen und Leipzig, 1911.

Mérimée, Prosper. *Demetrius the Impostor,* trans. Andrew R. Scoble. London, 1853.

Meščerskij, Elim. "L'Agonie du Faux-Dmitri," *Les Roses Noires.* Paris, 1845.

Metastio, Pietro, Antonio Domenico Bonaventura. Drama Per Musica. *Demetrio.* n.p., 1796.

Mosenthal, S. H. *Maryna.* Histor. Drama. Leipzig, 1871.

Narežnij, Vasilij N. *Boris Godunov.* Moscow, 1804.

Novgorod, G. R. *"Lžedimitrij" Tragedija v 10 bylinax.* Moscow, 1835.

Ostrovskij, Alexsandr N. "Dmitrij Samozvanec i Vasilij Šujskij," *Sobranie sočinenij.* 10 vols. Moscow: Gosizdatel xudožest. lit., 1960.

Pallavicino, C. *Demetrio.* Opera. Venice, n.d. Probably second half of the seventeenth century.

Pix, Mary. *The Czar of Moscow.* London, 1701.

Pogodin, Mixail M. *Boris Godunov.* Moscow, 1835.

————. *Istorija v licax o Dimitrii Samozvance.* Moscow, 1835.

————. *Istorija v licax o Care Borise Godunove.* Moscow, 1864.

Polozov, N. *Dimitrij Samozvanec.* Moscow, 1858.

Puškin, A. S. "Boris Godunov," *Sočinenija.* 3 vols. Moscow: Gosizdat. xudožest. literatury, 1954.

Romains, Jules. *Le dictateur Demetrios.* A novel. Paris: Gallimard, 1926.

Schaarschmidt, Karl Emil. *Demetrius.* Leipzig: Verlag von Hermann Zieger, 1909.

Schaeffer, Albrecht. *Demetrius.* Tragoedie. Berlin: Ernst Rohwolt Verlag, 1923.

Schiller, Friedrich. *Schillers Demetrius,* Gustav Kettner, ed. Weimar: Schriften der Goethe Gesellschaft, 1894.

Schreyvogel, Friedrich. *Der Gott in Kreml.* Berlin-Wien-Leipzig: Paul Zsolnay Verlag, 1937.

Sievers, Otto. *Demetrius.* Geschichtliches Trauerspiel in vier Aufzuegen. Mit Benutzung des Schillerschen Bruchstueckes bis zur Verwandlung im zweiten Aufzug. Braunschweig, 1888.

Spaun, Wilhelm Anton von. *Demetrius.* Wien-Leipzig: Europaeischer Verlag, 1936.

Sumarokov, Aleksandr P. "Dimitrij Samozvanec," *Xrestomatija po russkoj literature XVIII veka,* A. V. Kokorev, ed. 3rd ed. Moscow: Gos. Učeb. pedag. izdat. min. prosv. RSFSR, 1961.

Suvorin, Aleksej S. *Car Dimitrij Samozvanec i Carevna Ksenija.* St. Petersburg, 1905.

Teodoli, Giuseppe. *Il Demetrio Moscovita.* Cesena, 1651.

Teweles, Heinrich. *Demetrius.* Trauerspiel in fuenf Aufzuegen und einem Vorspiel von Friedrich Hebbel. Ergaenzt und fuer die Buehne bearbeitet. Leipzig: Reclam Universalbibliothek, 1895.

Tolstoj, Aleksej K. "Car Boris," *Dramatičeskaja Trilogija.* St. Petersburg: Tip. M. M. Stasjuleviča, 1898.

Weimar, Auguste Goetze. *Demetrius.* Trauerspiel in fuenf Akten nach Schillers Entwurf mit Benutzung von Scenen der Gustav Kuehneschen Bearbeitung. First performed in Weimar. Dresden and Leipzig, 1897.

Wilhelmi, Adolf. *Dmitri Iwanowitsch.* Leipzig, 1869.

Wyrzykowski, *Moskienskie Godi, Legenda o Tajemniczem Carze.* A novel. Warszawa, 1930.

Xomjakov, Aleksej S. "Dimitrij Samozvanec," *Sobranie sočinenij.* 6 vols. Moscow: Univ. tipogr., 1900.

Zimmermann, Heinrich von. *Demetrius.* Trauerspiel in fuenf Aufzuegen als freie Vollendung des gleichlautenden Schillerschen Fragmentes. Prag, 1885.

B. Secondary Sources

1. General Historical

Altamira y Crevea, Rafael. *Historia de España y de la civilización española.* Ed. Cuarta, corregida y aumentada. 3 vols. Barcelona: Sucesores de J. Gili, s.a., 1928.

Arcybašev, N. S. "O končine Careviča Dimitrija," *Vestnik Evropy,* Nos. 9-12 (1830), pp. 241-66.

Baer, Martin. *Chronicon Moscovitum continens res a morte Joannis Basilidis Tyranni.* See Ustrjalov, *Skazanija,* Vol. I.

Barbour, Philip L. *Dimitry Called the Pretender, Tsar and Great Prince of All Russia, 1605-1606.* Boston: Houghton Mifflin Company, 1966.

Baxrušin, C. *Ivan Groznij.* Moscow: Gosizdat, 1945.

Belov, E. A. "O smerti Careviča Dimitrija," *Žurn. Min. Narod. Prosv.* 168 (1873): 1-44, 279-320.

Ciampi, S. *Esame critico con documenti inediti della storia di Demetrio di Iwan Wassiliewitsch.* Florence, 1827.

Cilli, Alessandro. *Historia di Moscovia.* Pistoia, 1627.

Graham, Stephen. *Ivan the Terrible.* New Haven: Yale University Press, 1933.

————. *Boris Godunov.* London: Ernest Benn, 1933.

Tragoedia Muscovitica, sive de vita et morte Demetrii, apud G. Grevenbruch. Coeln, 1608.

Grunwald, Constantin de. *La vraie histoire de Boris Godunov.* Paris: A. Fayard, 1961.

Hamel, Joseph. *England and Russia.* London, 1854.

Hirschberg, Aleksandr. *Maryna Mniszchowna,* Lvov, 1927.

Howe, Sonia E. *Some Russian Heroes, Saints and Sinners.* London: Williams and Norgate, 1913.

————. *The False Dmitri.* London: Williams and Norgate, 1916.

Karamzin, N. M. *Istorija Gosudarstva Rossijskago.* 11 vols. 5th ed. St. Petersburg, 1845.

Klejn, Vladimir. "Ugličskoe sledstvennoe delo," *Zapiski imp. Moskovs. arxeolog. instituta* 25 (1913).

Ključevskij, Vasilij O. *A History of Russia,* trans. C. J. Hogarth. 5 vols. New York: Russel and Russel, 1960. Originally published in the U. S. by E. P. Dutton & Co. Inc.

Kostomarov, N. I. *Kto byl pervij Lžedimitrij?* St. Petersburg, 1864.

————. *Sobranie sočinenij.* 21 vols. St. Petersburg: Izd. Lit. Fonda, 1903.

Le Clerc. *Histoire de la Russie Ancienne.* 2 vols. Paris, 1783.

Levesque, P. Ch. *Histoire de Russie.* 5 vols. Paris, 1782.

Margeret, Jacques. *Estat de l'Empire de Russie et Grande Duche de Moscovie.* Paris, 1606.

Massa, Isaac. *Histoire des Guerres de la Moscovie (1601-1610).* 2 vols. Brussels, 1866.

Maszkiewicz, Samuel. *Dnevnik Samuila Maskieviča.* See Ustrjalov, *Skazanija,* Vol. 5.

Merimée, Prosper. *Épisode de l'histoire de Russie. Les faux Démétrius.* Paris, 1953.

Mniszek, Marina. *Dnevnik Mariny Mniseka.* See Ustrjalov, *Skazanija,* Vol. 4.

Mueller, Gerhard F. *Sammlung Russischer Geschichte.* 9 vols. St. Petersburg, 1732-1763.

Outline History of the USSR. Moscow: Foreign Languages Publishing House, 1960.

Pantenius, Theodor H. *Der Falsche Demetrius.* Bielefeld-Leipzig, 1904.

Peyerle, George. *Beschreibung der Moscowitterischen Rayse.* See Ustryalov, *Skazanija,* Vol. 2.

Pierling, Pavel D. *Rome et Démétrius.* Paris: E. Leroux, 1878.

―――. *La Russie et le Saint-Siège.* 3 vols. Paris: Plon-Nourrit et Cie., 1896-1901.

Platon, Metropolit. *Kratkaja Cerkovnaja Istorija.* Moscow, 1823.

Platonov, S. F. *Drevnerusskije skazanija i povesti o smutnom vremeni XVII veka.* 2nd ed. St. Petersburg: Tip. M. A. Aleksandrova, 1903.

―――. *Ivan Groznij.* St. Petersburg, 1923.

―――. *Boris Godunov.* Prague, 1924.

―――. *History of Russia,* trans. E. Aronsberg. New York: The Macmillan Co., 1925.

Pogodin, Mixail M. "Ob učastii Godunova v ubienii Careviča Dimitrija," *Istoriko-kritičeskie otryvki.* Moscow, 1846.

Pokrovskij, M. N. *History of Russia,* trans and ed. J. D. Clarkson and M. R. M. Griffiths. New York: International Publishers, 1931.

Rochelle, de la. *Le Czar Demetrius. Histoire Moscovite.* Paris, 1716.

Russkaja Istoričeskaja Biblioteka, izd. Arxeog. Kommissii, Vol. 1. St. Petersburg, 1872.

Ščepkin, Evgenij. "Wer war Pseudodemetrius I?" *Archiv der Slavischen Philologie* 20 (1898):224-325; 21 (1899): 99-169, 558-606; 22 (1900):321-432.

Ščerbatov, M. M. *Istorija Rossiskaja ot drevnejšix vremen.* 7 vols. St. Petersburg, 1790-1791.

Seredonin, S. M. *Sočinenija Dzilsa Fletčera kak istoričeskij istočnik.* St. Petersburg, 1891.

Skribanowitz, Herman. *Pseudo-Demetrius I.* Inaugural Dissertation, Friedrich Wilhelm Universitaet, Berlin, 1913.

Šmurlo, E. "Le Saint Siège et l'Orient Orthodox Russe 1609-1654," *Publications des Archives du Ministère des Affaires Etrangères* 4. Première Série. Prague, 1928.

Sobranija gos. gramot i dogovorov (1819) Vol. 2.

Solov'ev, S. M. *Istorija Rossii s drevnejšix vremen.* 11 bks. Moscow: Izd. social'no-ekonom. lit., 1960.

Staehlin, Karl. *Geschichte Russlands.* 2 vols. Berlin, 1923.

Suvorin, Aleksej S. *O Dimitrii Samozvance.* St. Petersburg, 1906.

Tatiščev, E. V. "K voprosu o smerti Careviča Dimitrija," *Sbornik statei po russkoj istorii posvjaščennix S. F. Platonovu.*

Thou, Jacques-Auguste de. *Historiarium sui temporis.* See Ustrjalov, *Skazanija,* Vol. 3.

Turgenev, A. I. *Historica Russiae Monumenta ex antiquis exterarum gentium archivis et bibliotecis deprompta.* 2 vols. St. Petersburg: v. tip. Eduarda Pratsa, 1842-1848.

Ustrjalov, Nikolaj. *Skazanija sovremennikov o Dimitrii Samozvance.* 5 vols. St. Petersburg, 1834-1837.

Vallotton, H. *Ivan le Terrible.* Paris: A. Fayard, 1959.

Vernadsky, George. "The Death of Tsarevich Dimitry: a Reconsideration of the Case," *Oxford Slavonic Papers 5* (1954): 1-19.

Veselovskij, S. V. *Issledovanija po istorii opričniny.* Moscow: Ak. Nauk, 1963.

Vipper, R. *Ivan Grozny,* trans. J. Fineberg. Moscow: Foreign Languages Publishing House, 1947.

Waliszewski, K. *La crise revolutionnaire.* 2nd ed. Paris: Plon-Nourrit et Cie, 1906.

Ziegler, Charles. *Ivan IV dit le terrible.* Paris: Science Historique, 1957.

Zimin, A. A. *Opričnina Ivana Groznogo.* Moscow: Mysl', 1964.

Żółkiewski, Hetman Stanislav. *Expedition to Moscow, a Memoir.* trans. M. W. Stephen. London: Polonia Publications, 1959.

2. General Literary

Alekseev, M. P. "Boris Godunov i Dimitrij Samozvanec v zapadnoevro-pejskoj drame," *"Boris Godunov" A. S. Puškina,* K. N. Deržavin, ed. Leningrad, 1936.

———. *Očerki istorii ispano-russkix literaturnyx otnošenij XVI-XIX vv.* Izd. Leningradskogo universiteta, 1964.

Blagoj, D. D. *Tvorčeskij put' Puškina.* Moscow-Leningrad: Izd. Akad. Nauk SSSR, 1950.

Boas, Frederick S. *An Introduction to Stuart Drama*. London: Oxford University Press, 1964.

Boxberger, R. "Ueber Schillers Demetrius," *Zeitschrift fuer vergleichende Literaturgeschichte* 5 (1892) : 56.

Brenan, Gerald. *Literature of the Spanish People*. New York: Meridian Books, 1957.

Castle, Eduard. "Der falsche Demetrius in der Auffassung Schillers und Hebbels," *Jahrbuch des Freien Deutschen Hochstifts*. Frankfurt-am-Mein, 1930, p. 237.

Čebysev, A. A. "Tragedija Šillera iz russkoj istorii," *Žurn. Min. Narod. Prosv.* No. 7 (1898), pp. 49-95.

Clarke, H. Butler. *Spanish Literature*. London: Swan Sonnenschein & Co. Ltd., 1909.

Coleridge, Samuel T. *Lectures and Notes on Shakespear and Other English Poets*. London, 1914.

––––––. *Shakespeare's Criticism*. ed. Thomas Middleton, 2 vols. London: Raysor, 1930.

Courthope, W. J. *A History of English Poetry*. 6 vols. London: Macmillan and Co., 1904-1925.

Fleay, Fr. G. *Biographical Chronicles of the English Drama, 1559-1642*. 2 vols. London: Reeves and Turner, 1890-1891.

Flex, Walter. *Die Entwicklung des tragischen Problems in den deutschen Demetriusdramen von Schiller bis auf die Gegenwart*. Dissertation. Friedrich Alexander Universitaet, Erlangen, Hofbuchdruckerei, Eisenach H. Kahle, 1912.

González-Lopez, Emilio. *Historia de la literature española. Edad Media y Siglo de Oro*. New York: Las Americas Publishing Co., 1962.

Gorodeckij, V. P. "Boris Godunov v tvorčestve Puškina," *"Boris Godunov"* A. S. Puškina, K. N. Deržavin, ed. Leningrad, 1936.

Gottschall, Rudolf von. "Die Demetrius Dramen," *Studien zur neuen deutschen Literatur*. Berlin, 1892. pp. 95-133.

Hallam, Henry. *Literature of Europe in the Fifteenth, Sixteenth, and Seventeenth Centuries*. 3 vols. London: J. Murray, 1843.

Ikonnikov, V. S. *Neskol'ko zametok po voprosam smutnago vremeni*. Kiev: Tip. Imper. Universiteta, 1916.

Klein, J. K. *Geschichte des spanischen Dramas*. 12 Bks. Leipzig, 1874.

Kridl, Manfred. *A Survey of Polish Literature and Culture.* 'S-Gravenhage: Mouton & Co., 1956.

Langbaine, Gerald. *Account of the English Dramatick Poets.* London, 1691.

Lavrin, Janko. *Pushkin and Russian Literature,* London, 1947.

Lieder, F. W. C. "The Don Carlos Theme," *Harvard Studies and Notes in Philology and Literature* 12 (1930).

Mincoff, M. "Baroque Literature in English," *Annuaire de l'Université de Sofia,* Faculté Hist. Philol. 1947.

Nikolaev, N. I. "O tak nazyvaemom pervom Lžedimitrii v istorii i drame," *Efemeridy* (Kiev, 1912), pp. 467-69.

Ott, Adele. *Die italianische Novelle im Englischen Drama vom 1600 bis zur Restauration.* Zuerich: Universitaet, 1904.

Painter, William. *Palace of Pleasure.* London, 1890.

Parrott, Thomas M. and Ball, Robert H. *A Short View of Elizabethan Drama together with some accounts of the principal playwrights and the conditions under which it was produced.* New York: Charles Scribner's Sons, 1943.

Pfandl, Ludwig. *Geschichte der spanischen Nationalliteratur in ihrer Bluetezeit.* Freiberg im Bresgau, 1929.

Puškin, A. S. *Boris Godunov,* a drama in verse. Rendered into English verse by Alfred Hayes. London: K. Paul, Trench, Trubner & Co., Ltd., 1918.

Rapp, Moritz. *Studien ueber das englische Theater.* Tuebingen, 1862.

Salgaller, Emanuel. *The Demetrius-Godunof Theme in German and Russian Dramas of the Twentieth Century.* Ph. D. dissertation. New York University, 1956.

Schelling, F. E. *Elizabethan Drama 1558-1642, a history of the drama in England from the accession of Queen Elizabeth to the closing of the theaters, to which is prefixed a résumé of the earlier drama from its beginning.* 2 vols. Boston and New York: Houghton, Mifflin & Co., 1908.

Schiller, Friedrich. "Warbeck," *Saemtliche Werke.* 6 vols. Muenich: Carl Hanser Verlag, 1962. Vol. 3.

Shakespeare, William. *The Complete Works,* William G. Clark and William A. Wright eds. New York: Grosset & Dunlap, 1911. This includes *Richard III, Julius Caesar, Richard II, Henry IV* (two parts), *Henry V,* mentioned in this study.

Sibley, Gertrude M. *The Lost Plays and Masques 1500-1642.* Ithaca, N.Y.: Cornell University Press, 1933.

Slonimskij, A. L. "Boris Godunov i dramaturgija 20-x godov," *"Boris Godunov" A. S. Puškina*, K. N. Deržavin, ed. Leningrad, 1936.

Tolstoj, Aleksej K. *Knjaz' Serebranij*, trans. C. A. Manning, as *A Prince of Outlaws*. New York: A. A. Knopf, 1927.

Ward, A. W. *A History of English Dramatic Literature to the Death of Queen Anne*. 3 vols. London: Macmillan & Co., 1899.

3. On Lope de Vega

Alonso, Amado. "Lope de Vega y sus fuentes," *Thesaurus* 8 (Bogota, 1952): 3.

Andersen, Hans Christian. "The Emperor's New Clothes," *The Little Mermaid and Other Fairy Tales*. Odense: Flensted Publisher, 1960, pp. 78-93.

Arco y Garai, Ricardo del. "Lope de Vega," *Historia general de las literaturas hispánicas*, G. Guillermo Diaz-Plaja ed. Barcelona: Editorial Barna, 1953, p. 222.

Arsona, J. H. "La introducción del gracioso en el teatro de Lope de Vega," *Hispanic Review* 7 (January 1939): 1.

Balašov, N. I. "Lope de Vega i problematika ispanskoj dramy XVII. veka na vostočnoslavjanskie temy," *Izvestija*, Ak. Nauk Otdel. Lit. i Jaz. 22, Moscow, 1963.

————. "Renessansnaja problematika ispanskoj dramy XVII veka na vostočnoslavjanskie temy," *Slavjanskie Literatury*, Doklady sovetskoj delegacii, V. Mežnar. s' 'ezd slavistov. Moscow, 1963.

Barezzi, Barezzo. *Relazione della segnalata e como miracolosa conquista del paterno Imperio conseguita dal serenis. giovane Demetrio Gran Duca di Moscovia. L'anno 1605*. Venice, 1605.

Bavía, Luis de. *Historica Pontifical y Católica*, Compuesta y ordenada por el doctor Luis de Bavía, Capellan del Rey, nuestro Señor, en su Real Capilla de Granada. 5 vols. Madrid, 1652.

Bie, Cornelis de. *Den groten gerthoge van Moskovien oft gheweldighe heerschaapije*. A Dutch adaptation of Lope's *El Gran Duque*. Performed in Lierre in 1672.

Bruerton, Courtney. "Lope's Belardo-Lucinda Plays," *Hispanic Review* 5 (1937): 310.

Buchanan, Milton A. "The Chronology of Lope de Vega's Plays," *University of Toronto Studies,* Philological Series 6. Toronto: The University Library, 1922, p. 19.

Calderón, Pedro de la Barca. *La Vida es Sueño.* Toronto, 1909.

Castro, Américo. "Aluciones a Micaela Lucan. . . ," *Revista de Filología Española* 5 (1918) : 278.

Cervantes, Saavedra Miguel de. "El licenciado vidriero," *Novelas ejemplares.* London: Thomas Nelson, n. d.

Depta, Max Victor dr. *Lope de Vega.* Breslau: Ostdeutsche Verlagsanstalt, 1927.

Fichter, W. L. "Notes on the Chronology of Lope de Vega's *Comedias,*" *Modern Language Notes* 39 (1924) : 273.

Gigas, Emile. "Etudes sur quelques *comedias* de Lope. . . ," *Revue Hispanique* 81 (1933) : 177-89.

Grillparzer, Franz. "Studien zum Spanischen Theater," *Saemtliche Werke.* 20 vols. Stuttgart: Cotta, 1893.

——. "Ein treuer Diener seines Herrn," *Dramatische Werke.* 4 vols. Wien: Bergland Verlag, 1952.

Halstead, Frank G. "The Attitude of Lope de Vega Toward Astrology," *Hispanic Review* 7 (1939) : 205-20.

Herrero, Miguel. "Nueva Interpretación de la novela picaresca," *Revista Filología* 24 (1937).

Heseler, Maria dr. *Studien zur Figur des gracioso bei Lope de Vega und Vorgaengers.* Hildesheim, 1933.

Kennedy, Ruth L. "The Dramatic Art of Moreto," *Smith College Studies in Modern Languages* 13, Philadelphia, 1932.

Kovalevskaja, S. G. "Drama Lope de Vega 'Velikij Knjaz' Moskovskij'," *Minerva,* Kiev, 1913, pp. 87-138.

Lawson, Richard H. "El Gran Duque de Moscovia . . . A Likely Source for Lessing," *Romance Notes* 4 (1952) : 58-62.

Lope de Vega. "Peribañez," "Los novios de Hornachuelos," El Duque de Viseo," "Fuente-Ovejuna," "Las Vargas de Castello," Tomo Tres de las Comedias Escogidas, *Biblioteca de Autores Españoles* 52, Madrid, 1952.

——. "La tragedia del rey Don Sebastian y Bautismo del Principe de Marruecas," "El cerco de Viena por Carlos V," *Obras,* 14 vols. Madrid: Real academia española, 1890-1913. Vol. 12.

Menédez y Pelayo, Marcelino. *Estudios sobre el teatro de Lope de Vega.* Tomo 2. Madrid, 1921.

————. "Observaciones Preliminares," *Obras de Lope de Vega.* 7 vols. Madrid, 1896.

Montesinos, José F. "The Chronology of Lope de Vega's Plays," *Revista de Filología Española* 10 (1923) : 192.

————. *Estudios sobre Lope.* El Colegio de México, n.d.

Morley, S. Griswold and Bruerton, Courtney. *Los nombres de personajes en las comedias de Lope de Vega. Estudio de onomatologia.* Berkeley-Valencia : University of California Publications in Modern Philology, 1961.

Mosquera, Juan. *Relacion de la señalada y como milagrosa conquista del paterno imperio consequida del serenissimo principe Ivan Demetrio, Gran Duque de Moscovia, en el año de 1605. Juntamente con su coronacion, y con lo que a hecho despues que fue coronado, desde el ultimo del Mes de Julio, hasta agora, recogido todo de varios y verdaderos avisos, venidos de aquellas partes en diversas vezes traducido de lengua italiana en nuestro vulgar Castellano.* Por Juan Mosquera, religioso de la compania de Jesus. En Valladolid en casa de Andres de Merchan, año de 1606.

Obolenskij, K. M. Preface to the translation of Barezzi's "Relazione," *Čtenija v imper. obščestve istorii i drevnostej* 5. Moscow, 1845.

Parker, A. A. "The Approach to the Spanish Drama of the Golden Age," *Tulane Drama Review* 4, No. 1. (September 1959) : 45.

Plavskin, E. *Lope de Vega.* Moscow : Izd. Vses. knižnoj palaty, 1962.

Poehl, Gertrude von. "La fuente de El Gran Duque. . . ," *Revista de Filología Española* 19 (1932) : 47-63.

————. "Quellenkundliches zur Geschichte des Ersten Falschen Demetrius, Mosquera-Barezzo Barezzi," *Zeitschrift fuer Osteuropaeische Geschichte* 7 (1933) : 73-85.

Possevino, Antonio. *La Moscovia.* Ferrarra, 1592.

Praag, J. A. van. "Más noticias sobre la fuente de el Gran Duque. . . ," *Bulletine Hispanique* 39 (1937) : 356-66.

Pring-Mill, R. D. *Lope de Vega 5 Plays,* trans. Jill Booty. New York : Hill and Wang, 1961.

Pušnov, A. "Lope de Vega o Rossii," *Teatral'naja Žizn',* No. 15. (August, 1960), p. 27.

Quijano, Pedro M. G. "Una vez más Lope y Calderón," *Fenix* 5 (Madrid, October 27, 1935) : 622.

Rapp, Moritz. "Einleitung zu Lope de Vega," *Spanisches The-
ater.* 4 vols. Leipzig, 1868.
Rennert, Hugo A. *The Life of Lope de Vega.* New York: G. E.
Stechart & Co., 1937.
Romanos, Ramón de Mesonero. "Dramáticos Posteriores a
Lope de Vega," *Biblioteca de Autores Españoles* 47 Ma-
drid, 1858, p. 49.
Rostockij, B. and Čuškin, N. *Car Feodor Ivannovič na scene
MXAT,* n.p., 1940.
Schewill, Rudolf. "The Dramatic Art of Lope de Vega." *Mod-
ern Philology,* Berkeley: University of California, 1918.
Varneke, B. *Lope de Vega "Dimitrij Samozvanec,"* n.p., 1903.
Vernet, J. "Las fuentes de El Gran Duque," *Cuadernos de Lite-
ratura* 5-6 (1949): 17-36.
Villarejo, Oscar M. *Lope de Vega and Elizabethan and Jaco-
bean Drama.* Ph. D. dissertation, Columbia University,
1953.
Vossler, Karl. *Lope de Vega und sein Zeitalter.* Muenchen: C.
H. Beck'sche Verlagsbuchhandlung (Oscar Beck), 1932.
Wilson, E. M. "Did John Fletcher read Spanish?" *Philological
Quarterly* 18 (1948): 187-90.
————. "Rule a Wife and Have a Wife" and "El sagaz
Estacio," *Review of English Studies* 24 (1948): 189-94.
Yurramendi, Maximo. *Lope de Vega y la Teología.* Madrid,
1935.
Anonymous. "Hados y Lados hacen dichosos y desdichosos.
Parecido de Rusia," Dramáticos posteriores a Lope de
Vega, por Ramón de Mesonero Romanos, Part 1, *Bib-
lioteca de Autores Españoles* 47 (Madrid, 1858): 49, and
Part 2, *Biblioteca de Autores Españoles* 49: 35.

4. On John Fletcher

Appleton, William W. *Beaumont and Fletcher. A Critical Study.*
London: George Allen and Unwin Ltd., 1956.
Bald, Robert C. *Bibliographical Studies in Beaumont and
Fletcher.* Folio of 1647. Oxford: University Press, 1938.
Bandello, Matteo. "Ariobarzane seniscalco del Re di Persia
quello vuol vincer de cortesia ove vari accidenti inter-
vengono," *Novelle.* 2 vols. Milano, 1813.

Bentley, Gerald E. *The Jacobean and Caroline Stage*. Oxford: The Clarendon Press, 1956.

Bond, Warwick R. "Introduction to John Fletcher's *The Loyal Subject*" John Masefield, ed. *The Works of Francis Beaumont and John Fletcher*, A. H. Bullen ed. Variorum ed. 4 vols. London: George Bell & Sons and A. H. Bullen, 1908.

Brooke, Tucker. "The Royal Fletcher and the Loyal Heywood," *Elizabethan Studies and Other Essays in Honor of George F. Reynolds* 2, No. 4. Boulder: University of Colorado Studies, 1945: 193.

Darley, George, ed. *The Works of Beaumont and Fletcher*. 2 vols. London, New York: Routledge, 1851.

Dibdin, Charles. *A Complete History of the Stage*. London, 1800.

Dietrich, E. Th. *Heywoods "The Royal King and the Loyal Subject" und John Fletcher's "The Loyal Subject" in ihren Beziehungen zu einander und zu ihren Quellen*. Dissertation. Koenigsberg i. Pr.: Albertus Universitaet, 1916.

Dyce, Rev. Alexander. "Some Account of the Lives and Writings of Beaumont and Fletcher," *The Works of Beaumont and Fletcher*. 11 vols. London: E. Moxon, 1843-1846.

Fletcher, Dr. Giles. "Of the Russe Commonwealth," *The English Works of Giles Fletcher, the Elder*, Lloyd E. Berry, ed. Madison: University of Wisconsin Press, 1964.

Fletcher and Beaumont. *Fifty comedies and tragedies*. 1 vol. London: J. Macock for J. Martyn, H. Harrington, Richard Marriot, 1679. This volume includes *A King or No King, Bonduca, The Humorous Lieutenant. The Faithful Shepherdess, The Maid's Tragedy, Thierry and Theodoret, The Mad Lover, Valentinian, The Island Princess, Wife for a Month, The Knight of Malta, Wild Goose Chase, Philaster,* and *Bloody Brother,* mentioned in this study.

————. *The tragedy of Sir John Van Olden Barnavelt*. 'S-Gravenhage: Nijhoff, 1884.

Gregg, W. W. "The Bakings of Betsy," *The Library* 2. Third Series, No. 7 (July, 1911): 225-28.

Grosart, Rev. Alexander B. *The Poems of Phineas Fletcher*. London, 1869.

Guarini, Giovanni B. *Il Pastor Fido*. Londra, 1812.

Hakluyt, Richard. *Principal Navigations, Voyages, Traffiques, & Discoveries of the English Nation* . . . London, 1598.

Hatcher, Orie L. *John Fletcher: A Study in Dramatic Method.* Chicago: University of Chicago Press, 1905.

Heywood, Thomas. *The Royal King and the Loyal Subject,* J. Payne Collier, Esq. ed. London: Printed for the Shakespeare Society, 1850.

Horsey, Sir Jerome. "A Relacion of Memoriall Abstracted owt of Sir Jerome Horsey, His Travels," *Russia at the Close of the Sixteenth Century,* Edward E. Bond, ed. London: Hakluyt Society 20, 1857.

Knight, L. C. *Drama and Society in the Age of Jonson.* London, 1937.

Koeppel, Emil. *Quellen-Studien zu den Dramen Ben Jonson's, John Marston's und Beaumont's und Fletcher's.* Erlangen und Leipzig, 1895.

Konovalov, S. "Anglo-Russian Relations, 1620-1624," *Oxford Slavonic Papers* 2 (1951):142-44; 4 (1953):103-4, 124-27; 7 (1957):118-34.

Malone, Edmond. *The Plays and Poems of William Shakespeare.* 21 vols. London, 1821.

Massinger, Philip. *Believe as You List.* London: Printed for the Malone Society, Oxford University Press, 1928.

———. *The Plays of Philip Massinger,* W. Gifford, ed. London, 1813.

Oliphant, E. H. "Problems of Authorship in Elizabethan Dramatic Literature," *Modern Philology* 8 (1910-1911):413.

Ornstein, Robert. *The Moral Vision of Jacobean Tragedy.* Madison: The University of Wisconsin Press, 1960.

Proells, Robert. *Geschichte des neueren Dramas.* Vol. 2. Part 2. Leipzig, 1882.

Purchas, Samuel. *Hakluytus Posthumus or Purchas His Pilgrimes.* London, 1625.

Seccombe, Thomas, and Allen, J. W. *The Age of Shakespeare.* 2 vols. London: G. Bell and Sons Ltd., 1911.

Sera Tomasa Smita putesestvie i prebyvanie v Rossii, I. M. Baldakov, ed. St. Petersburg, 1893.

Strachey, Leo. *Introduction to The Works of Beaumont and Fletcher,* London, 1887.

Swinburne, Algernon Ch. "Thomas Middleton," *The Age of Shakespeare,* New York and London: Harper Brothers Publishers, 1908.

Waith, Eugene W. "The Pattern of Tragicomedy in Beaumont and Fletcher," *Yale Studies,* No. 120 (1952), p. 42.

————. "A Tragi-Comedy of Humors: Fletcher's The Loyal Subject," *Modern Language Quarterly* (September, 1945).

Wallis, Lawrence B. *Fletcher, Beaumont and Company. Entertainers to the Jacobean Gentry.* New York: King's Crown Press, 1947.

The Faithful General. A Tragedy written by a Young Lady. London, 1706.

"The Reporte of a Bloudie and Terrible Massacre in the Citty of Mosco with the fearefull and tragicall end of Demetrius the last Duke, before him raigning at this present." Sonia E. Howe, *The False Dmitri.* London: Williams and Norgate, 1916.

Index